Save **50% OFF** the cover price!

THE WORLD'S MOST POPULAR MANGA

Each issue of SHONEN JUMP contains the coolest manga available in the U.S., anime news, and info on video & card games, toys AND more!

☑ **YES!** Please enter my one-year subscription (12 HUGE issues) to **SHONEN JUMP** at the LOW SUBSCRIPTION RATE of **$29.95!**

NAME

ADDRESS

CITY   STATE · ZIP

E-MAIL ADDRESS   P7GNC1

☐ **MY CHECK IS ENCLOSED** (PAYABLE TO SHONEN JUMP)   ☐ **BILL ME LATER**

CREDIT CARD: ☐ **VISA**   ☐ **MASTERCARD**

ACCOUNT #   EXP. DATE

SIGNATURE

CLIP AND MAIL TO ➤   SHONEN JUMP
                         Subscriptions Service Dept.
                         P.O. Box 515
                         Mount Morris, IL 61054-0515

Make checks payable to: **SHONEN JUMP**. Canada price for 12 issues: $41.95 USD, including GST, HST and QST. US/CAN orders only. Allow 6-8 weeks for delivery.

BLEACH © 2001 by Tite Kubo/SHUEISHA Inc. NARUTO © 1999 by Masashi Kishimoto/SHUEISHA Inc.
ONE PIECE © 1997 by Eiichiro Oda/SHUEISHA Inc.

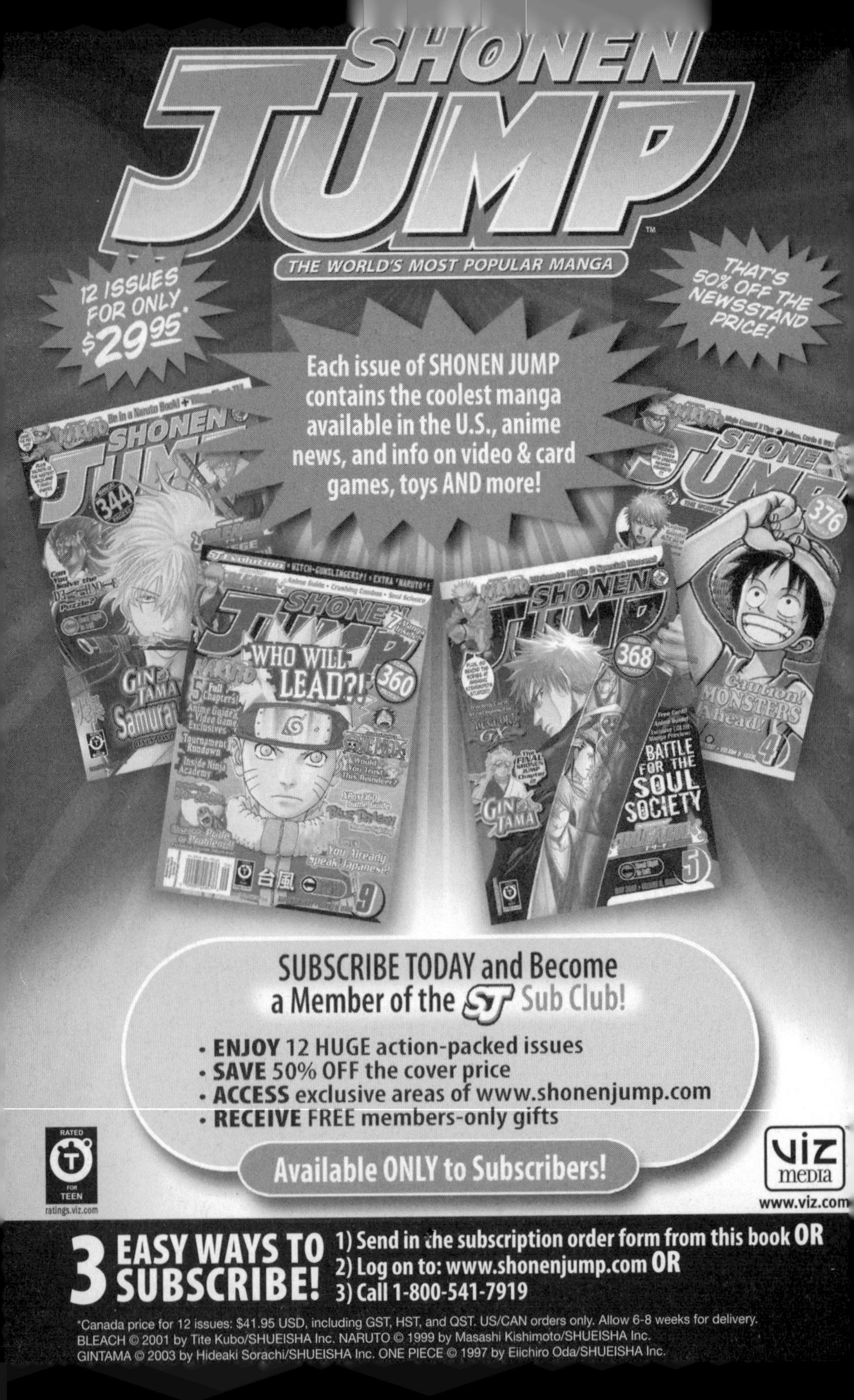
SHONEN JUMP
THE WORLD'S MOST POPULAR MANGA
12 ISSUES FOR ONLY $29.95*
THAT'S 50% OFF THE NEWSSTAND PRICE!
Each issue of SHONEN JUMP contains the coolest manga available in the U.S., anime news, and info on video & card games, toys AND more!
WHO WILL LEAD?!
BATTLE FOR THE SOUL SOCIETY
SUBSCRIBE TODAY and Become a Member of the SJ Sub Club!
• ENJOY 12 HUGE action-packed issues
• SAVE 50% OFF the cover price
• ACCESS exclusive areas of www.shonenjump.com
• RECEIVE FREE members-only gifts
Available ONLY to Subscribers!
RATED T FOR TEEN
ratings.viz.com
viz media
www.viz.com
3 EASY WAYS TO SUBSCRIBE!
1) Send in the subscription order form from this book OR
2) Log on to: www.shonenjump.com OR
3) Call 1-800-541-7919
*Canada price for 12 issues: $41.95 USD, including GST, HST, and QST. US/CAN orders only. Allow 6-8 weeks for delivery.
BLEACH © 2001 by Tite Kubo/SHUEISHA Inc. NARUTO © 1999 by Masashi Kishimoto/SHUEISHA Inc.
GINTAMA © 2003 by Hideaki Sorachi/SHUEISHA Inc. ONE PIECE © 1997 by Eiichiro Oda/SHUEISHA Inc.

Some things just make you feel good.
This one makes noise and it looks
silly – my favorite combo! I pick it up
and think, "Ah... so silly! So nice. Tee hee."
Before I know it, the tension just runs
right out of me. But then I remember
that deadline... Yikes!

–Yoshiyuki Nishi

Yoshiyuki Nishi was born in Tokyo. Two of
his favorite manga series are *Dragon Ball* and
the robot-cat comedy *Doraemon*. His latest
series, *Muhyo & Roji's Bureau of Supernatural
Investigation*, debuted in Japan's *Akamaru
Jump* magazine in 2004 and went on to be
serialized in *Weekly Shonen Jump*.

MUHYO & ROJI'S

BUREAU OF SUPERNATURAL INVESTIGATION

VOL. 3
The SHONEN JUMP Manga Edition

STORY AND ART BY
YOSHIYUKI NISHI

Translation & Adaptation/Alexander O. Smith
Touch-up Art & Lettering/Brian Bilter
Design/Izumi Hirayama
Editor/Amy Yu

Editor in Chief, Books/Alvin Lu
Editor in Chief, Magazines/Marc Weidenbaum
VP of Publishing Licensing/Rika Inouye
VP of Sales/Gonzalo Ferreyra
Sr. VP of Marketing/Liza Coppola
Publisher/Hyoe Narita

Printed in the U.S.A.

Published by VIZ Media, LLC
P.O. Box 77010
San Francisco, CA 94107

SHONEN JUMP Manga Edition
10 9 8 7 6 5 4 3 2 1
First printing, February 2008

www.viz.com

www.shonenjump.com

THE WORLD'S
MOST POPULAR MANGA

Muhyo & Roji's Bureau of Supernatural Investigation

BSI

Vol.3 Into the Arcanum

Story & Art by Yoshiyuki Nishi

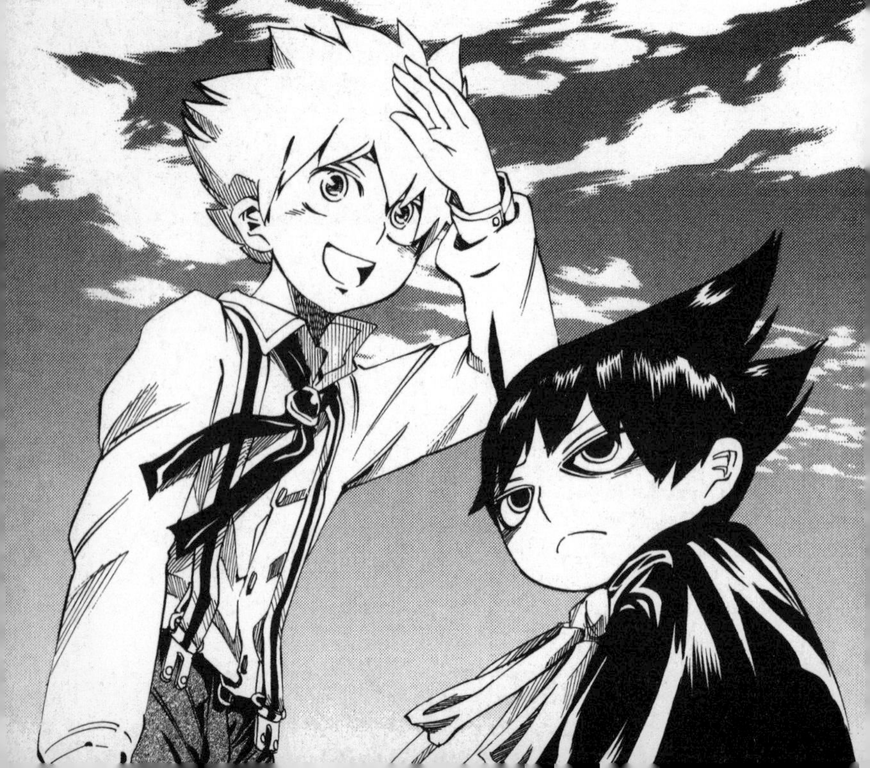

Dramatis Personae

Toru Muhyo (Muhyo)

Genius elite practitioner of magic law, one of the youngest to achieve the highest rank of "Executor." Always calm and collected (though sometimes considered cold due to his tendency to make harsh comments), Muhyo possesses a strong sense of justice and has even been known to show kindness at times. Sleeps a lot to recover from the exhaustion caused by his practice. Likes: *Jabin* (a manga). Dislikes: interruptions while sleeping.

Jiro Kusano (Roji)

Assistant at Muhyo's office and a "Second Clerk," the lowest of the five ranks of practitioners of magic law. Roji cries easily, is meek and gentle, and has been known to freak out in the presence of spirits. Irritated at his own inability to help Muhyo, Roji has devoted himself to studying magic law. Likes: tea and cakes. Dislikes: scary ghosts and scary Muhyo.

The Story

Magic law is a newly established practice for judging and punishing the increasing crimes committed by spirits; those who use it are called "practitioners." One day, Roji receives a package from the Magic Law Association containing two things: a Pen of Wards (used to create wards for fighting ghosts) and an invitation to take part in the annual advancement test. When Muhyo tells him he has to wait at least three years, Roji takes a risk so that Muhyo will notice him, inadvertently putting Nana in danger. Muhyo acknowledges the now-repentant Roji's determination, so the two leave for the association's headquarters. Waiting for them is Enchu, summoner of evil spirits and Muhyo's former classmate. Hopes were high for Enchu during his Magic Law School days, but Muhyo took the only available Executor position once his talent blossomed. The death of Enchu's mother was the last straw. His personality collapsed, leaving only twisted spite for Muhyo and a desire for revenge. Since then, he has been scheming to bring down Muhyo, Muhyo's friends, and the Magic Law Association itself. With the help of Muhyo's old classmate, Judge Yoichi, Muhyo and Roji are able to fend off Enchu's attack. The two return home unharmed...for now.

Yoichi Himukai (Yoichi)

Judge and Muhyo's former classmate. Expert practitioner of all magic law except execution.

Nana Takenouchi (Nana)

Kenji's neighbor and aspiring photographer. Doesn't get along well with Muhyo but is a fan of Roji's tea.

Kenji

Friend of Muhyo and Roji since they saved him from a marauding ghost. A bit of a troublemaker.

Muhyo & Roji's Bureau of Supernatural Investigation BSI

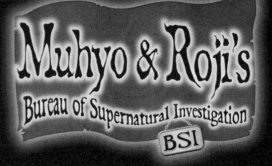

CONTENTS

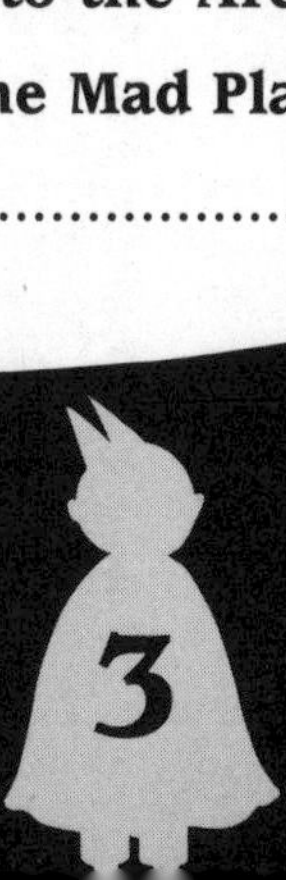
3

ARTICLE 15
SOMEONE'S THERE

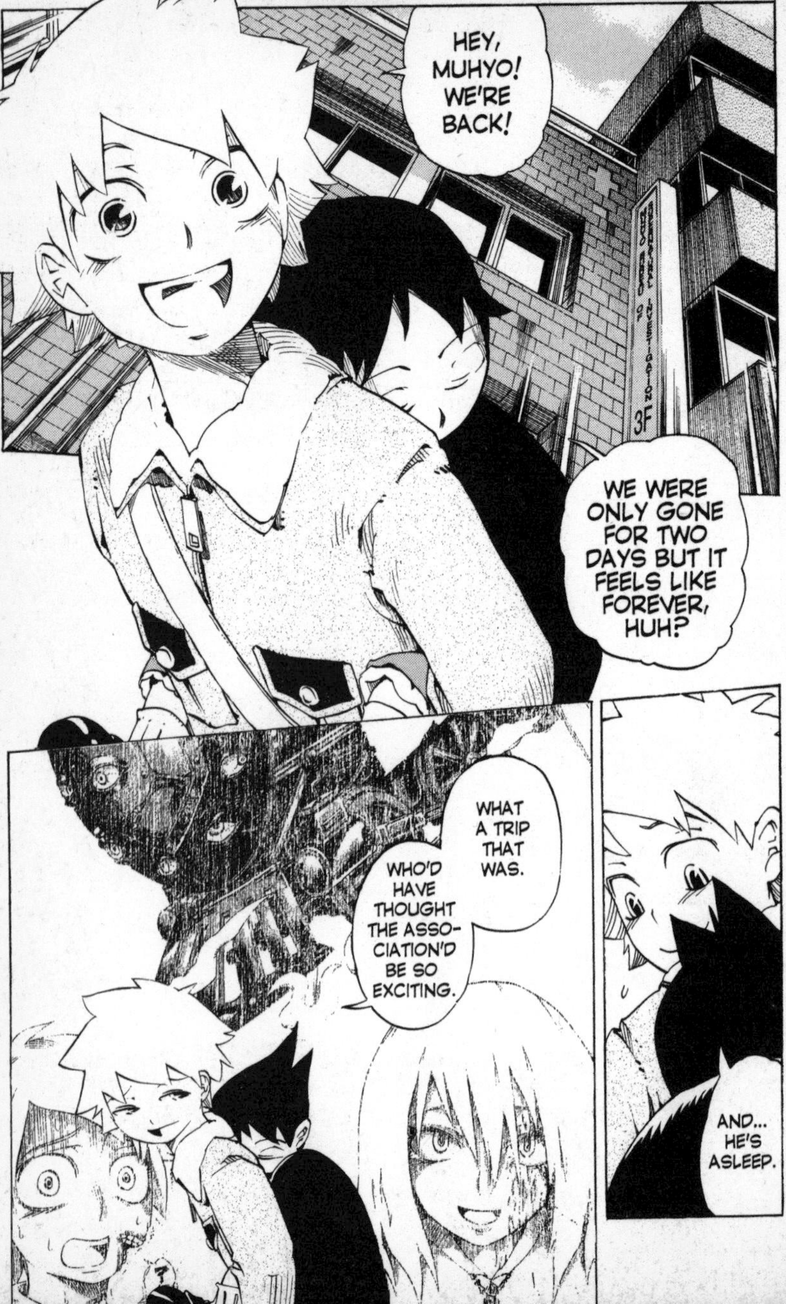
HEY, MUHYO! WE'RE BACK!
WE WERE ONLY GONE FOR TWO DAYS BUT IT FEELS LIKE FOREVER, HUH?
AND... HE'S ASLEEP.
WHAT A TRIP THAT WAS.
WHO'D HAVE THOUGHT THE ASSO-CIATION'D BE SO EXCITING.

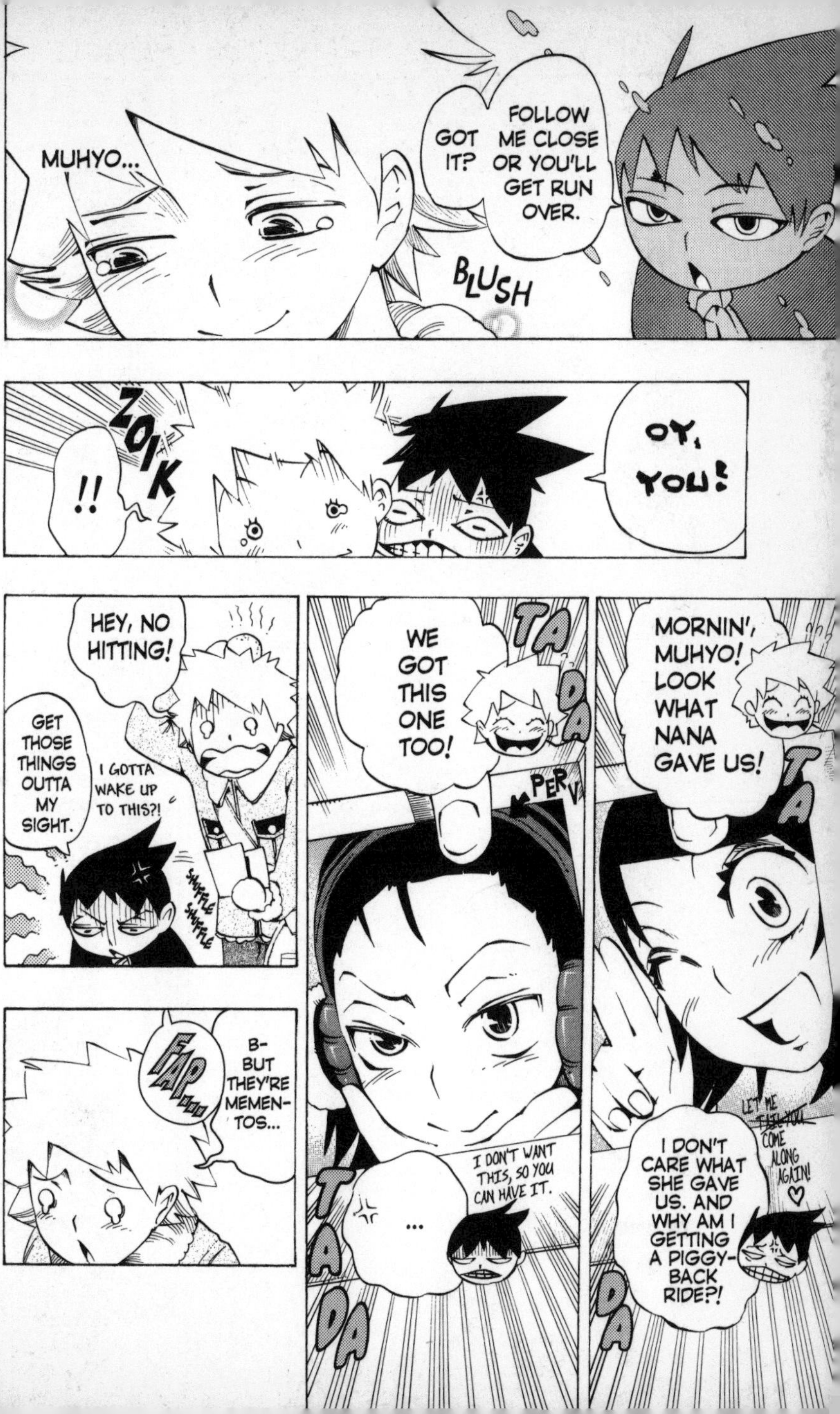
FOLLOW ME CLOSE OR YOU'LL GET RUN OVER.
GOT IT?
BLUSH
MUHYO...
OY, YOU!
ZOIK
!!
MORNIN', MUHYO! LOOK WHAT NANA GAVE US!
TA
DA
TA
LET ME COME ALONG AGAIN! ♡
I DON'T CARE WHAT SHE GAVE US. AND WHY AM I GETTING A PIGGY-BACK RIDE?!
DA
TA
DA
WE GOT THIS ONE TOO!
PERV
I DON'T WANT THIS, SO YOU CAN HAVE IT.
...
TA
DA
HEY, NO HITTING!
GET THOSE THINGS OUTTA MY SIGHT.
I GOTTA WAKE UP TO THIS?!
SHUFFLE SHUFFLE
B-BUT THEY'RE MEMENTOS...
FAP

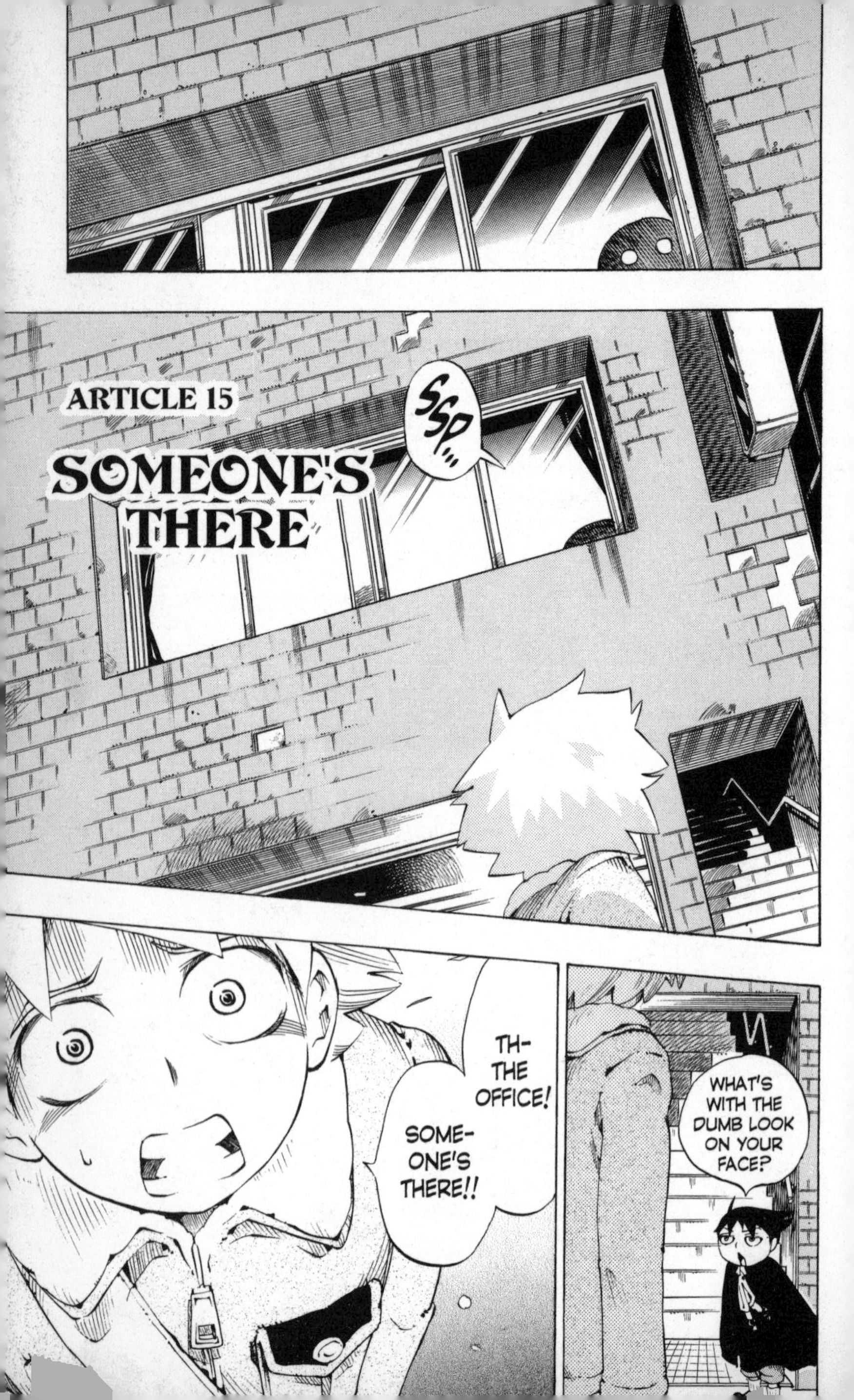
ARTICLE 15
SOMEONE'S THERE
SSP...
TH- THE OFFICE!
SOME-ONE'S THERE!!
WHAT'S WITH THE DUMB LOOK ON YOUR FACE?

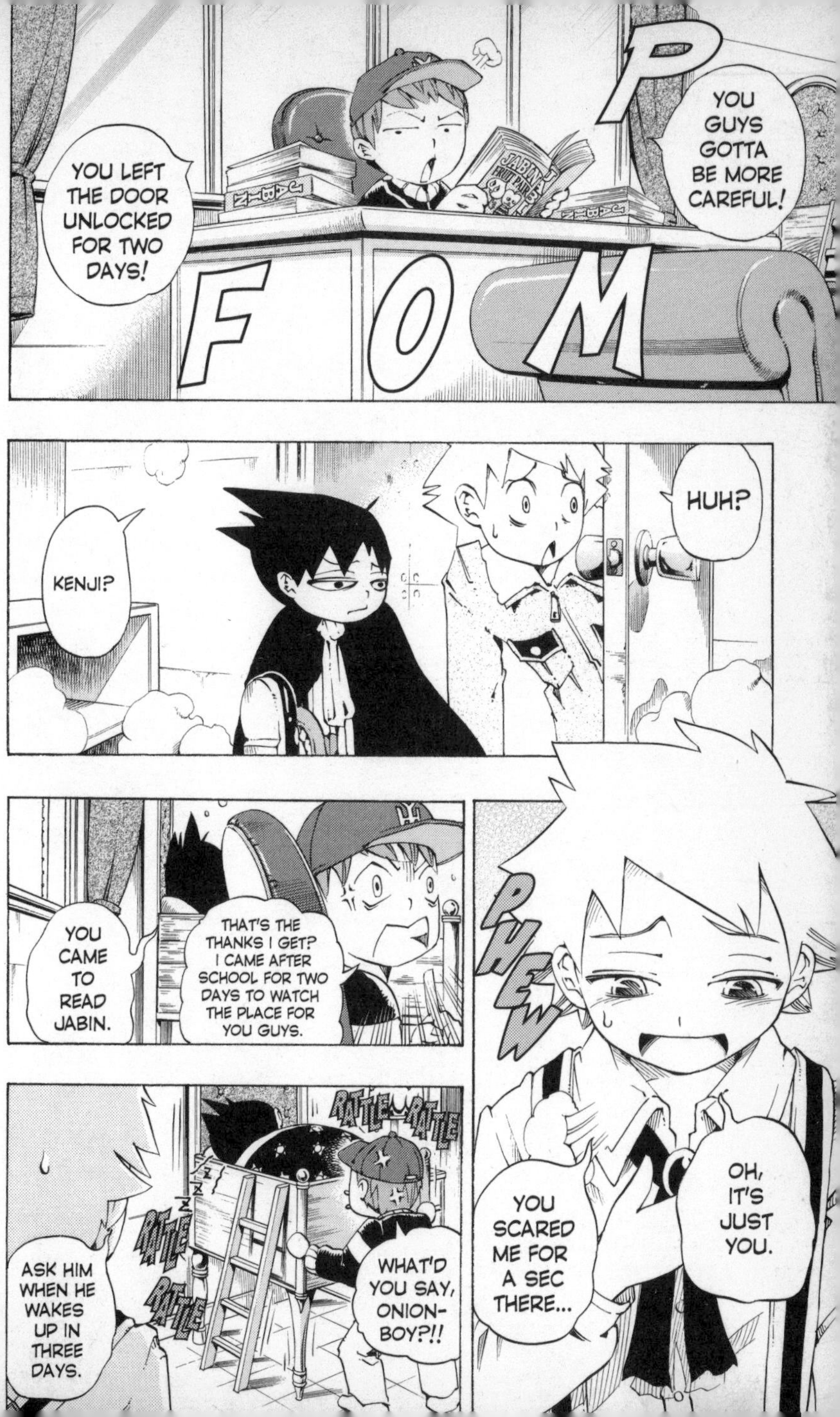
PFOM
YOU GUYS GOTTA BE MORE CAREFUL!
YOU LEFT THE DOOR UNLOCKED FOR TWO DAYS!
HUH?
KENJI?
PHEW
OH, IT'S JUST YOU.
YOU SCARED ME FOR A SEC THERE...
THAT'S THE THANKS I GET? I CAME AFTER SCHOOL FOR TWO DAYS TO WATCH THE PLACE FOR YOU GUYS.
YOU CAME TO READ JABIN.
RATTLE RATTLE
WHAT'D YOU SAY, ONION-BOY?!!
RATTLE RATTLE
ASK HIM WHEN HE WAKES UP IN THREE DAYS.

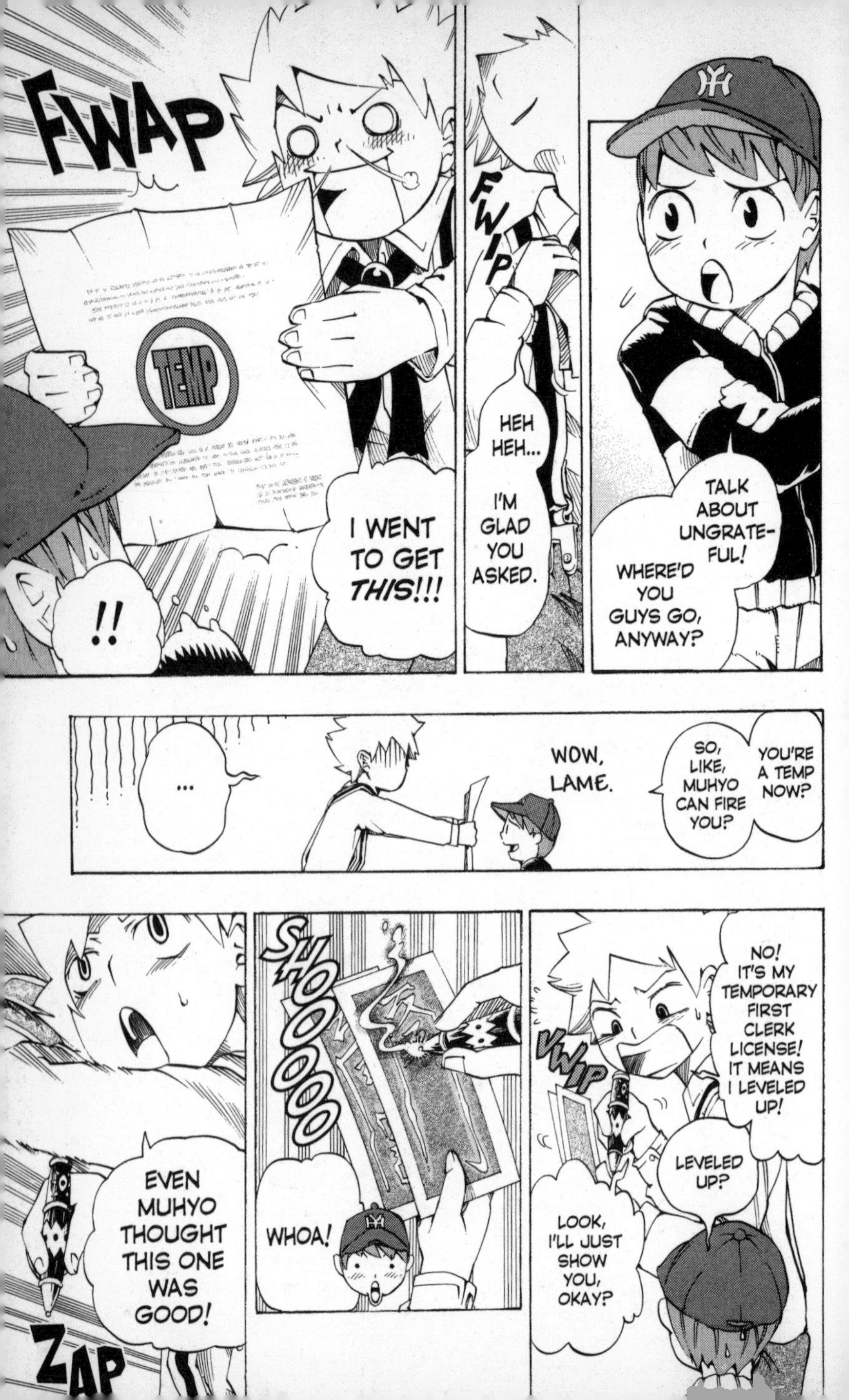
TALK ABOUT UNGRATEFUL!
WHERE'D YOU GUYS GO, ANYWAY?
FWIP
HEH HEH...
I'M GLAD YOU ASKED.
FWAP
I WENT TO GET THIS!!!
TEMP
!!
YOU'RE A TEMP NOW?
SO, LIKE, MUHYO CAN FIRE YOU?
WOW, LAME.
...
NO! IT'S MY TEMPORARY FIRST CLERK LICENSE! IT MEANS I LEVELED UP!
VWIP
LEVELED UP?
LOOK, I'LL JUST SHOW YOU, OKAY?
SHOOOOO
WHOA!
EVEN MUHYO THOUGHT THIS ONE WAS GOOD!
ZAP

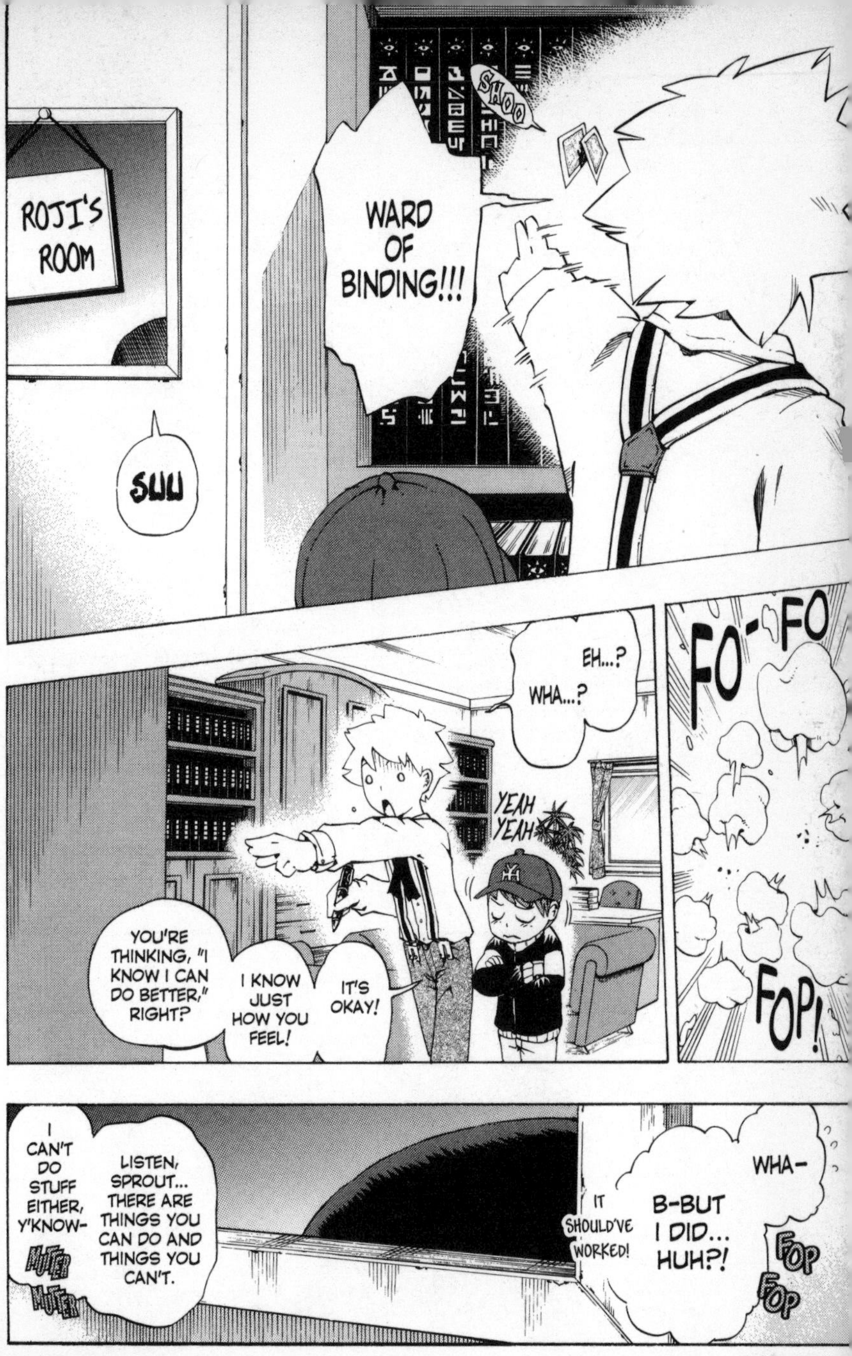
SHOO
WARD OF BINDING!!!
ROJI'S ROOM
SUU
FO-FO
FOP!
EH...? WHA...?
YEAH YEAH
IT'S OKAY!
I KNOW JUST HOW YOU FEEL!
YOU'RE THINKING, "I KNOW I CAN DO BETTER," RIGHT?
WHA-
B-BUT I DID... HUH?!
FOP FOP
IT SHOULD'VE WORKED!
LISTEN, SPROUT... THERE ARE THINGS YOU CAN DO AND THINGS YOU CAN'T.
I CAN'T DO STUFF EITHER, Y'KNOW-
MUTTER MUTTER

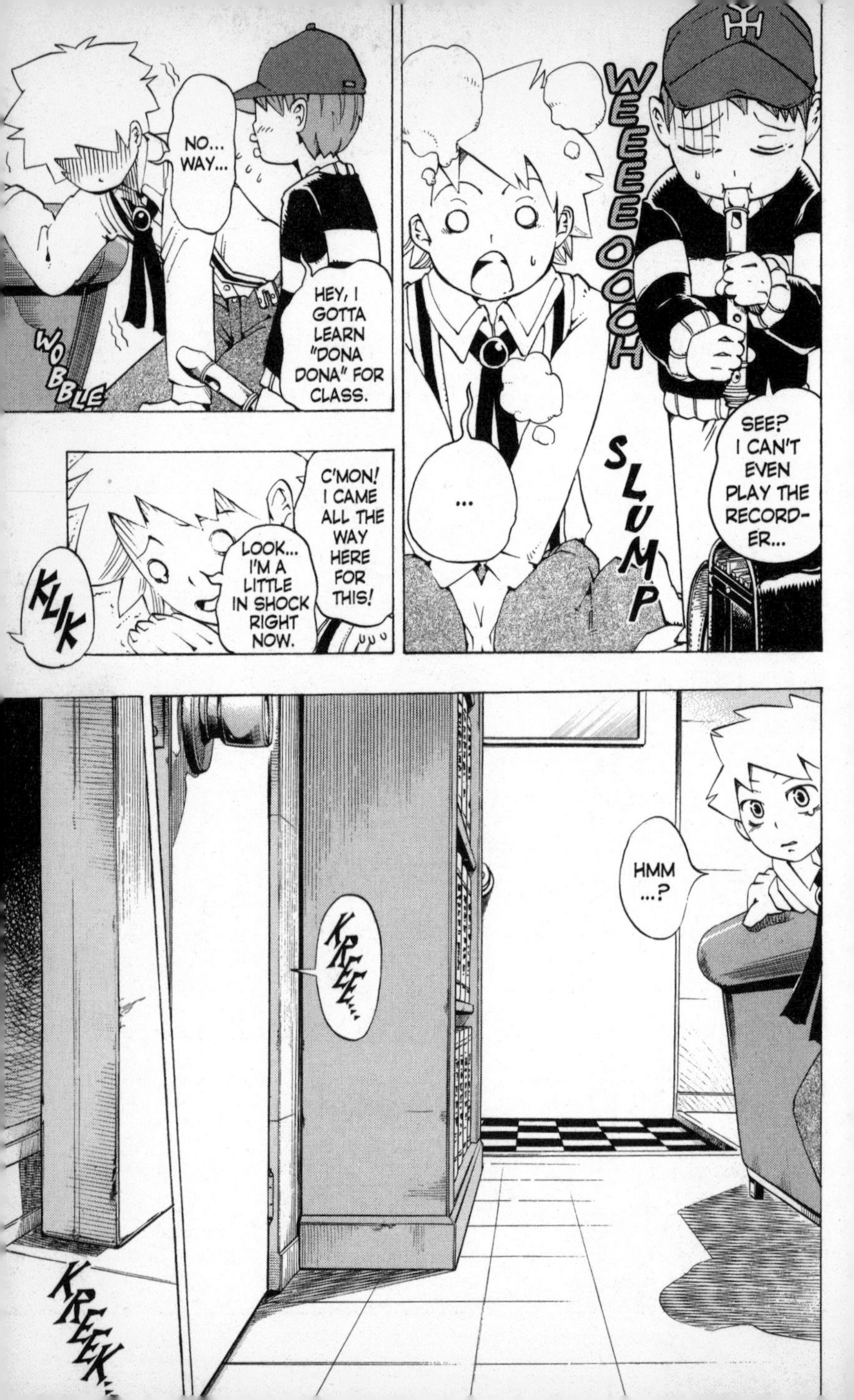
WEEEEOOOOH
SEE? I CAN'T EVEN PLAY THE RECORDER...
SLUMP
...
HEY, I GOTTA LEARN "DONA DONA" FOR CLASS.
NO... WAY...
WOBBLE
C'MON! I CAME ALL THE WAY HERE FOR THIS!
LOOK... I'M A LITTLE IN SHOCK RIGHT NOW.
KLIK
HMM ...?
KREEE...
KREEK...

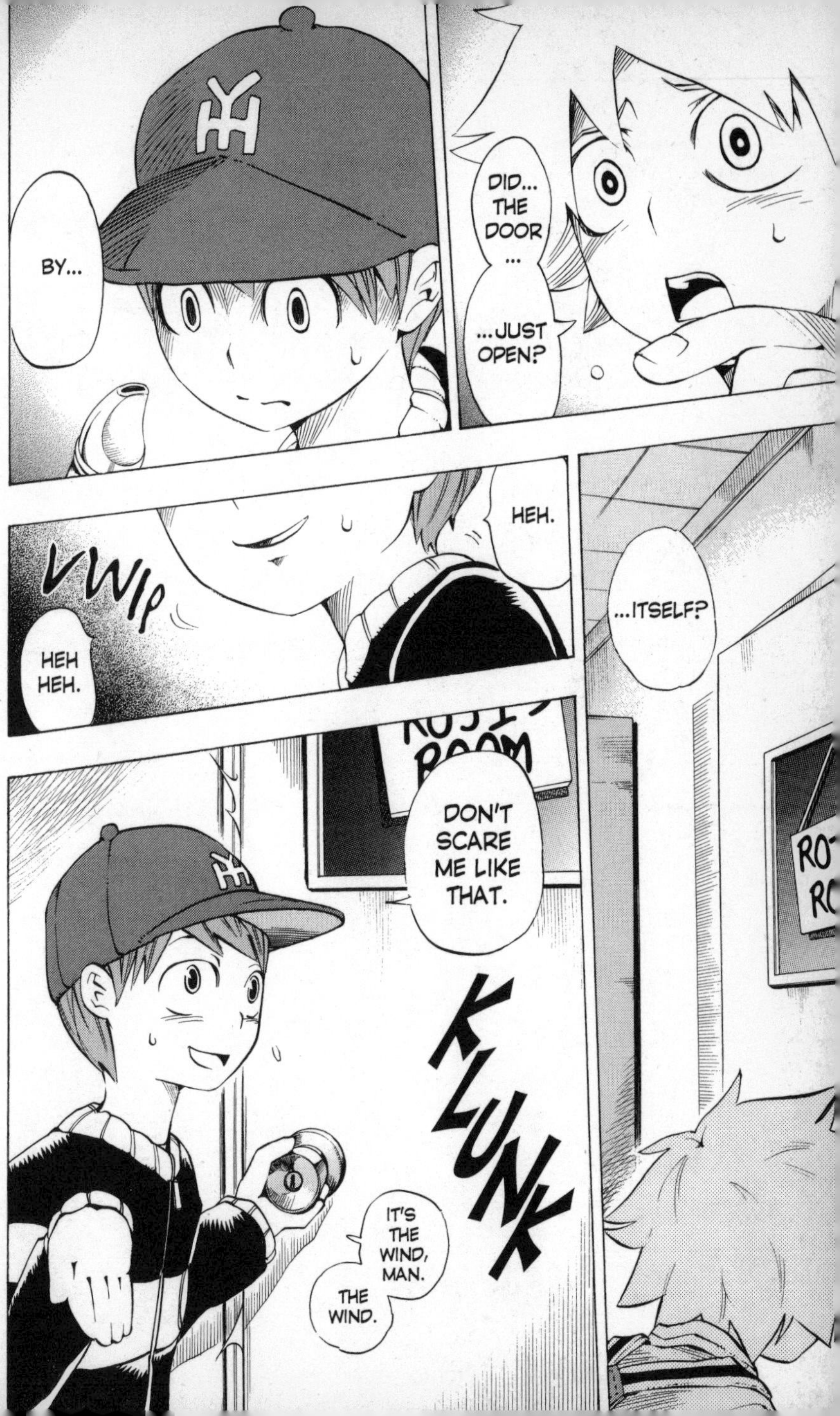

DID... THE DOOR ...
...JUST OPEN?
BY...
...ITSELF?
HEH.
VWIR
HEH HEH.
DON'T SCARE ME LIKE THAT.
KLUNK
IT'S THE WIND, MAN.
THE WIND.

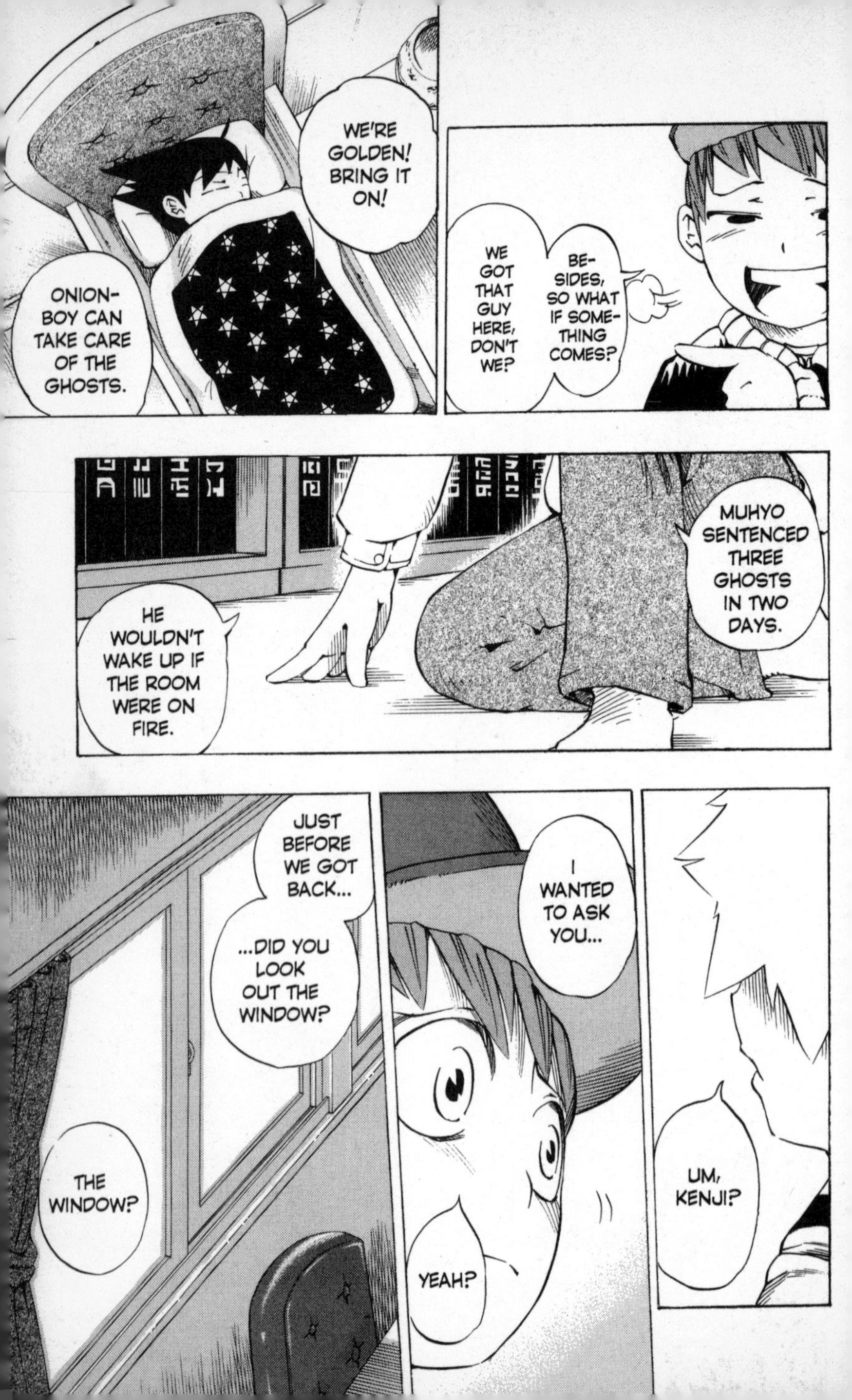
BESIDES, SO WHAT IF SOMETHING COMES?
WE GOT THAT GUY HERE, DON'T WE?
WE'RE GOLDEN! BRING IT ON!
ONION-BOY CAN TAKE CARE OF THE GHOSTS.
MUHYO SENTENCED THREE GHOSTS IN TWO DAYS.
HE WOULDN'T WAKE UP IF THE ROOM WERE ON FIRE.
UM, KENJI?
YEAH?
I WANTED TO ASK YOU...
JUST BEFORE WE GOT BACK...
...DID YOU LOOK OUT THE WINDOW?
THE WINDOW?

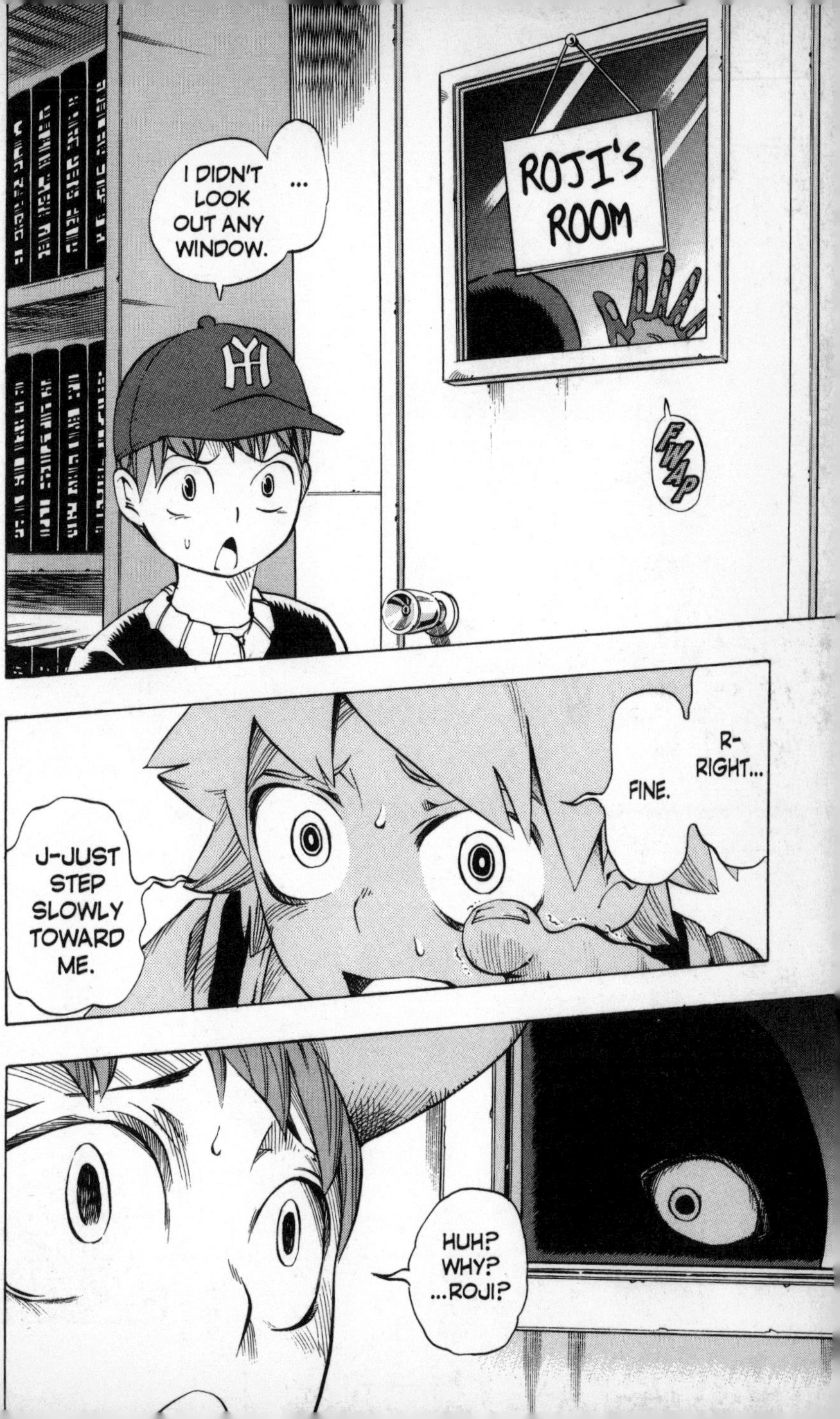
ROJI'S ROOM
...
I DIDN'T LOOK OUT ANY WINDOW.
FWAP
R- RIGHT... FINE.
J-JUST STEP SLOWLY TOWARD ME.
HUH? WHY? ...ROJI?

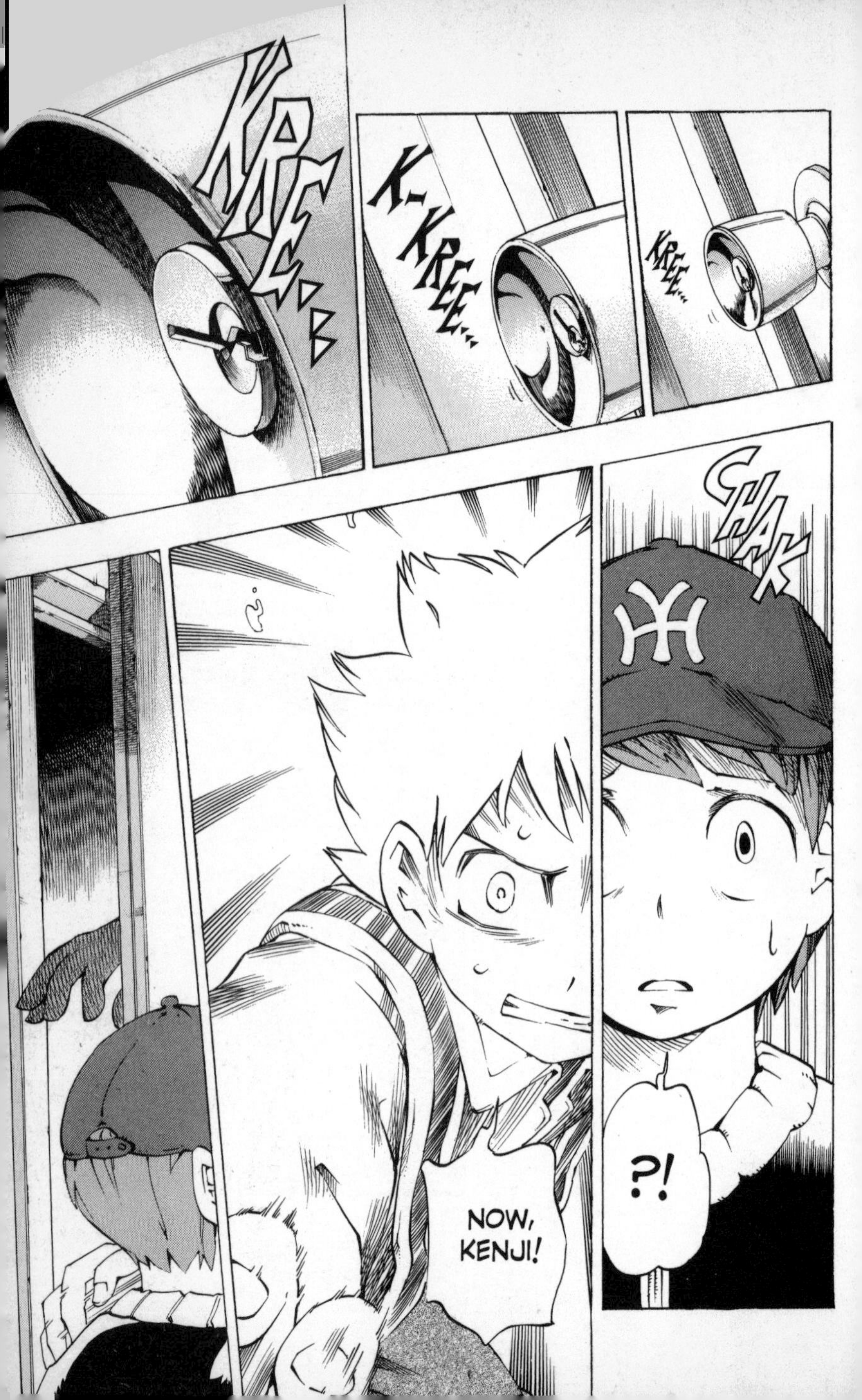
KREE...
K-KREE...
KREE...
CHAK
?!
NOW, KENJI!

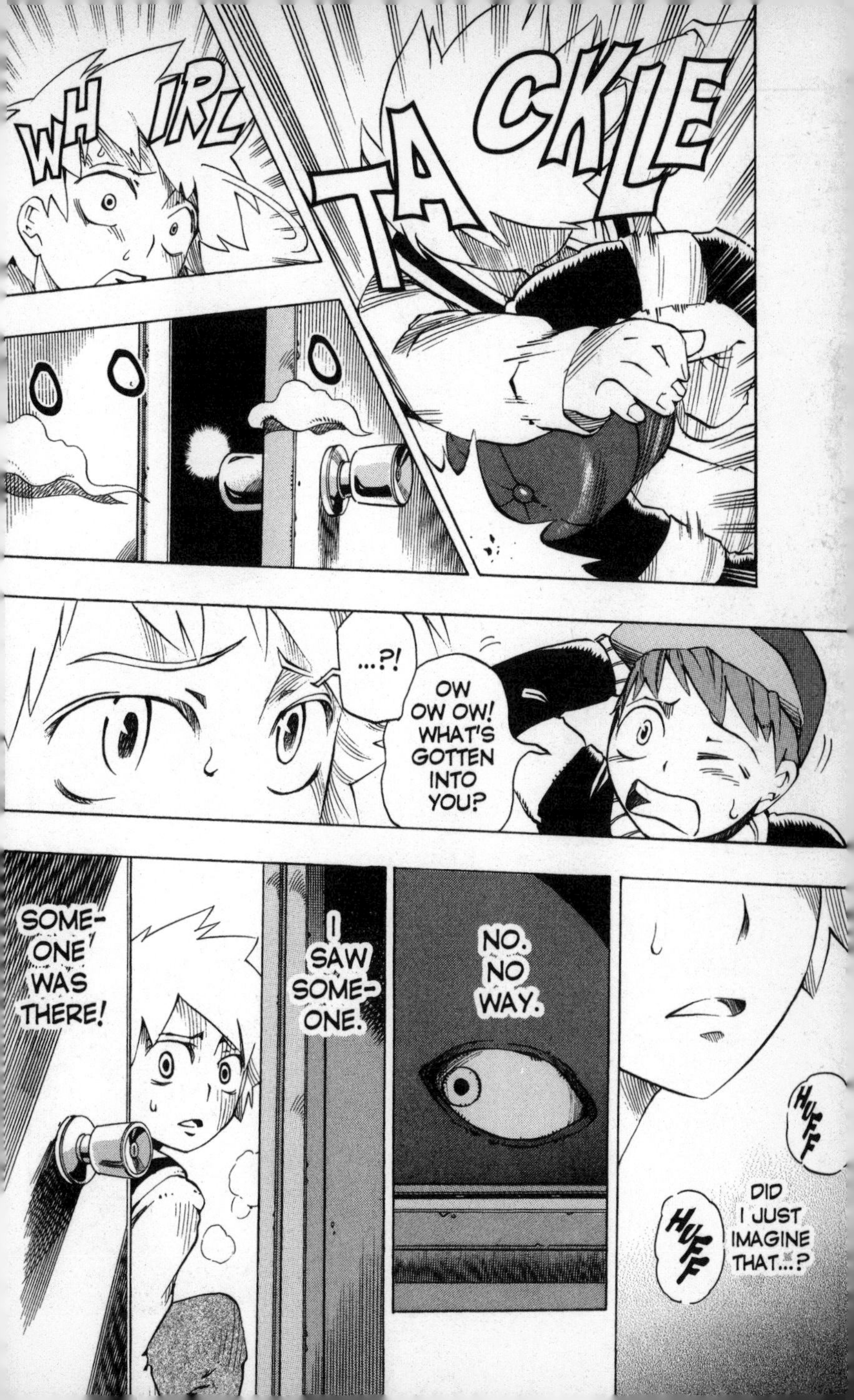
TACKLE
WHIRL
...?!
OW OW OW! WHAT'S GOTTEN INTO YOU?
HUFF
HUFF
DID I JUST IMAGINE THAT...?
NO. NO WAY.
I SAW SOME-ONE.
SOME-ONE WAS THERE!

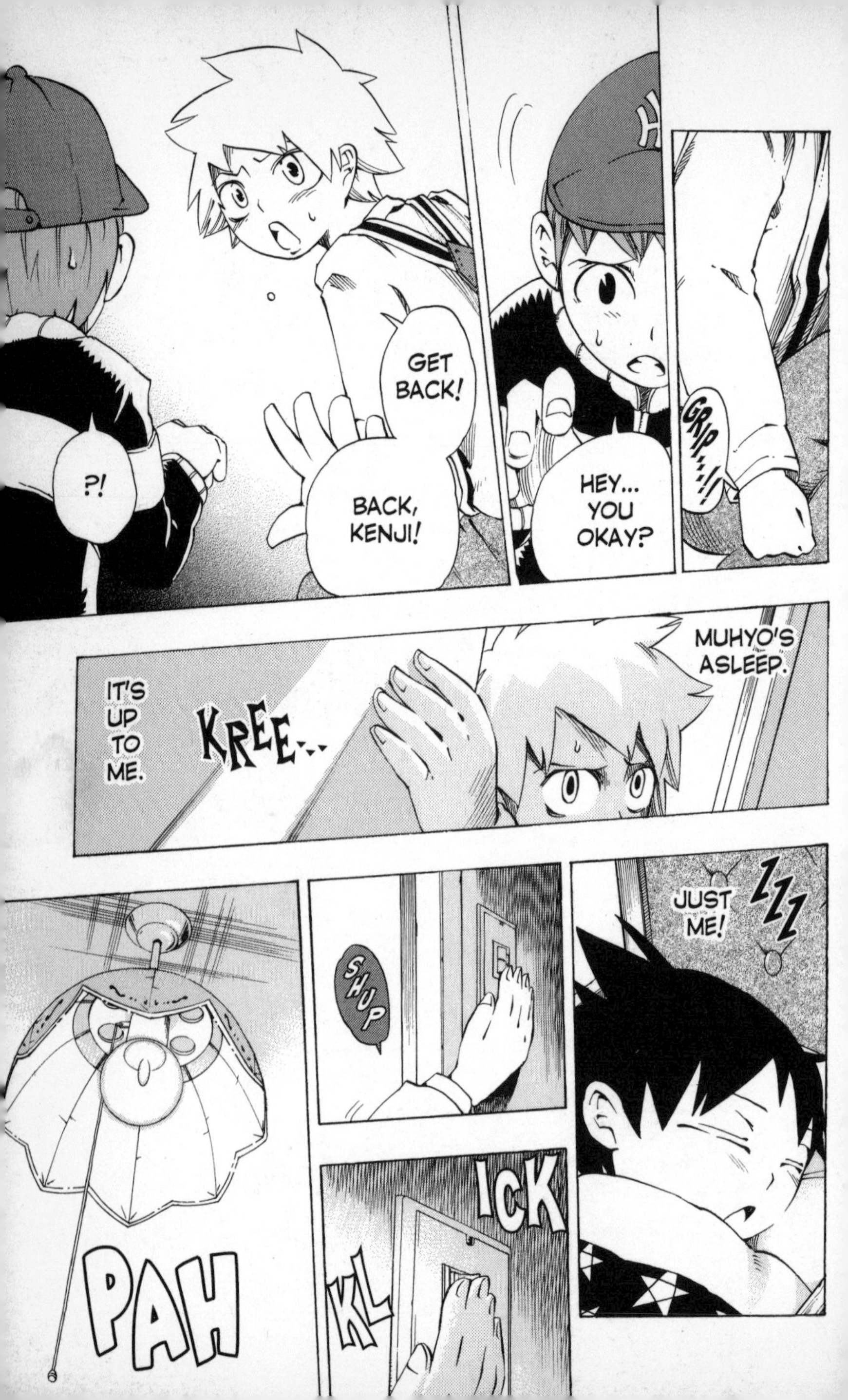
GRIP...!!
HEY... YOU OKAY?
GET BACK!
BACK, KENJI!
?!
MUHYO'S ASLEEP.
KREE...
IT'S UP TO ME.
JUST ME!
ZZZ
SHUP
KL
ICK
PAH

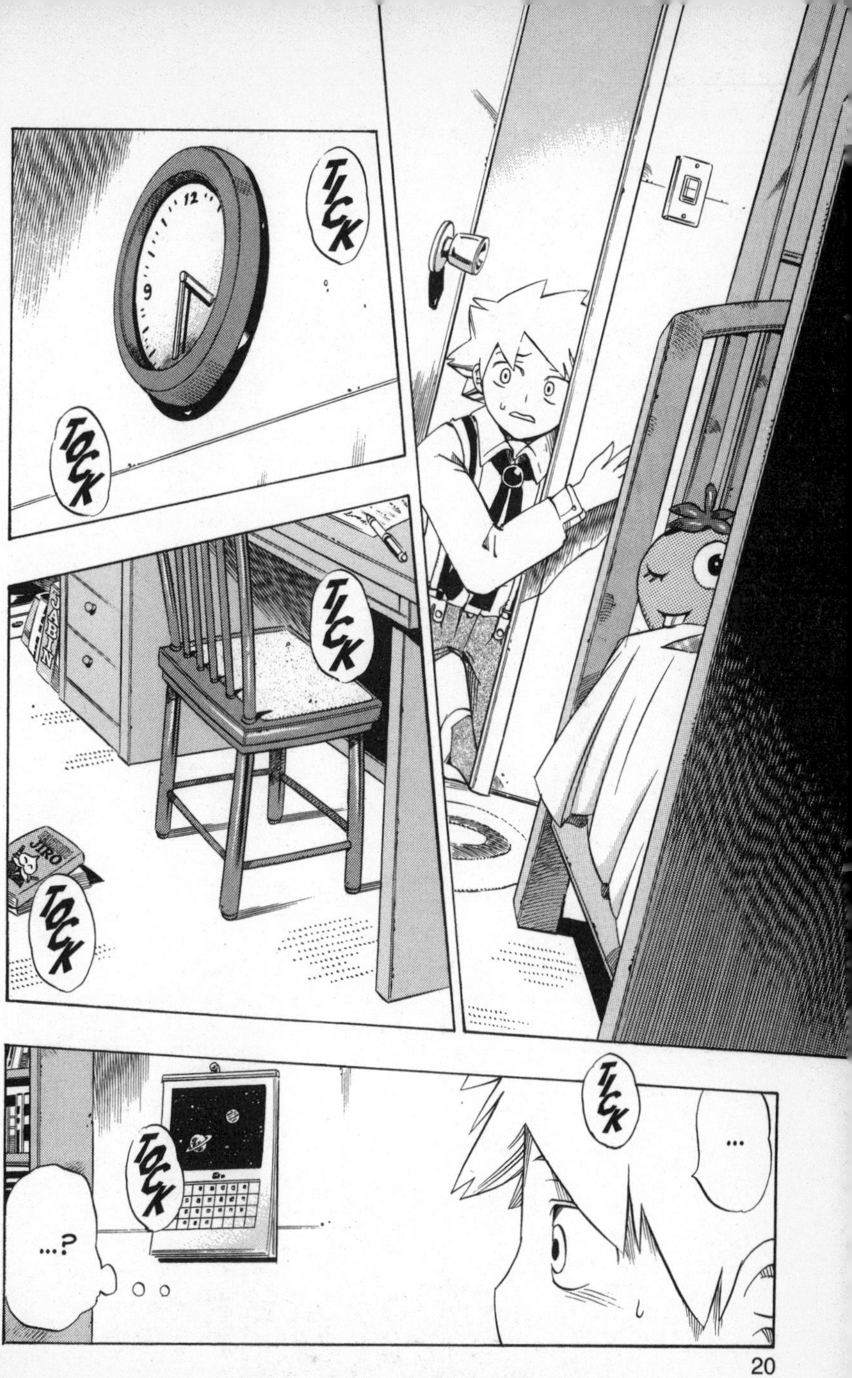
TICK
TOCK
TICK
JIRO
TOCK
TICK
...
TOCK
...?

READ THIS WAY

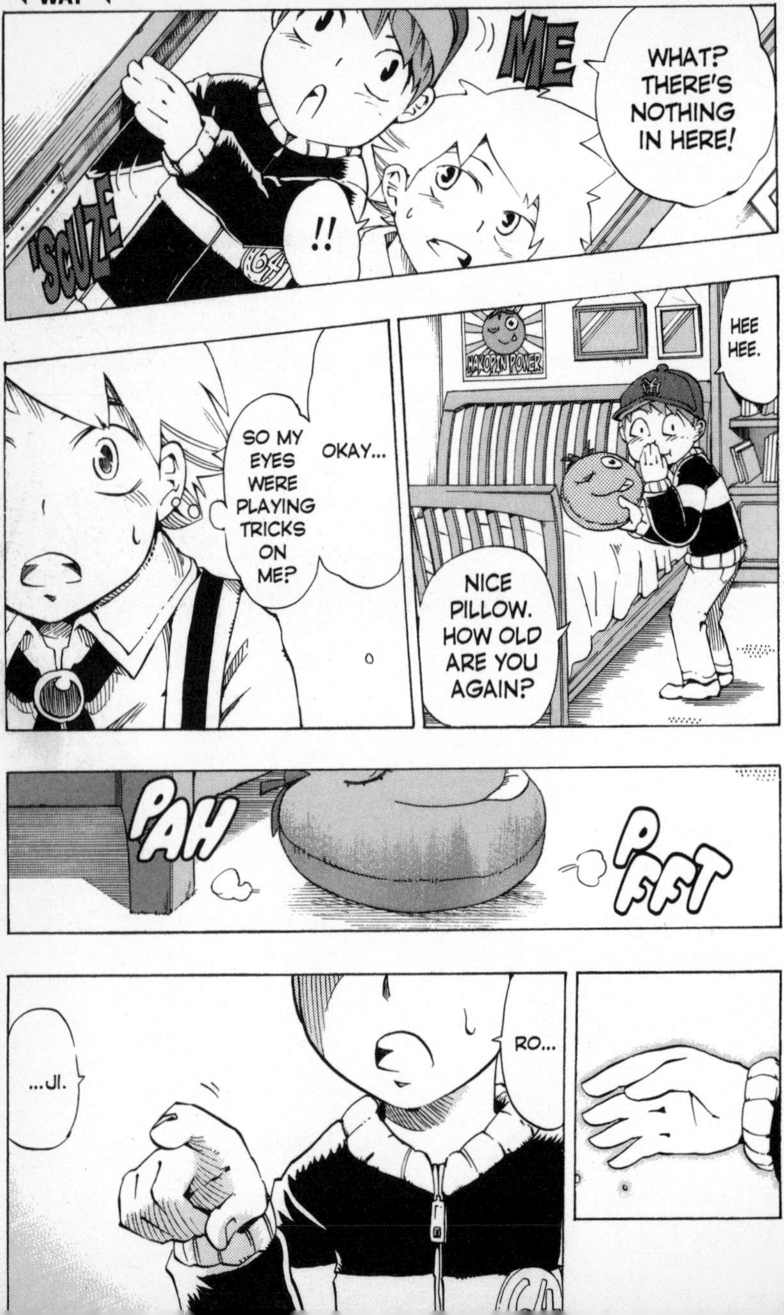
WHAT? THERE'S NOTHING IN HERE!
ME
!!
'SCUZE
HEE HEE.
HAKOPIN POWER
NICE PILLOW. HOW OLD ARE YOU AGAIN?
OKAY...
SO MY EYES WERE PLAYING TRICKS ON ME?
PFFT
PAH
RO...
...JI.

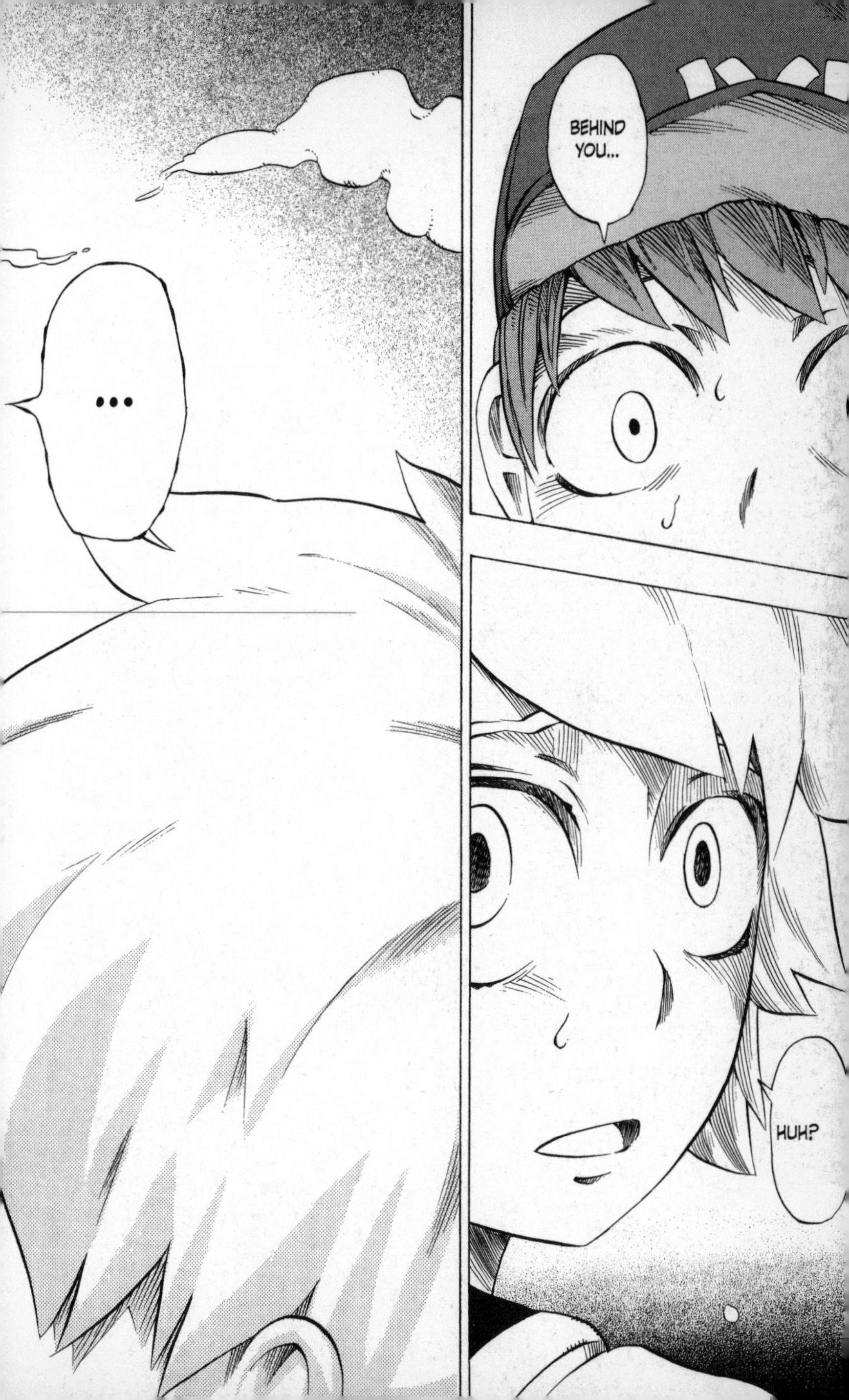
BEHIND YOU...
HUH?
...

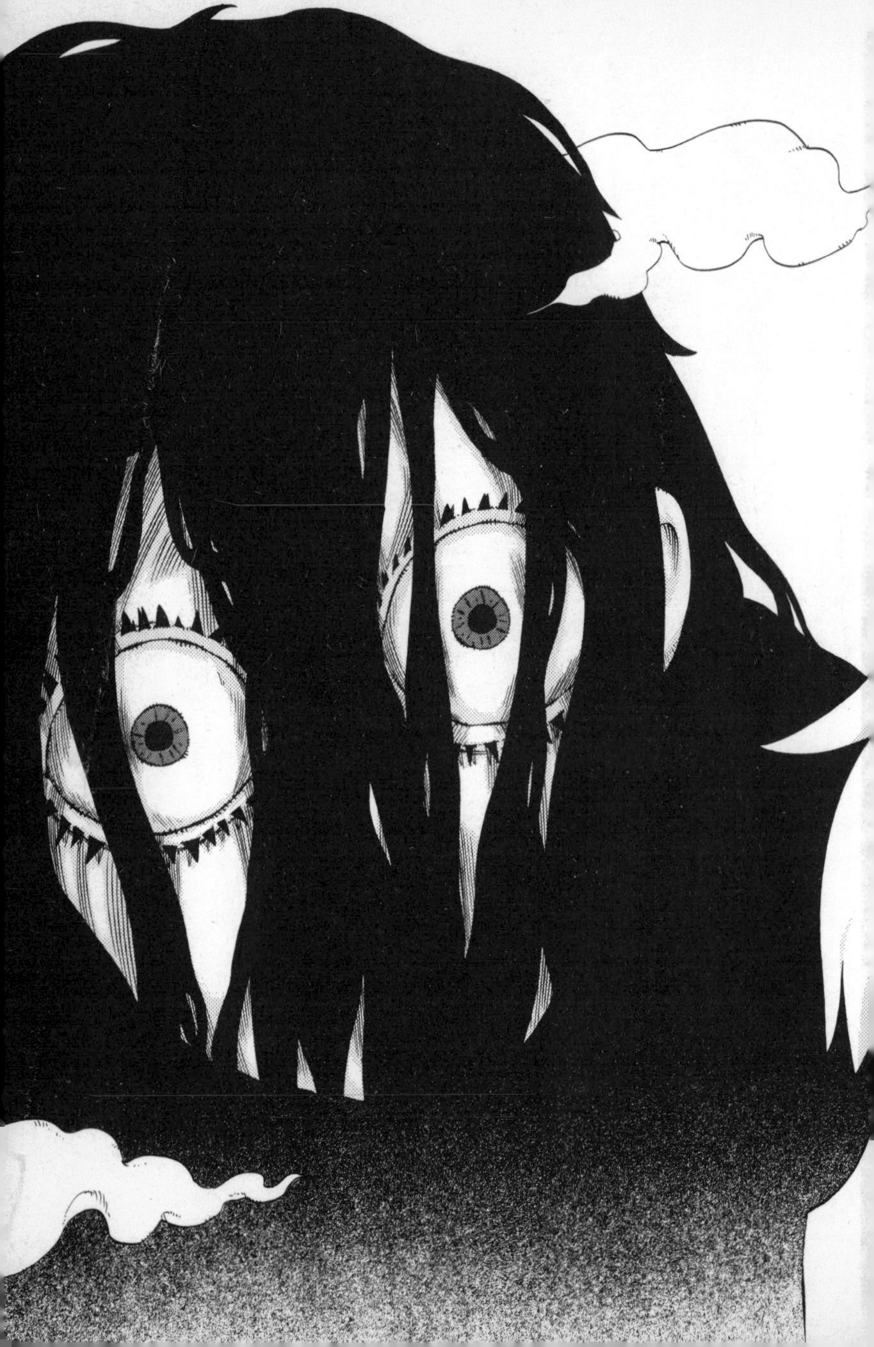

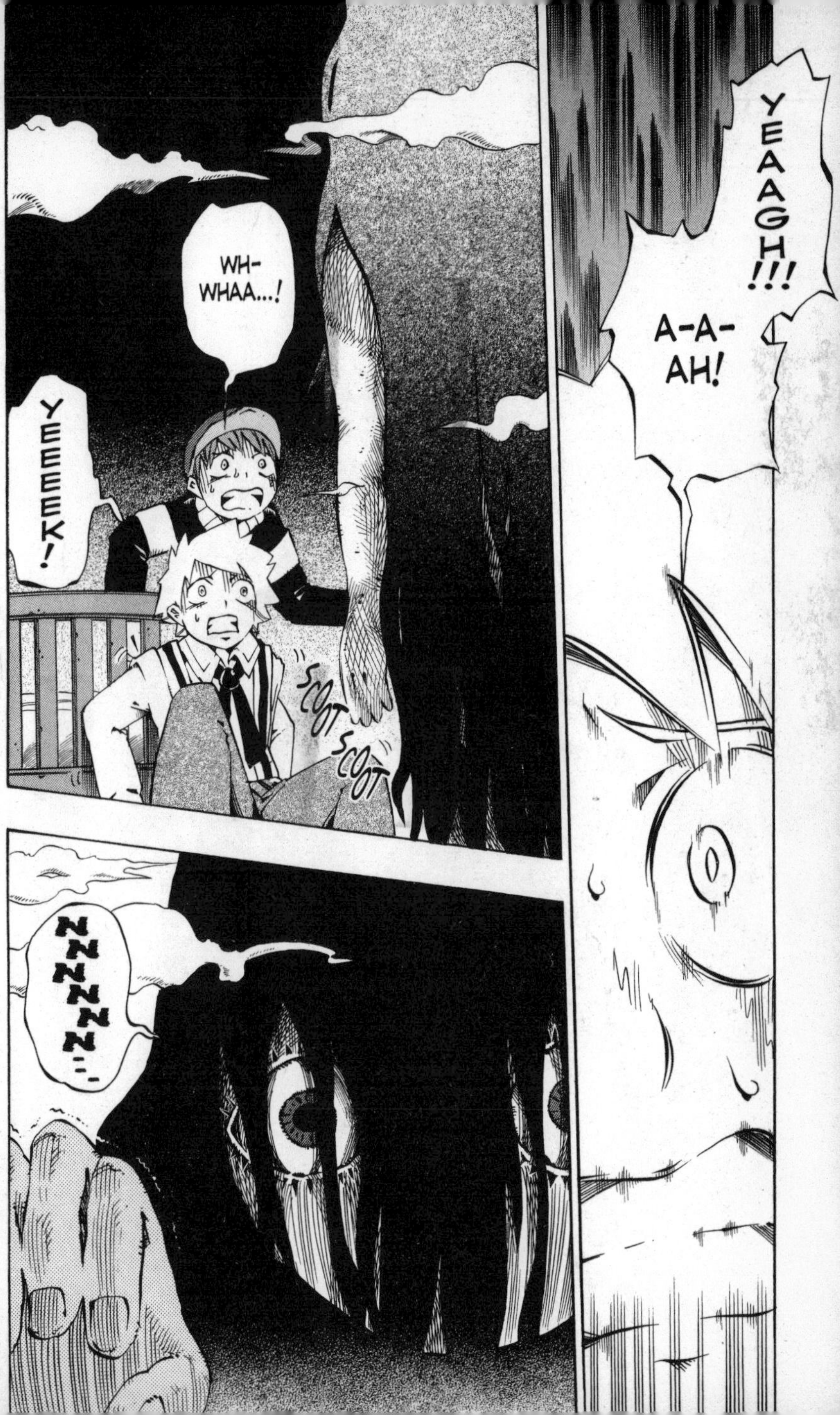
YEAAAGH!!!
A-A-AH!
WH-WHAA...!
YEEEEK!
SCOOT SCOOT
NNNNN--

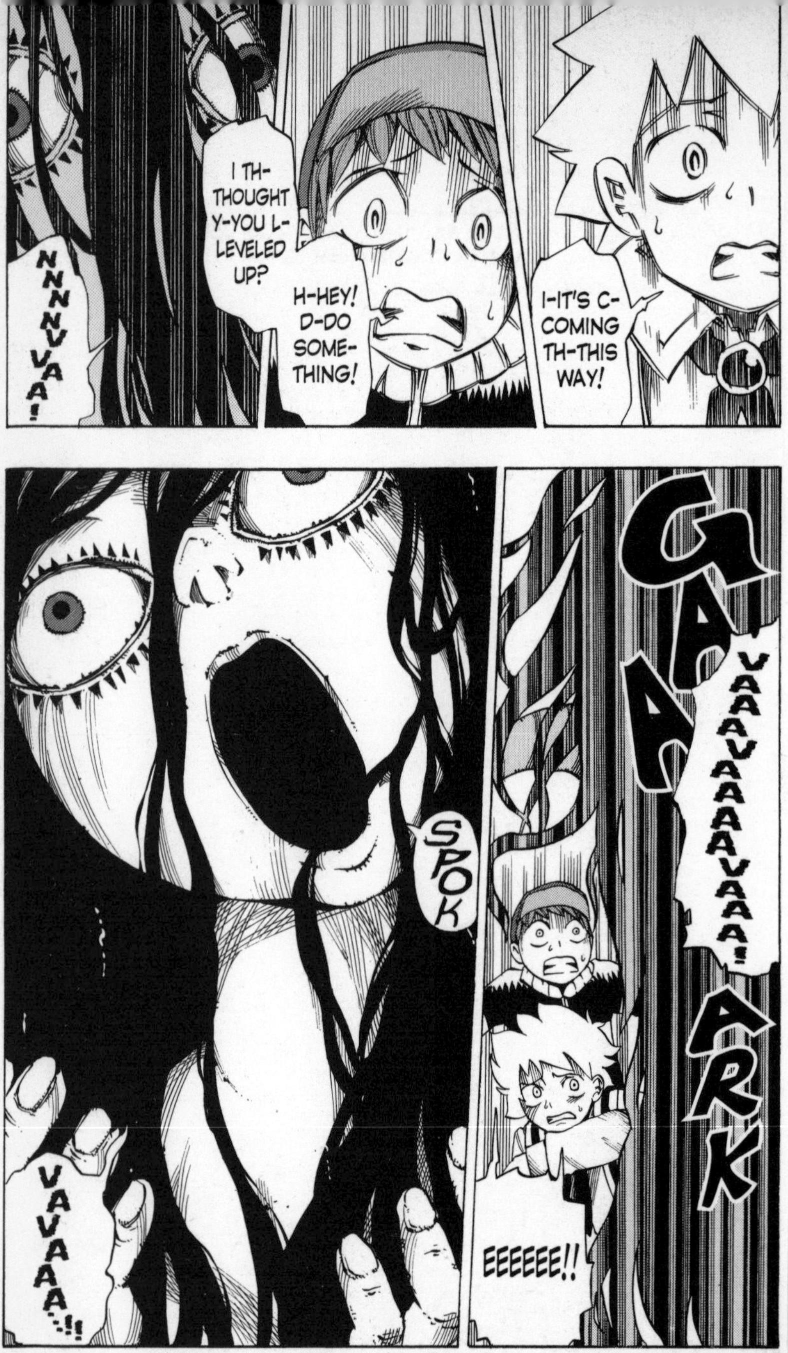
I-IT'S C-COMING TH-THIS WAY!
H-HEY! D-DO SOME-THING!
I TH-THOUGHT Y-YOU L-LEVELED UP?
NNNNVAA!
GAAA
VAAAVAAAAAVAAAA!
ARK
EEEEEE!!
SPOK
VAVAAA..!!

KENJI SATO

BIRTHDAY: DECEMBER 7
HEIGHT: 135 CM

LIKES: HAMBURGERS
BALLS (WILL THROW ANYTHING ROUND)
JABIN (A DEVOTED READER FOR TWO YEARS)

TALENTS: ALL SPORTS
RUNNING AWAY
PLAYING PRANKS

NOT GOOD WITH: STUDYING
SITTING AT A DESK
PLAYING THE RECORDER
CARROTS
ALL KINDS OF ONIONS

CURVE BALL!

GRIP

SO HOW COME MY INTRO CAME AFTER YOURS, NANA? I WAS FIRST!

HMM, I WONDER...

ARTICLE 16
LURKER IN THE GRASS

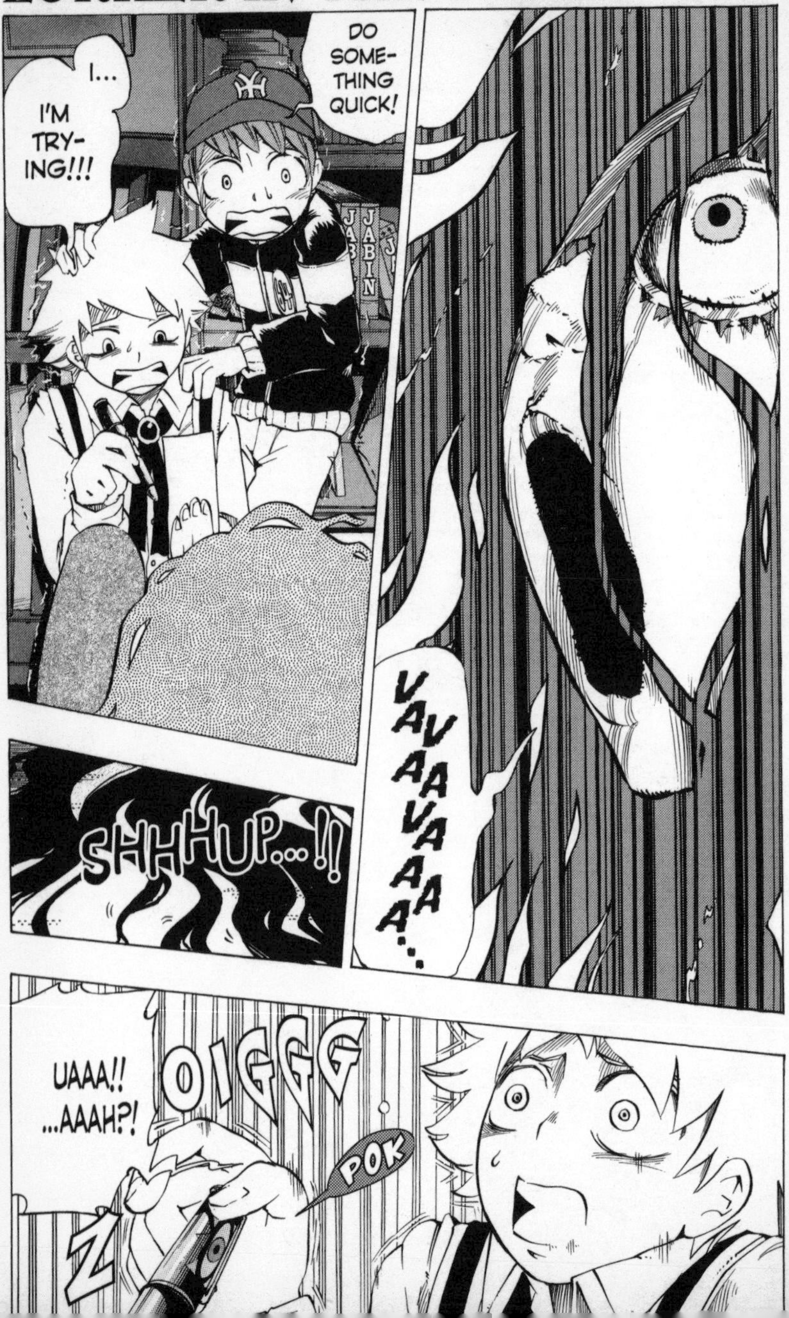
VAVAAAVAAAAA...
DO SOME-THING QUICK!
I... I'M TRY-ING!!!
SHHHUP...!!
OIGGG
UAAA!! ...AAAH?!
POK
Z

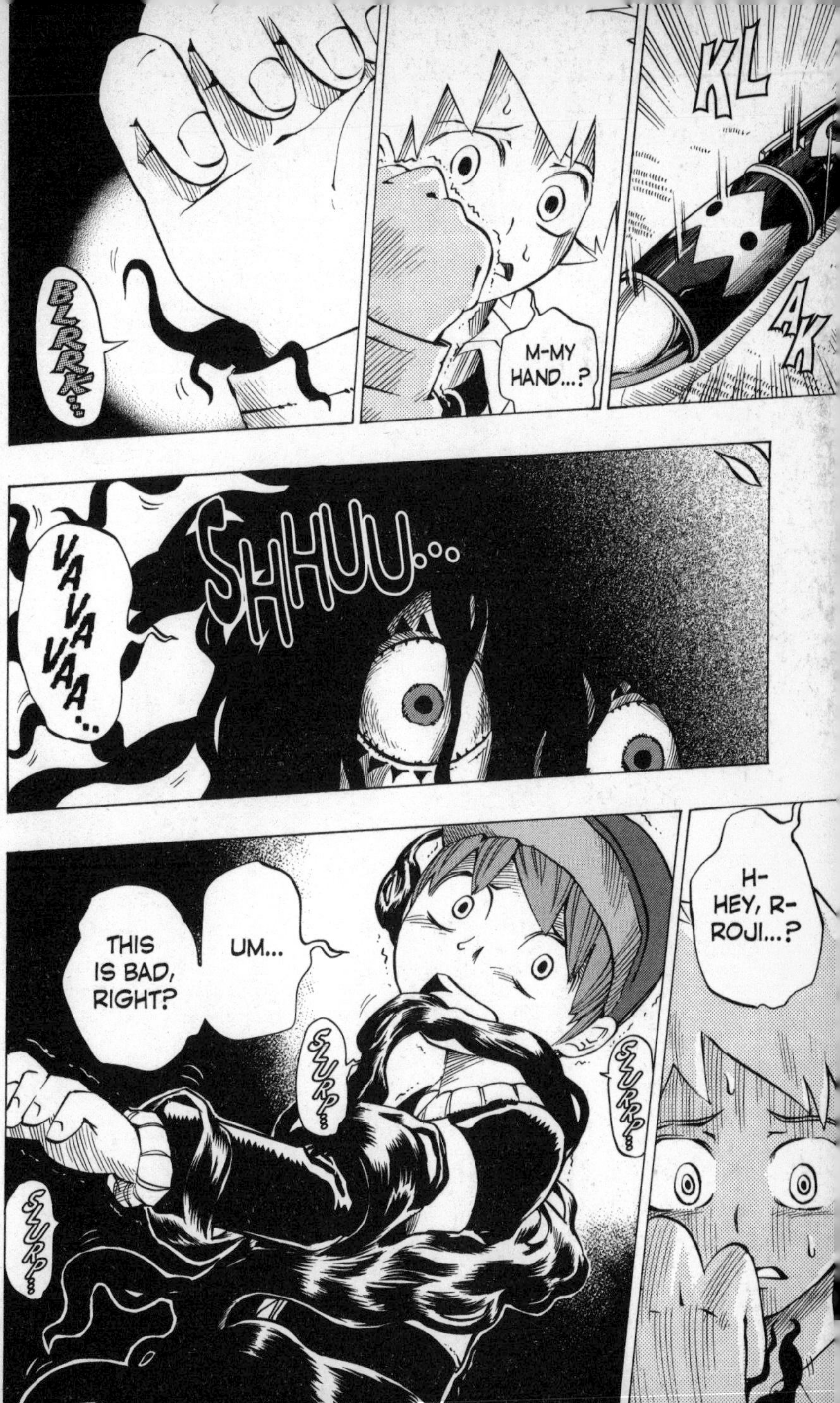
KL
AK
M-MY HAND...?
BLRRK...
SHHUU...
VAVAVAVAA...
H-HEY, R-ROJI...?
SLURP...
UM...
THIS IS BAD, RIGHT?
SLURP...
SLURP...

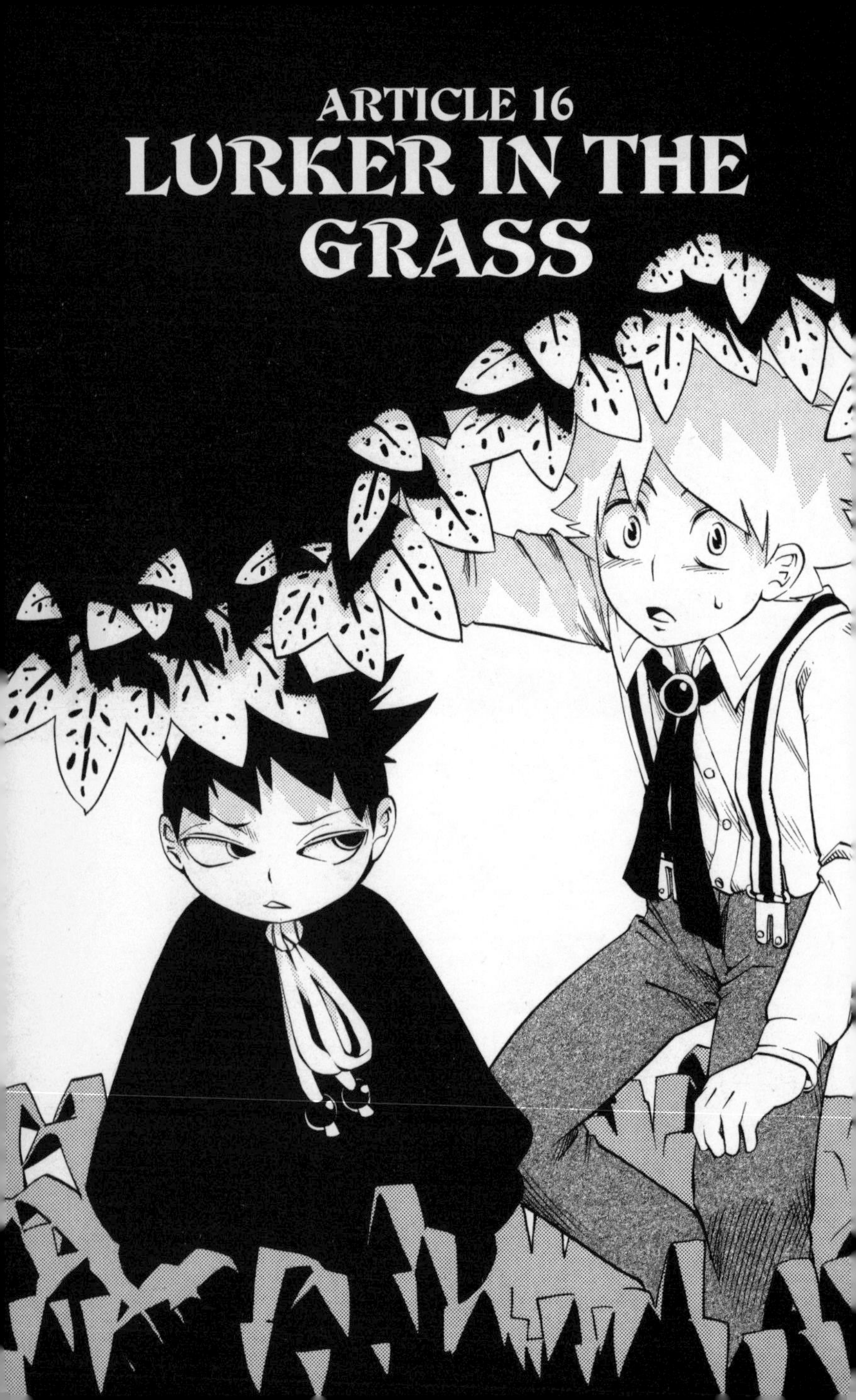
ARTICLE 16
LURKER IN THE GRASS

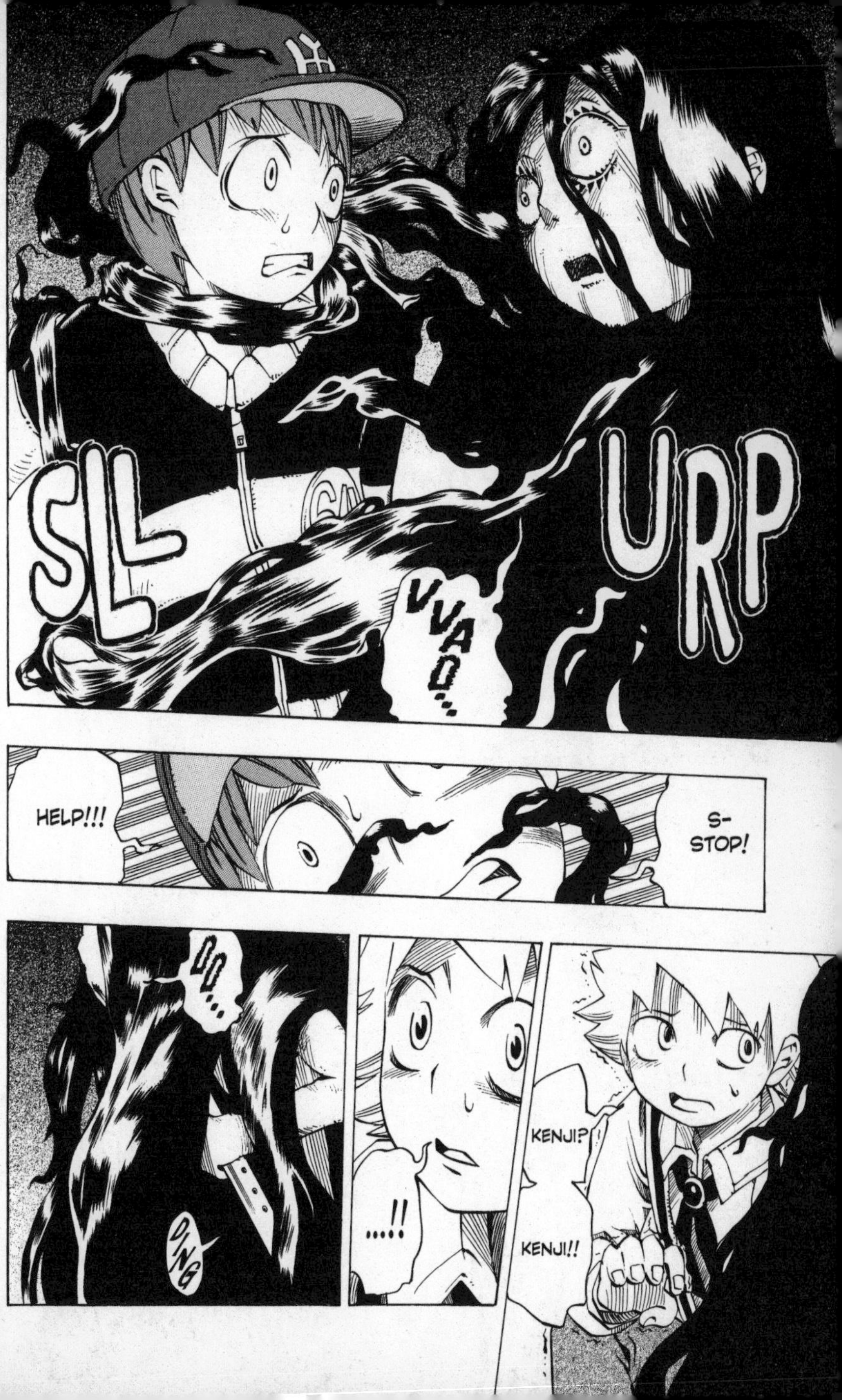
SL URP
VVAQ...
S-STOP!
HELP!!!
KENJI?
KENJI!!
....!!
DO...
DING

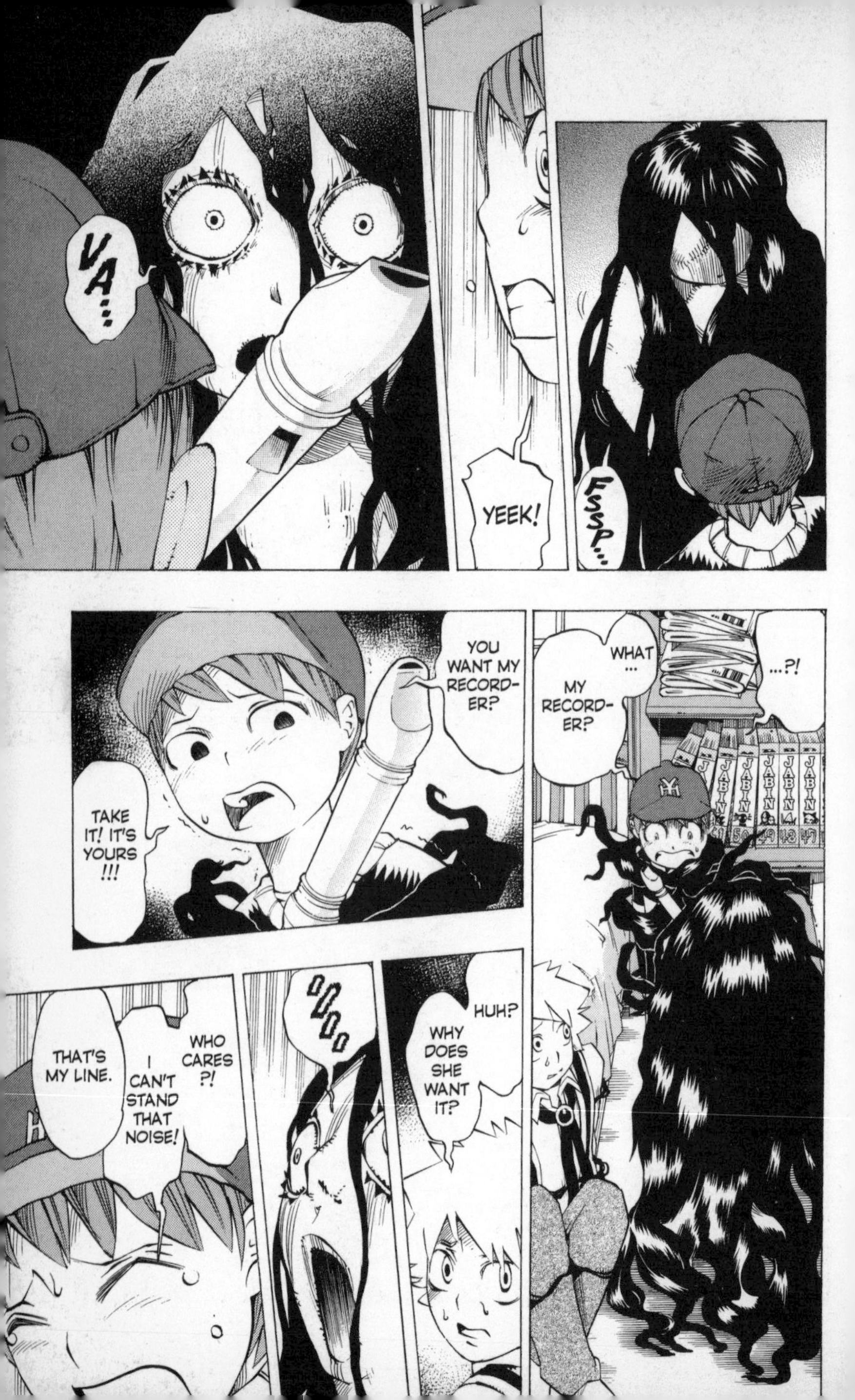
FSSP...
YEEK!
VA...
WHAT...
MY RECORDER?
...?!
YOU WANT MY RECORDER?
TAKE IT! IT'S YOURS!!!
HUH?
WHY DOES SHE WANT IT?
OOOO
WHO CARES?!
I CAN'T STAND THAT NOISE!
THAT'S MY LINE.

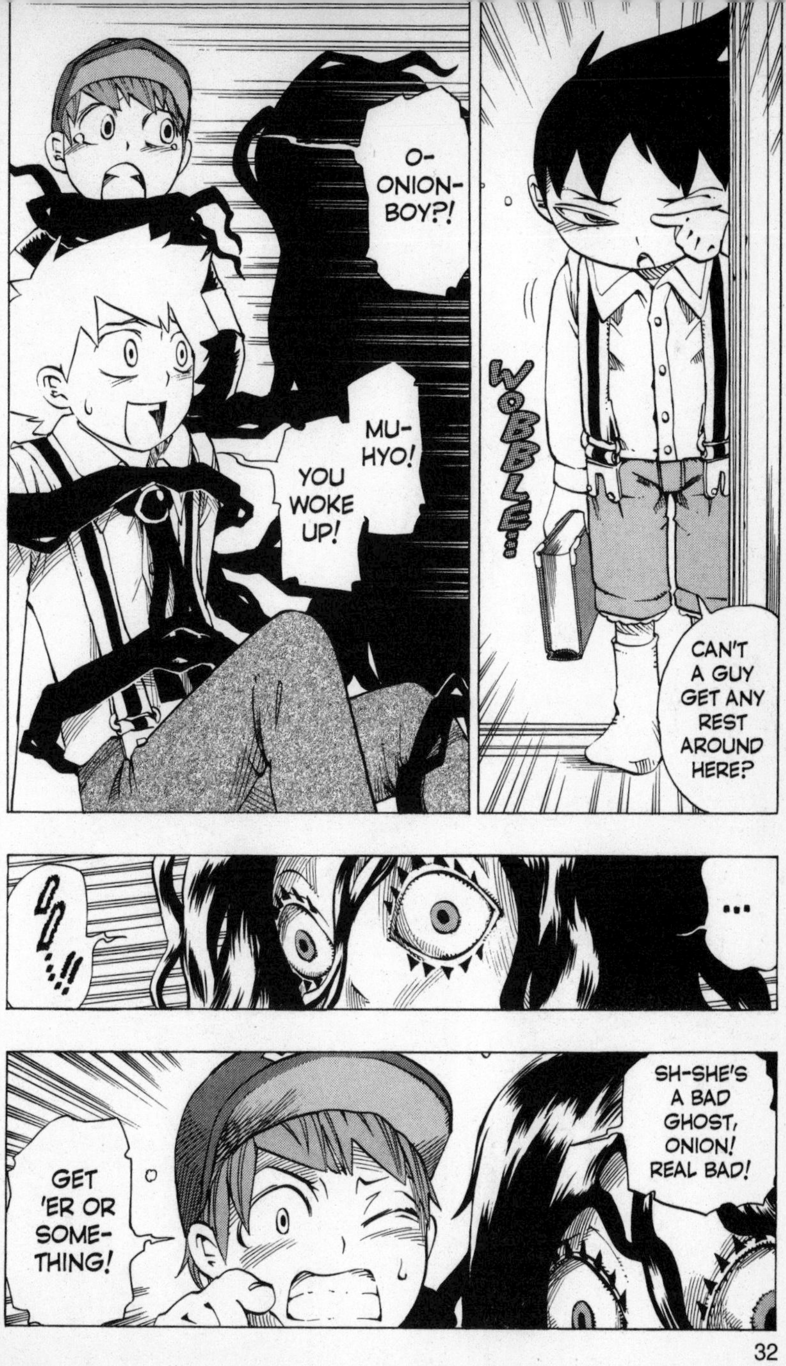
WOBBLE...
CAN'T A GUY GET ANY REST AROUND HERE?
O-ONION-BOY?!
MU-HYO! YOU WOKE UP!
...
SH-SHE'S A BAD GHOST, ONION! REAL BAD!
GET 'ER OR SOMETHING!

READ THIS WAY

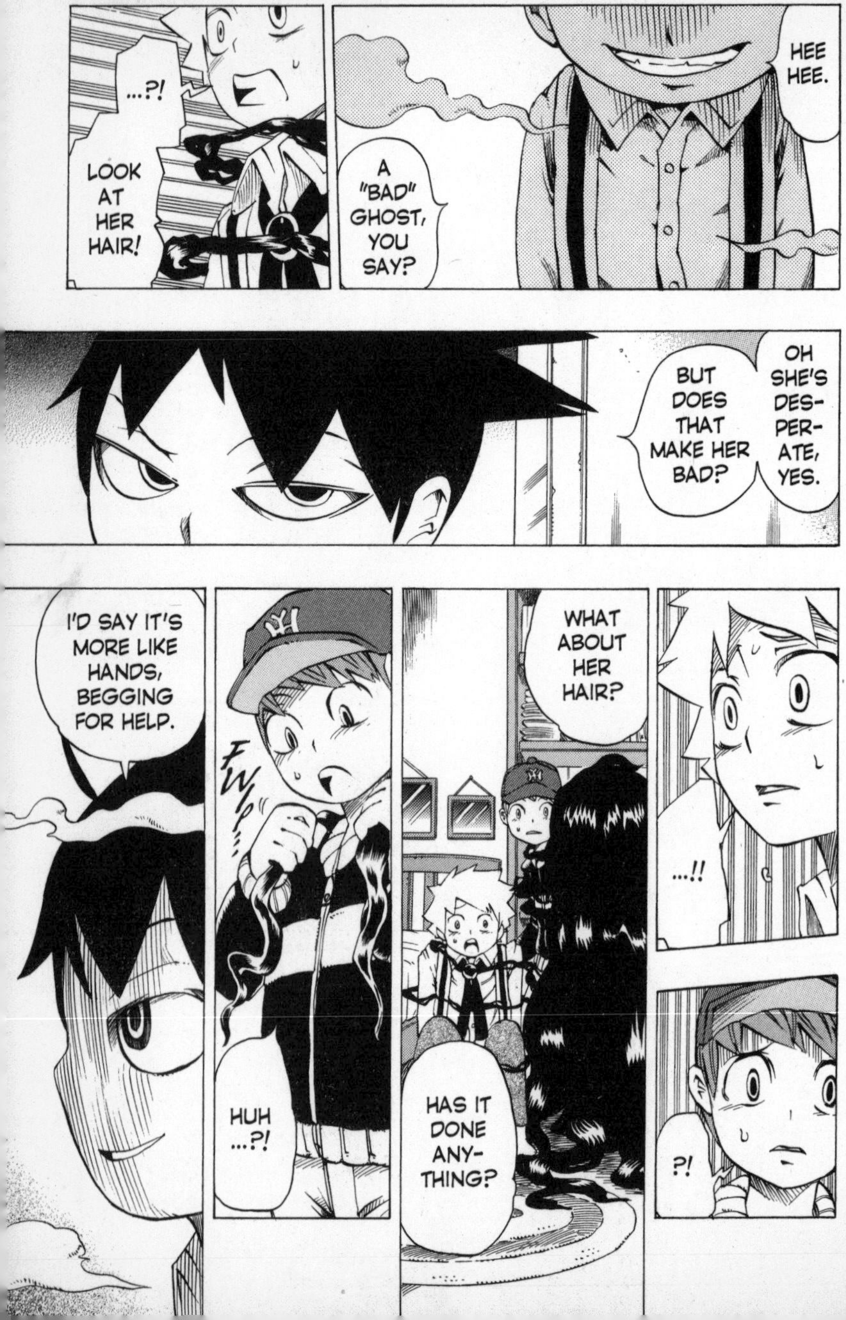

HEE HEE.
A "BAD" GHOST, YOU SAY?
...?!
LOOK AT HER HAIR!
OH SHE'S DESPERATE, YES.
BUT DOES THAT MAKE HER BAD?
...!!
?!
WHAT ABOUT HER HAIR?
HAS IT DONE ANYTHING?
FWIP
HUH ...?!
I'D SAY IT'S MORE LIKE HANDS, BEGGING FOR HELP.

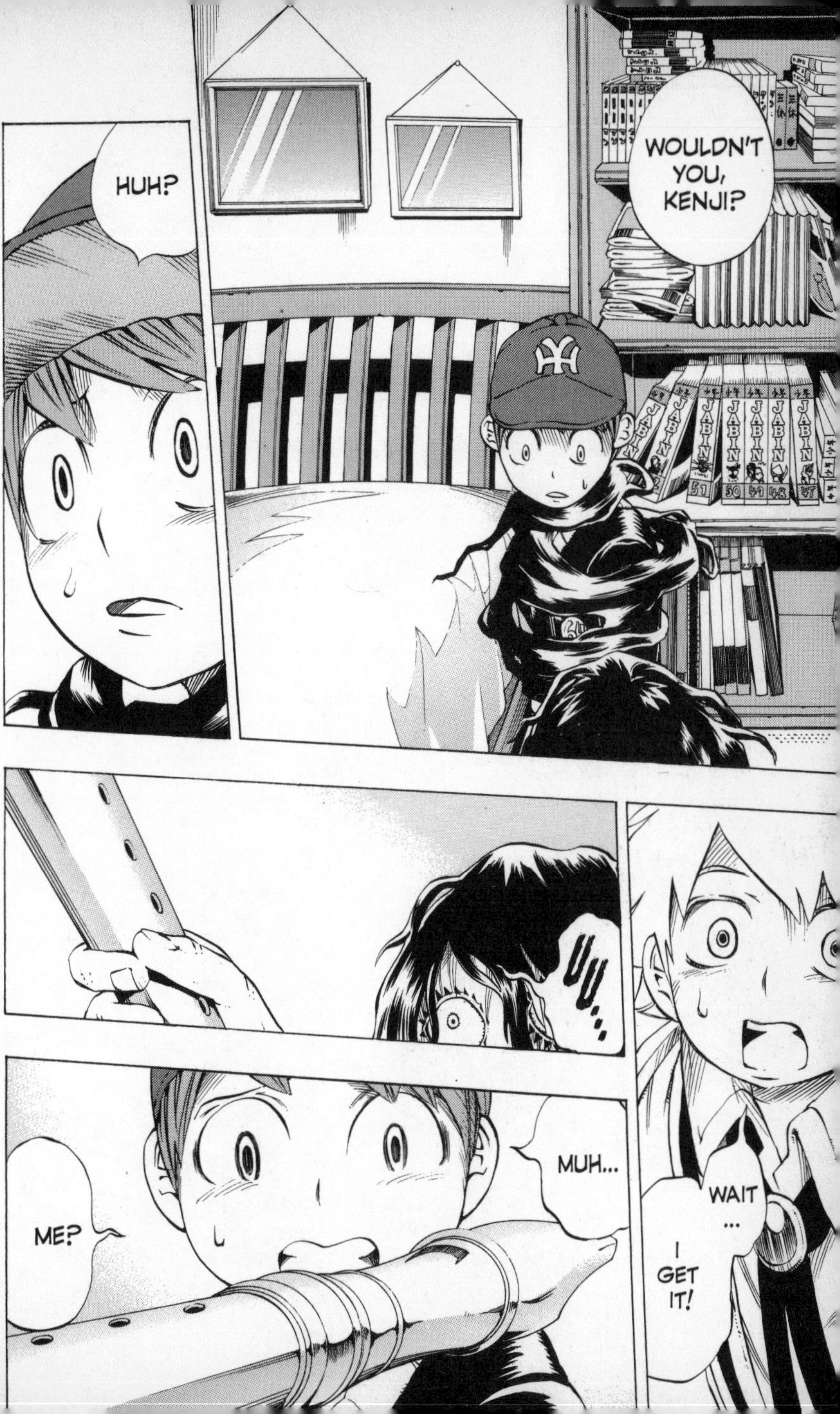
WOULDN'T YOU, KENJI?
HUH?
WAIT ... I GET IT!
UU...
MUH...
ME?

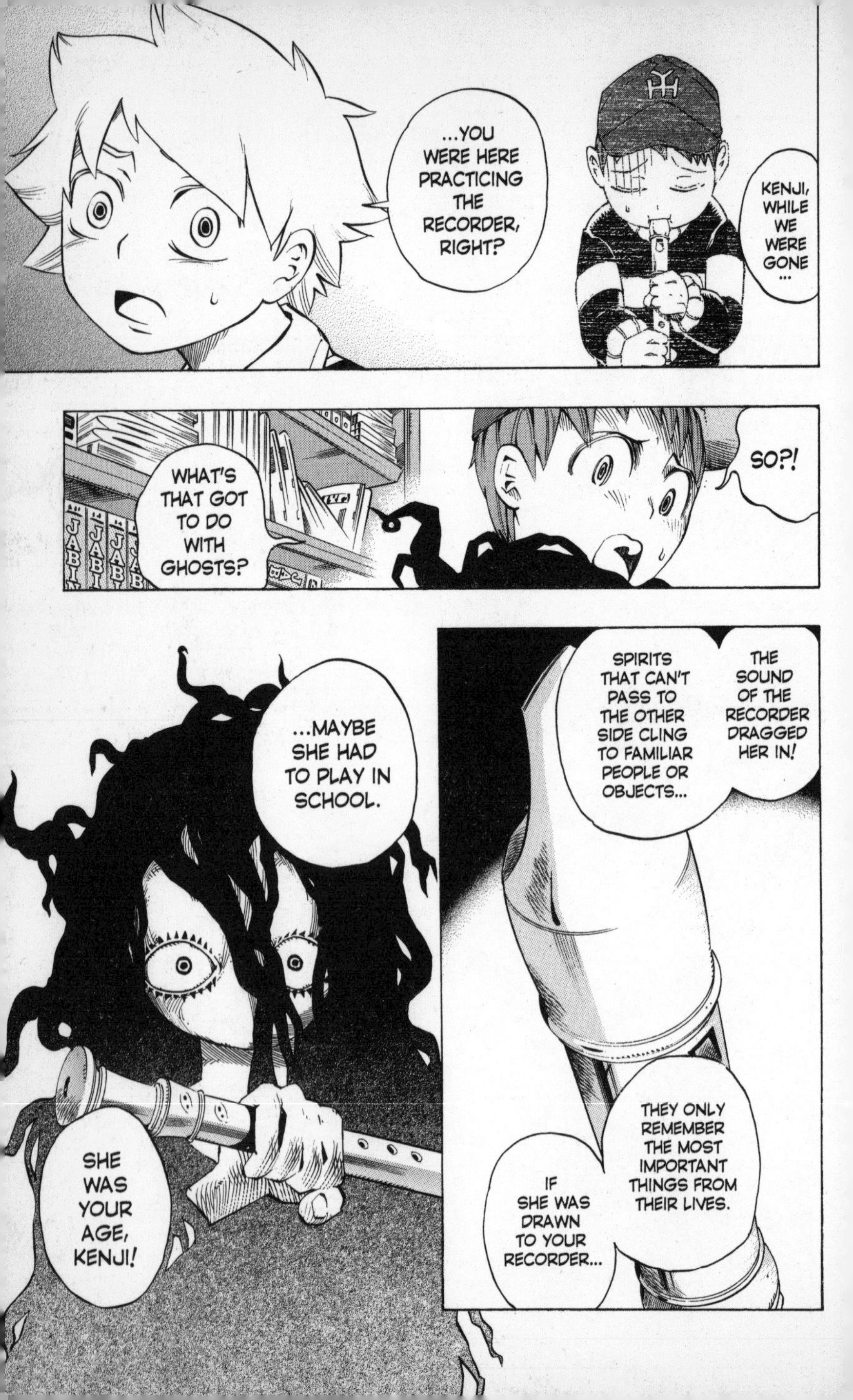
KENJI, WHILE WE WERE GONE ...
...YOU WERE HERE PRACTICING THE RECORDER, RIGHT?
SO?!
WHAT'S THAT GOT TO DO WITH GHOSTS?
THE SOUND OF THE RECORDER DRAGGED HER IN!
SPIRITS THAT CAN'T PASS TO THE OTHER SIDE CLING TO FAMILIAR PEOPLE OR OBJECTS...
THEY ONLY REMEMBER THE MOST IMPORTANT THINGS FROM THEIR LIVES.
IF SHE WAS DRAWN TO YOUR RECORDER...
...MAYBE SHE HAD TO PLAY IN SCHOOL.
SHE WAS YOUR AGE, KENJI!

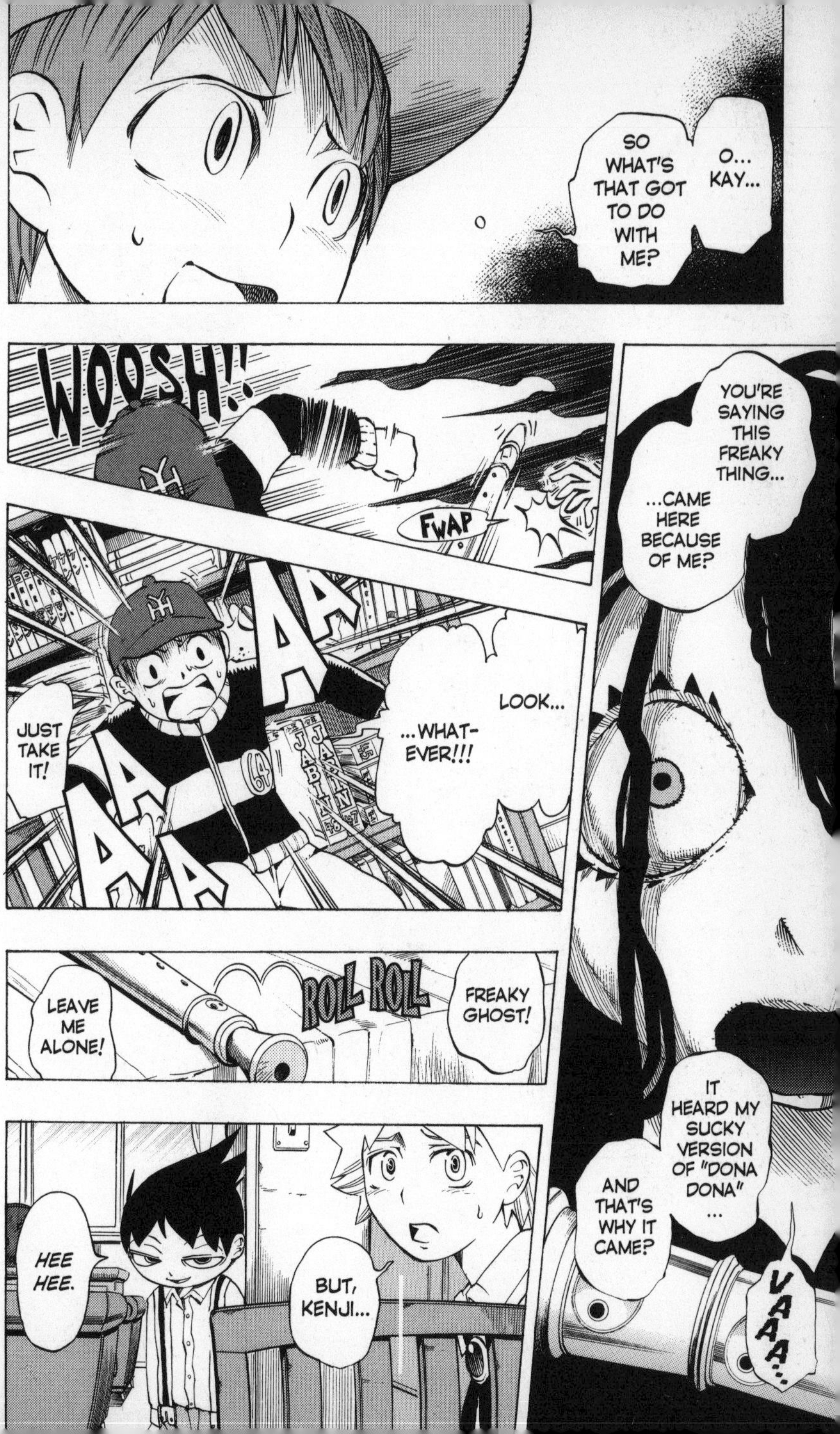
O... KAY...
SO WHAT'S THAT GOT TO DO WITH ME?
YOU'RE SAYING THIS FREAKY THING...
...CAME HERE BECAUSE OF ME?
IT HEARD MY SUCKY VERSION OF "DONA DONA"...
AND THAT'S WHY IT CAME?
VAAA...
WOOSH!!
FWAP
AAAAA
LOOK...
...WHAT-EVER!!!
JUST TAKE IT!
FREAKY GHOST!
ROLL ROLL
LEAVE ME ALONE!
BUT, KENJI...
HEE HEE.

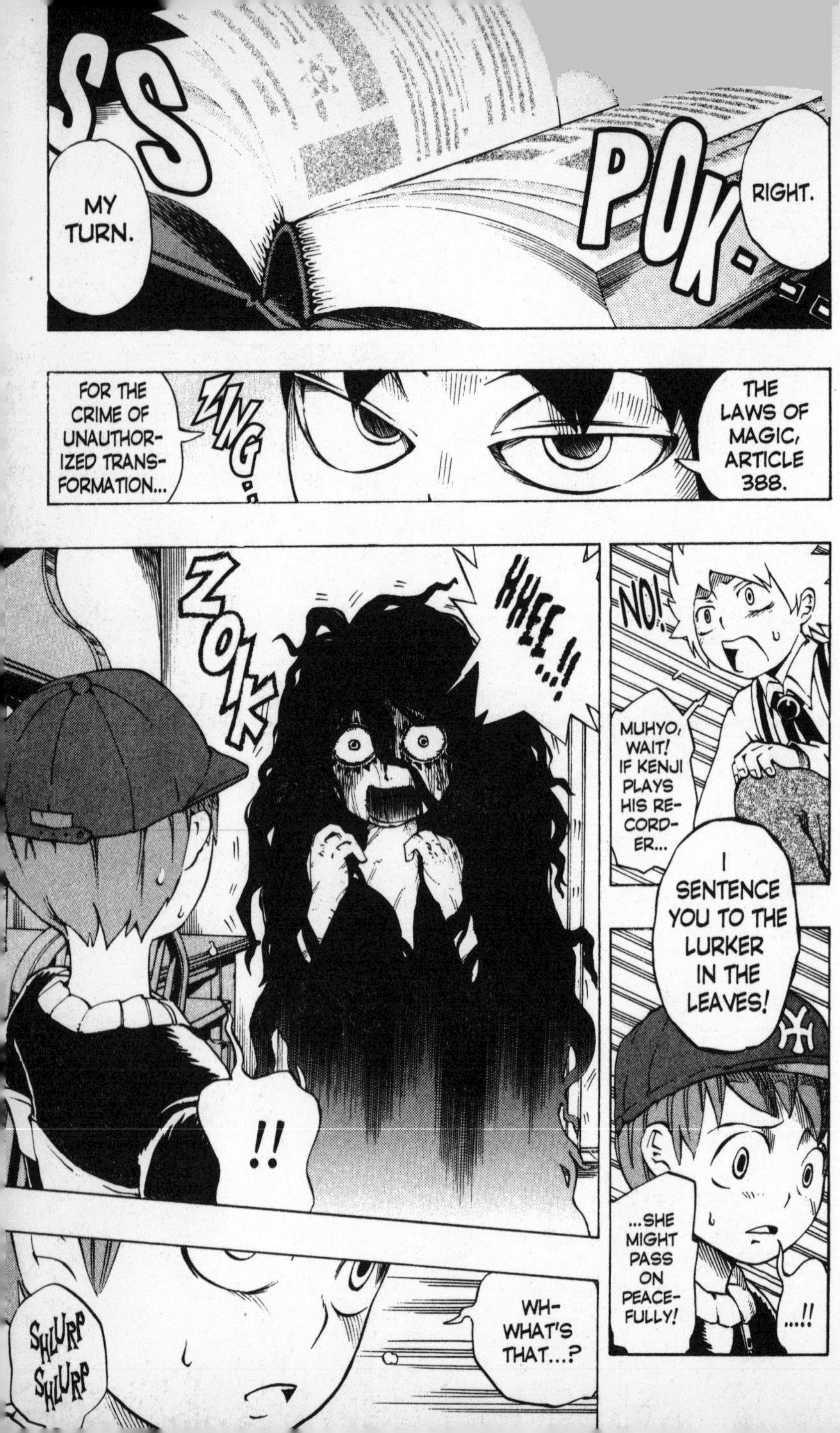
RIGHT.
POK-
SS
MY TURN.
THE LAWS OF MAGIC, ARTICLE 388.
ZING
FOR THE CRIME OF UNAUTHORIZED TRANSFORMATION...
NO!
MUHYO, WAIT! IF KENJI PLAYS HIS RECORDER...
I SENTENCE YOU TO THE LURKER IN THE LEAVES!
...SHE MIGHT PASS ON PEACEFULLY!
...!!
HHEE..!!
ZOK
!!
WH-WHAT'S THAT...?
SHLURP
SHLURP

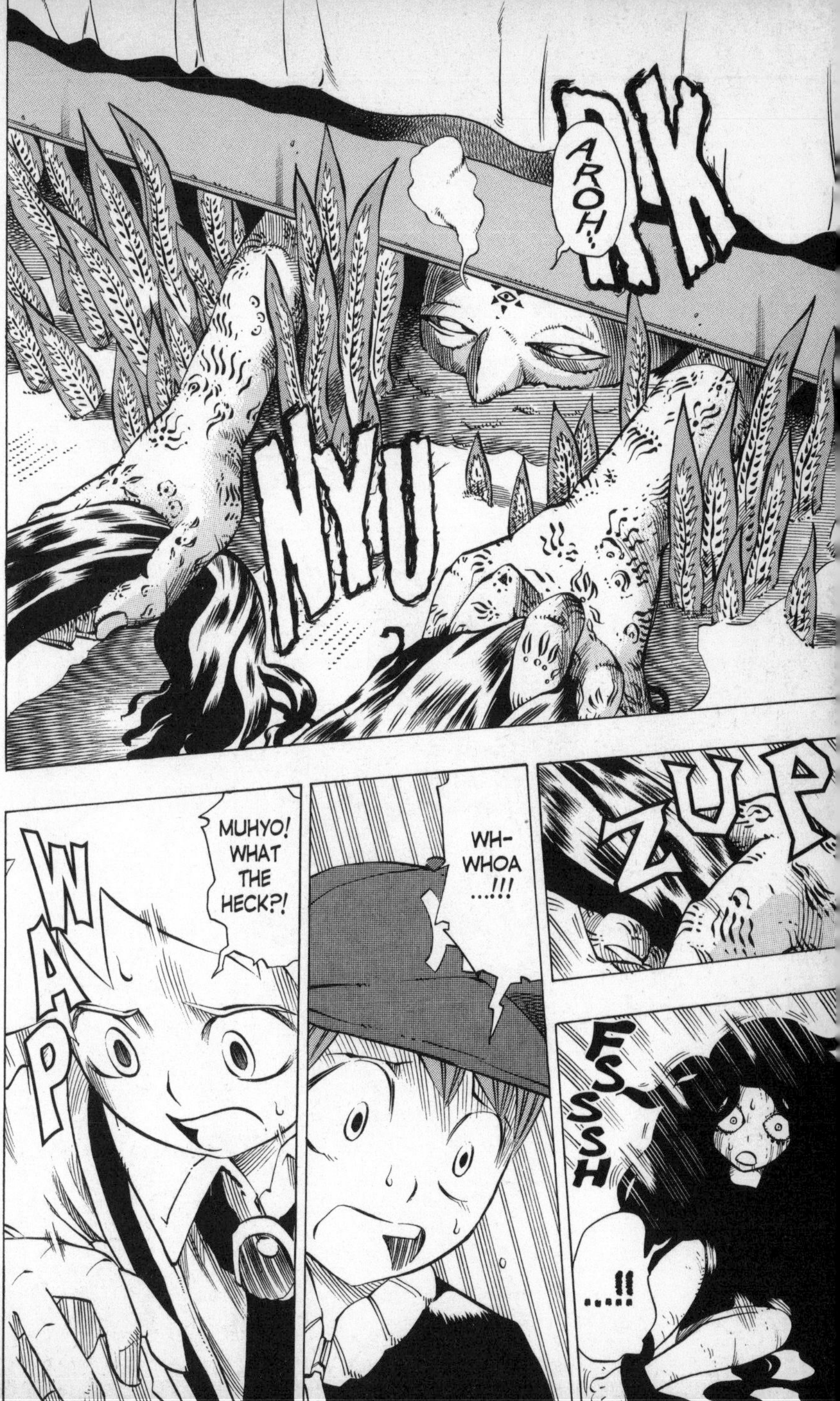
DK
AROH...
NYU
ZUP
FSSSH
...!!
WH-WHOA ...!!!
MUHYO! WHAT THE HECK?!
WAP

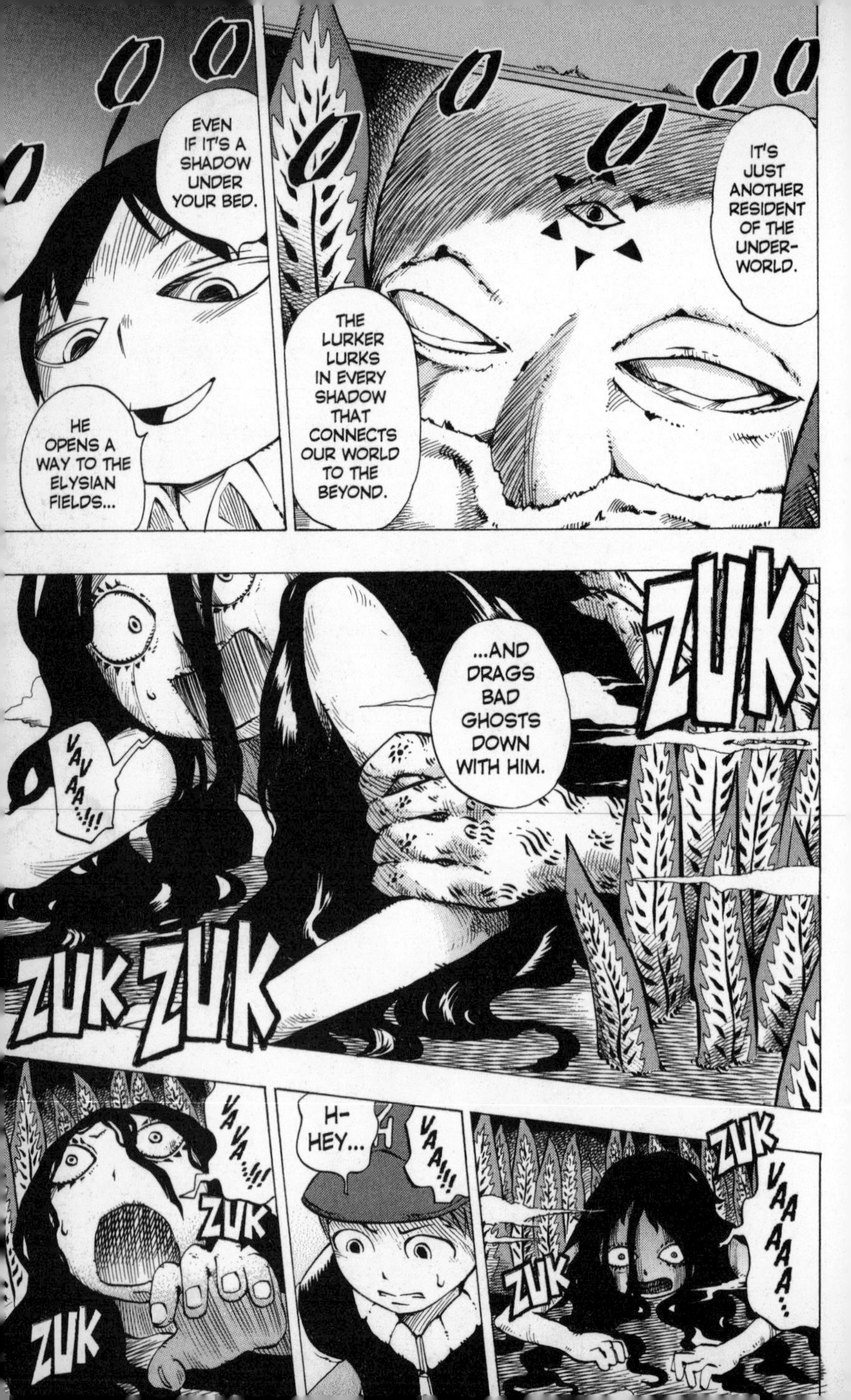
IT'S JUST ANOTHER RESIDENT OF THE UNDER-WORLD.
THE LURKER LURKS IN EVERY SHADOW THAT CONNECTS OUR WORLD TO THE BEYOND.
EVEN IF IT'S A SHADOW UNDER YOUR BED.
HE OPENS A WAY TO THE ELYSIAN FIELDS...
ZUK
...AND DRAGS BAD GHOSTS DOWN WITH HIM.
VAVAA...!!!
ZUK ZUK
ZUK
VAAAAAA...
ZUK
VAA!!!
H-HEY...
VAVA...!!!
ZUK
ZUK

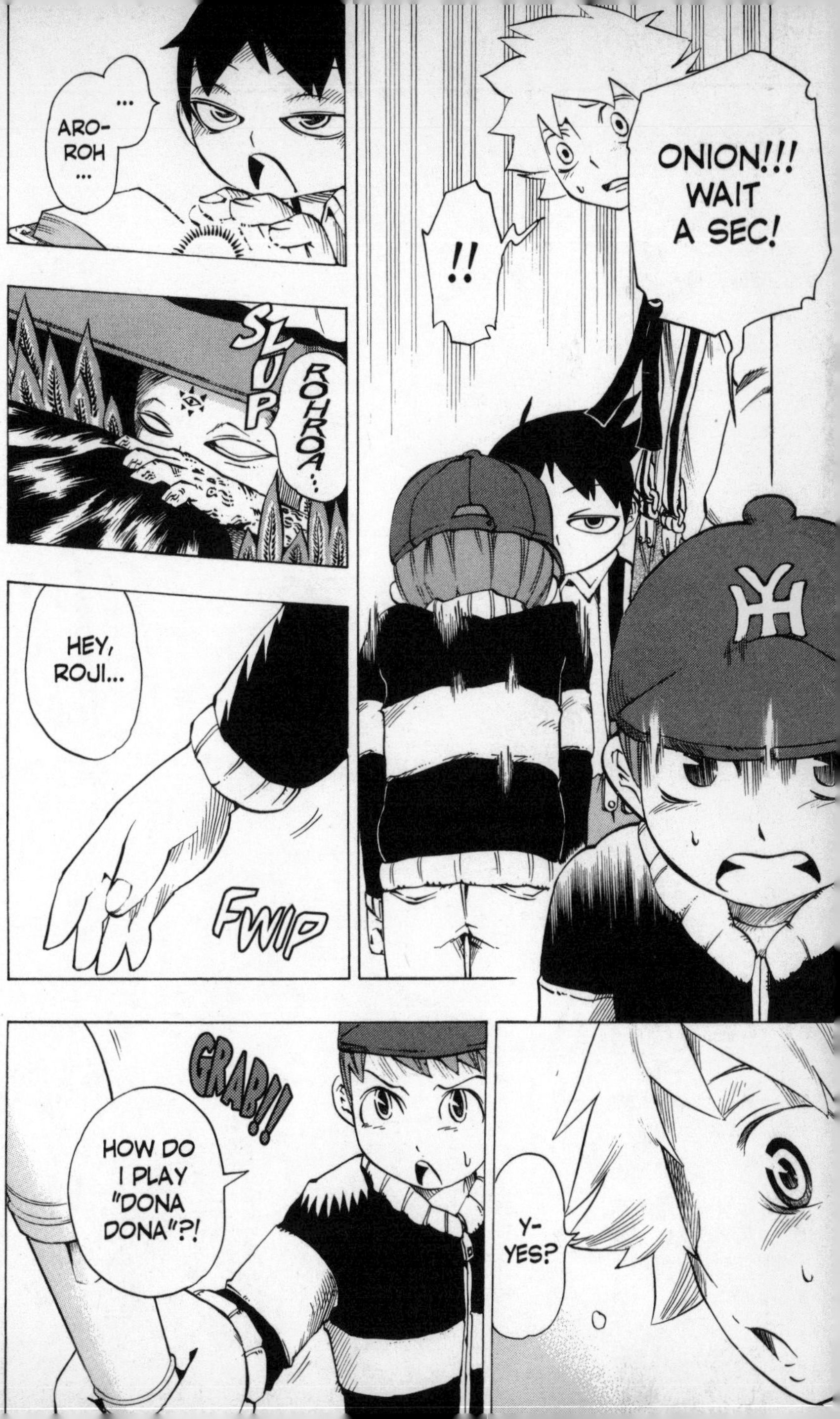
ONION!!! WAIT A SEC!
!!
... ARO- ROH ...
SLUP
ROHROA...
HEY, ROJI...
FWIP
Y- YES?
GRAB!!
HOW DO I PLAY "DONA DONA"?!

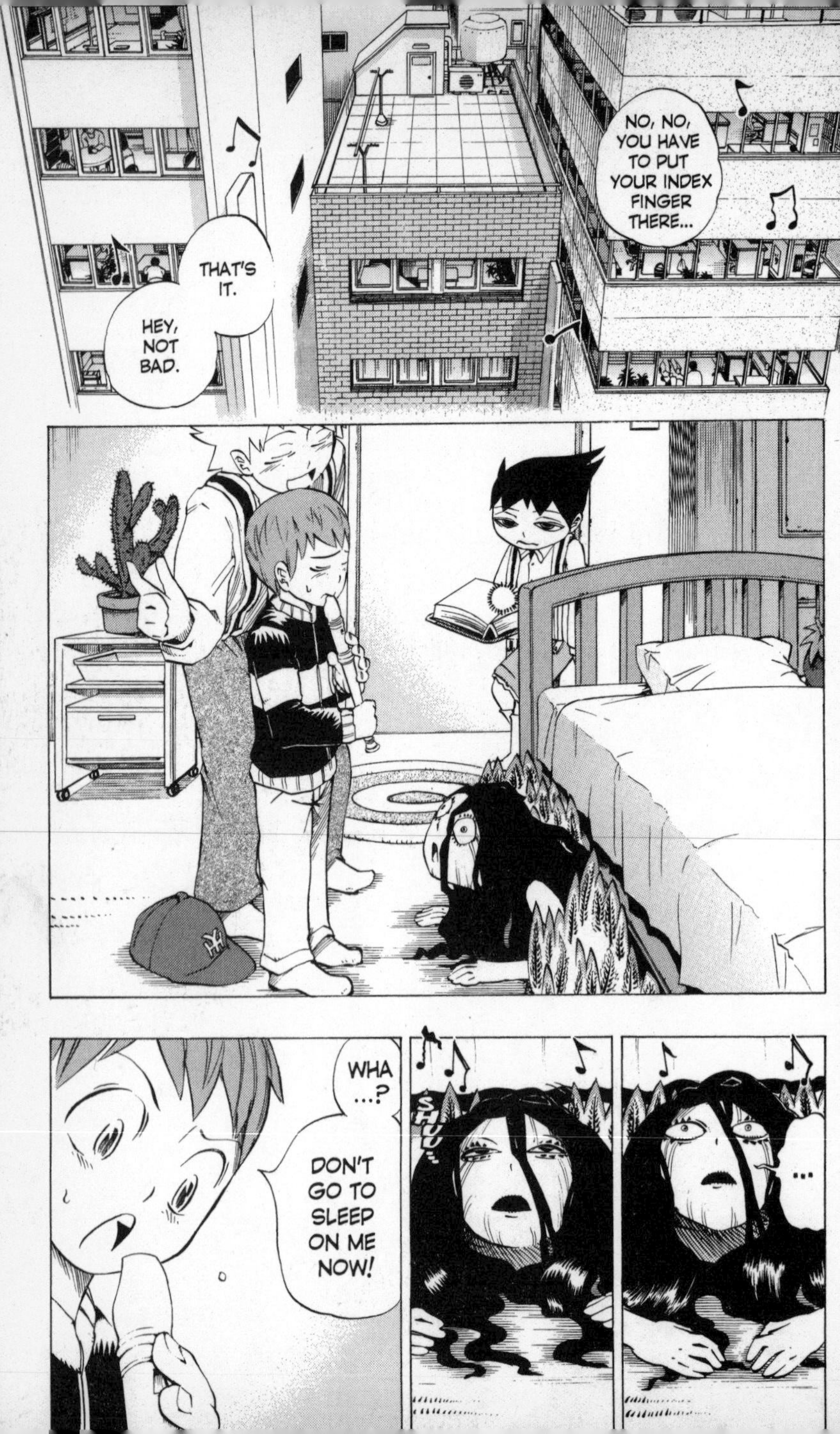
NO, NO, YOU HAVE TO PUT YOUR INDEX FINGER THERE...
THAT'S IT.
HEY, NOT BAD.
...
SHUU...
WHA ...?
DON'T GO TO SLEEP ON ME NOW!

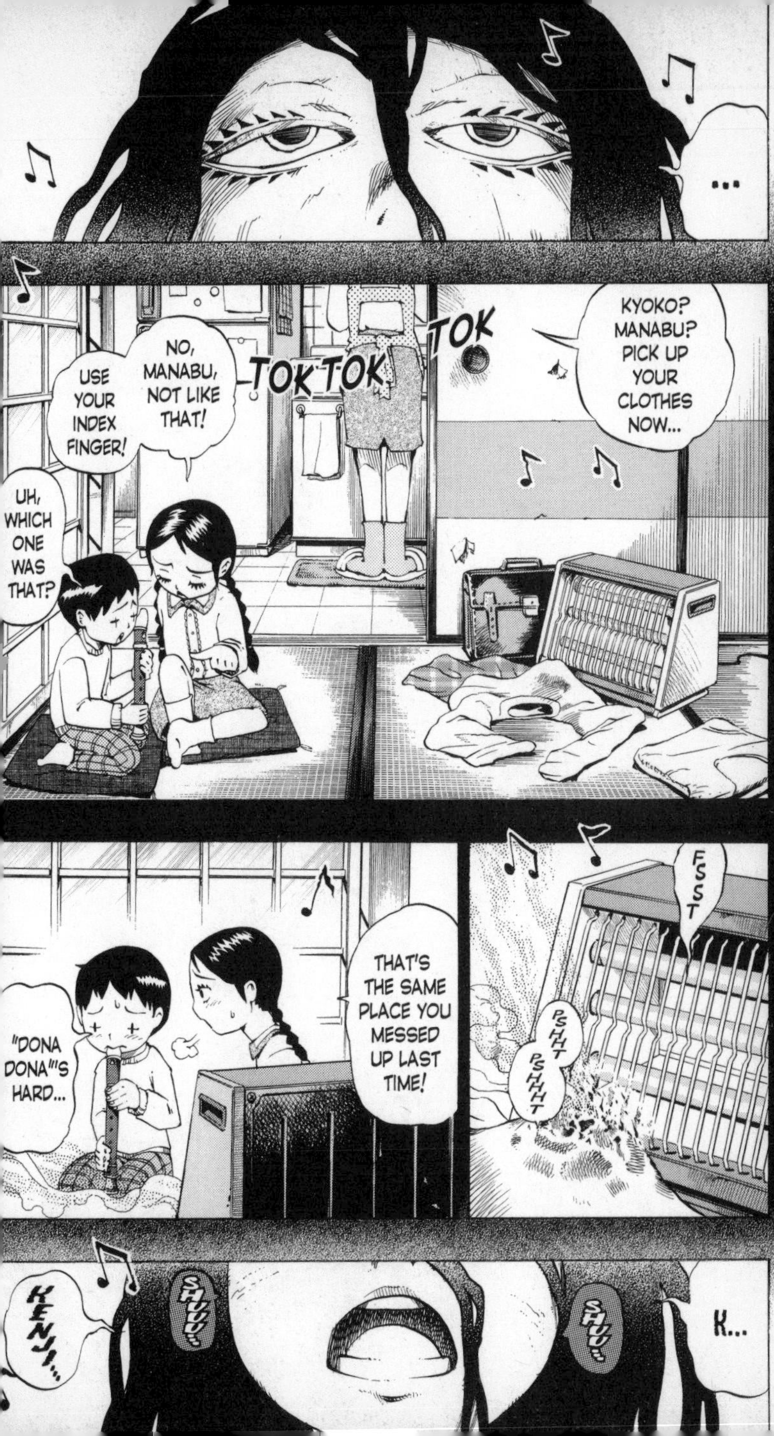
...
KYOKO? MANABU? PICK UP YOUR CLOTHES NOW...
TOK TOK TOK
NO, MANABU, NOT LIKE THAT!
USE YOUR INDEX FINGER!
UH, WHICH ONE WAS THAT?
FSST
PSHHT PSHHHT
THAT'S THE SAME PLACE YOU MESSED UP LAST TIME!
"DONA DONA"'S HARD...
K...
SHUUU...
SHUUU...
KENJI...

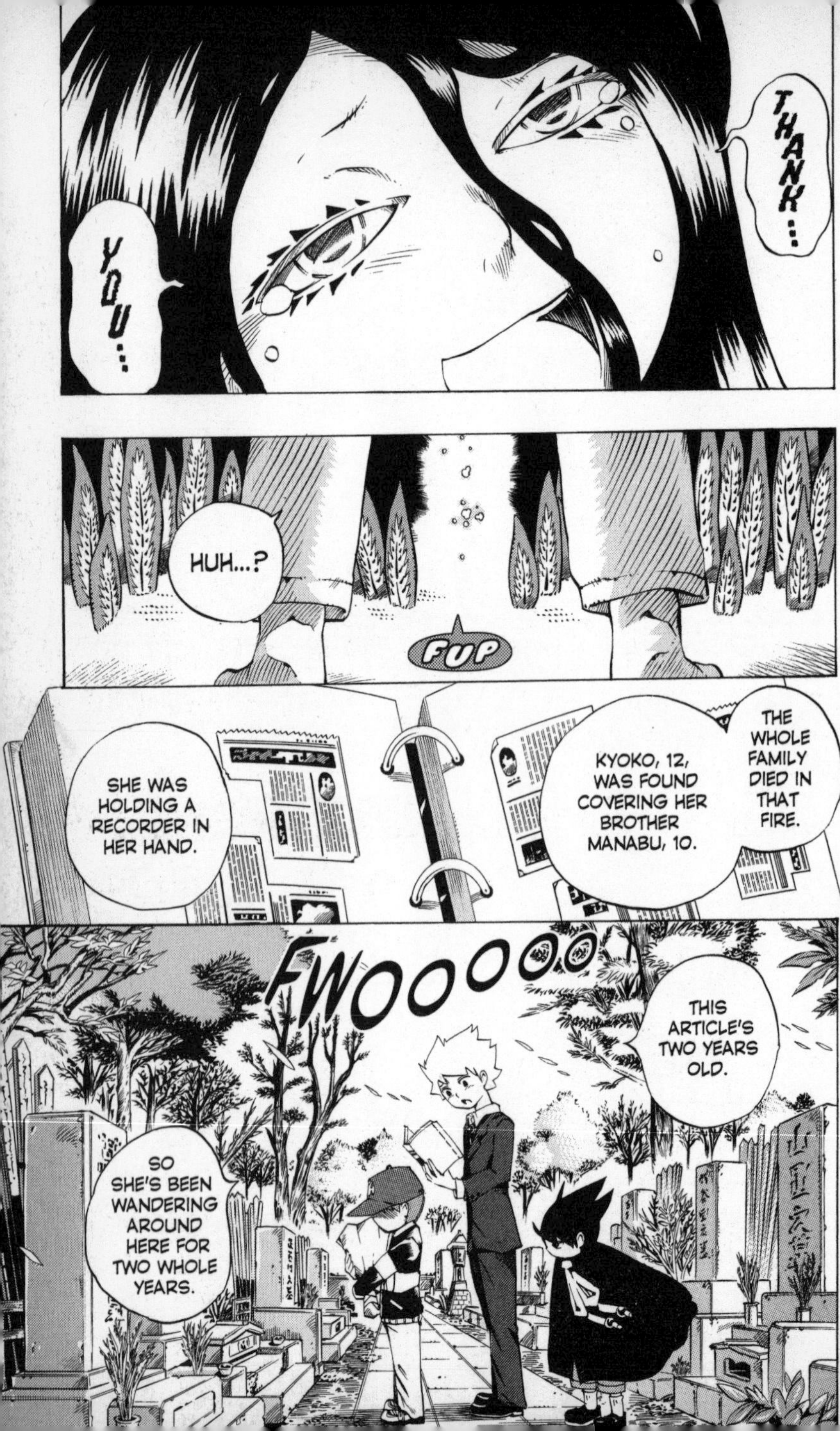
THANK...
YOU...
HUH...?
FUP
THE WHOLE FAMILY DIED IN THAT FIRE.
KYOKO, 12, WAS FOUND COVERING HER BROTHER MANABU, 10.
SHE WAS HOLDING A RECORDER IN HER HAND.
FWOOOOO
THIS ARTICLE'S TWO YEARS OLD.
SO SHE'S BEEN WANDERING AROUND HERE FOR TWO WHOLE YEARS.

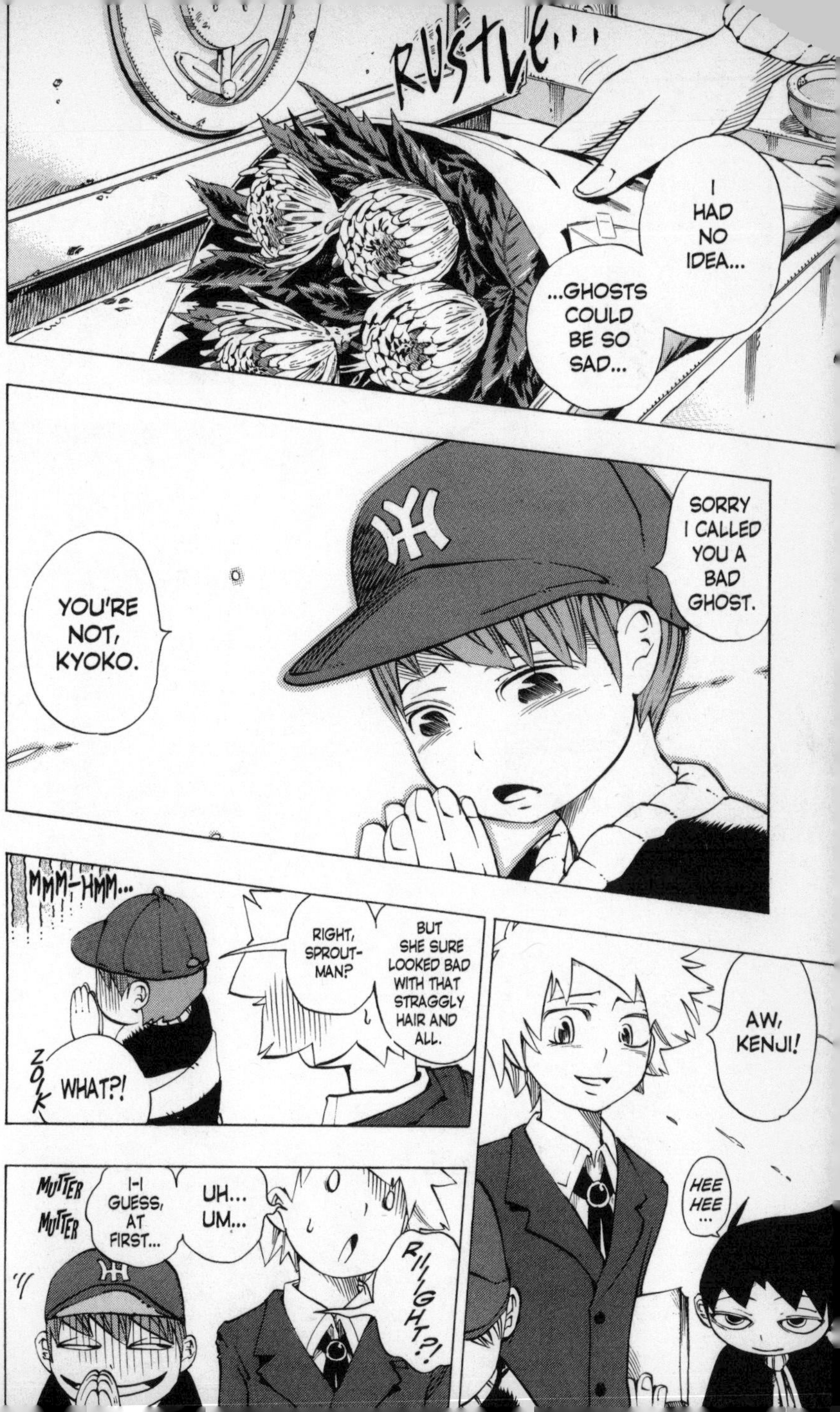
RUSTLE...
I HAD NO IDEA...
...GHOSTS COULD BE SO SAD...
SORRY I CALLED YOU A BAD GHOST.
YOU'RE NOT, KYOKO.
AW, KENJI!
HEE HEE ...
BUT SHE SURE LOOKED BAD WITH THAT STRAGGLY HAIR AND ALL.
RIGHT, SPROUT-MAN?
MMM-HMM...
ZOIK
WHAT?!
RIIIGHT?!
UH... UM...
I-I GUESS, AT FIRST...
MUTTER MUTTER

READ THIS WAY

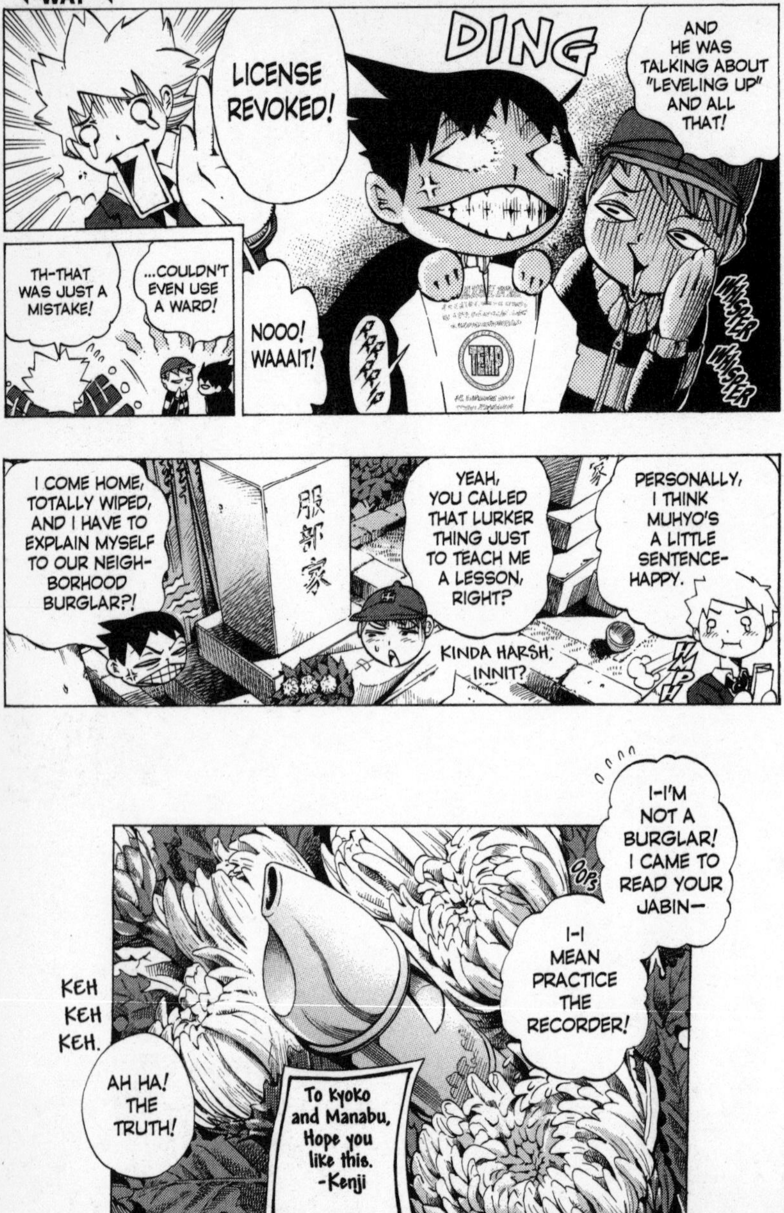
AND HE WAS TALKING ABOUT "LEVELING UP" AND ALL THAT!
DING
LICENSE REVOKED!
WHISPER WHISPER
RRRRIP
NOOO! WAAAIT!
...COULDN'T EVEN USE A WARD!
TH-THAT WAS JUST A MISTAKE!
PERSONALLY, I THINK MUHYO'S A LITTLE SENTENCE-HAPPY.
YEAH, YOU CALLED THAT LURKER THING JUST TO TEACH ME A LESSON, RIGHT?
KINDA HARSH, INNIT?
HMPH
I COME HOME, TOTALLY WIPED, AND I HAVE TO EXPLAIN MYSELF TO OUR NEIGHBORHOOD BURGLAR?!
服部家
I-I'M NOT A BURGLAR! I CAME TO READ YOUR JABIN—
OOPS
I-I MEAN PRACTICE THE RECORDER!
To Kyoko and Manabu, Hope you like this. -Kenji
KEH KEH KEH.
AH HA! THE TRUTH!

INTRODUCING
THE Q & A CORNER,
WHERE I ANSWER SOME
FREQUENTLY ASKED
QUESTIONS AND SOME
UNUSUAL ONES.
LET'S BEGIN...

Q: ARE YOU A GIRL?
YOUR MANGA STYLE'S
KIND OF...GIRLISH.

A: I'M VERY MUCH A *DUDE*.
BUT MAYBE INSIDE I'M
A GIRL. HMM...

ARTICLE 17
THE GHOST WRITER

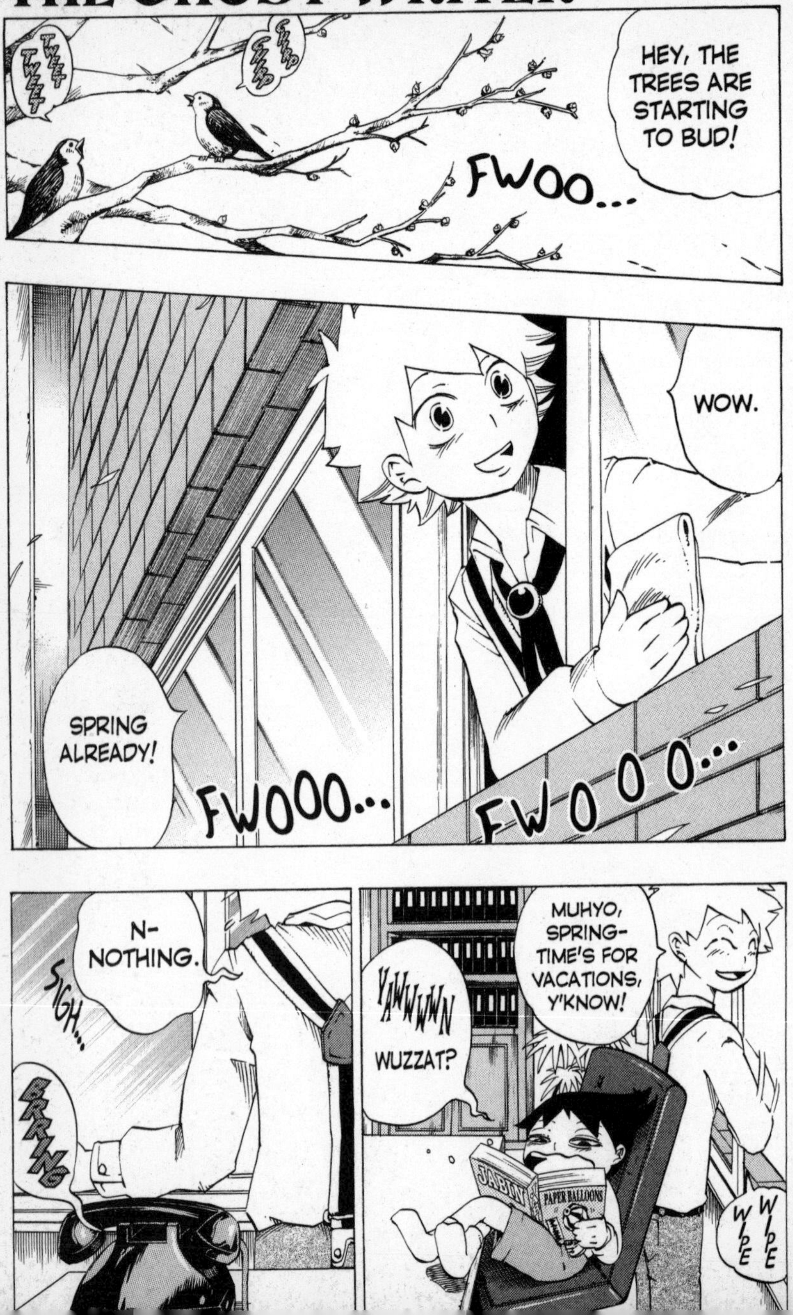
HEY, THE TREES ARE STARTING TO BUD!
CHIRP CHIRP
TWEET TWEET
FWOO...
WOW.
FWOOO...
FWOOO...
SPRING ALREADY!
MUHYO, SPRING-TIME'S FOR VACATIONS, Y'KNOW!
YAWWWWN
WUZZAT?
JABIN
PAPER BALLOONS
WIPE WIPE
N-NOTHING.
SIGH...
BRRING

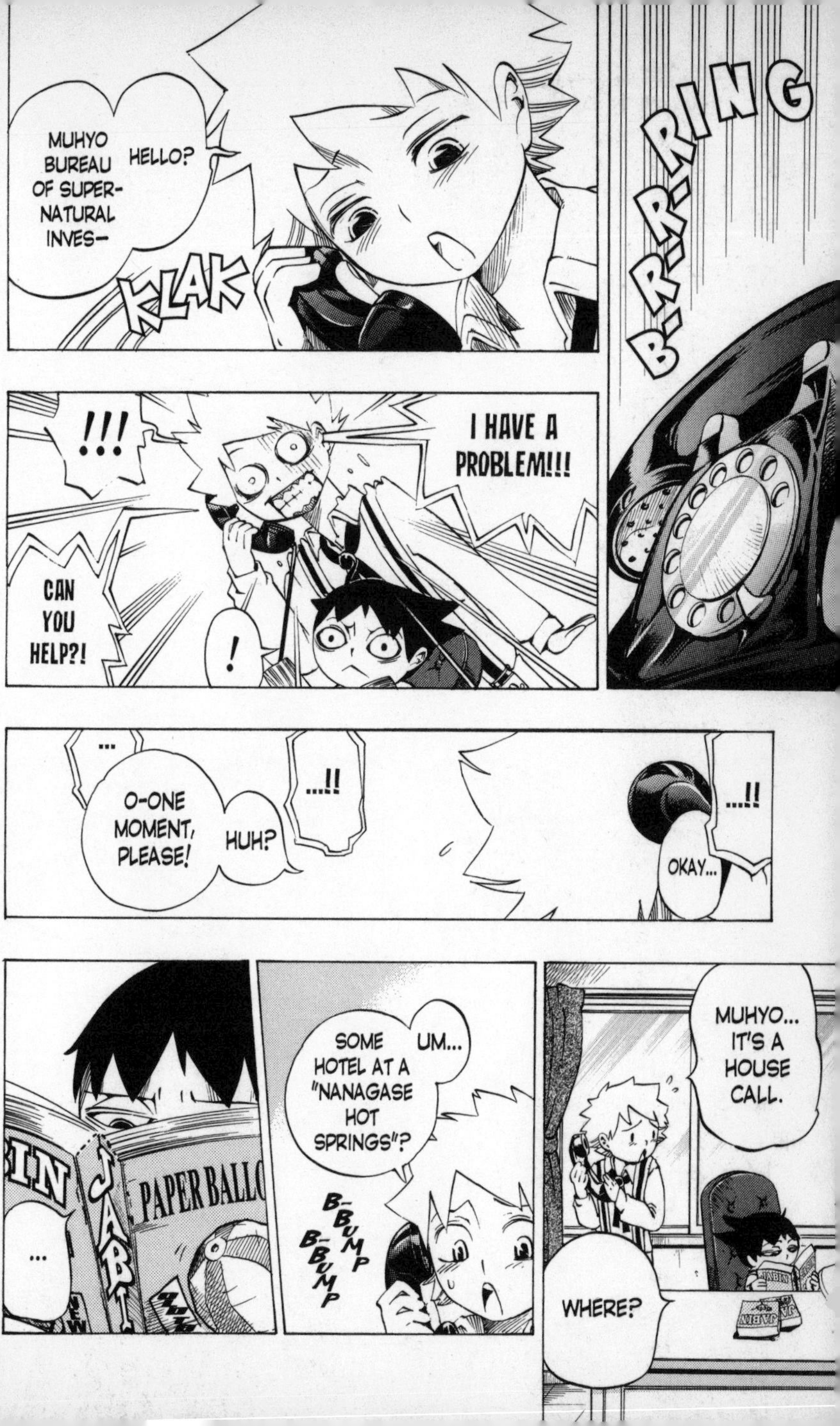
B-R-R-RING
HELLO?
MUHYO BUREAU OF SUPER-NATURAL INVES—
KLAK
I HAVE A PROBLEM!!!
!!!
CAN YOU HELP?!
!
...!!
OKAY...
...!!
...
O-ONE MOMENT, PLEASE!
HUH?
MUHYO... IT'S A HOUSE CALL.
WHERE?
UM...
SOME HOTEL AT A "NANAGASE HOT SPRINGS"?
B-BUMP B-BUMP
...

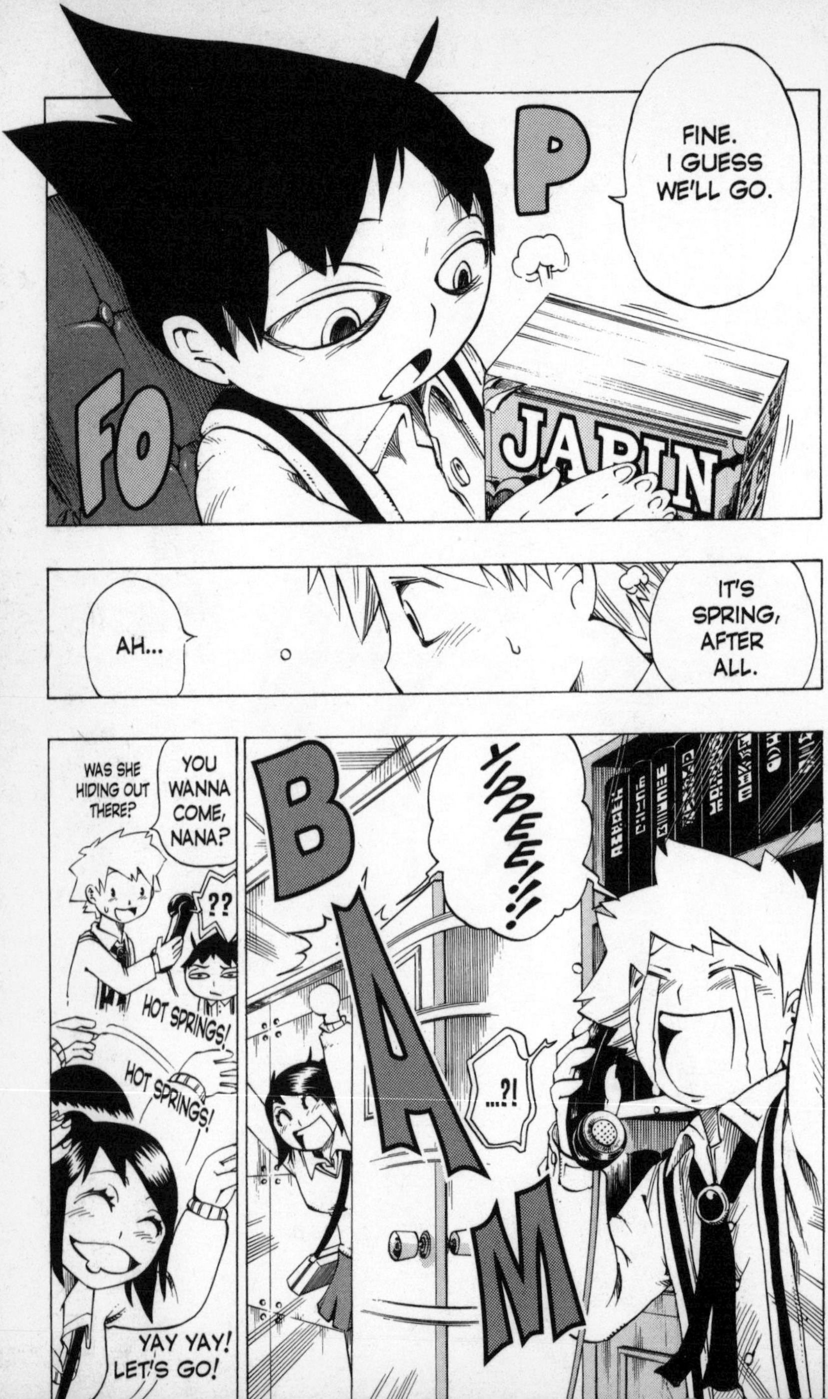
FINE. I GUESS WE'LL GO.
FOP
JAPIN
IT'S SPRING, AFTER ALL.
AH...
YIPPEE!!!
BAM
...?!
YOU WANNA COME, NANA?
WAS SHE HIDING OUT THERE?
??
HOT SPRINGS!
HOT SPRINGS!
YAY YAY! LET'S GO!

ARTICLE 17
THE GHOST WRITER

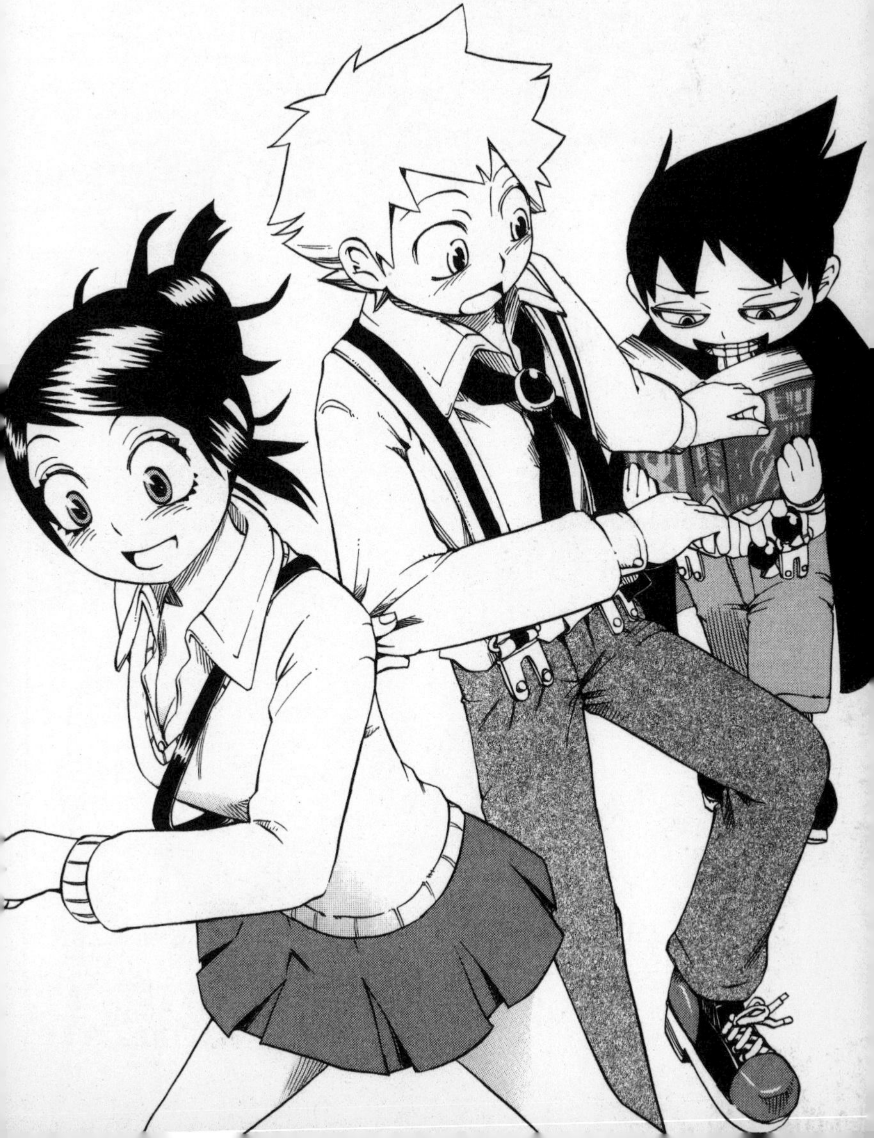

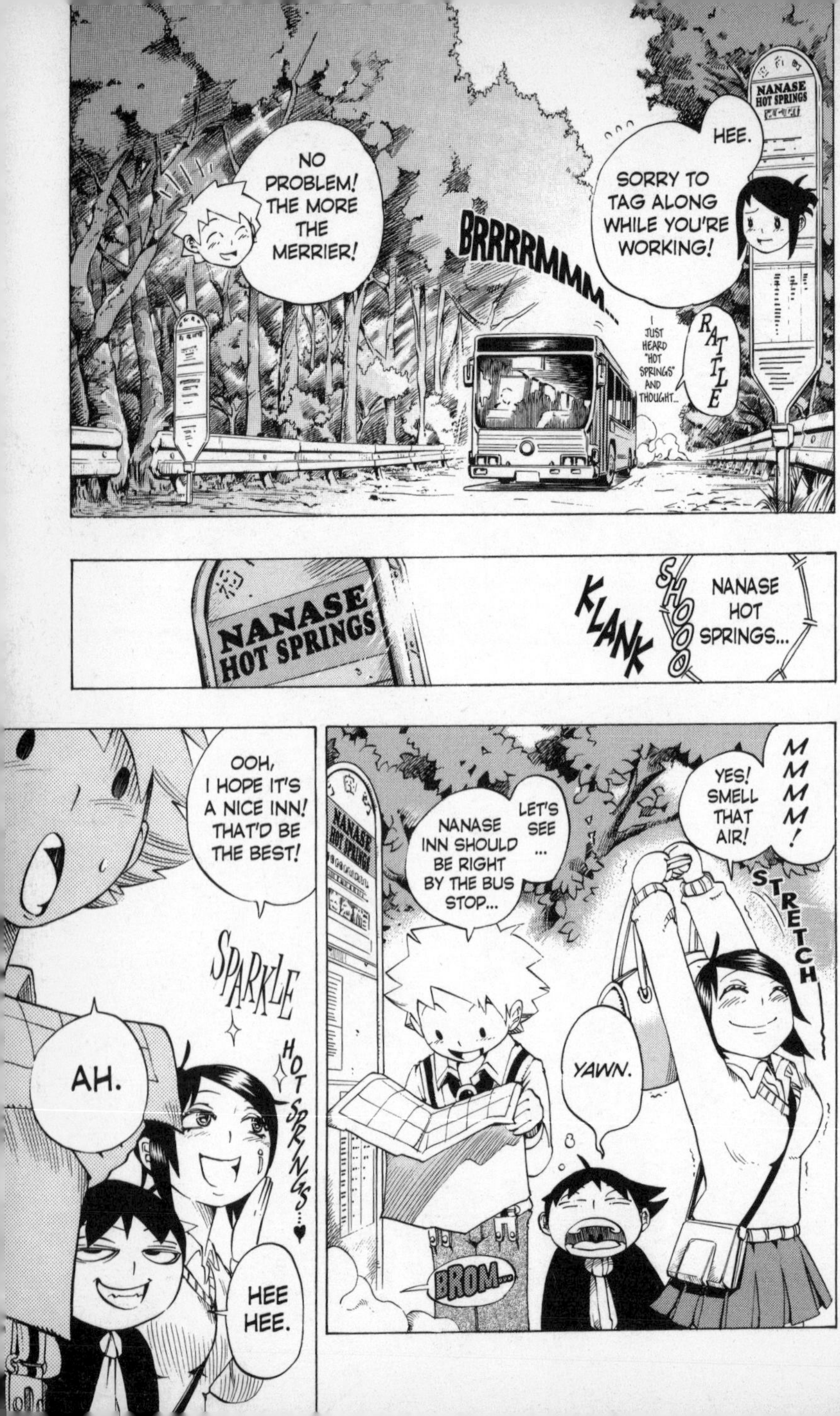
NANASE HOT SPRINGS
HEE.
SORRY TO TAG ALONG WHILE YOU'RE WORKING!
RATTLE
I JUST HEARD "HOT SPRINGS" AND THOUGHT...
BRRRRMMMM...
NO PROBLEM! THE MORE THE MERRIER!
NANASE HOT SPRINGS...
SHOOO
KLANK
NANASE HOT SPRINGS
MMMM!
YES! SMELL THAT AIR!
STRETCH
LET'S SEE...
NANASE INN SHOULD BE RIGHT BY THE BUS STOP...
NANASE HOT SPRINGS
YAWN.
BROM...
OOH, I HOPE IT'S A NICE INN! THAT'D BE THE BEST!
SPARKLE
AH.
HOT SPRINGS...
HEE HEE.

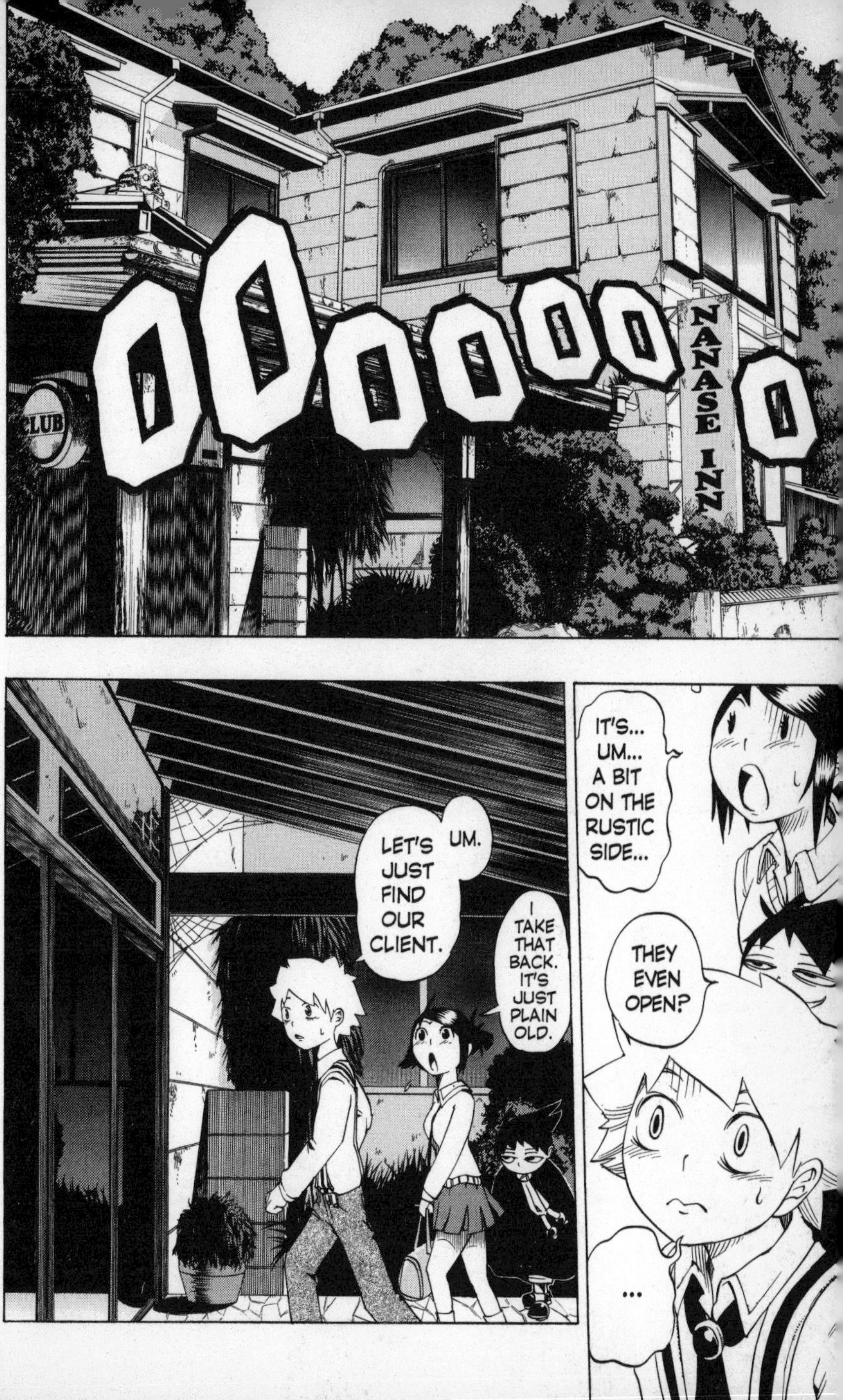
OOOOOOOO
CLUB
NANASE INN
IT'S... UM... A BIT ON THE RUSTIC SIDE...
THEY EVEN OPEN?
...
I TAKE THAT BACK. IT'S JUST PLAIN OLD.
UM. LET'S JUST FIND OUR CLIENT.

READ THIS WAY

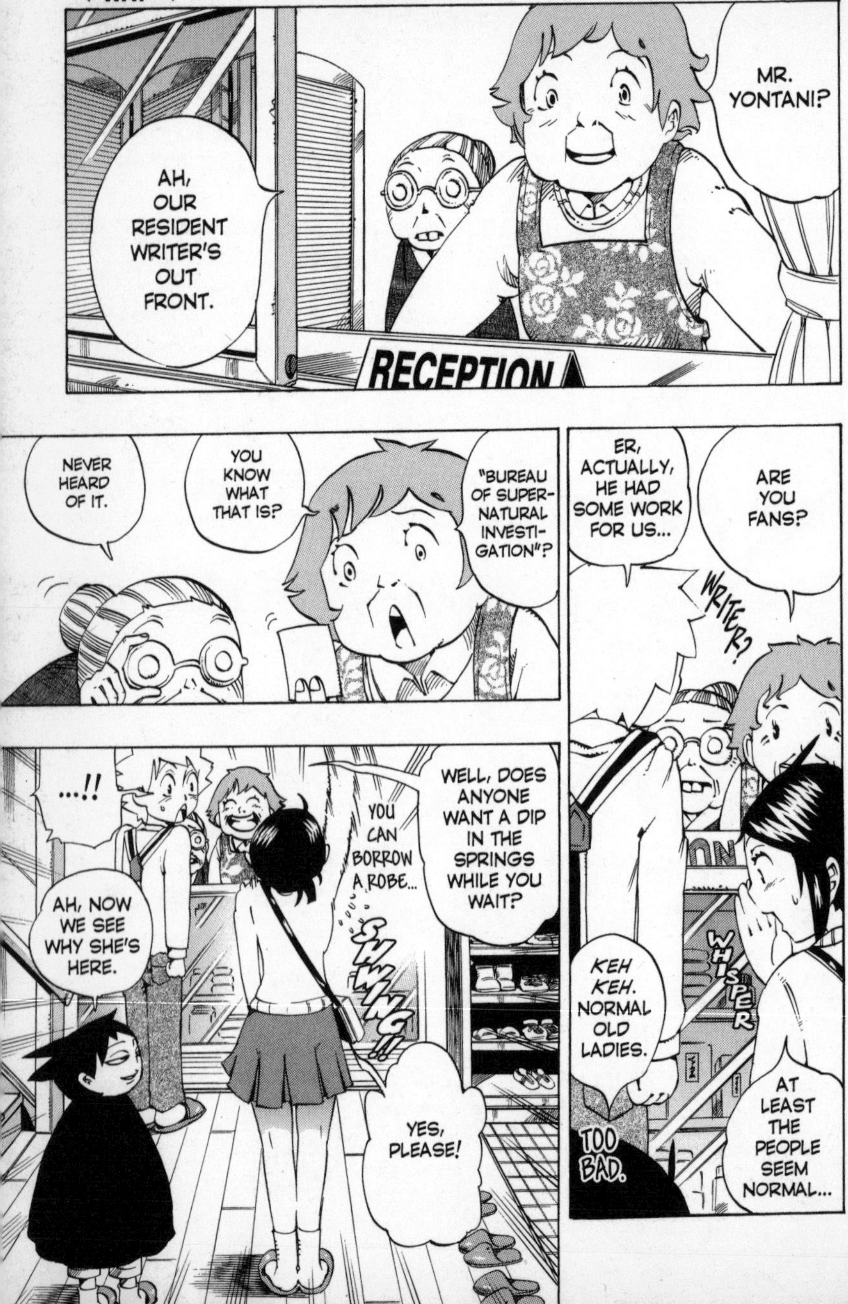
MR. YONTANI?
AH, OUR RESIDENT WRITER'S OUT FRONT.
RECEPTION
ARE YOU FANS?
ER, ACTUALLY, HE HAD SOME WORK FOR US...
WRITER?
WHISPER
AT LEAST THE PEOPLE SEEM NORMAL...
KEH KEH. NORMAL OLD LADIES.
TOO BAD.
"BUREAU OF SUPER-NATURAL INVESTI-GATION"?
YOU KNOW WHAT THAT IS?
NEVER HEARD OF IT.
WELL, DOES ANYONE WANT A DIP IN THE SPRINGS WHILE YOU WAIT?
YOU CAN BORROW A ROBE...
SHWING!!
...!!
YES, PLEASE!
AH, NOW WE SEE WHY SHE'S HERE.

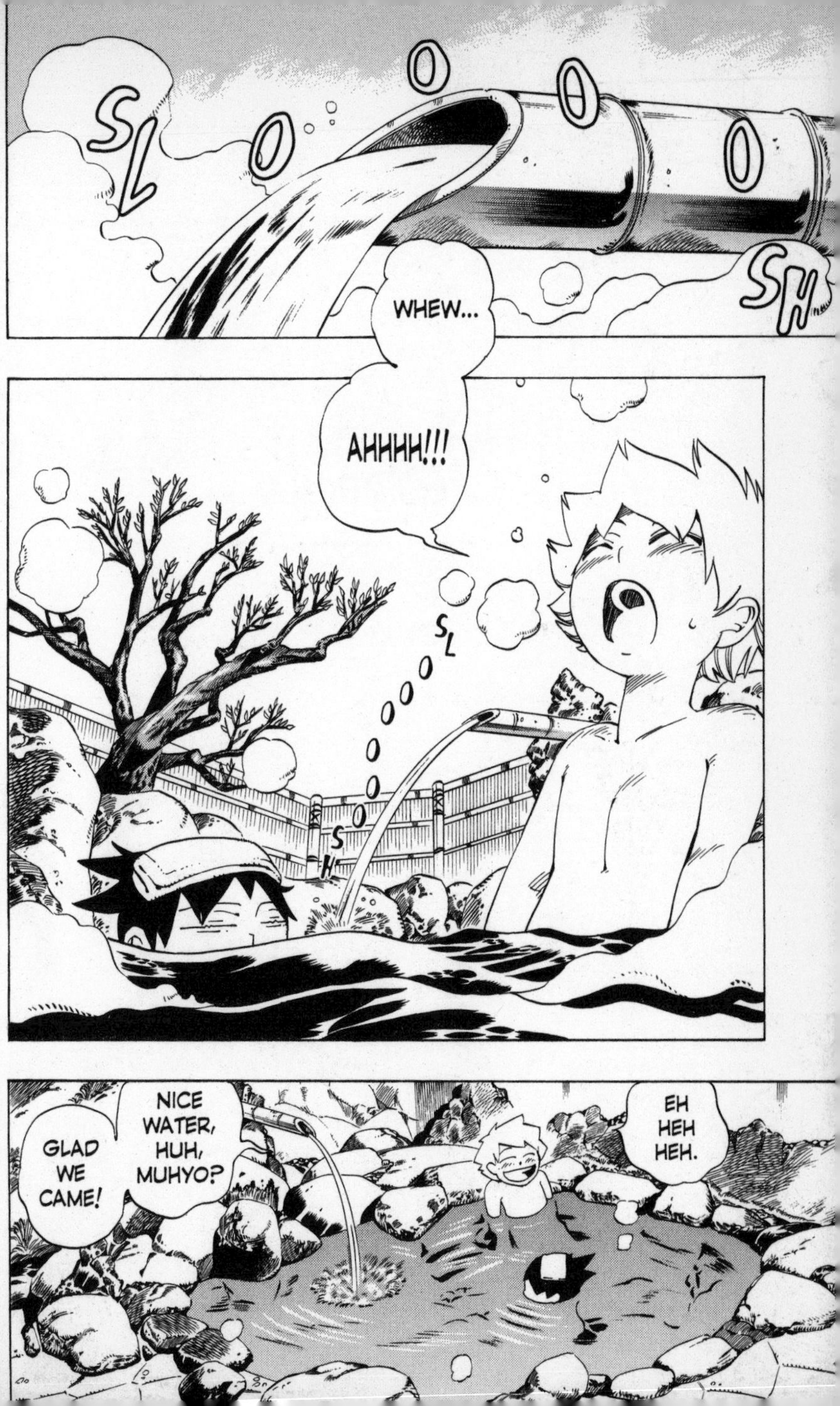
SLOOOOSH
WHEW...
AHHHH!!!
SLOOOOOOSH
EH HEH HEH.
NICE WATER, HUH, MUHYO?
GLAD WE CAME!

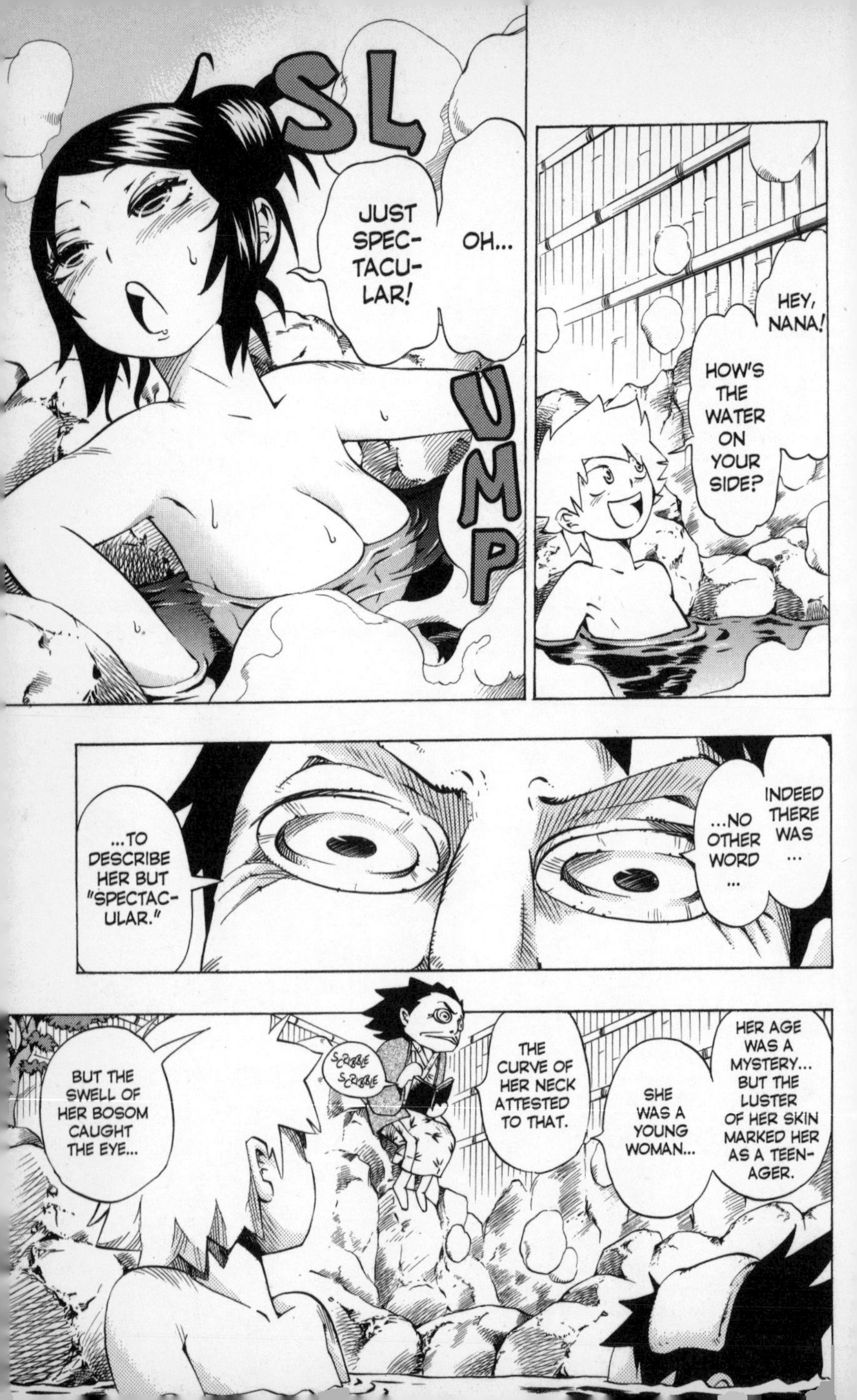
HEY, NANA!
HOW'S THE WATER ON YOUR SIDE?
OH...
JUST SPECTACULAR!
SLUMP
INDEED THERE WAS...
...NO OTHER WORD...
...TO DESCRIBE HER BUT "SPECTACULAR."
HER AGE WAS A MYSTERY... BUT THE LUSTER OF HER SKIN MARKED HER AS A TEENAGER.
SHE WAS A YOUNG WOMAN...
THE CURVE OF HER NECK ATTESTED TO THAT.
SCRIBBLE SCRIBBLE
BUT THE SWELL OF HER BOSOM CAUGHT THE EYE...

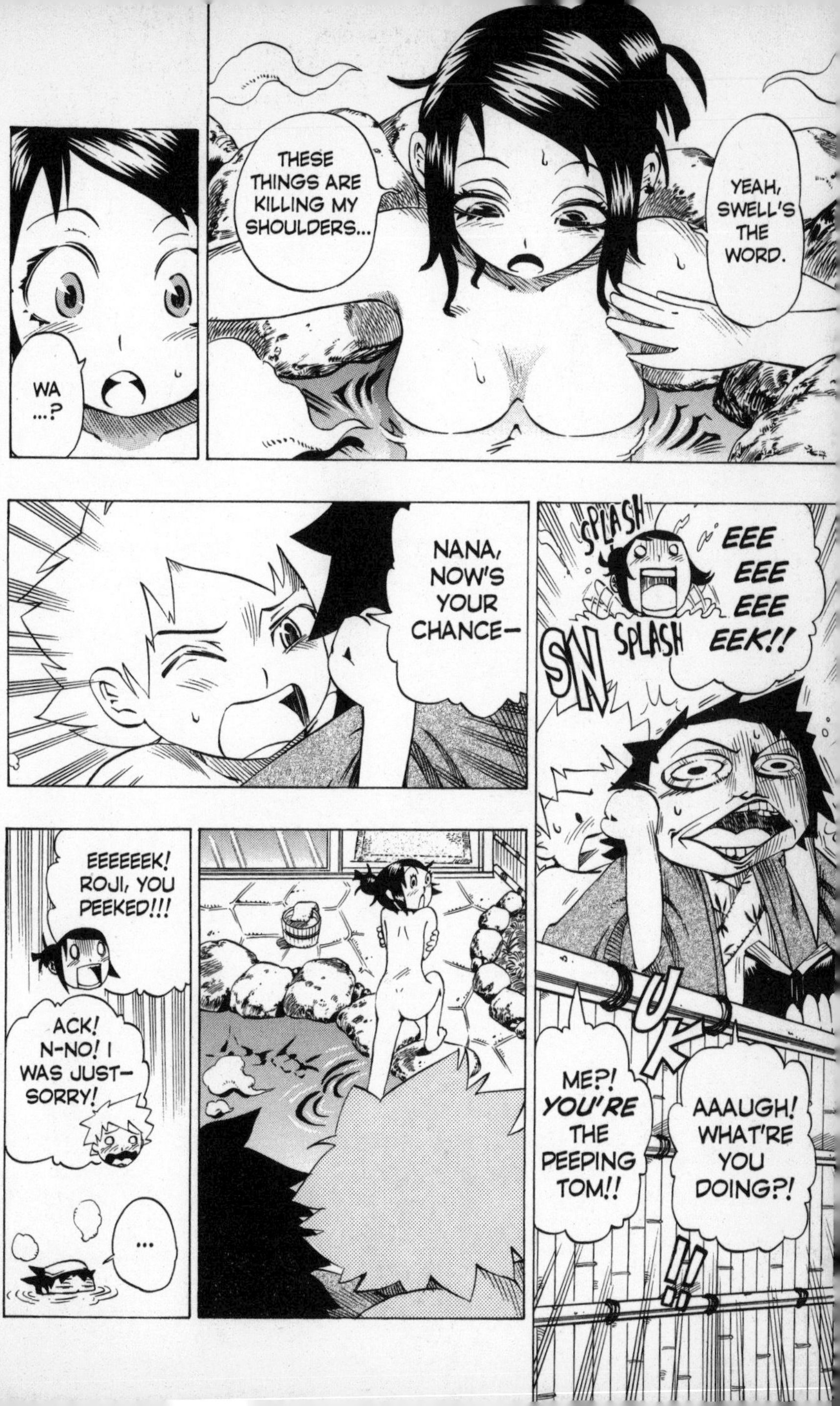
YEAH, SWELL'S THE WORD.
THESE THINGS ARE KILLING MY SHOULDERS...
WA ...?
SPLASH
EEE EEE EEE EEK!!
SPLASH
SN
UK
AAAUGH! WHAT'RE YOU DOING?!
ME?! YOU'RE THE PEEPING TOM!!
!!
NANA, NOW'S YOUR CHANCE—
EEEEEEK! ROJI, YOU PEEKED!!!
ACK! N-NO! I WAS JUST— SORRY!
...

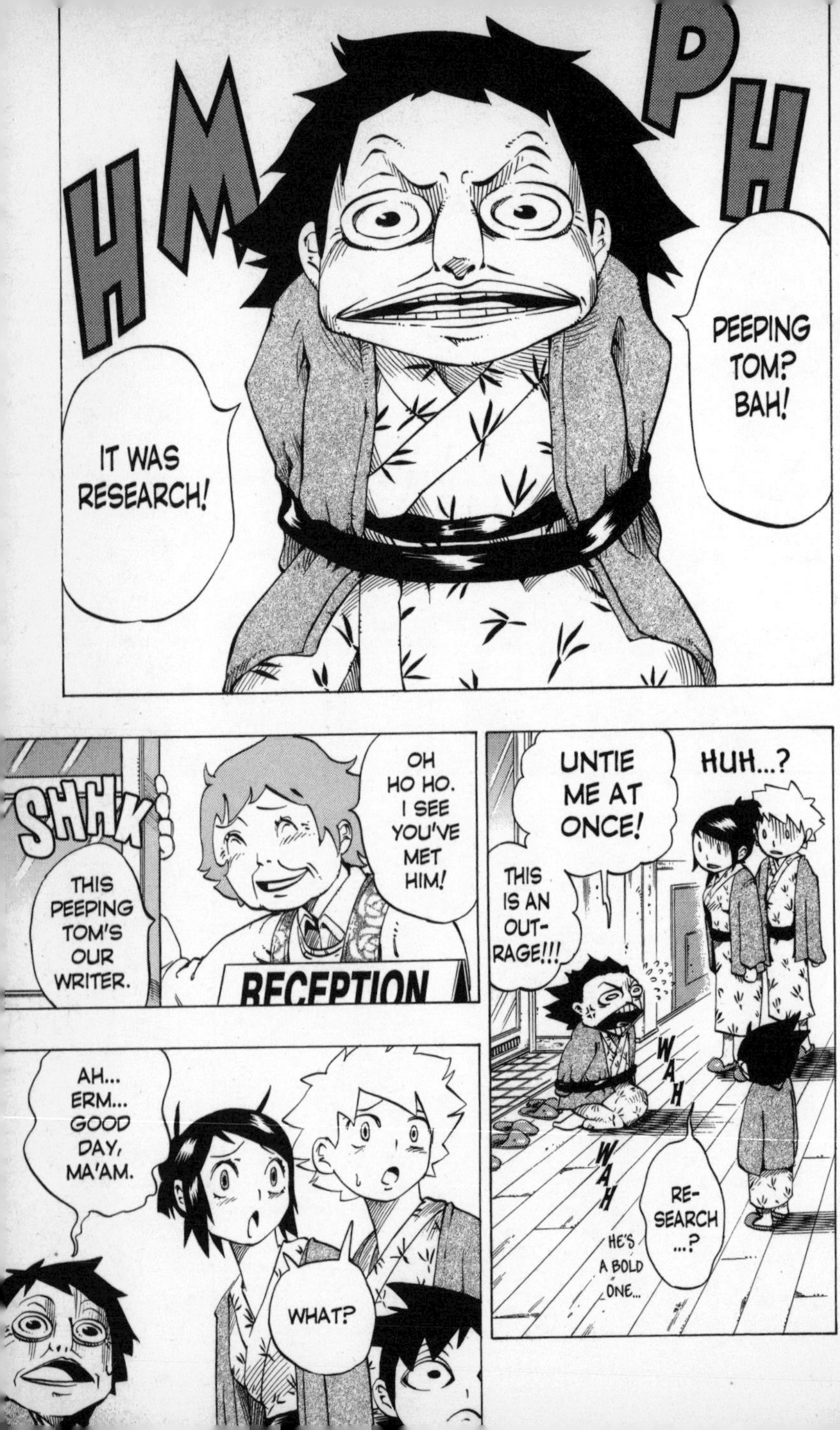
HMPH
PEEPING TOM? BAH!
IT WAS RESEARCH!
HUH...?
UNTIE ME AT ONCE!
THIS IS AN OUT-RAGE!!!
WAH
WAH
RE-SEARCH...?
HE'S A BOLD ONE...
OH HO HO. I SEE YOU'VE MET HIM!
SHHK
THIS PEEPING TOM'S OUR WRITER.
RECEPTION
WHAT?
AH... ERM... GOOD DAY, MA'AM.

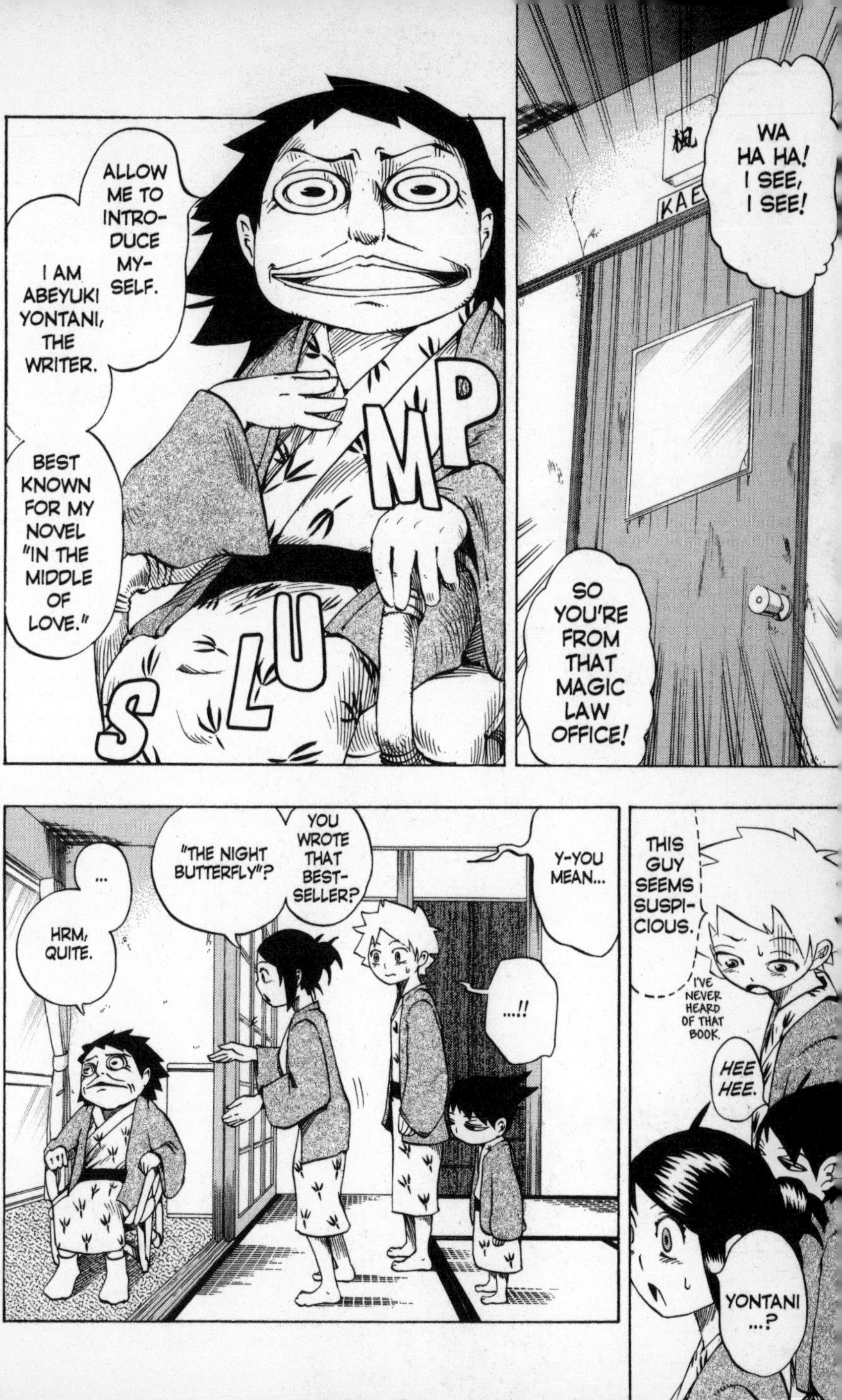
KAE
WA HA HA! I SEE, I SEE!
SO YOU'RE FROM THAT MAGIC LAW OFFICE!
ALLOW ME TO INTRODUCE MYSELF.
I AM ABEYUKI YONTANI, THE WRITER.
BEST KNOWN FOR MY NOVEL "IN THE MIDDLE OF LOVE."
SLUMP
THIS GUY SEEMS SUSPICIOUS.
I'VE NEVER HEARD OF THAT BOOK.
HEE HEE.
YONTANI ...?
Y-YOU MEAN...
YOU WROTE THAT BEST-SELLER?
"THE NIGHT BUTTERFLY"?
...!!
...
HRM, QUITE.

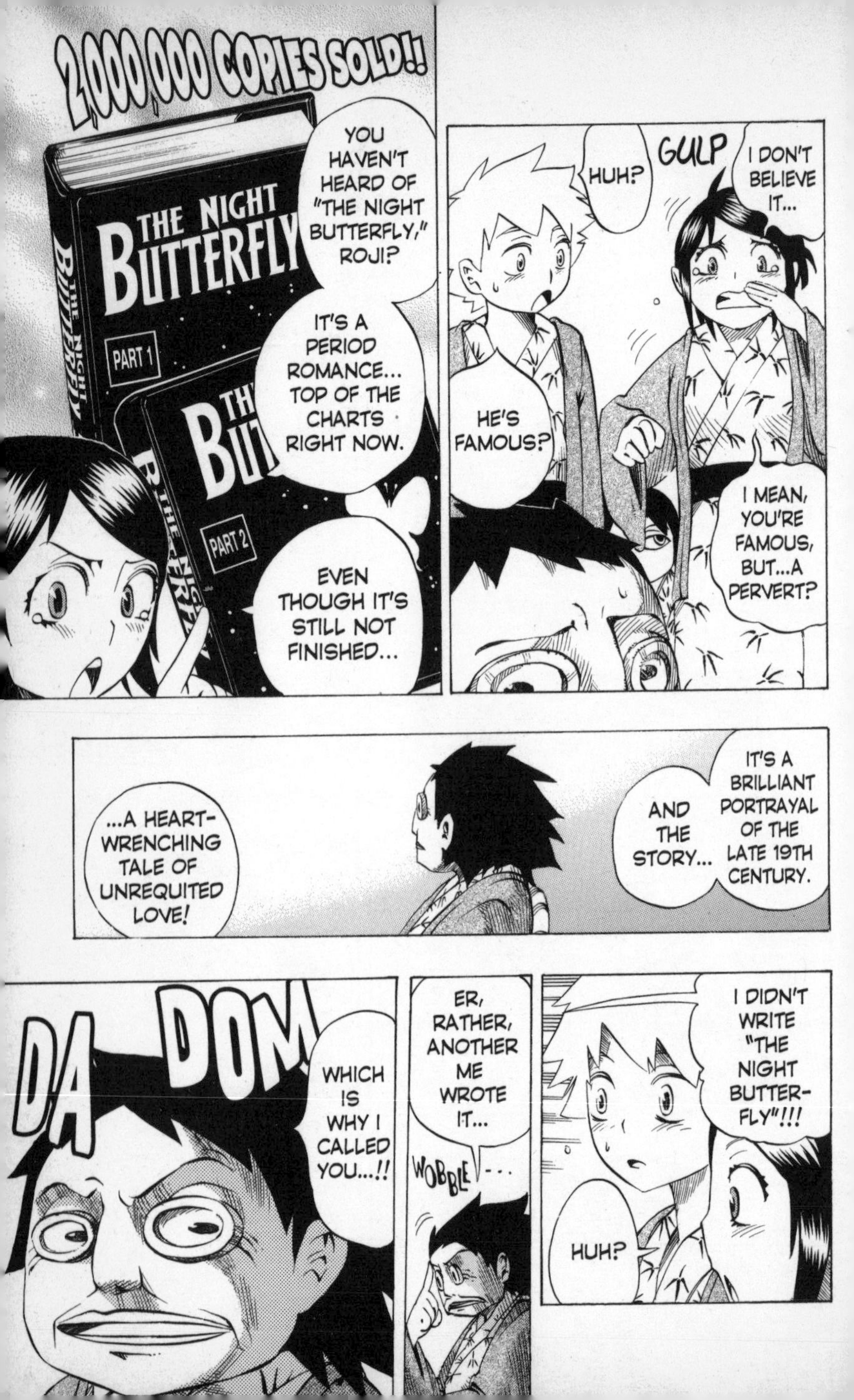
I DON'T BELIEVE IT...
GULP
HUH?
I MEAN, YOU'RE FAMOUS, BUT...A PERVERT?
HE'S FAMOUS?
2,000,000 COPIES SOLD!!
YOU HAVEN'T HEARD OF "THE NIGHT BUTTERFLY," ROJI?
THE NIGHT BUTTERFLY
PART 1
PART 2
IT'S A PERIOD ROMANCE... TOP OF THE CHARTS RIGHT NOW.
EVEN THOUGH IT'S STILL NOT FINISHED...
IT'S A BRILLIANT PORTRAYAL OF THE LATE 19TH CENTURY.
AND THE STORY...
...A HEART-WRENCHING TALE OF UNREQUITED LOVE!
I DIDN'T WRITE "THE NIGHT BUTTER-FLY"!!!
HUH?
ER, RATHER, ANOTHER ME WROTE IT...
WOBBLE...
DA DOM
WHICH IS WHY I CALLED YOU...!!

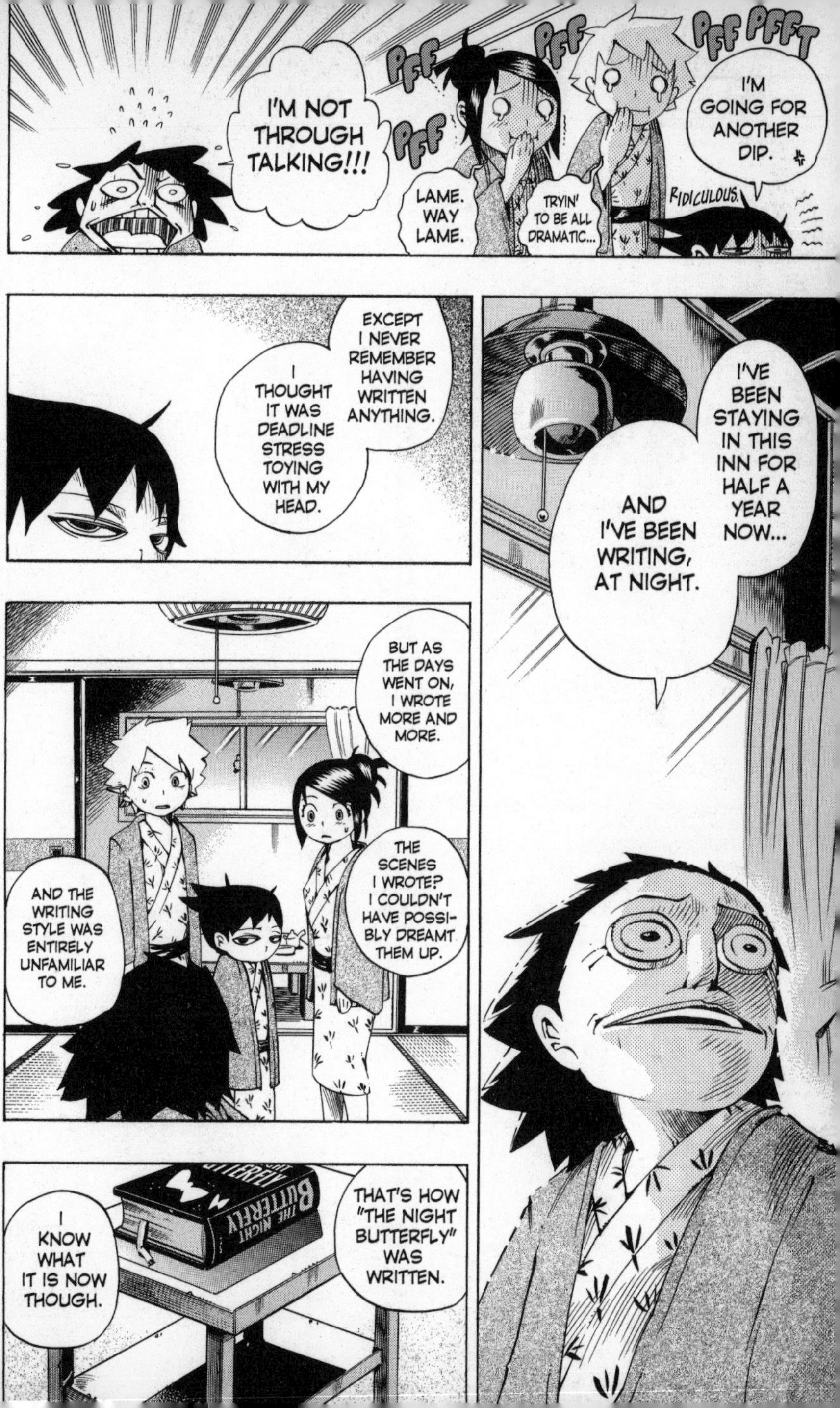
PFF PFFT
I'M GOING FOR ANOTHER DIP.
PFF
RIDICULOUS.
PFF
TRYIN' TO BE ALL DRAMATIC...
LAME. WAY LAME.
PFF
I'M NOT THROUGH TALKING!!!
I'VE BEEN STAYING IN THIS INN FOR HALF A YEAR NOW...
AND I'VE BEEN WRITING, AT NIGHT.
EXCEPT I NEVER REMEMBER HAVING WRITTEN ANYTHING.
I THOUGHT IT WAS DEADLINE STRESS TOYING WITH MY HEAD.
BUT AS THE DAYS WENT ON, I WROTE MORE AND MORE.
THE SCENES I WROTE? I COULDN'T HAVE POSSI-BLY DREAMT THEM UP.
AND THE WRITING STYLE WAS ENTIRELY UNFAMILIAR TO ME.
THE NIGHT BUTTERFLY
THAT'S HOW "THE NIGHT BUTTERFLY" WAS WRITTEN.
I KNOW WHAT IT IS NOW THOUGH.

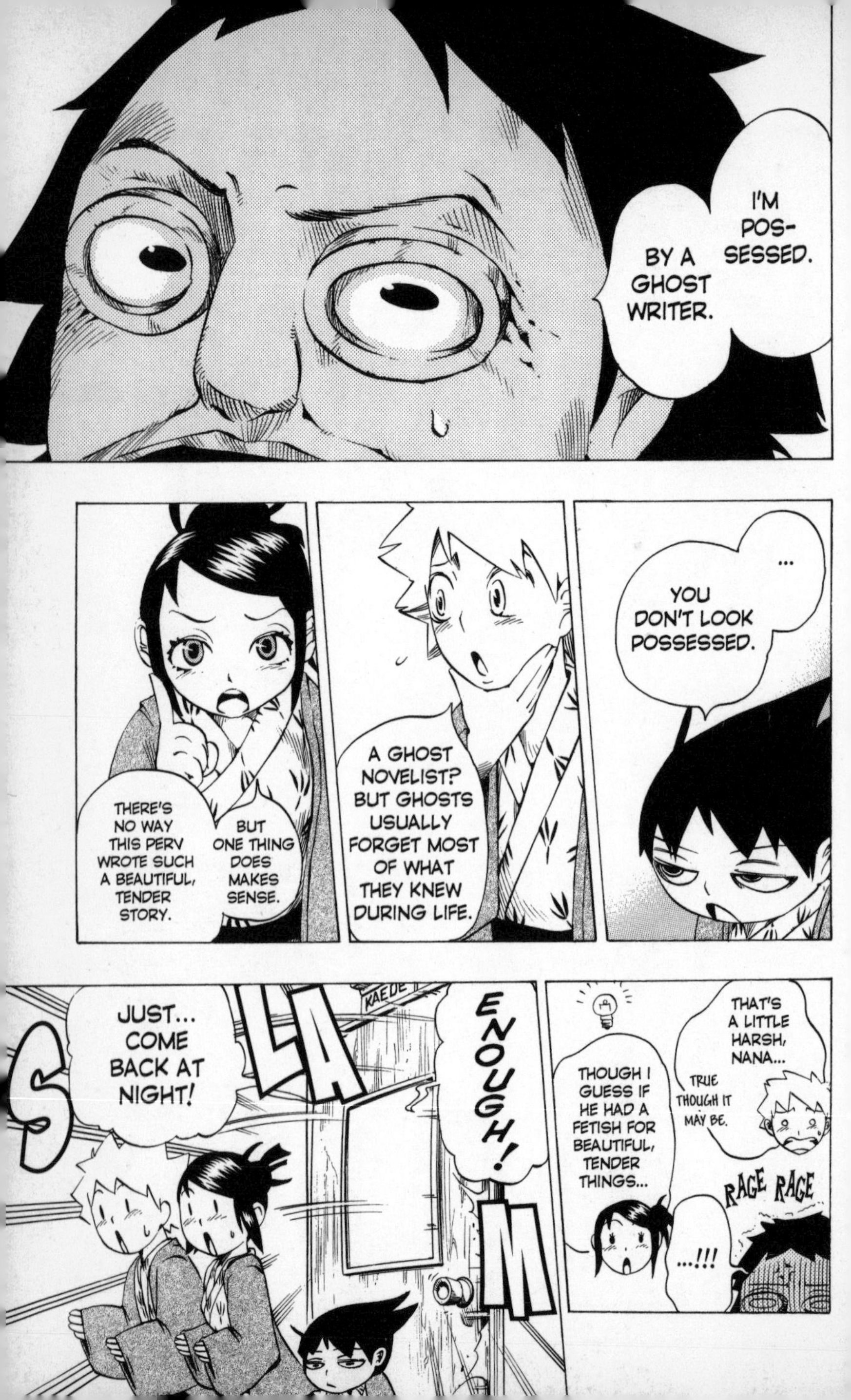
I'M POSSESSED.
BY A GHOST WRITER.
... YOU DON'T LOOK POSSESSED.
A GHOST NOVELIST? BUT GHOSTS USUALLY FORGET MOST OF WHAT THEY KNEW DURING LIFE.
BUT ONE THING DOES MAKES SENSE.
THERE'S NO WAY THIS PERV WROTE SUCH A BEAUTIFUL, TENDER STORY.
THAT'S A LITTLE HARSH, NANA...
TRUE THOUGH IT MAY BE.
THOUGH I GUESS IF HE HAD A FETISH FOR BEAUTIFUL, TENDER THINGS...
RAGE RAGE
...!!!
ENOUGH!
SLAM
KAEDE
JUST... COME BACK AT NIGHT!

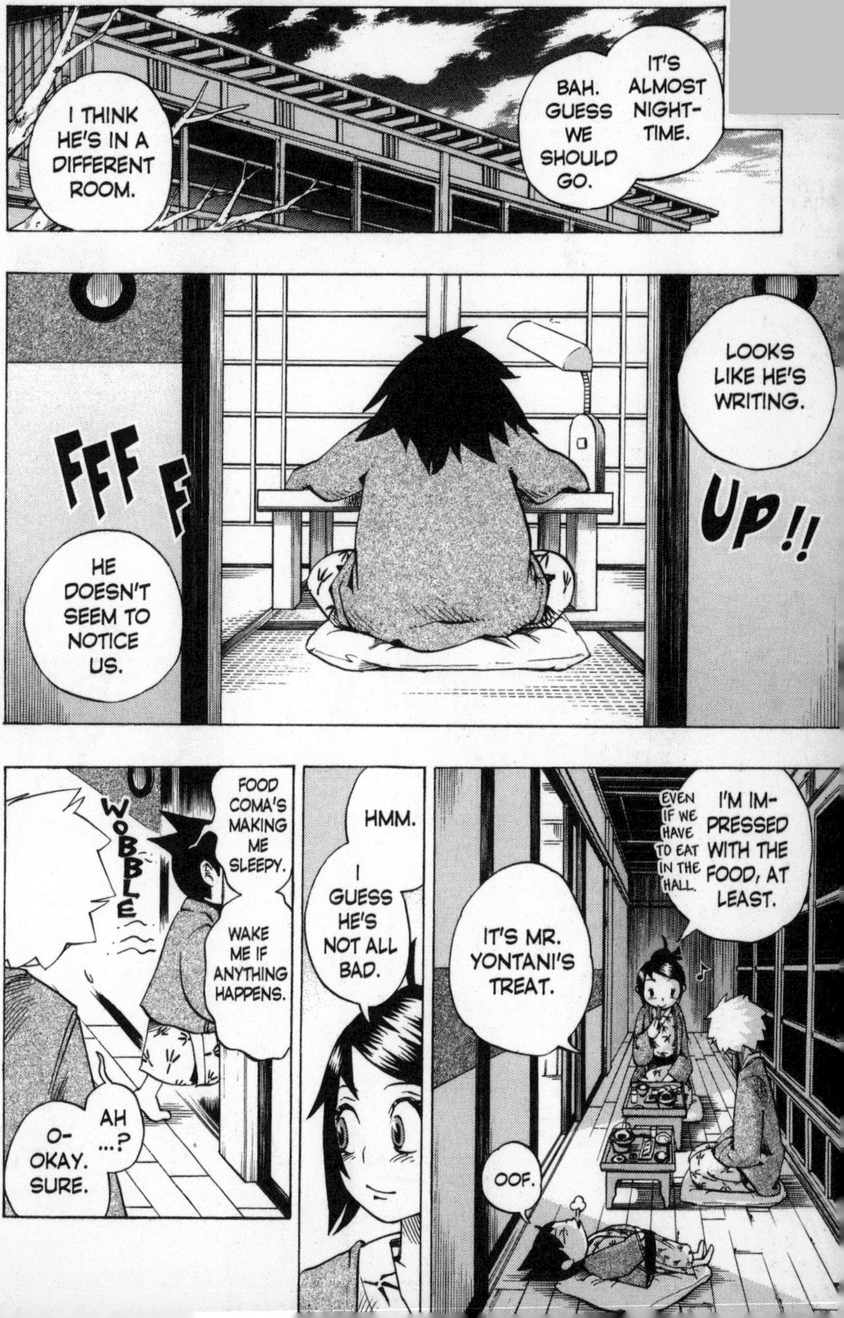
IT'S ALMOST NIGHT-TIME.
BAH. GUESS WE SHOULD GO.
I THINK HE'S IN A DIFFERENT ROOM.
LOOKS LIKE HE'S WRITING.
UP!!
FFF F
HE DOESN'T SEEM TO NOTICE US.
I'M IM-PRESSED WITH THE FOOD, AT LEAST.
EVEN IF WE HAVE TO EAT IN THE HALL.
IT'S MR. YONTANI'S TREAT.
OOF.
HMM.
I GUESS HE'S NOT ALL BAD.
FOOD COMA'S MAKING ME SLEEPY.
WOBBLE
WAKE ME IF ANYTHING HAPPENS.
AH ...?
O-OKAY. SURE.

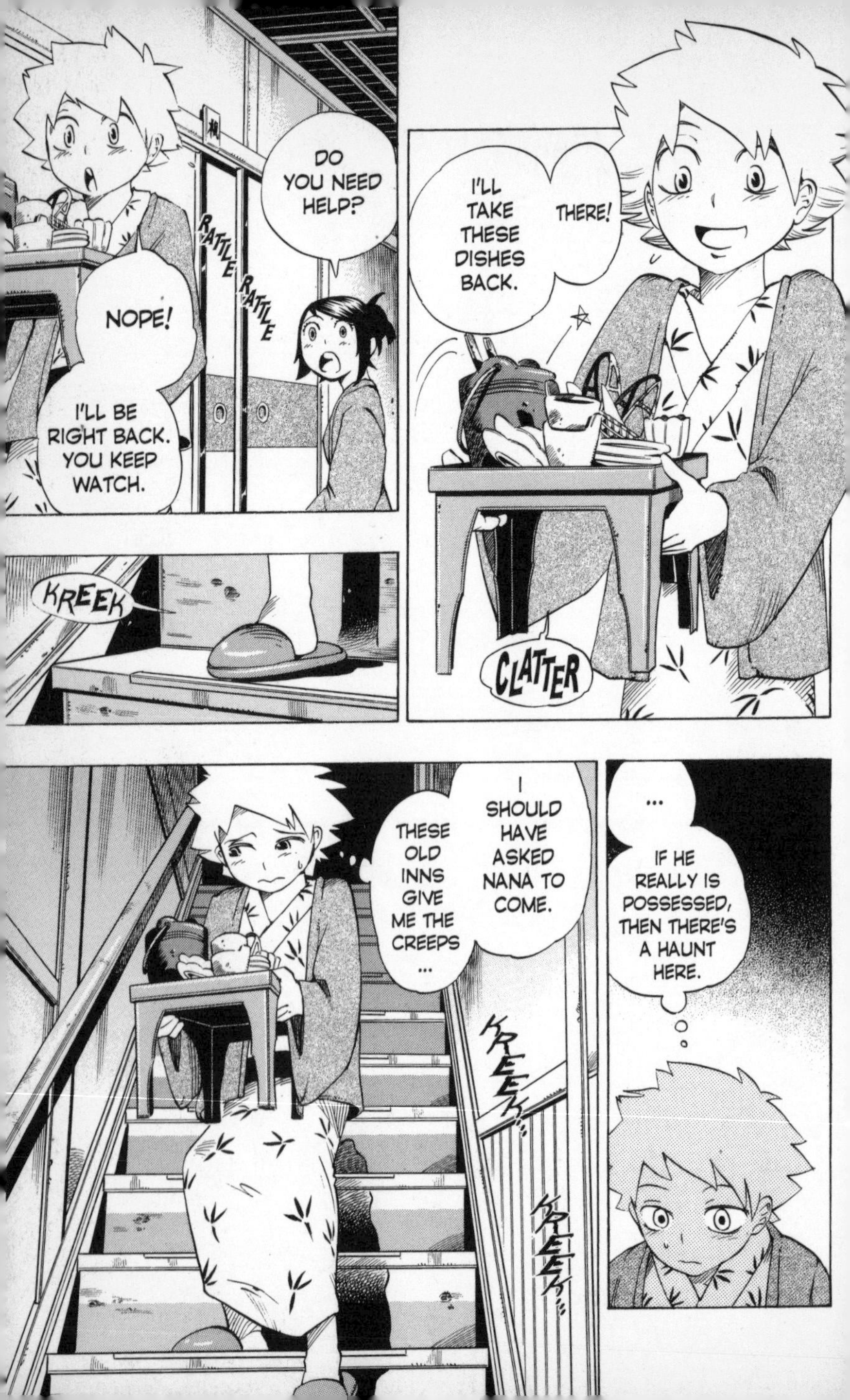
THERE!
I'LL TAKE THESE DISHES BACK.
CLATTER
DO YOU NEED HELP?
RATTLE RATTLE
NOPE!
I'LL BE RIGHT BACK. YOU KEEP WATCH.
KREEK
...
IF HE REALLY IS POSSESSED, THEN THERE'S A HAUNT HERE.
I SHOULD HAVE ASKED NANA TO COME.
THESE OLD INNS GIVE ME THE CREEPS ...
KREEEK...
KREEEK...

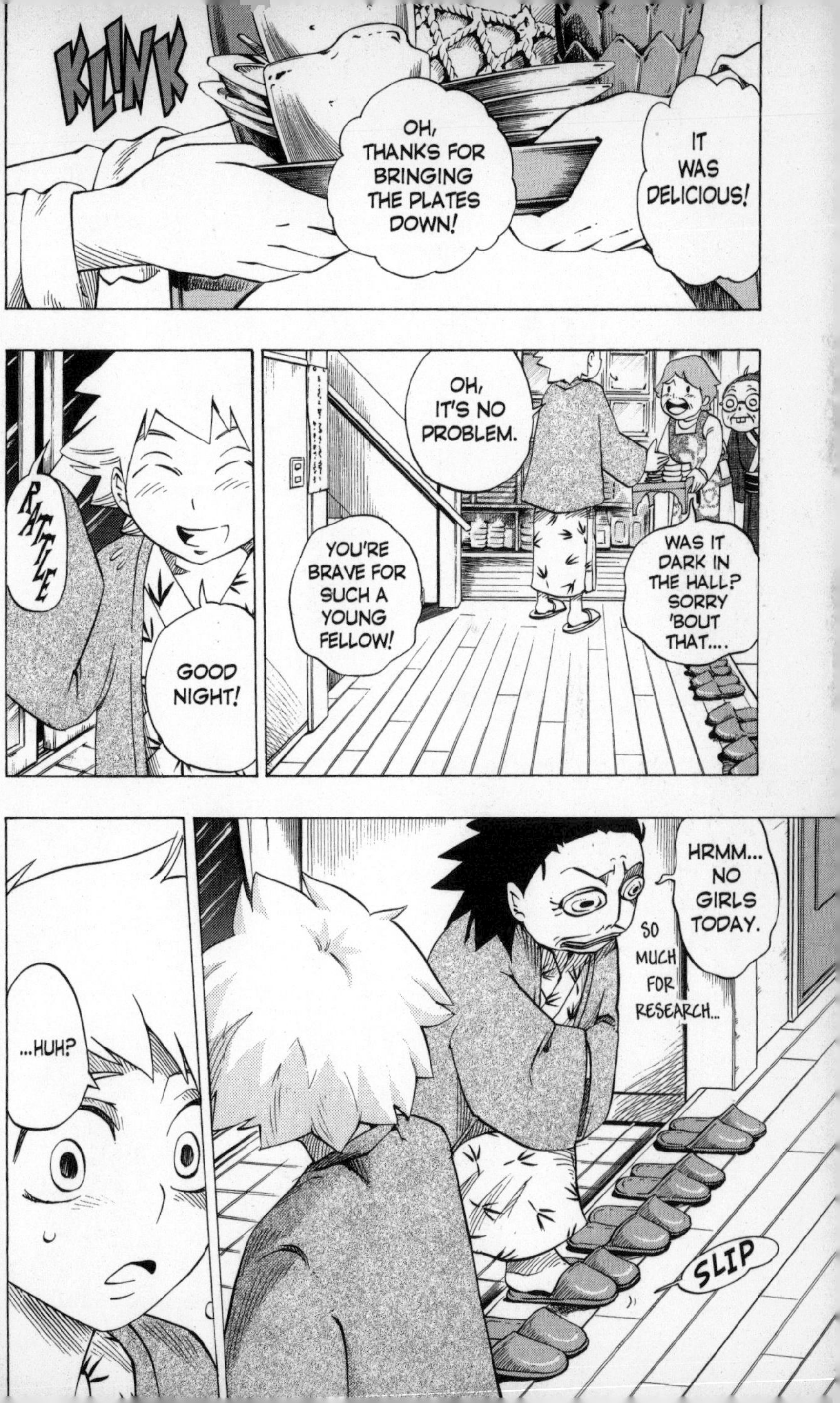
IT WAS DELICIOUS!
OH, THANKS FOR BRINGING THE PLATES DOWN!
KLINK
WAS IT DARK IN THE HALL? SORRY 'BOUT THAT....
OH, IT'S NO PROBLEM.
YOU'RE BRAVE FOR SUCH A YOUNG FELLOW!
RATTLE
GOOD NIGHT!
HRMM... NO GIRLS TODAY.
SO MUCH FOR RESEARCH...
SLIP
...HUH?

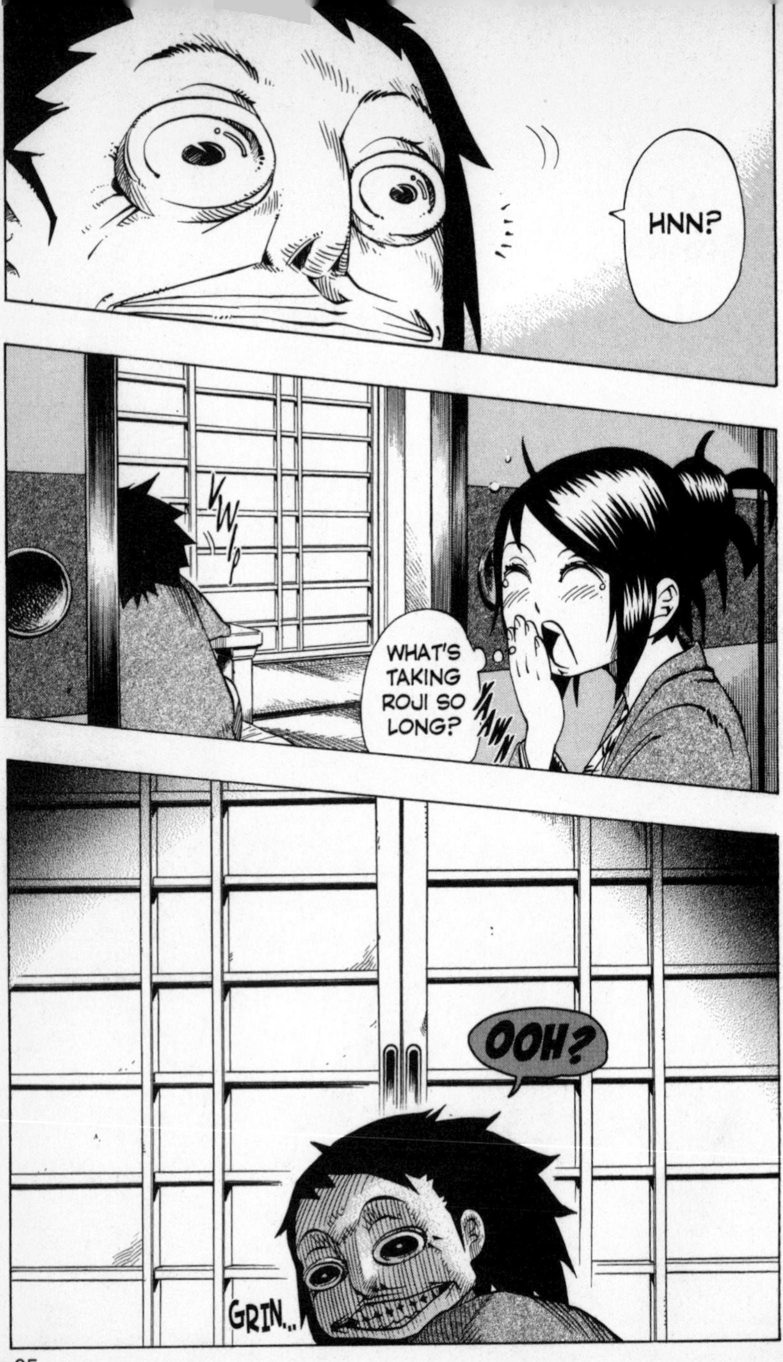
HNN?
VWIP
WHAT'S TAKING ROJI SO LONG?
YAWN
OOH?
GRIN...

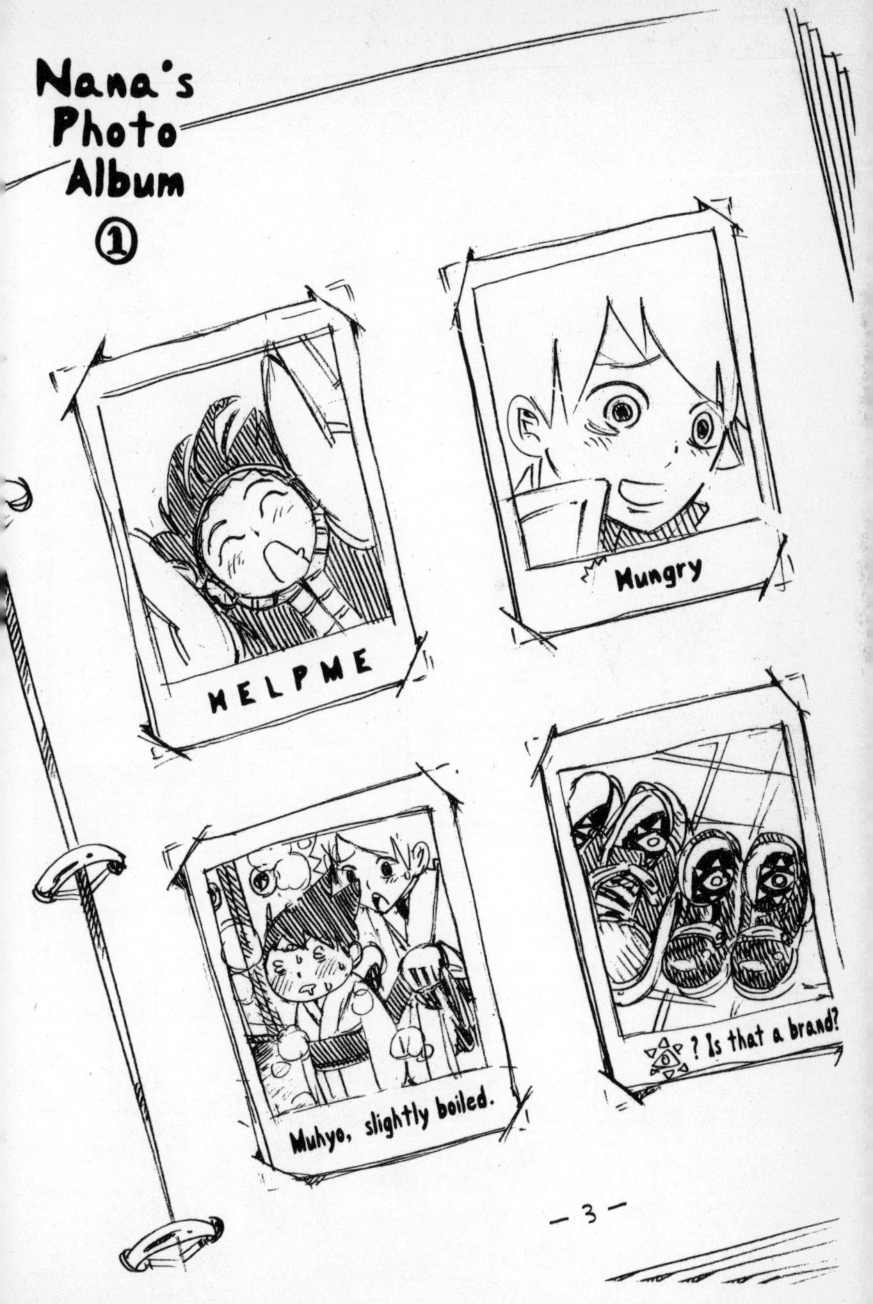
Nana's Photo Album ①
Hungry
HELPME
? Is that a brand?
Muhyo, slightly boiled.

ARTICLE 18
ZANSETSU HIRATA

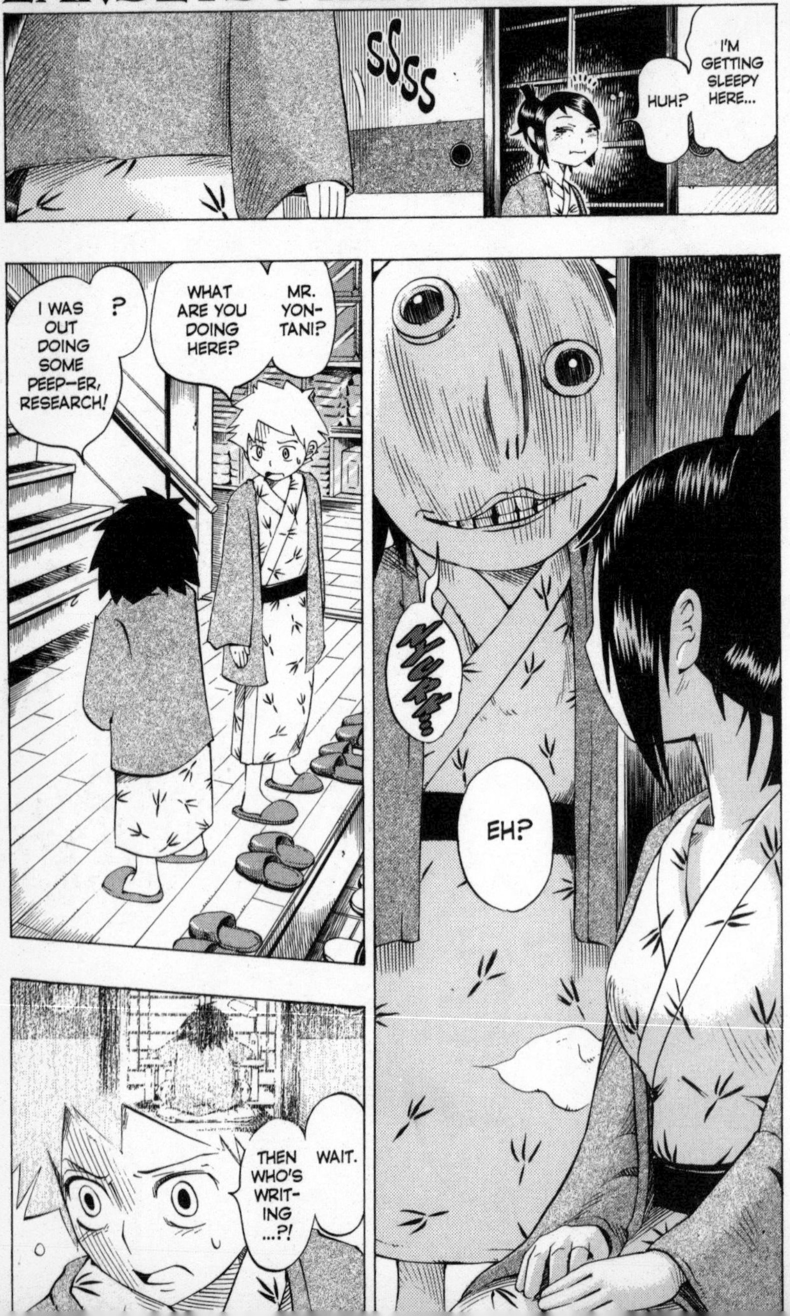
I'M GETTING SLEEPY HERE...
HUH?
SSSS
EH?
MR. YON-TANI?
WHAT ARE YOU DOING HERE?
?
I WAS OUT DOING SOME PEEP—ER, RESEARCH!
WAIT.
THEN WHO'S WRITING ...?!

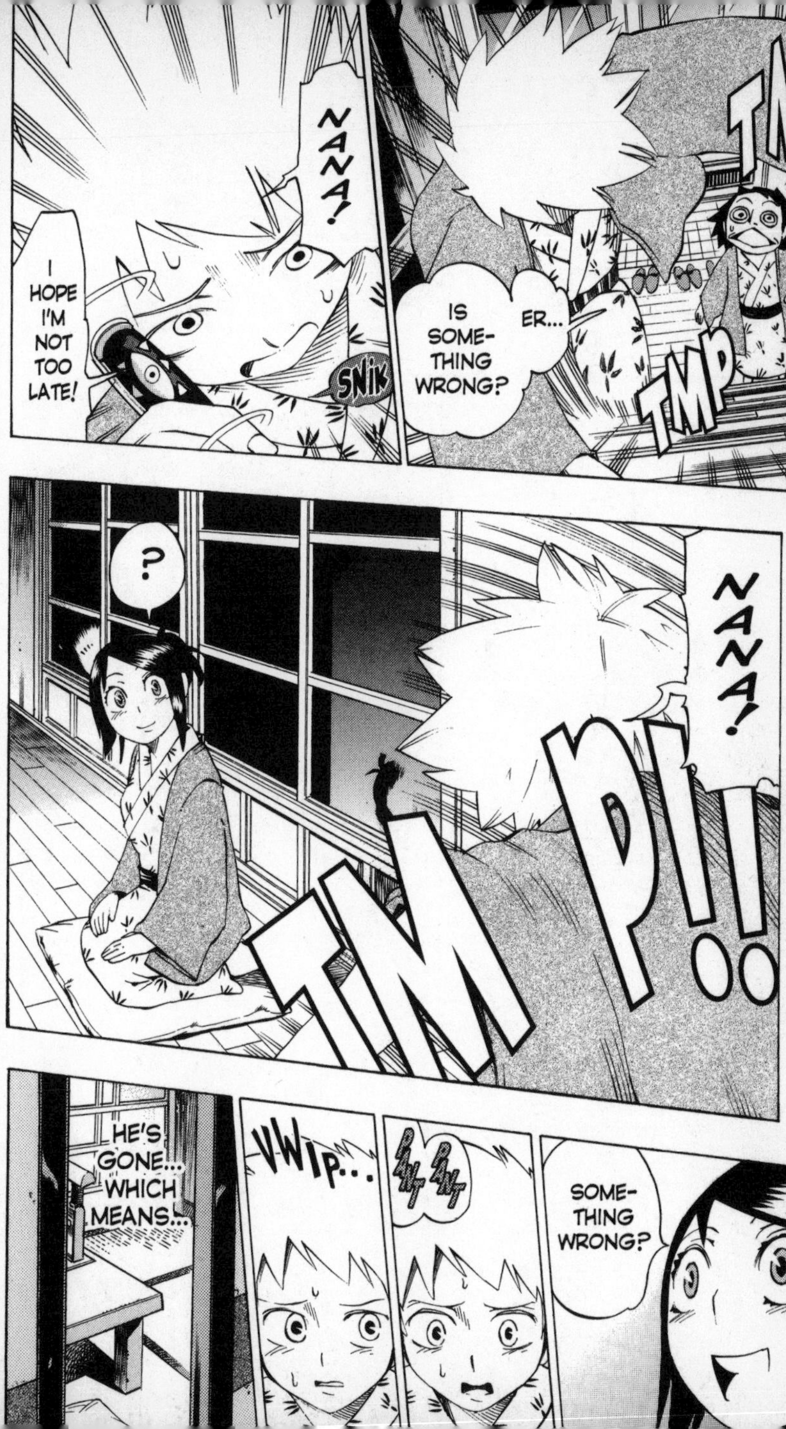
TMP
ER...
IS SOMETHING WRONG?
TMP
NANA!
I HOPE I'M NOT TOO LATE!
SNIK
NANA!
TMP!!
?
SOME-THING WRONG?
VWIP...
HE'S GONE... WHICH MEANS...

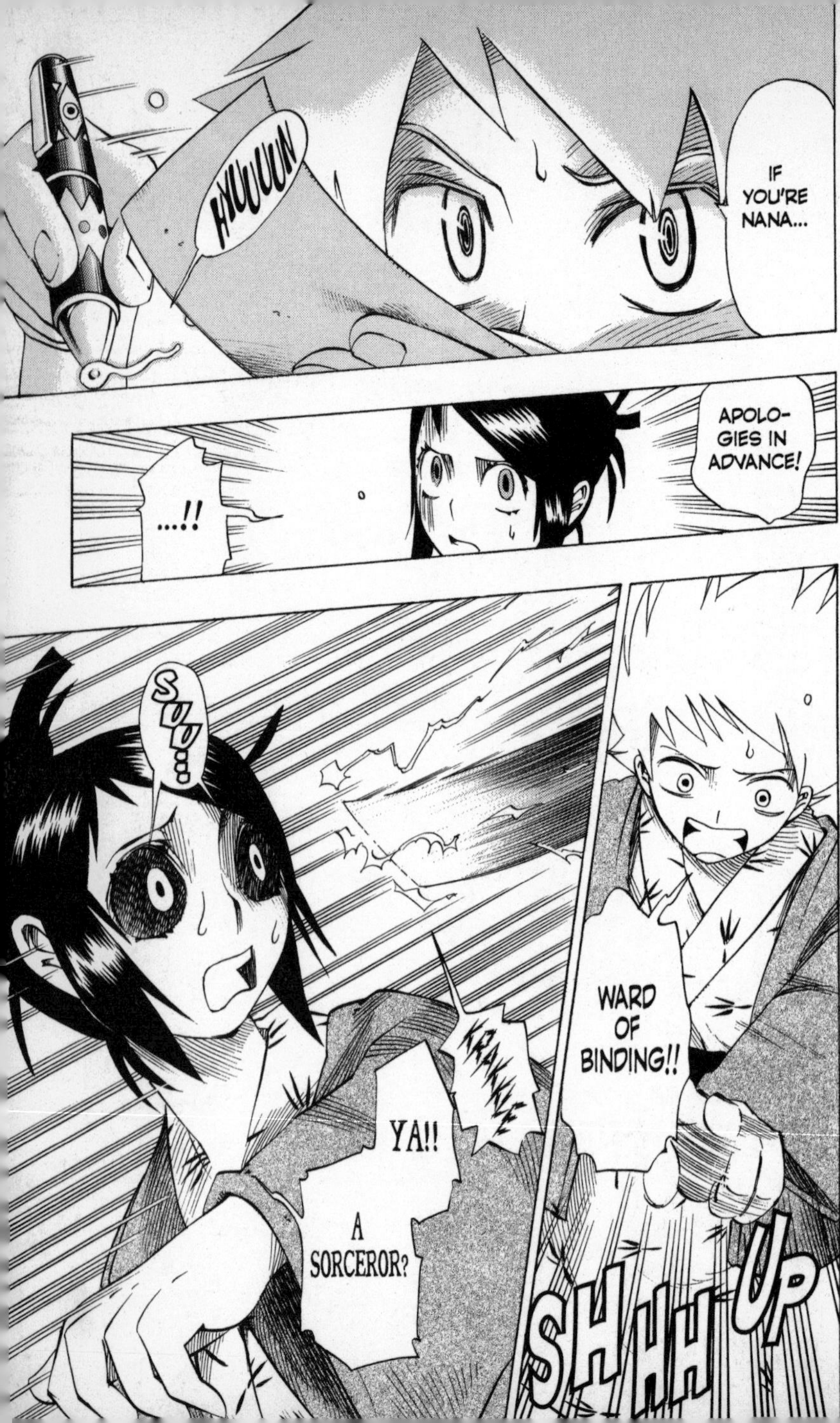
IF YOU'RE NANA...
HYUUUUN
APOLOGIES IN ADVANCE!
...!!
WARD OF BINDING!!
SHHHUP
SUU...
KRAKKLE
YA!!
A SORCEROR?

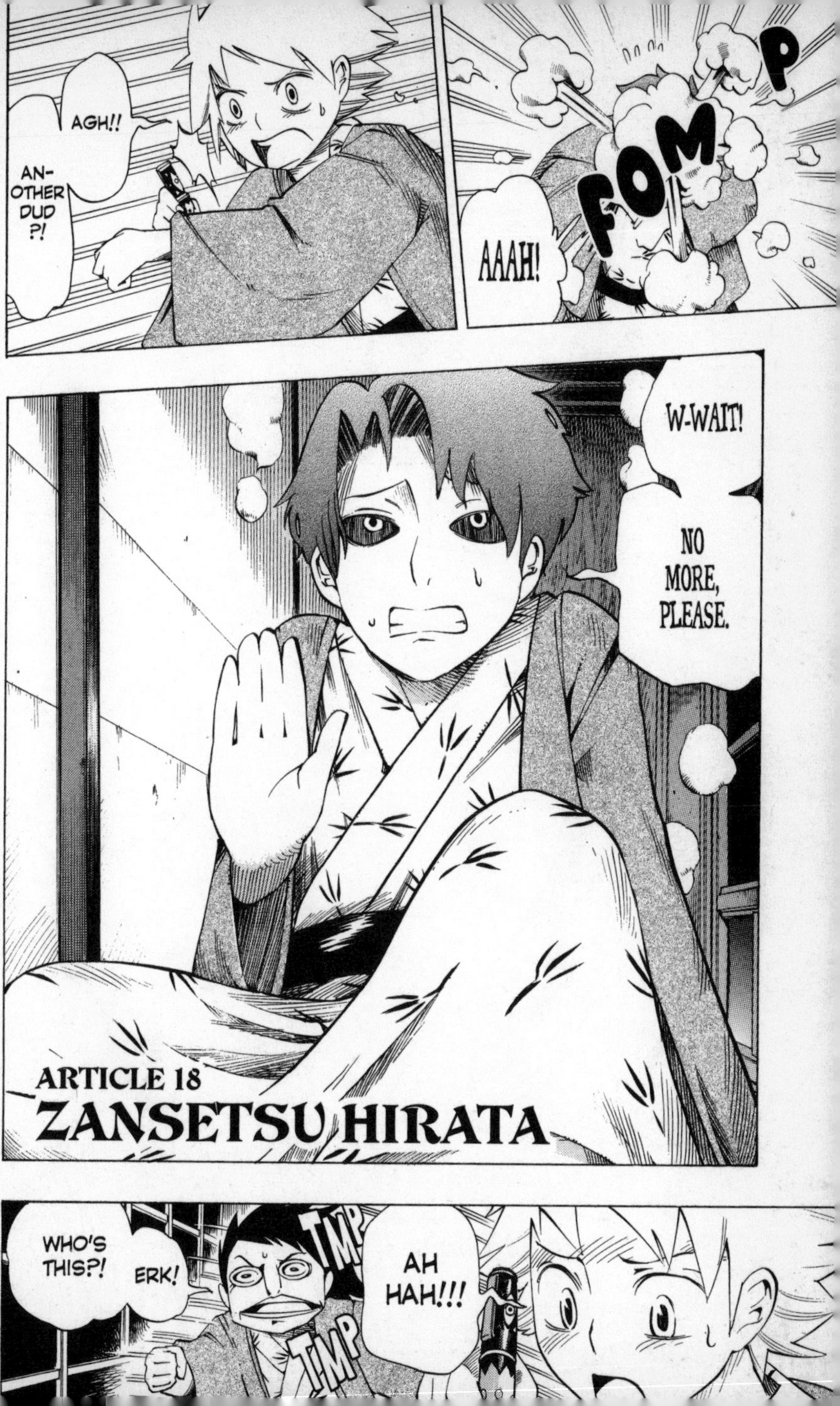
FOMP
AAAH!
AGH!!
AN-OTHER DUD ?!
W-WAIT!
NO MORE, PLEASE.
ARTICLE 18
ZANSETSU HIRATA
AH HAH!!!
TMP
TMP
ERK!
WHO'S THIS?!

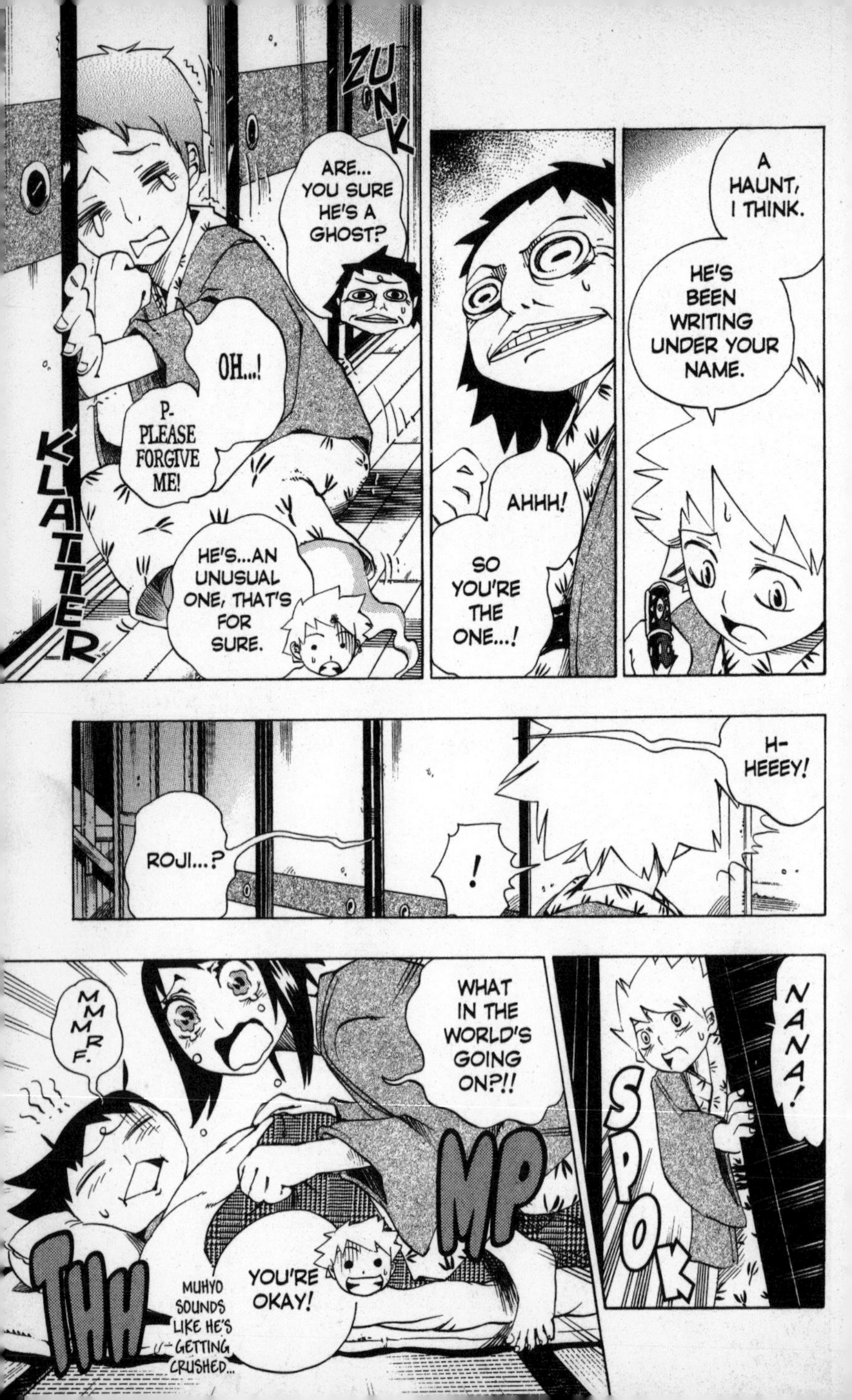
A HAUNT, I THINK.
HE'S BEEN WRITING UNDER YOUR NAME.
AHHH!
SO YOU'RE THE ONE...!
ZUNK
ARE... YOU SURE HE'S A GHOST?
OH...!
P-PLEASE FORGIVE ME!
KLATTER
HE'S...AN UNUSUAL ONE, THAT'S FOR SURE.
H-HEEEY!
!
ROJI...?
NANA!
SPOK
WHAT IN THE WORLD'S GOING ON?!!
THHMP
MMMRF.
YOU'RE OKAY!
MUHYO SOUNDS LIKE HE'S GETTING CRUSHED...

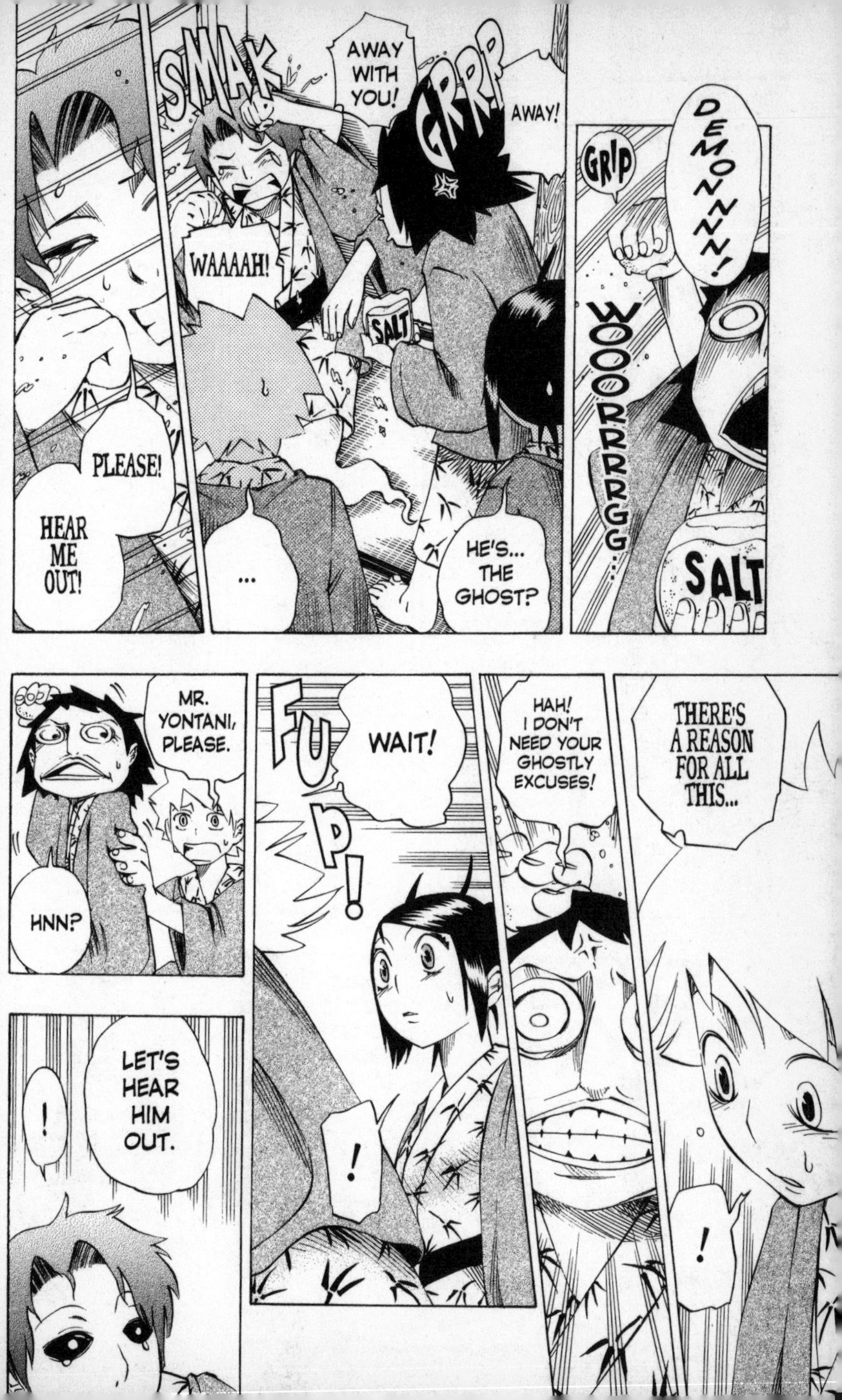
GRIP
DEMONNNN!
WOOORRRRGG...
SALT
SMAK
AWAY WITH YOU!
GRRR
AWAY!
SALT
WAAAAH!
HE'S... THE GHOST?
...
PLEASE!
HEAR ME OUT!
THERE'S A REASON FOR ALL THIS...
!
HAH! I DON'T NEED YOUR GHOSTLY EXCUSES!
WAIT!
FUP!
!
MR. YONTANI, PLEASE.
HNN?
LET'S HEAR HIM OUT.
!

READ THIS WAY

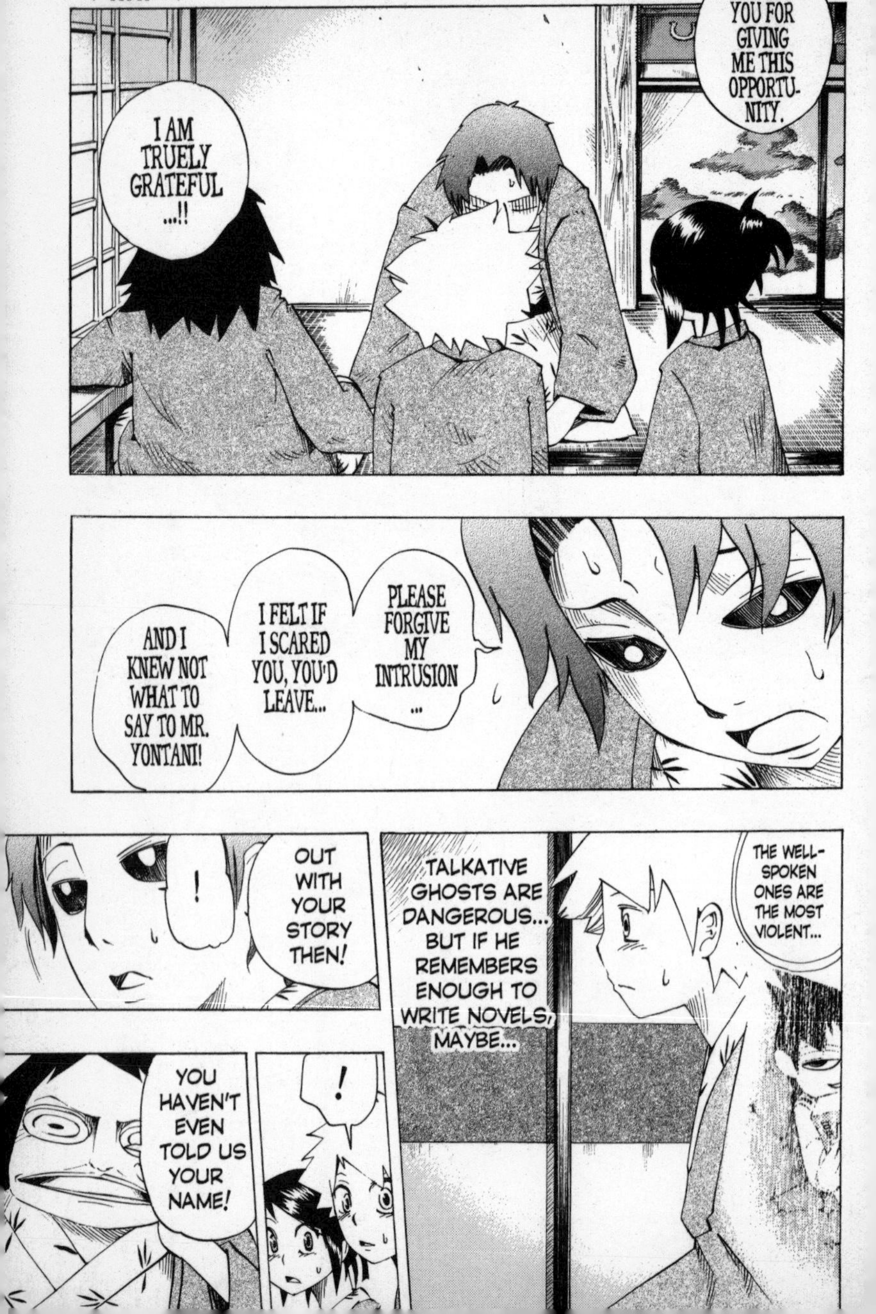
THANK YOU FOR GIVING ME THIS OPPORTUNITY.
I AM TRUELY GRATEFUL ...!!
PLEASE FORGIVE MY INTRUSION ...
I FELT IF I SCARED YOU, YOU'D LEAVE...
AND I KNEW NOT WHAT TO SAY TO MR. YONTANI!
THE WELL-SPOKEN ONES ARE THE MOST VIOLENT...
TALKATIVE GHOSTS ARE DANGEROUS... BUT IF HE REMEMBERS ENOUGH TO WRITE NOVELS, MAYBE...
OUT WITH YOUR STORY THEN!
!
!
YOU HAVEN'T EVEN TOLD US YOUR NAME!

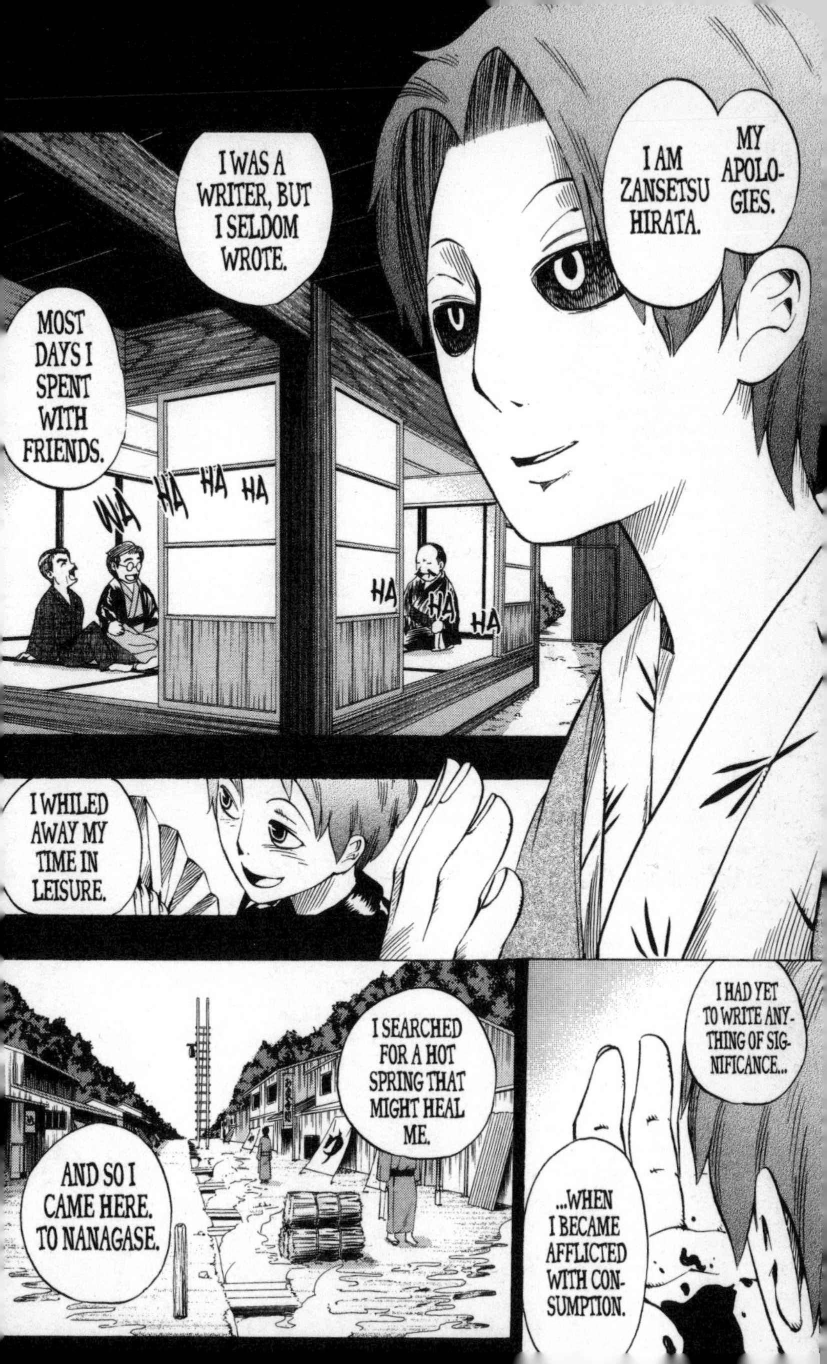
MY APOLOGIES.
I AM ZANSETSU HIRATA.
I WAS A WRITER, BUT I SELDOM WROTE.
MOST DAYS I SPENT WITH FRIENDS.
WA HA HA HA
HA HA HA
I WHILED AWAY MY TIME IN LEISURE.
I HAD YET TO WRITE ANYTHING OF SIGNIFICANCE...
...WHEN I BECAME AFFLICTED WITH CONSUMPTION.
I SEARCHED FOR A HOT SPRING THAT MIGHT HEAL ME.
AND SO I CAME HERE. TO NANAGASE.

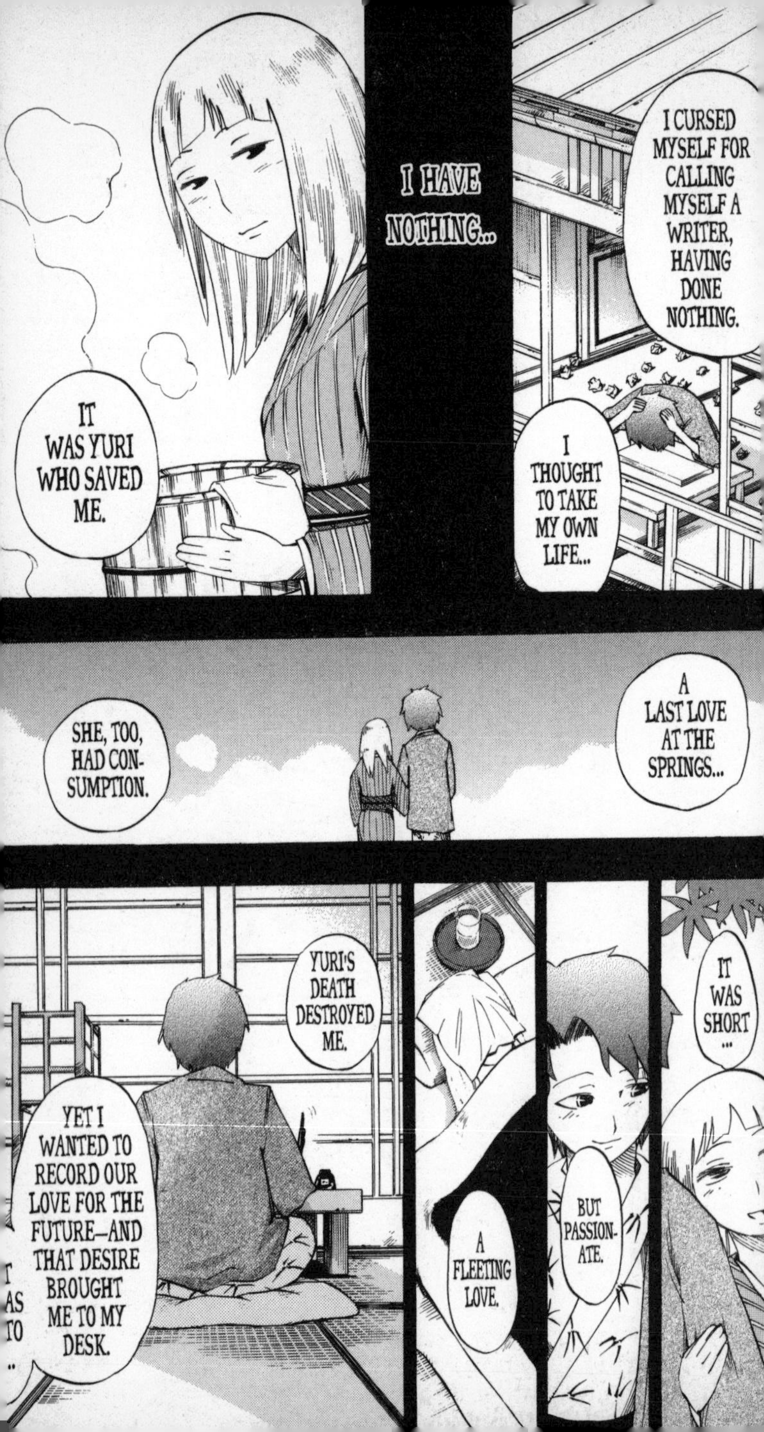
I CURSED MYSELF FOR CALLING MYSELF A WRITER, HAVING DONE NOTHING.
I THOUGHT TO TAKE MY OWN LIFE...
I HAVE NOTHING...
IT WAS YURI WHO SAVED ME.
A LAST LOVE AT THE SPRINGS...
SHE, TOO, HAD CON-SUMPTION.
IT WAS SHORT...
BUT PASSION-ATE.
A FLEETING LOVE.
YURI'S DEATH DESTROYED ME.
YET I WANTED TO RECORD OUR LOVE FOR THE FUTURE—AND THAT DESIRE BROUGHT ME TO MY DESK.

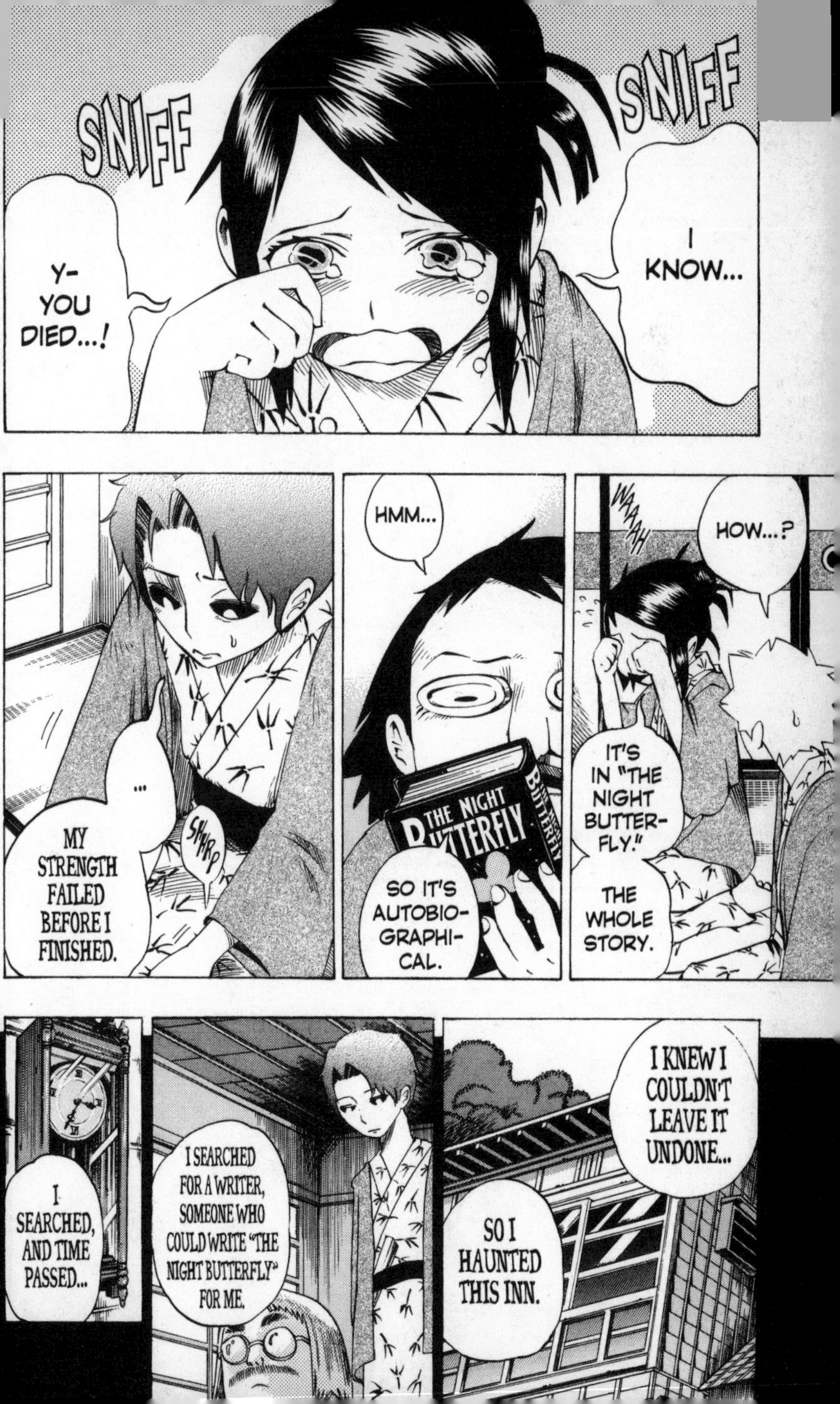
SNIFF
I KNOW...
SNIFF
Y-YOU DIED...!
WAAAH
HOW...?
IT'S IN "THE NIGHT BUTTER-FLY."
THE WHOLE STORY.
HMM...
THE NIGHT BUTTERFLY
SO IT'S AUTOBIO-GRAPHI-CAL.
...
SHHRP
MY STRENGTH FAILED BEFORE I FINISHED.
I KNEW I COULDN'T LEAVE IT UNDONE...
SO I HAUNTED THIS INN.
I SEARCHED FOR A WRITER, SOMEONE WHO COULD WRITE "THE NIGHT BUTTERFLY" FOR ME.
I SEARCHED, AND TIME PASSED...

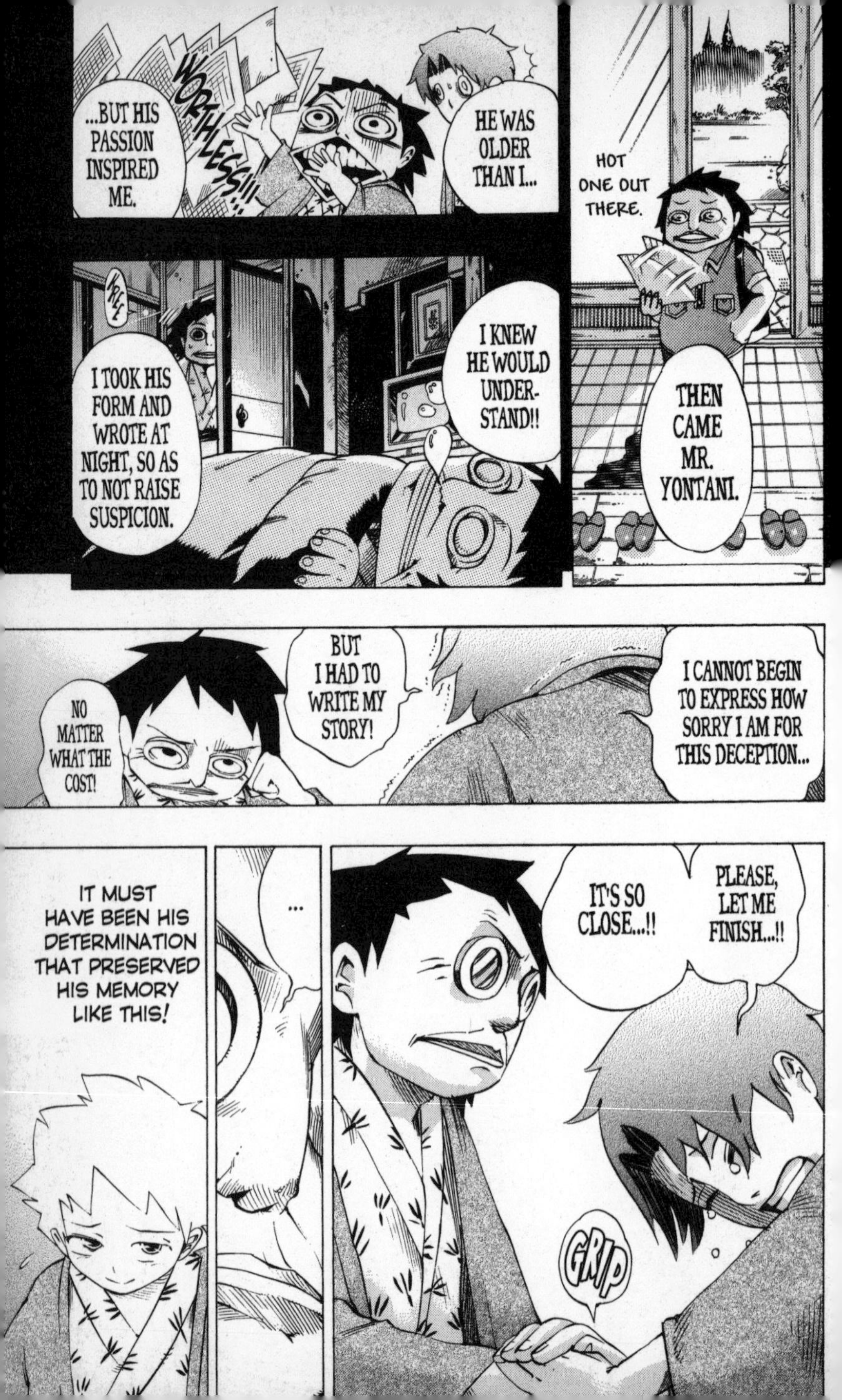
HOT ONE OUT THERE.
THEN CAME MR. YONTANI.
HE WAS OLDER THAN I...
WORTHLESS!!!
...BUT HIS PASSION INSPIRED ME.
I KNEW HE WOULD UNDER-STAND!!
KREE
I TOOK HIS FORM AND WROTE AT NIGHT, SO AS TO NOT RAISE SUSPICION.
I CANNOT BEGIN TO EXPRESS HOW SORRY I AM FOR THIS DECEPTION...
BUT I HAD TO WRITE MY STORY!
NO MATTER WHAT THE COST!
PLEASE, LET ME FINISH...!!
IT'S SO CLOSE...!!
GRIP
...
IT MUST HAVE BEEN HIS DETERMINATION THAT PRESERVED HIS MEMORY LIKE THIS!

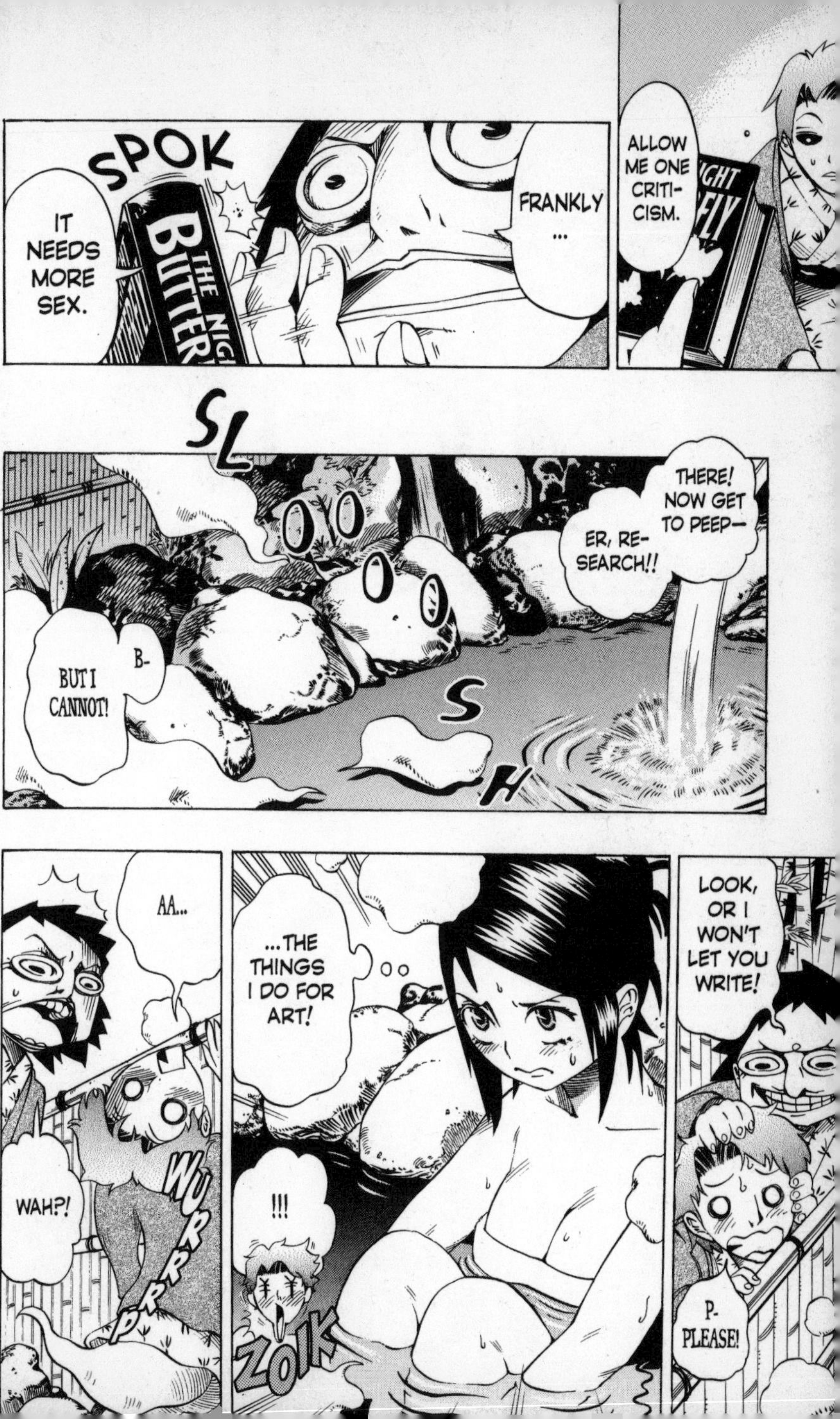
ALLOW ME ONE CRITI-CISM.
FRANKLY ...
SPOK
IT NEEDS MORE SEX.
SL
THERE! NOW GET TO PEEP—
ER, RE-SEARCH!!
S
H
B-
BUT I CANNOT!
LOOK, OR I WON'T LET YOU WRITE!
P-PLEASE!
...THE THINGS I DO FOR ART!
!!!
ZOIK
AA...
WAH?!
WURRRRP

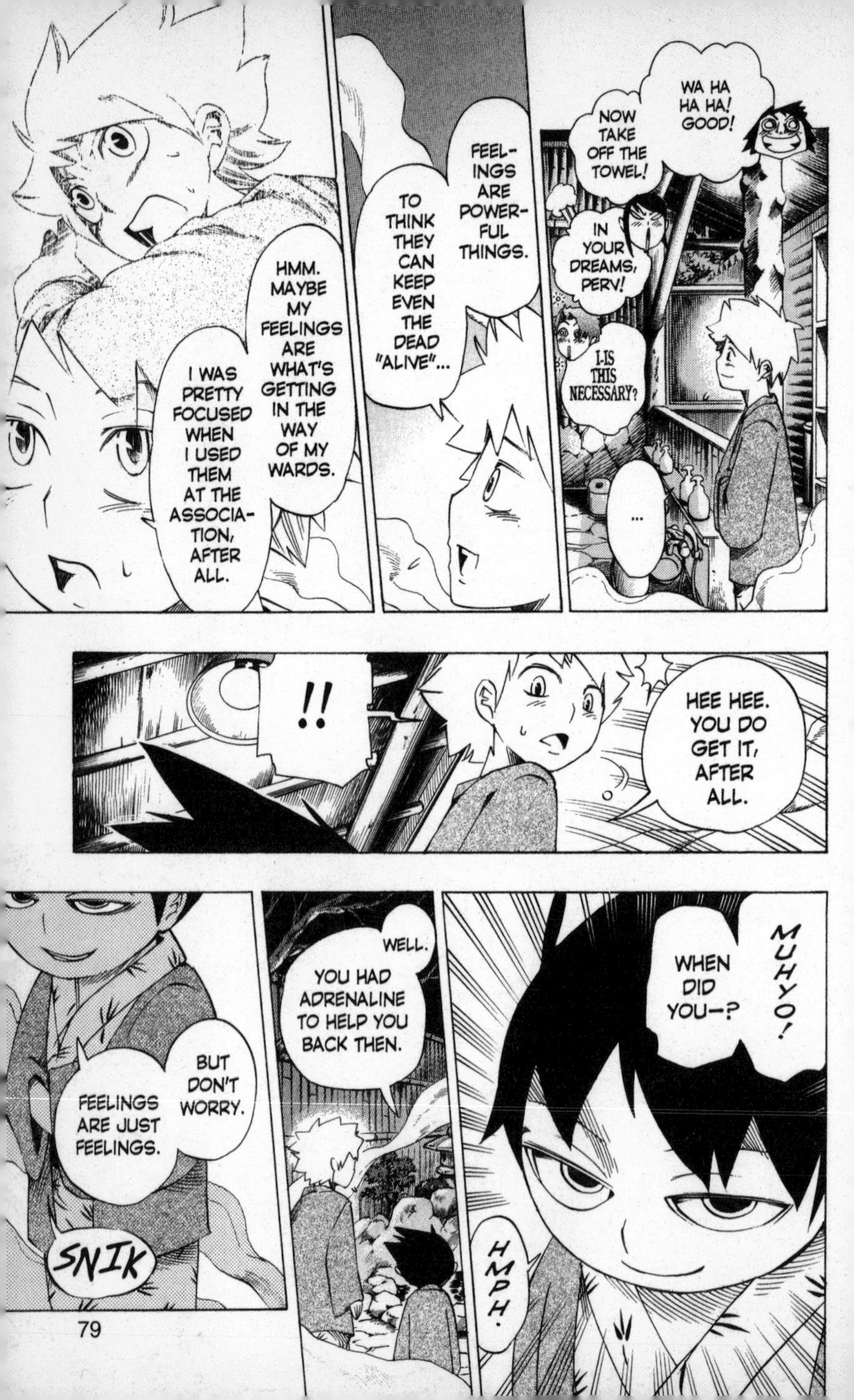
WA HA HA HA! GOOD!
NOW TAKE OFF THE TOWEL!
IN YOUR DREAMS, PERV!
I-IS THIS NECESSARY?
...
FEEL-INGS ARE POWER-FUL THINGS.
TO THINK THEY CAN KEEP EVEN THE DEAD "ALIVE"...
HMM. MAYBE MY FEELINGS ARE WHAT'S GETTING IN THE WAY OF MY WARDS.
I WAS PRETTY FOCUSED WHEN I USED THEM AT THE ASSOCIA-TION, AFTER ALL.
HEE HEE. YOU DO GET IT, AFTER ALL.
!!
MUHYO!
WHEN DID YOU—?
HMPH.
WELL.
YOU HAD ADRENALINE TO HELP YOU BACK THEN.
BUT DON'T WORRY.
FEELINGS ARE JUST FEELINGS.
SNIK

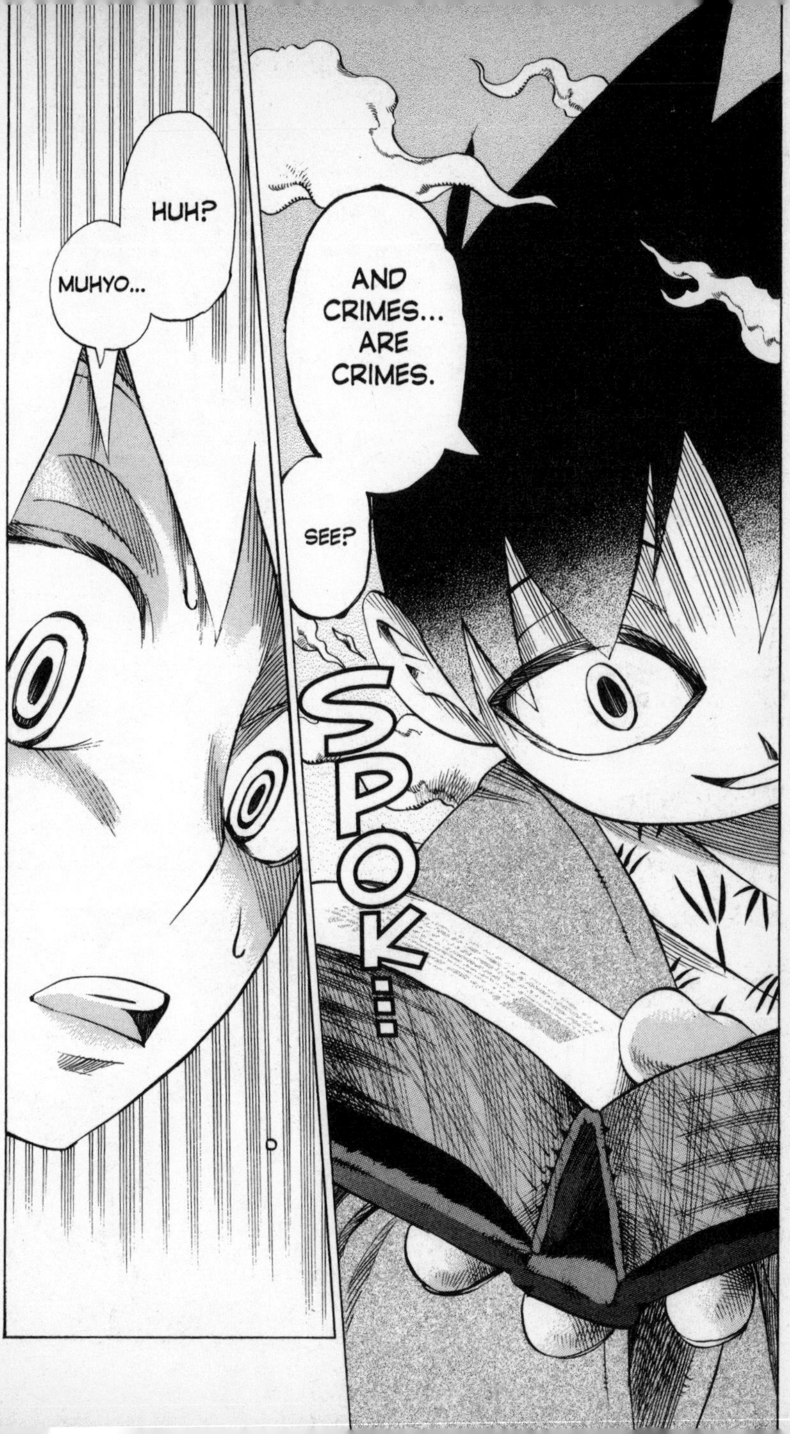
AND CRIMES... ARE CRIMES.
SEE?
SPOK...
HUH?
MUHYO...

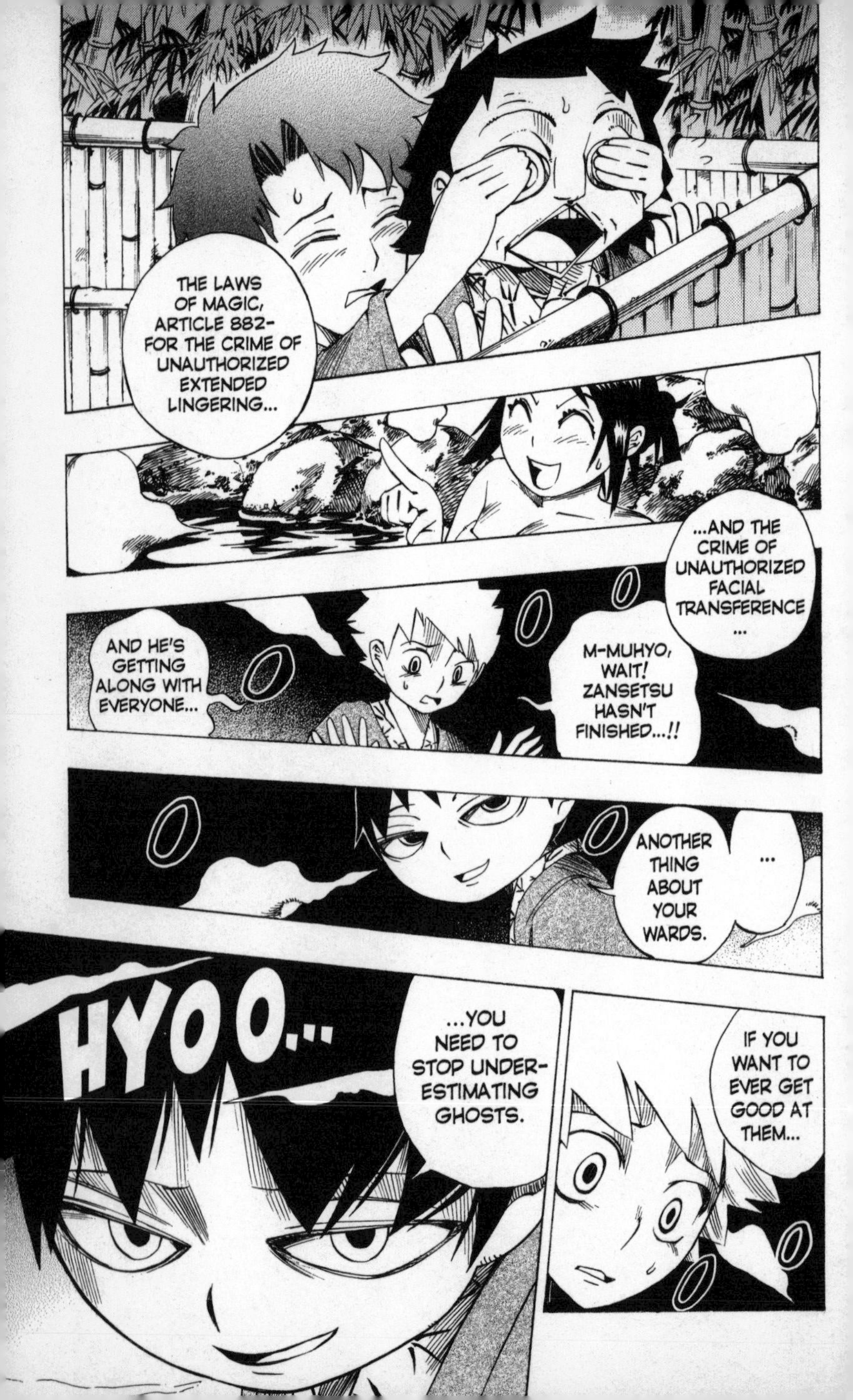
THE LAWS OF MAGIC, ARTICLE 882- FOR THE CRIME OF UNAUTHORIZED EXTENDED LINGERING...
...AND THE CRIME OF UNAUTHORIZED FACIAL TRANSFERENCE ...
M-MUHYO, WAIT! ZANSETSU HASN'T FINISHED...!!
AND HE'S GETTING ALONG WITH EVERYONE...
...
ANOTHER THING ABOUT YOUR WARDS.
IF YOU WANT TO EVER GET GOOD AT THEM...
...YOU NEED TO STOP UNDER-ESTIMATING GHOSTS.
HYOO...

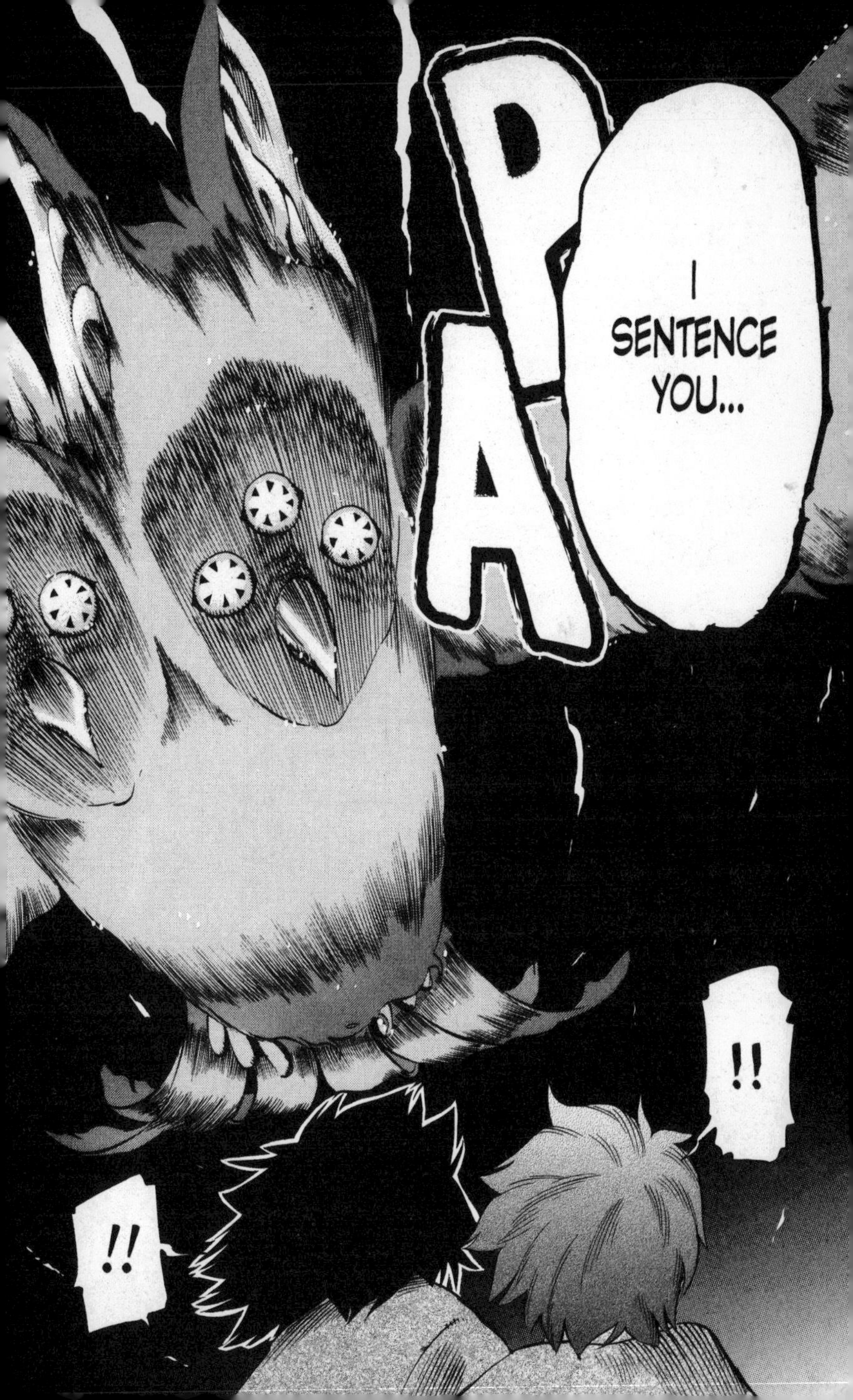
I SENTENCE YOU...
PA
!!
!!

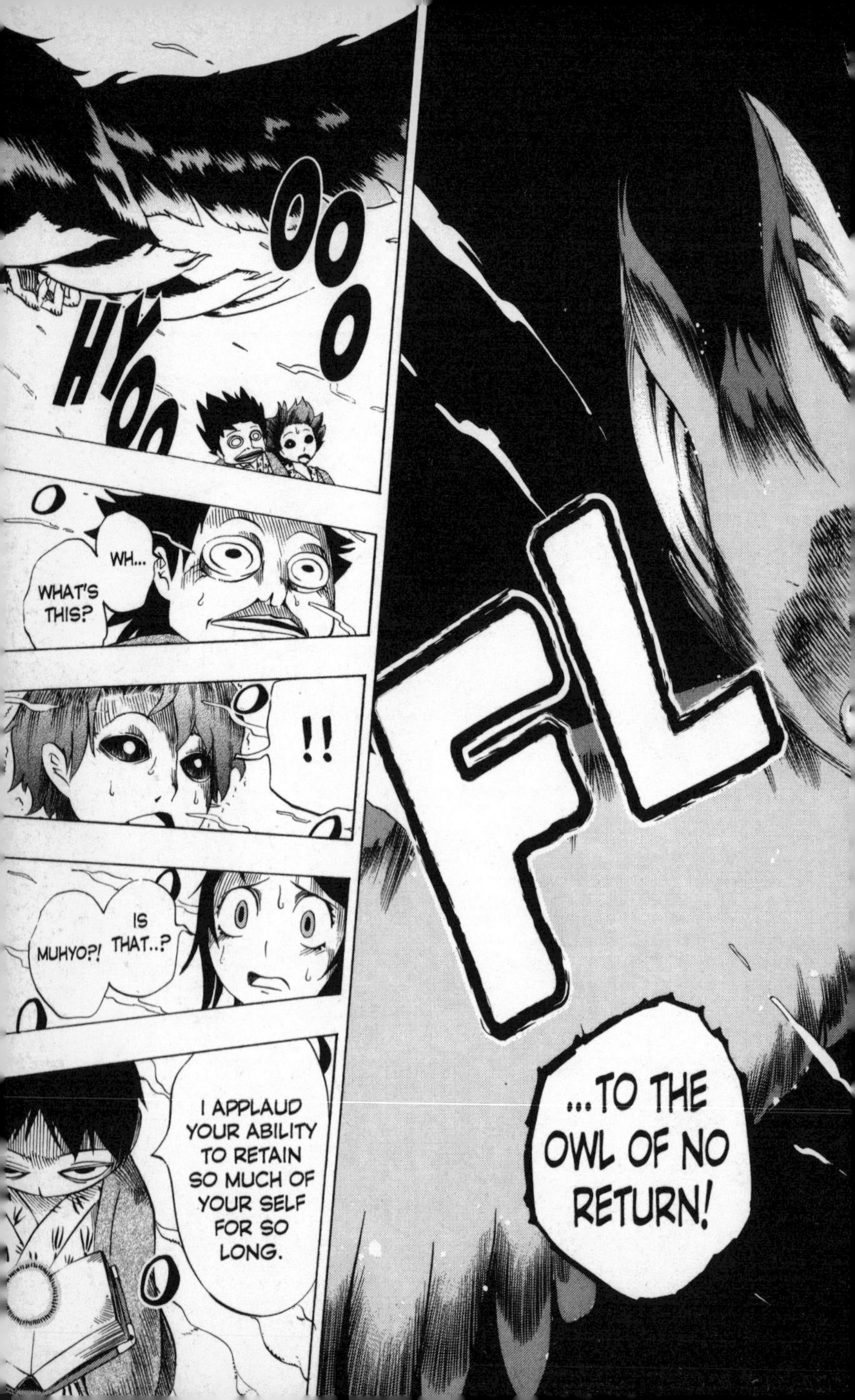
FL
...TO THE OWL OF NO RETURN!
HYOOOOO
WH...
WHAT'S THIS?
!!
IS THAT..?
MUHYO?!
I APPLAUD YOUR ABILITY TO RETAIN SO MUCH OF YOUR SELF FOR SO LONG.

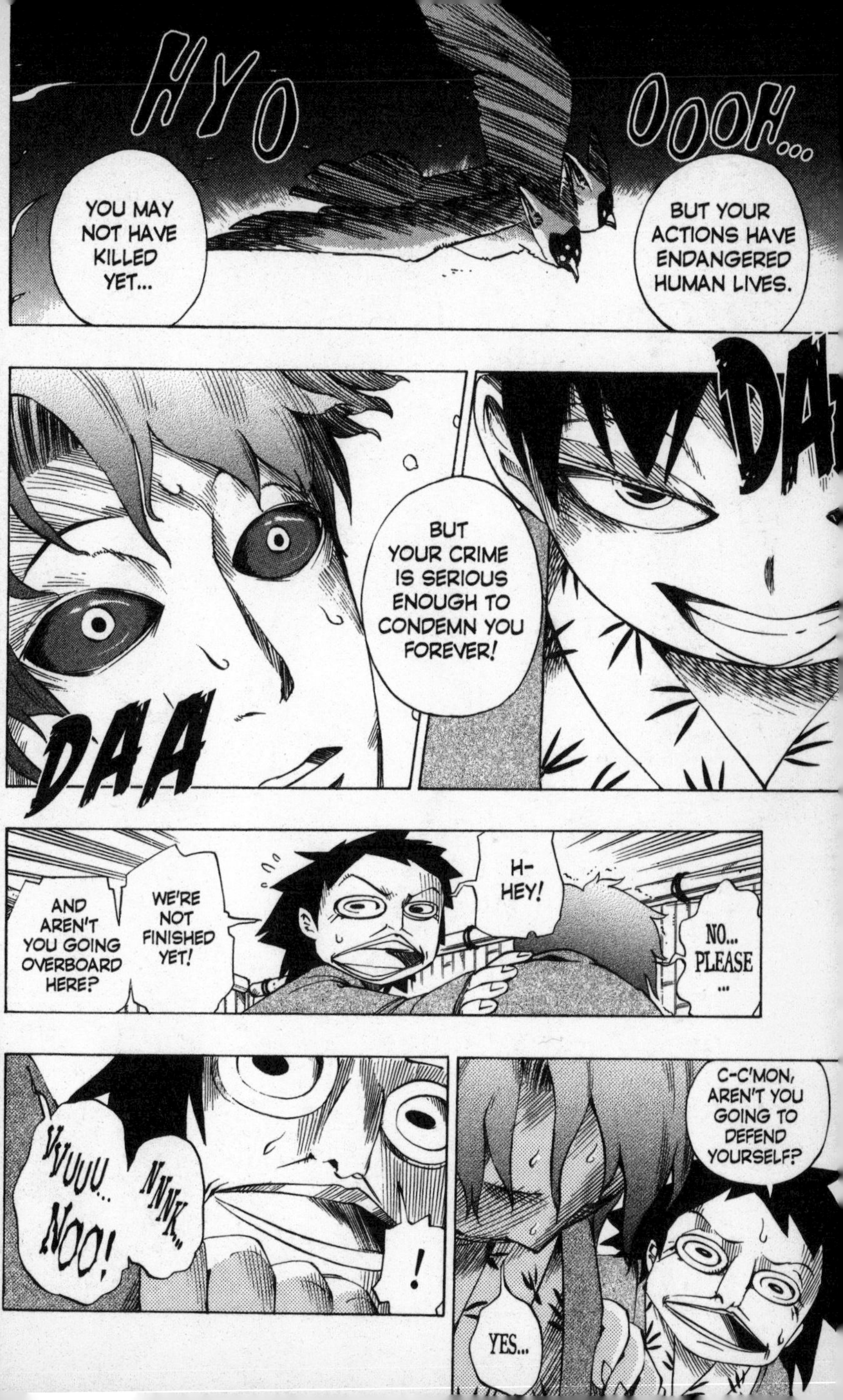
OOOH...
BUT YOUR ACTIONS HAVE ENDANGERED HUMAN LIVES.
HYO
YOU MAY NOT HAVE KILLED YET...
DAA
BUT YOUR CRIME IS SERIOUS ENOUGH TO CONDEMN YOU FOREVER!
DAA
NO... PLEASE ...
H-HEY!
WE'RE NOT FINISHED YET!
AND AREN'T YOU GOING OVERBOARD HERE?
C-C'MON, AREN'T YOU GOING TO DEFEND YOURSELF?
YES...
NNNK...
!
VVUUU... NOO!

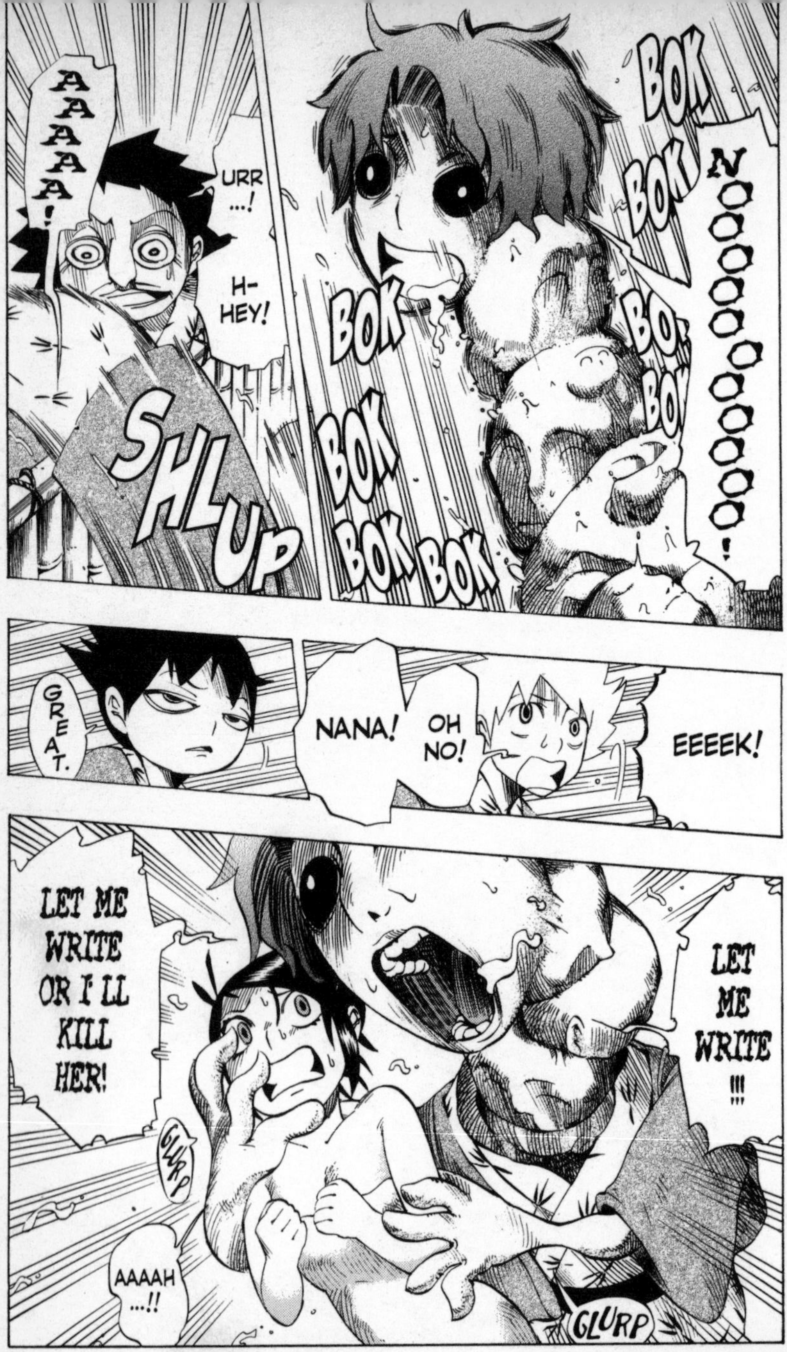
BOK
BOK
NOOOOOOOOOOOOO!
BOK
BOK
BOK
BOK
BOK
BOK
AAAAAA!
URR ...!
H-HEY!
SHLUP
EEEEK!
OH NO!
NANA!
GREAT.
LET ME WRITE!!!
LET ME WRITE OR I'LL KILL HER!
GLURP
GLURP
AAAAH ...!!

ARTICLE 19
THE NIGHT BUTTERFLY

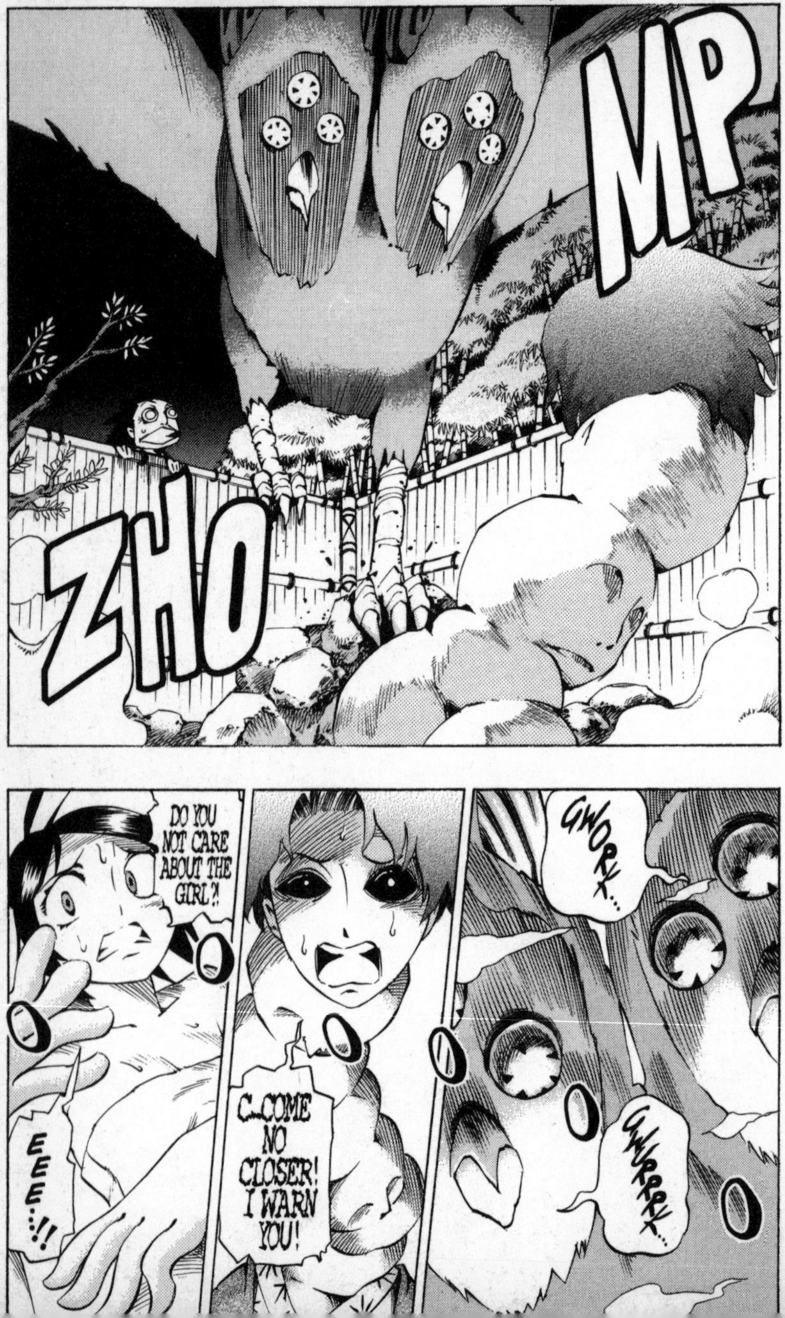
ZHO
MP
GWORK...
GWURRRK...
C..COME NO CLOSER! I WARN YOU!
DO YOU NOT CARE ABOUT THE GIRL?!
EEE...!!

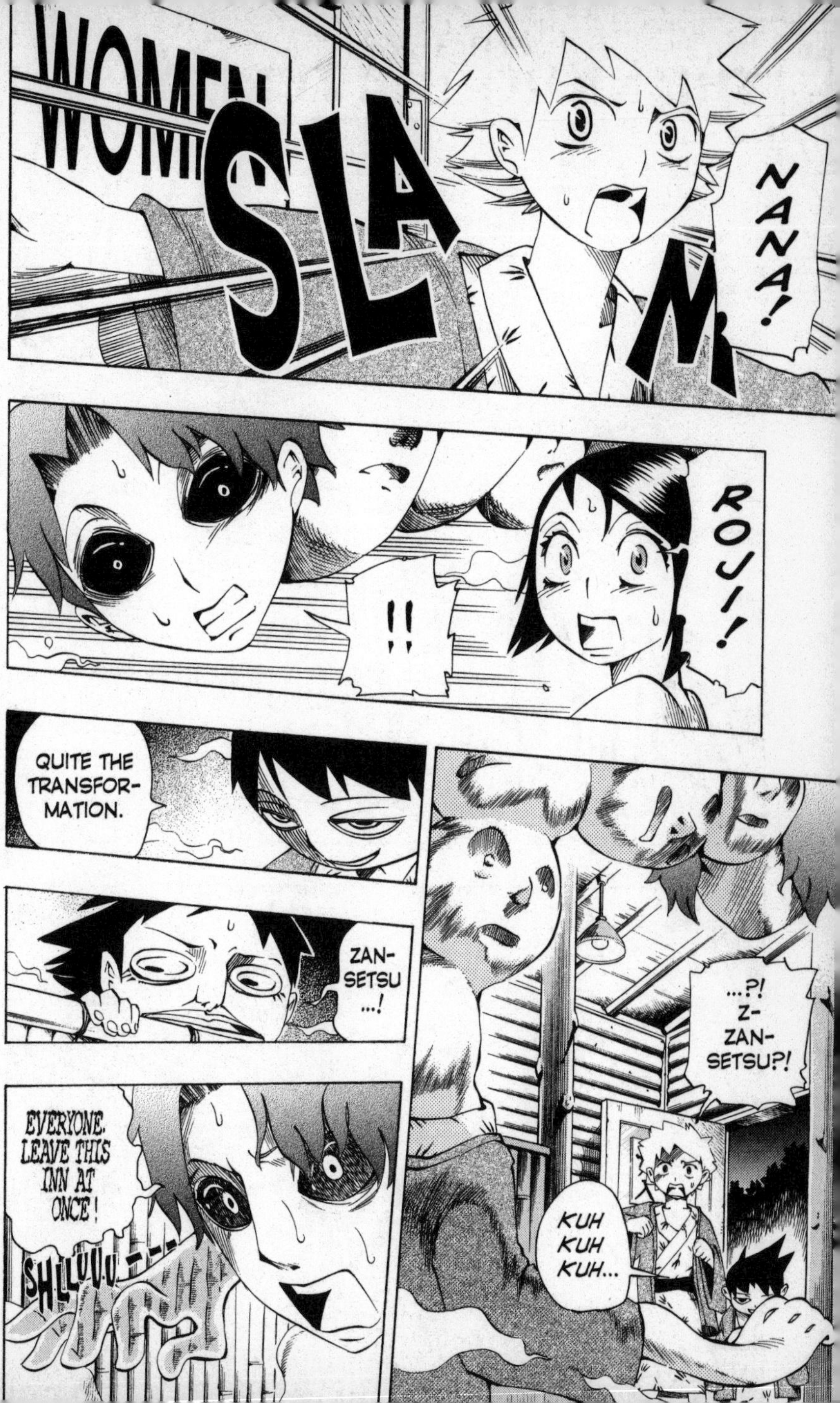
NANA!
SLAM
WOMEN
ROJI!
!!
...?! Z-ZAN-SETSU?!
KUH KUH KUH...
QUITE THE TRANSFORMATION.
ZAN-SETSU...!
EVERYONE. LEAVE THIS INN AT ONCE!
SHLLUUU---

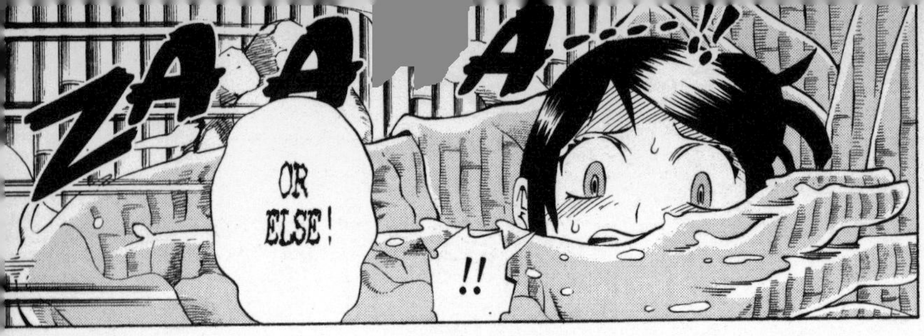
ZAAA...!!
OR ELSE!
!!

ARTICLE 19
THE NIGHT BUTTERFLY

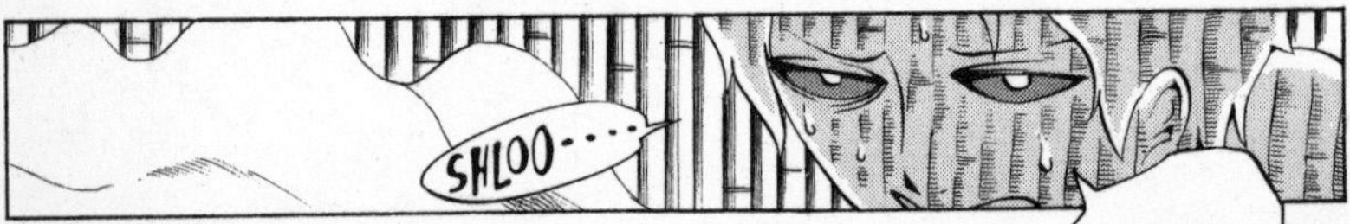
SHLOO....
SHE STAYS.

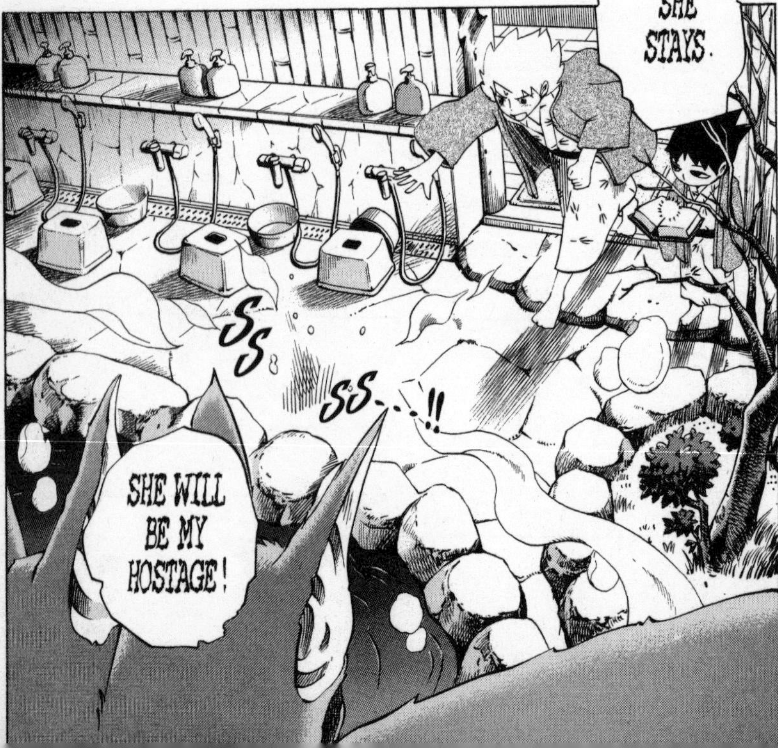
SS
SS...!!
SHE WILL BE MY HOSTAGE!

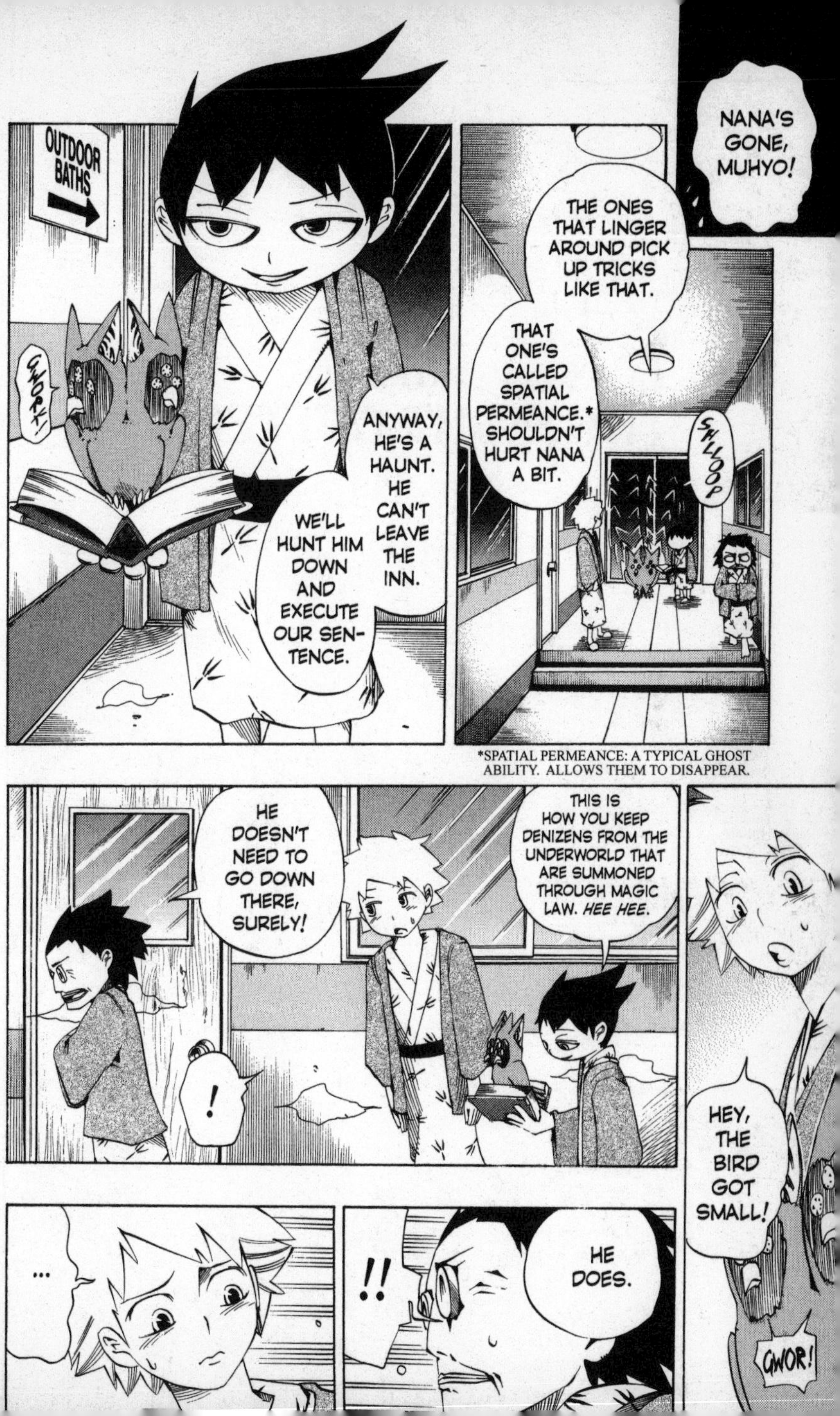
NANA'S GONE, MUHYO!
THE ONES THAT LINGER AROUND PICK UP TRICKS LIKE THAT.
THAT ONE'S CALLED SPATIAL PERMEANCE.* SHOULDN'T HURT NANA A BIT.
SHLOOP
GWORK!
ANYWAY, HE'S A HAUNT. HE CAN'T LEAVE THE INN.
WE'LL HUNT HIM DOWN AND EXECUTE OUR SEN- TENCE.
HEY, THE BIRD GOT SMALL!
GWOR!
THIS IS HOW YOU KEEP DENIZENS FROM THE UNDERWORLD THAT ARE SUMMONED THROUGH MAGIC LAW. *HEE HEE.*
HE DOESN'T NEED TO GO DOWN THERE, SURELY!
!
HE DOES.
!!
...
*SPATIAL PERMEANCE: A TYPICAL GHOST ABILITY. ALLOWS THEM TO DISAPPEAR.

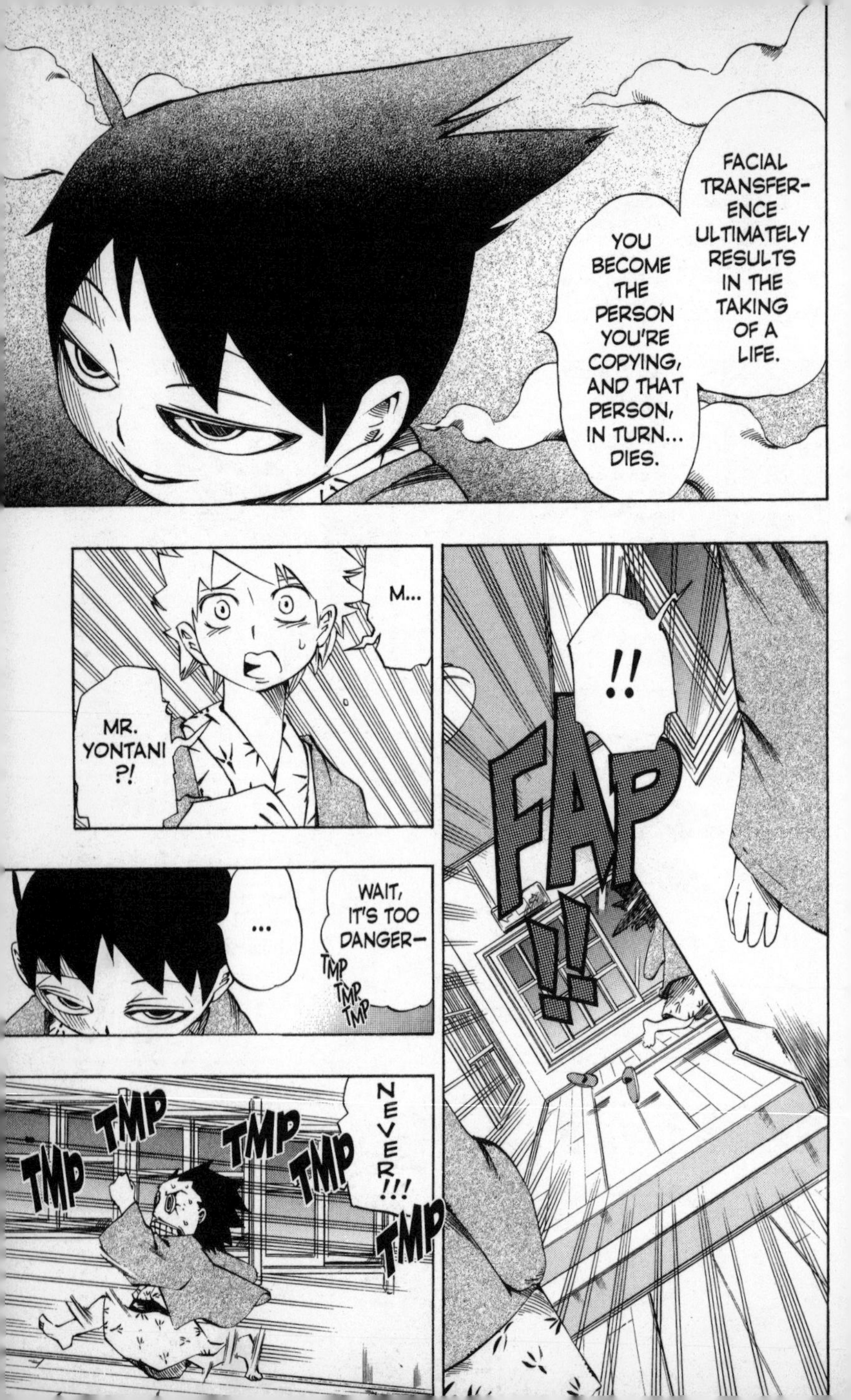
FACIAL TRANSFERENCE ULTIMATELY RESULTS IN THE TAKING OF A LIFE.
YOU BECOME THE PERSON YOU'RE COPYING, AND THAT PERSON, IN TURN... DIES.
!!
FAP
!!!
M...
MR. YONTANI ?!
WAIT, IT'S TOO DANGER—
TMP TMP TMP
...
TMP
NEVER!!!
TMP
TMP
TMP
TMP

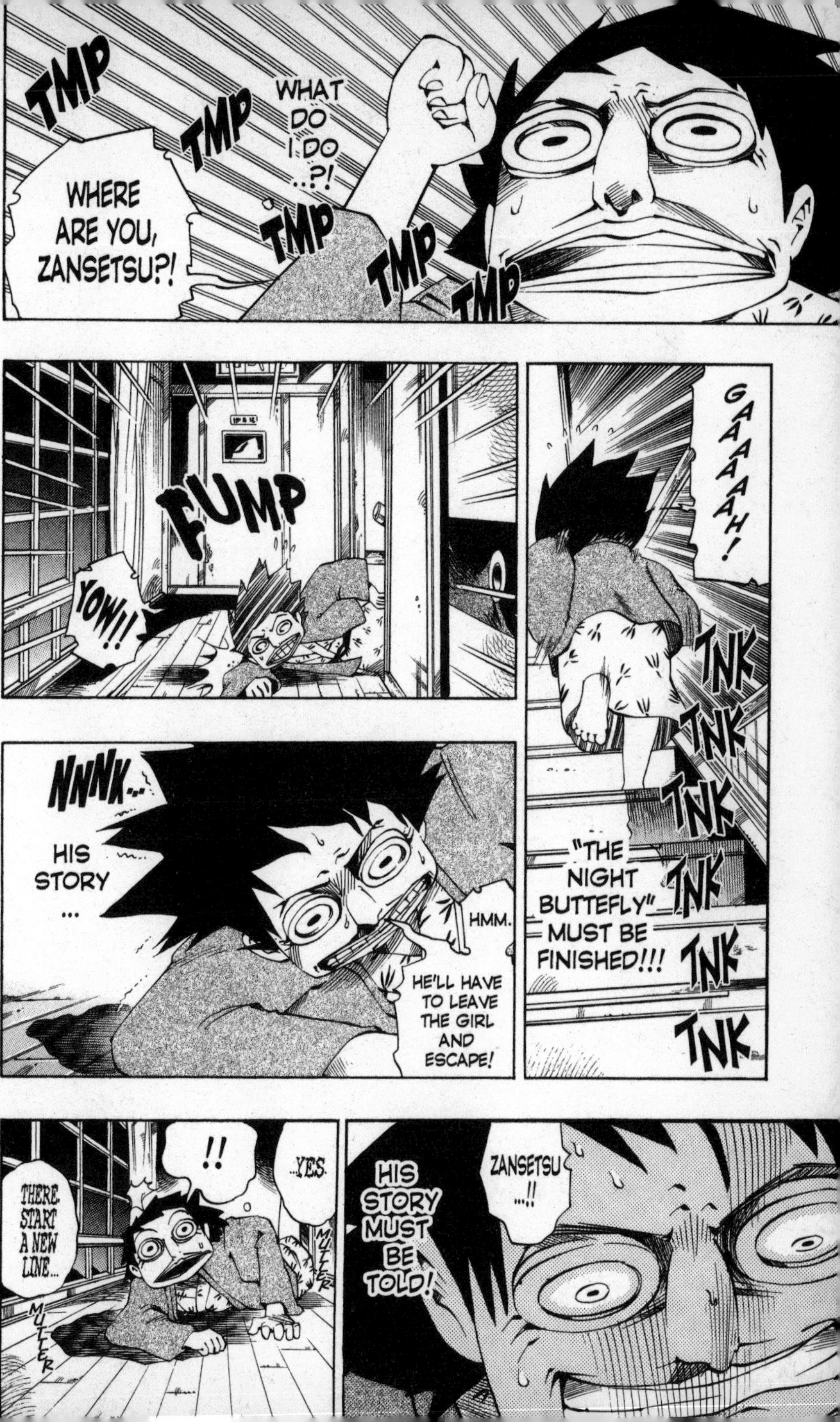
WHAT DO I DO ..?!
TMP
TMP
TMP
TMP
TMP
WHERE ARE YOU, ZANSETSU?!
GAAAAAH!
TNK
TNK
TNK
TNK
TNK
TNK
"THE NIGHT BUTTEFLY" MUST BE FINISHED!!!
FUMP
YOW!!
HMM.
HE'LL HAVE TO LEAVE THE GIRL AND ESCAPE!
NNNK...
HIS STORY ...
ZANSETSU ...!!
HIS STORY MUST BE TOLD!
...YES.
!!
MUTTER
THERE. START A NEW LINE...
MUTTER

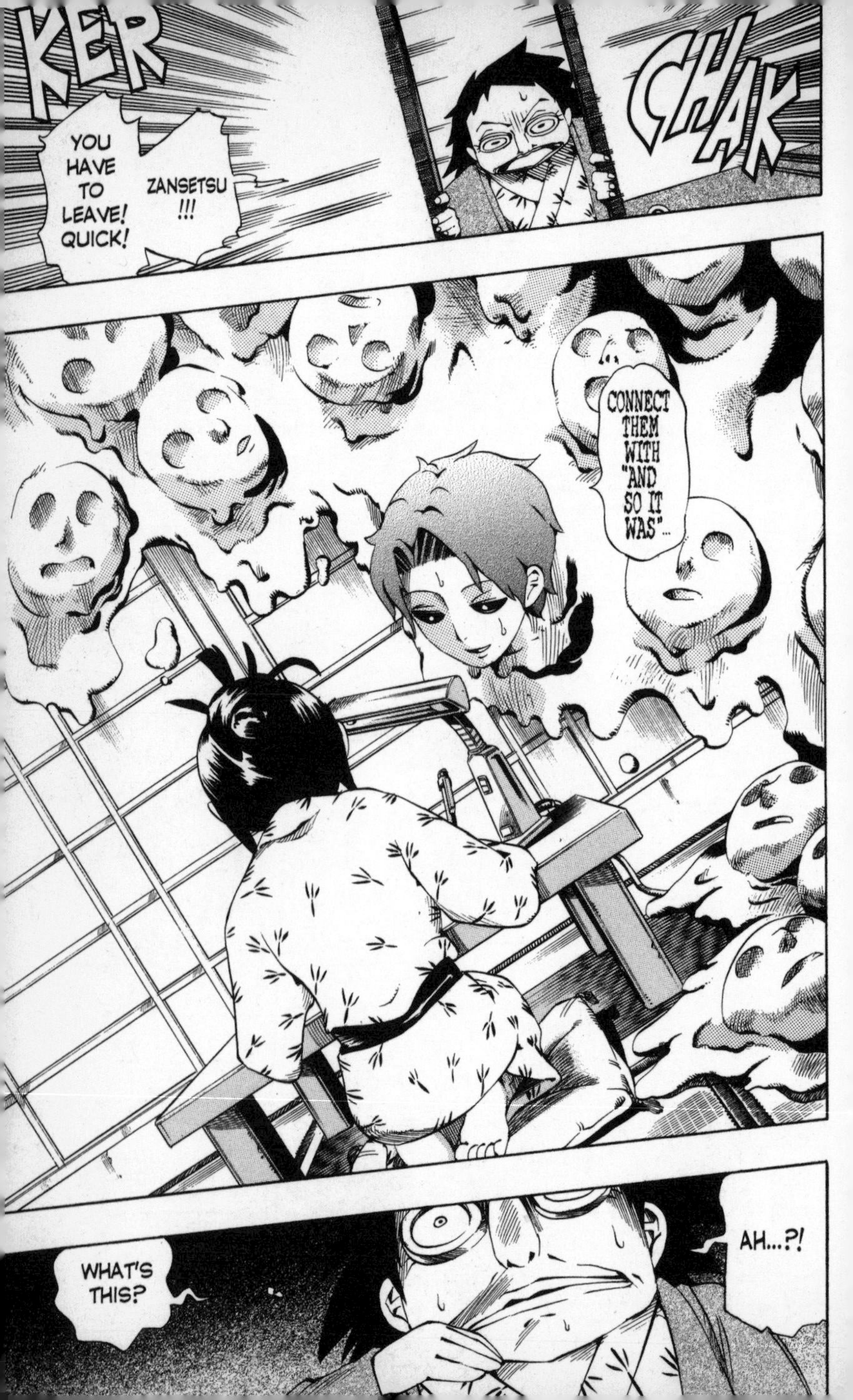
KER CHAK
ZANSETSU!!!
YOU HAVE TO LEAVE! QUICK!
CONNECT THEM WITH "AND SO IT WAS"...
AH...?!
WHAT'S THIS?

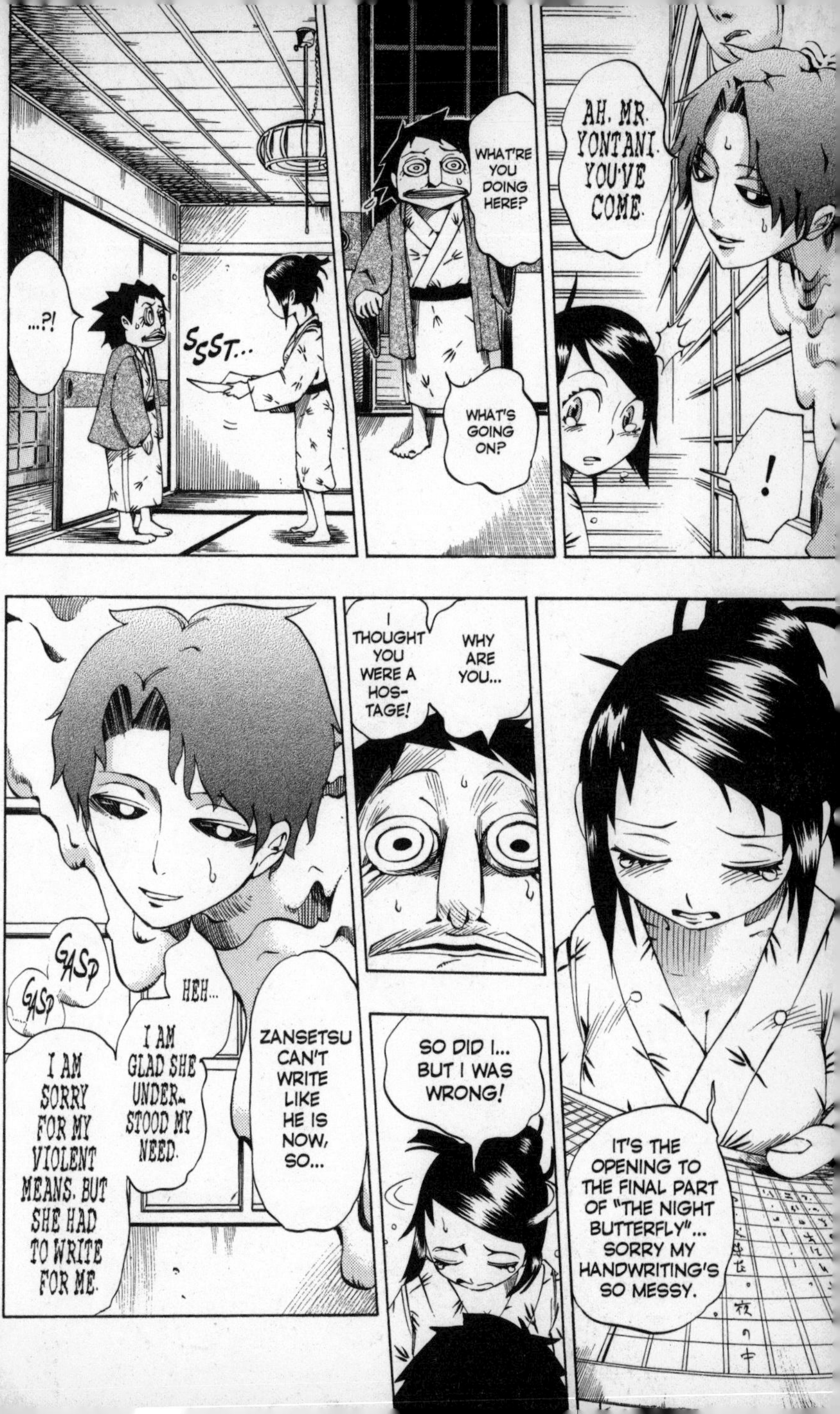
AH, MR. YONTANI. YOU'VE COME.
!
WHAT'RE YOU DOING HERE?
WHAT'S GOING ON?
SSST...
...?!
IT'S THE OPENING TO THE FINAL PART OF "THE NIGHT BUTTERFLY"... SORRY MY HANDWRITING'S SO MESSY.
WHY ARE YOU...
I THOUGHT YOU WERE A HOS-TAGE!
SO DID I... BUT I WAS WRONG!
ZANSETSU CAN'T WRITE LIKE HE IS NOW, SO...
HEH...
I AM GLAD SHE UNDER-STOOD MY NEED.
I AM SORRY FOR MY VIOLENT MEANS. BUT SHE HAD TO WRITE FOR ME.
GASP
GASP

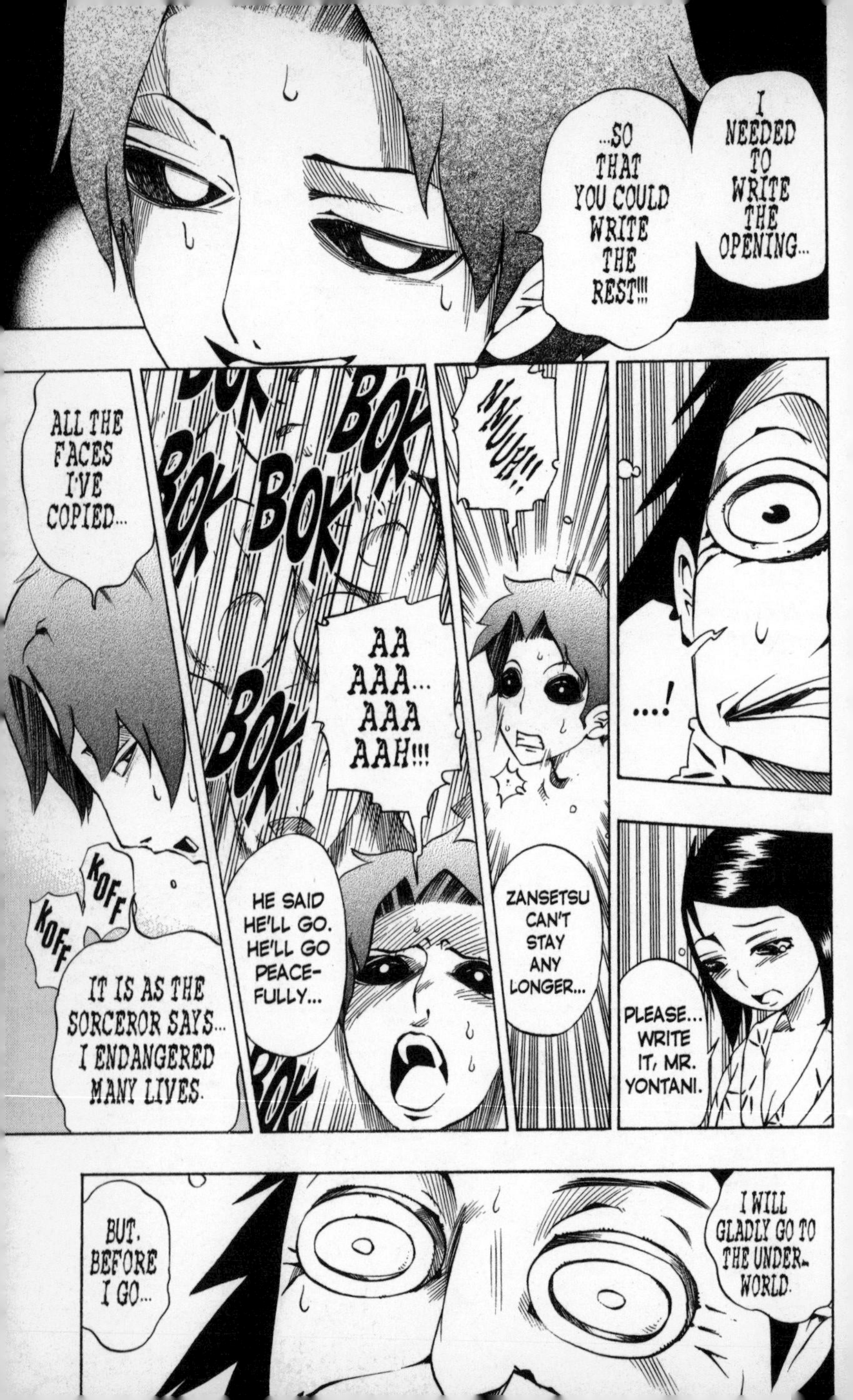
I NEEDED TO WRITE THE OPENING...
...SO THAT YOU COULD WRITE THE REST!!!
...!
PLEASE... WRITE IT, MR. YONTANI.
N'NUH!!
ZANSETSU CAN'T STAY ANY LONGER...
BOK
BOK
BOK
BOK
BOK
AA AAA... AAA AAH!!!
HE SAID HE'LL GO. HE'LL GO PEACE-FULLY...
ALL THE FACES I'VE COPIED...
KOFF
KOFF
IT IS AS THE SORCEROR SAYS... I ENDANGERED MANY LIVES.
I WILL GLADLY GO TO THE UNDER-WORLD.
BUT, BEFORE I GO...

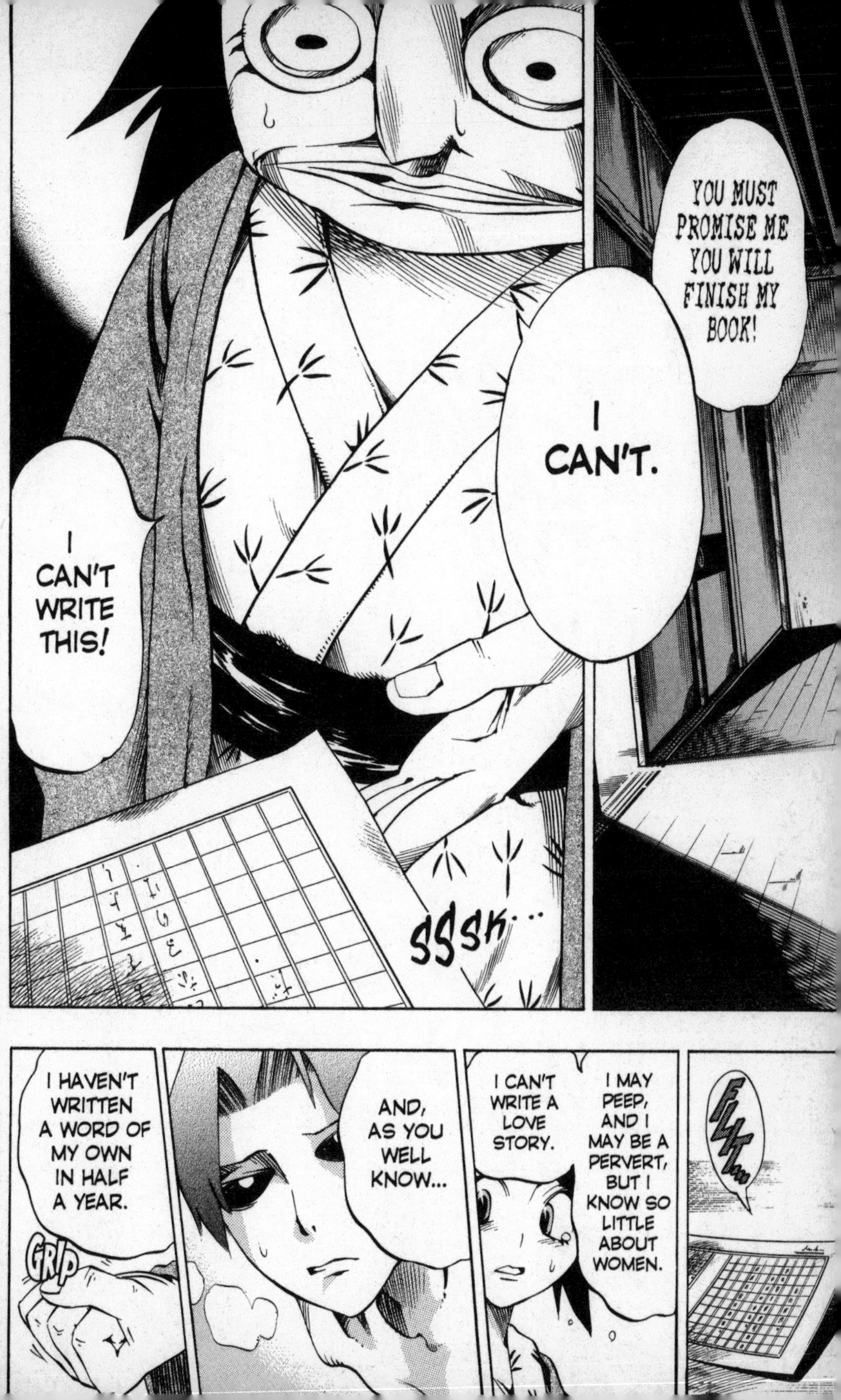
YOU MUST PROMISE ME YOU WILL FINISH MY BOOK!
I CAN'T.
I CAN'T WRITE THIS!
SSSK...
FLIK...
I MAY PEEP, AND I MAY BE A PERVERT, BUT I KNOW SO LITTLE ABOUT WOMEN.
I CAN'T WRITE A LOVE STORY.
AND, AS YOU WELL KNOW...
I HAVEN'T WRITTEN A WORD OF MY OWN IN HALF A YEAR.
GRIP

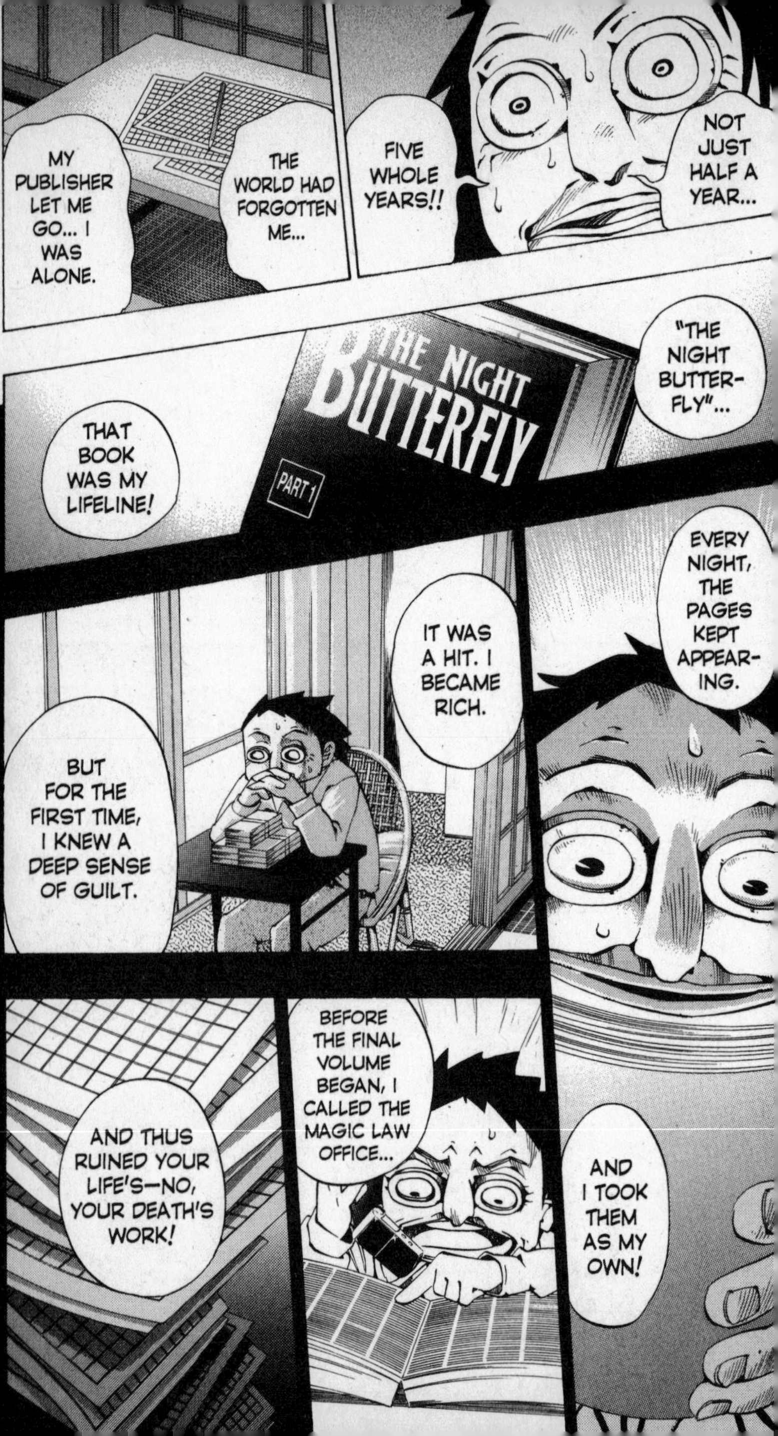
NOT JUST HALF A YEAR...
FIVE WHOLE YEARS!!
THE WORLD HAD FORGOTTEN ME...
MY PUBLISHER LET ME GO... I WAS ALONE.
"THE NIGHT BUTTERFLY"...
THE NIGHT BUTTERFLY
PART 1
THAT BOOK WAS MY LIFELINE!
EVERY NIGHT, THE PAGES KEPT APPEARING.
AND I TOOK THEM AS MY OWN!
IT WAS A HIT. I BECAME RICH.
BUT FOR THE FIRST TIME, I KNEW A DEEP SENSE OF GUILT.
BEFORE THE FINAL VOLUME BEGAN, I CALLED THE MAGIC LAW OFFICE...
AND THUS RUINED YOUR LIFE'S—NO, YOUR DEATH'S WORK!

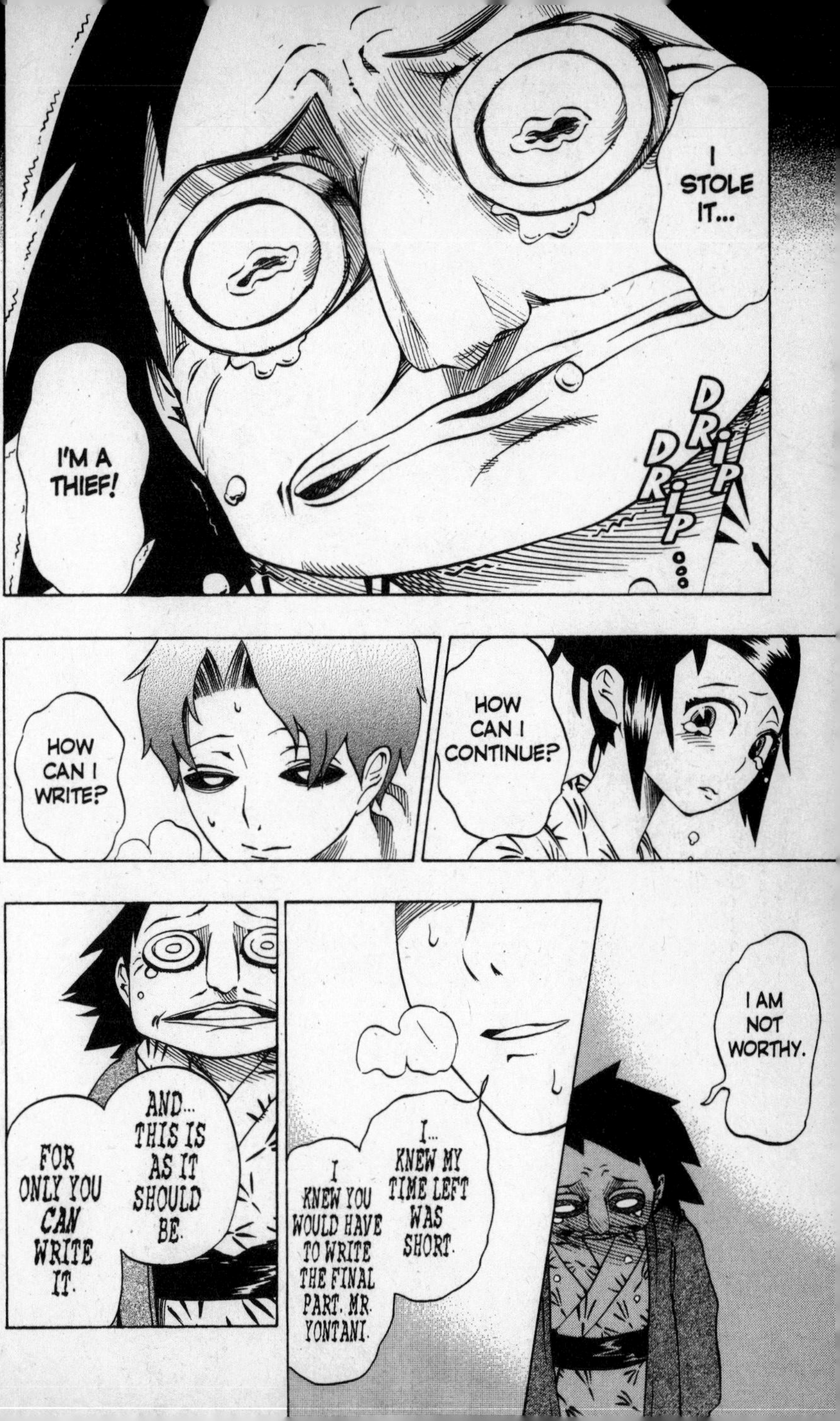
I STOLE IT...
DRIP DRIP...
I'M A THIEF!
HOW CAN I CONTINUE?
HOW CAN I WRITE?
I AM NOT WORTHY.
I... KNEW MY TIME LEFT WAS SHORT.
I KNEW YOU WOULD HAVE TO WRITE THE FINAL PART, MR. YONTANI.
AND... THIS IS AS IT SHOULD BE.
FOR ONLY YOU *CAN* WRITE IT.

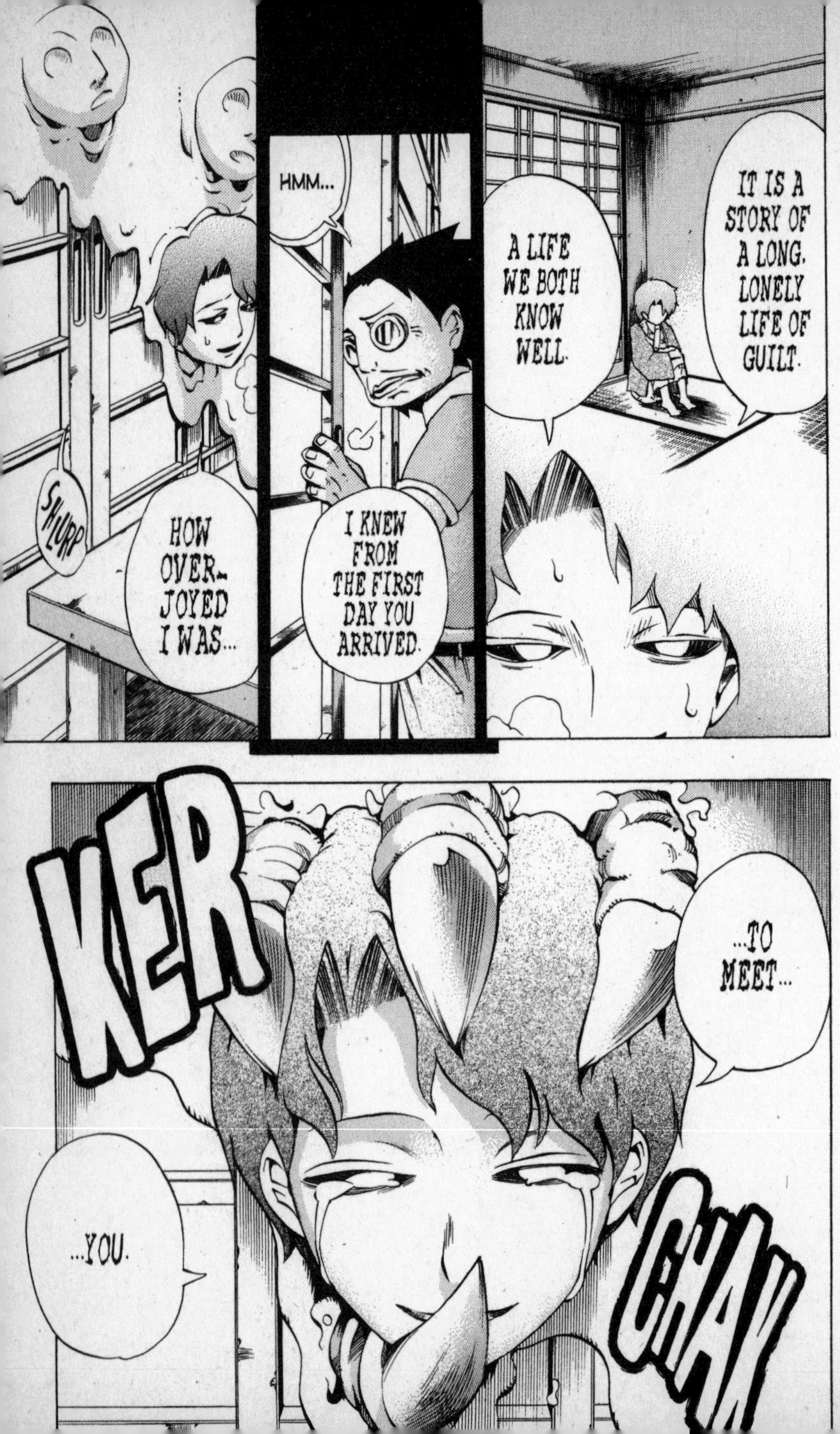
IT IS A STORY OF A LONG. LONELY LIFE OF GUILT.
A LIFE WE BOTH KNOW WELL.
HMM...
I KNEW FROM THE FIRST DAY YOU ARRIVED.
SHLURP
HOW OVER-JOYED I WAS...
...TO MEET...
KER
CHAK
...YOU.

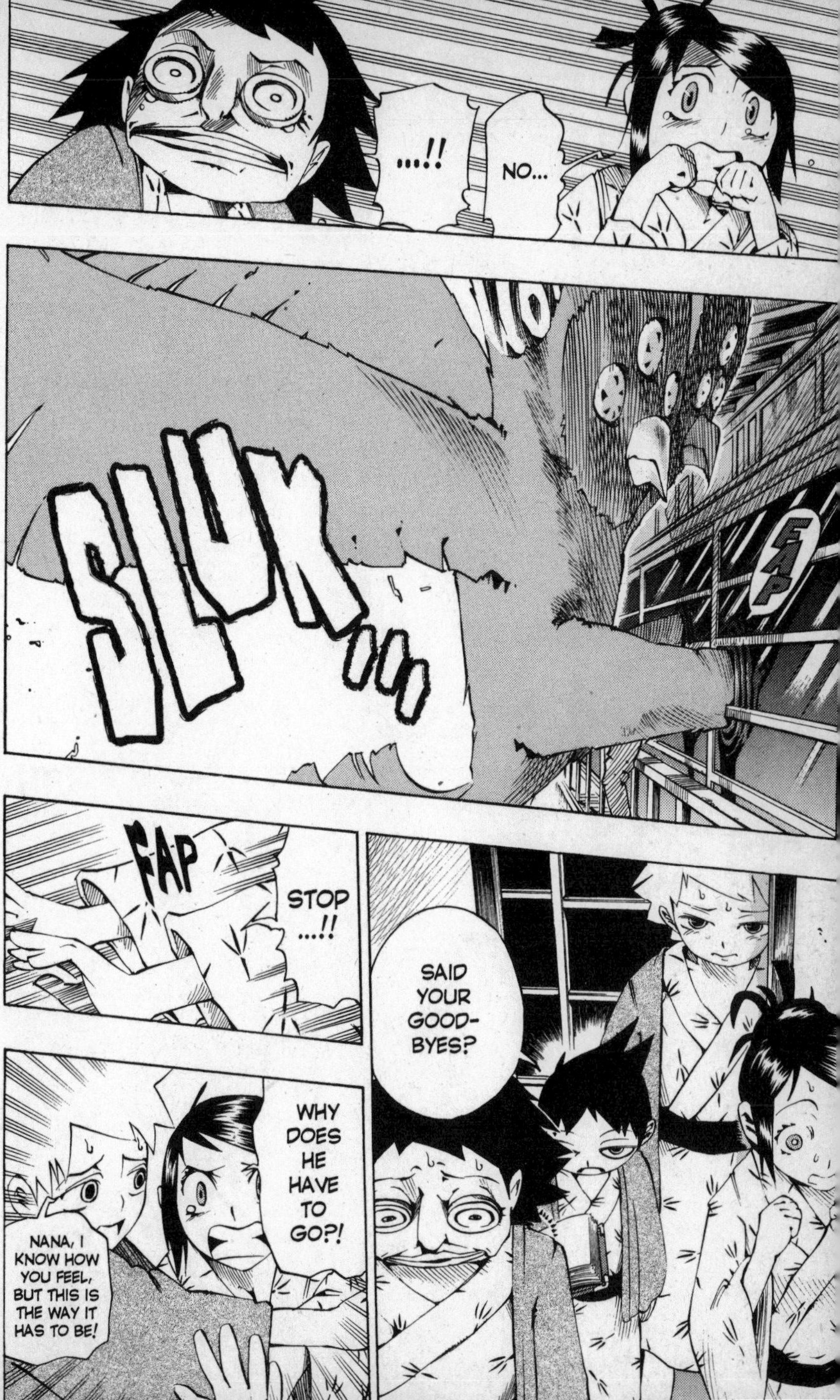
NO...
...!!
FAP
SLUK...
SAID YOUR GOOD-BYES?
FAP
STOP...!!
WHY DOES HE HAVE TO GO?!
NANA, I KNOW HOW YOU FEEL, BUT THIS IS THE WAY IT HAS TO BE!

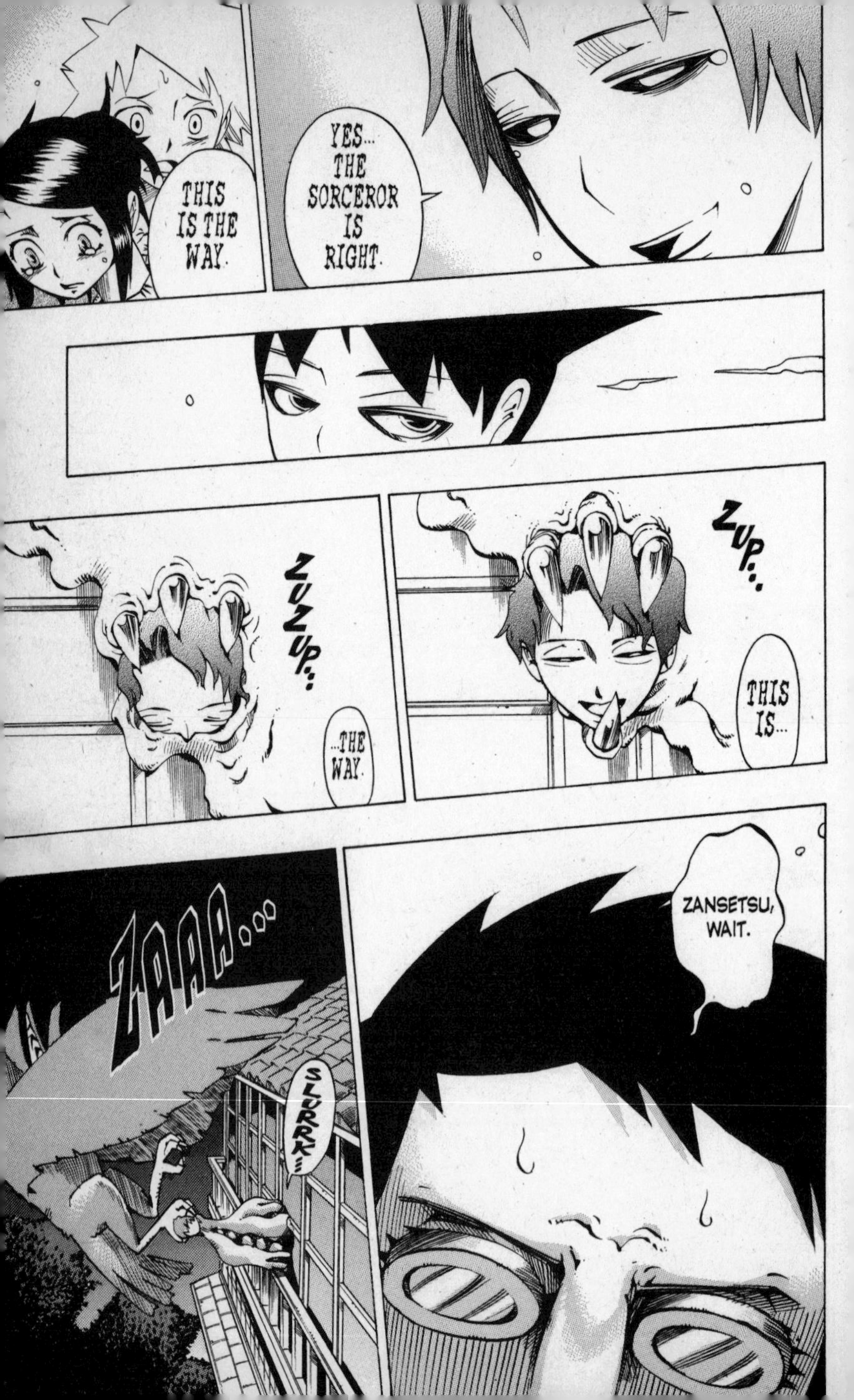
YES... THE SORCEROR IS RIGHT.
THIS IS THE WAY.
ZUP...
THIS IS...
ZUZUP...
...THE WAY.
ZANSETSU, WAIT.
ZAAA...
SLURRK!!

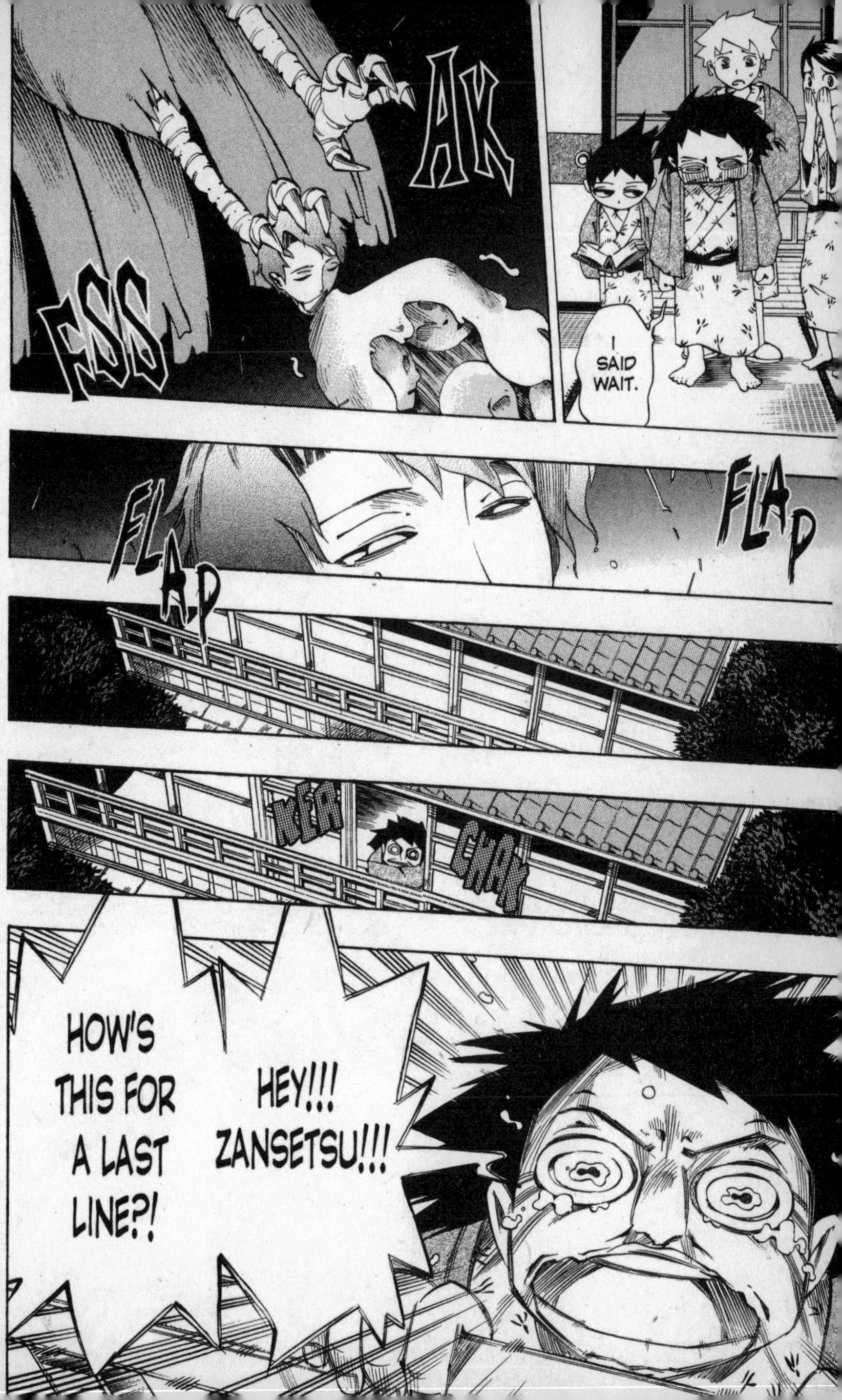
I SAID WAIT.
AK
FSS
FLAP
FLAP
KER
CHAK
HEY!!! ZANSETSU!!!
HOW'S THIS FOR A LAST LINE?!

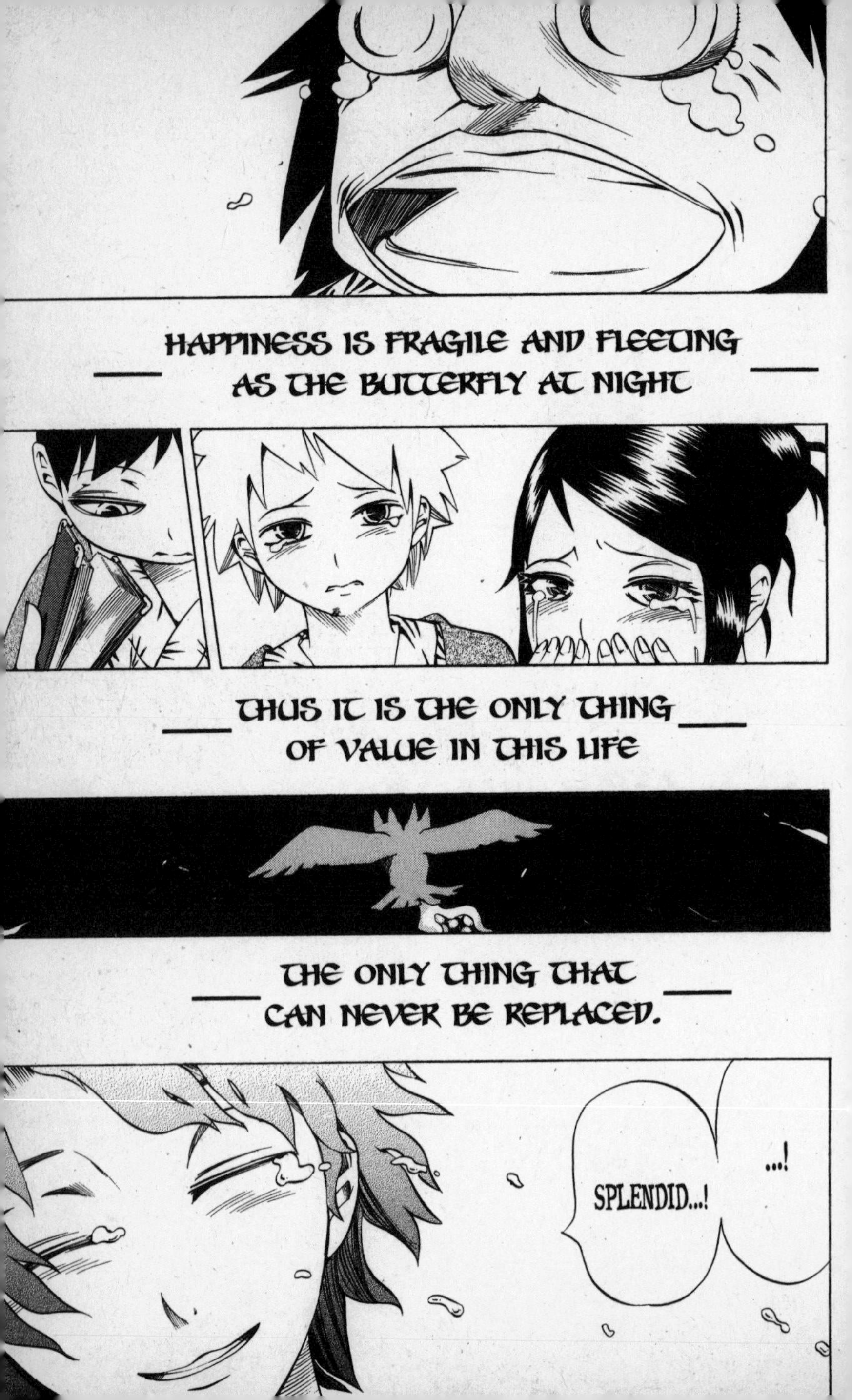
HAPPINESS IS FRAGILE AND FLEETING AS THE BUTTERFLY AT NIGHT
THUS IT IS THE ONLY THING OF VALUE IN THIS LIFE
THE ONLY THING THAT CAN NEVER BE REPLACED.
...!
SPLENDID...!

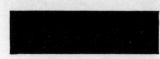

[redacted]

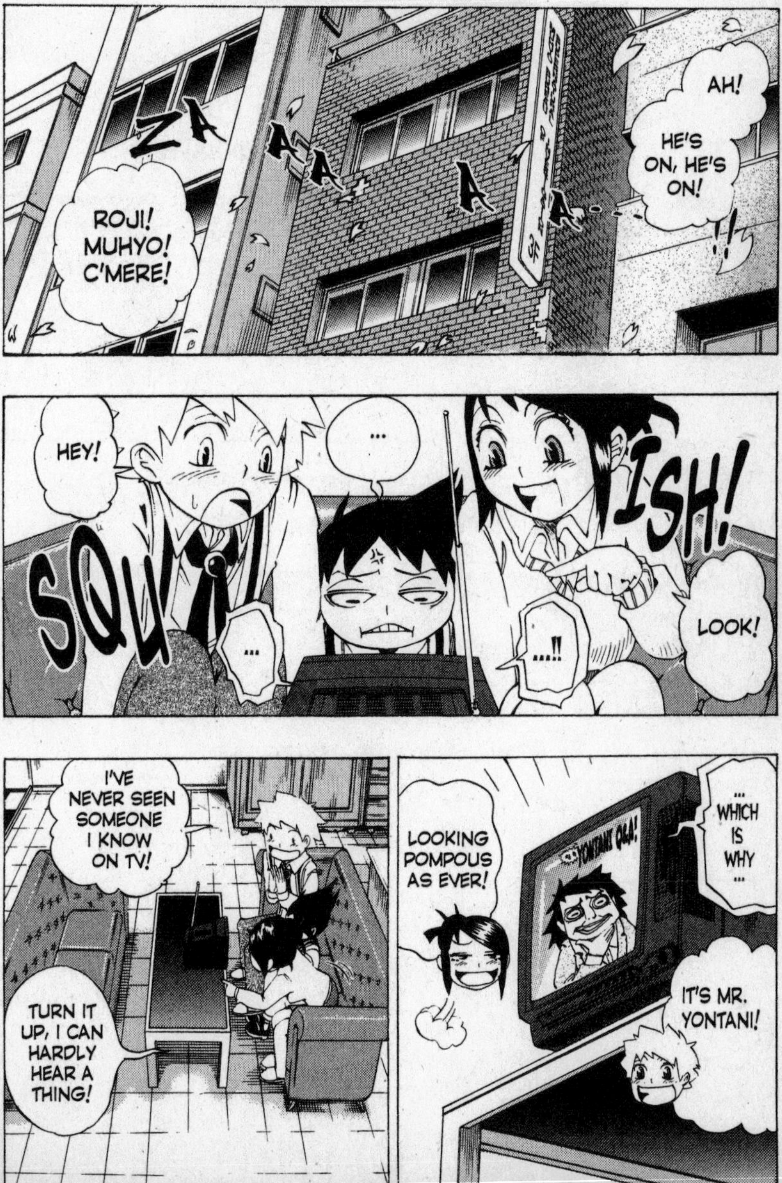
AH!
HE'S ON, HE'S ON!
ZAAAA...
ROJI! MUHYO! C'MERE!
ISH!
...
HEY!
LOOK!
...!!
...
SQU
... WHICH IS WHY ...
YONTANI Q&A!
LOOKING POMPOUS AS EVER!
IT'S MR. YONTANI!
I'VE NEVER SEEN SOMEONE I KNOW ON TV!
TURN IT UP, I CAN HARDLY HEAR A THING!

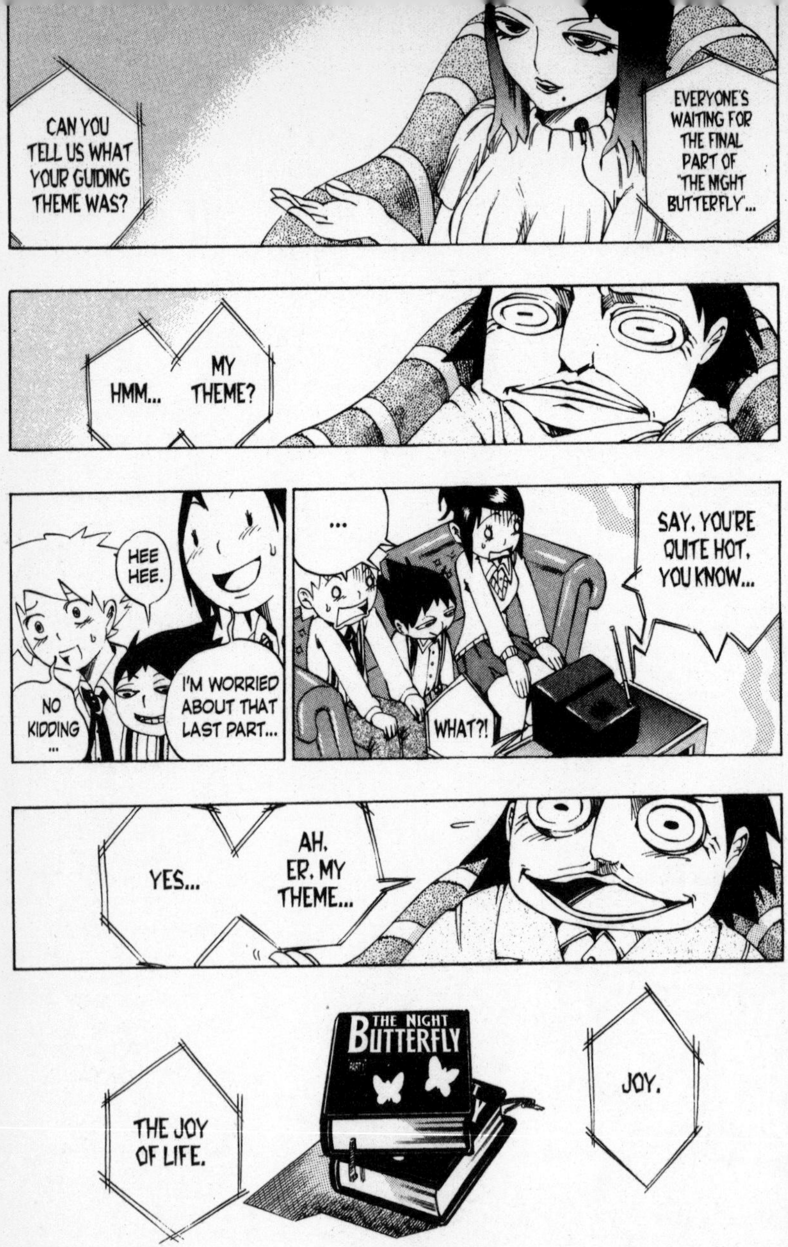
EVERYONE'S WAITING FOR THE FINAL PART OF "THE NIGHT BUTTERFLY"...
CAN YOU TELL US WHAT YOUR GUIDING THEME WAS?
MY THEME?
HMM...
SAY, YOU'RE QUITE HOT, YOU KNOW...
...
WHAT?!
HEE HEE.
I'M WORRIED ABOUT THAT LAST PART...
NO KIDDING...
AH, ER, MY THEME...
YES...
JOY.
THE NIGHT BUTTERFLY
THE JOY OF LIFE.

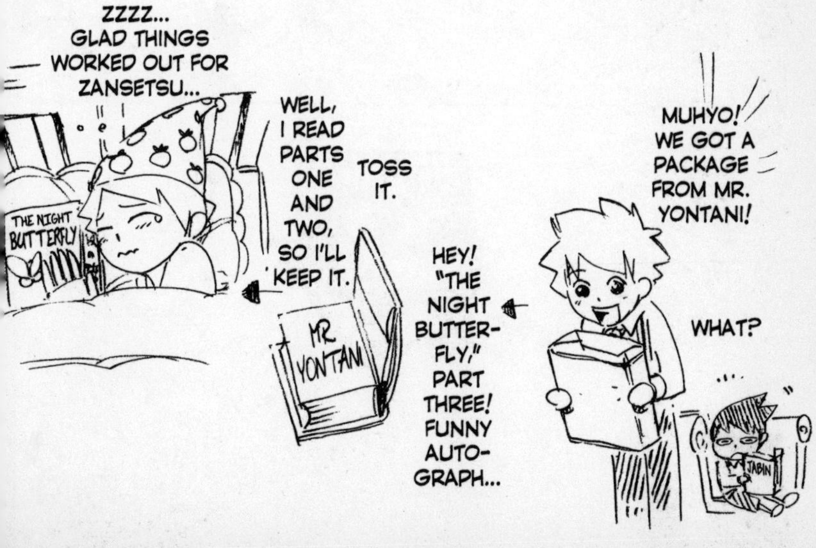
MUHYO! WE GOT A PACKAGE FROM MR. YONTANI!
WHAT?
...
JABIN
HEY! "THE NIGHT BUTTERFLY," PART THREE! FUNNY AUTOGRAPH...
MR YONTANI
TOSS IT.
WELL, I READ PARTS ONE AND TWO, SO I'LL KEEP IT.
ZZZZ... GLAD THINGS WORKED OUT FOR ZANSETSU...
THE NIGHT BUTTERFLY

ARTICLE 20
ARTIFICER BIKO

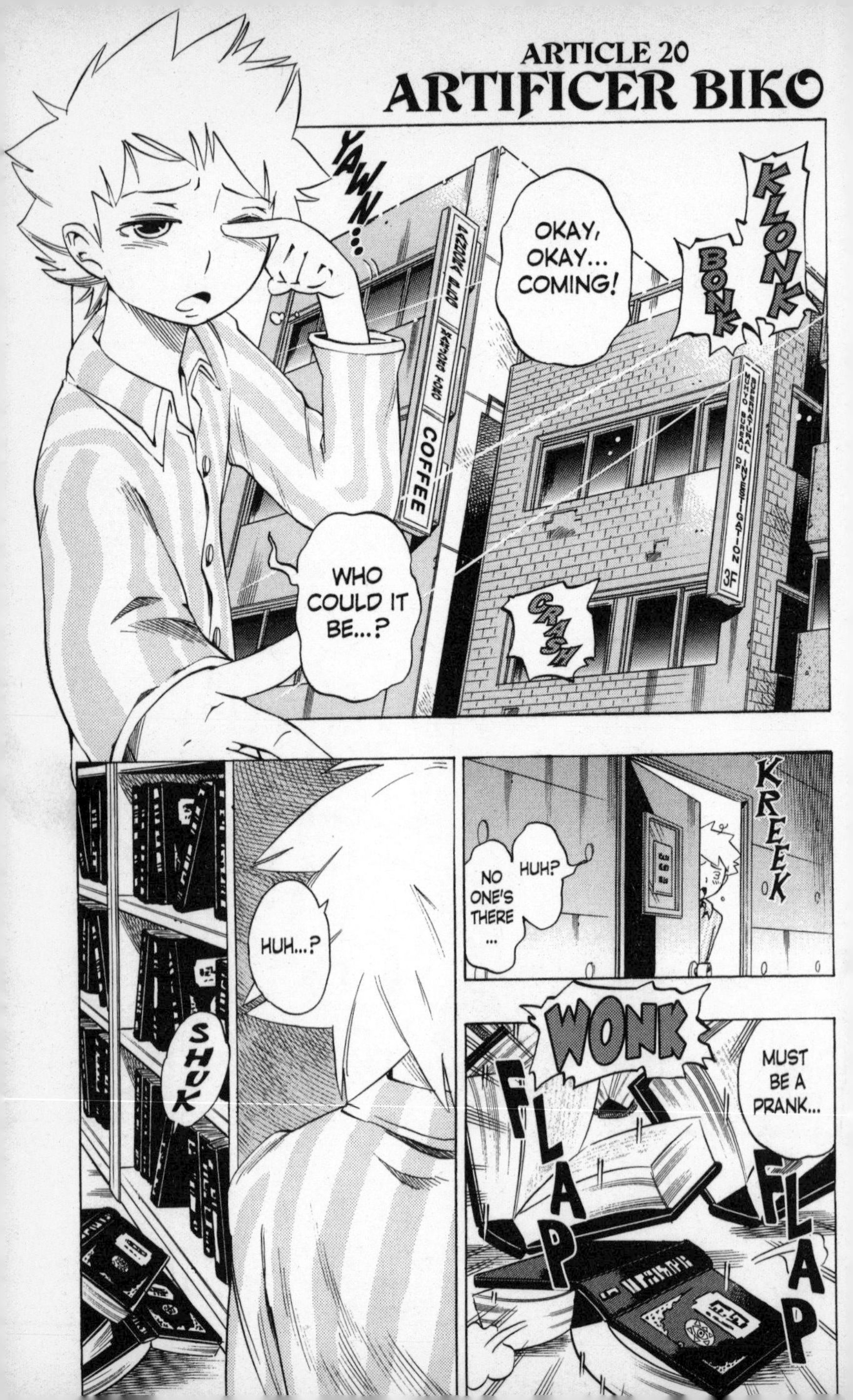
KLONK
BONK
OKAY, OKAY... COMING!
SUPERNATURAL MUHYO BUREAU OF INVESTIGATION 3F
CRASH
COFFEE
YAWN...
WHO COULD IT BE...?
KREEK
HUH?
NO ONE'S THERE ...
MUST BE A PRANK...
WONK
FLAP
FLAP
HUH...?
SHUK

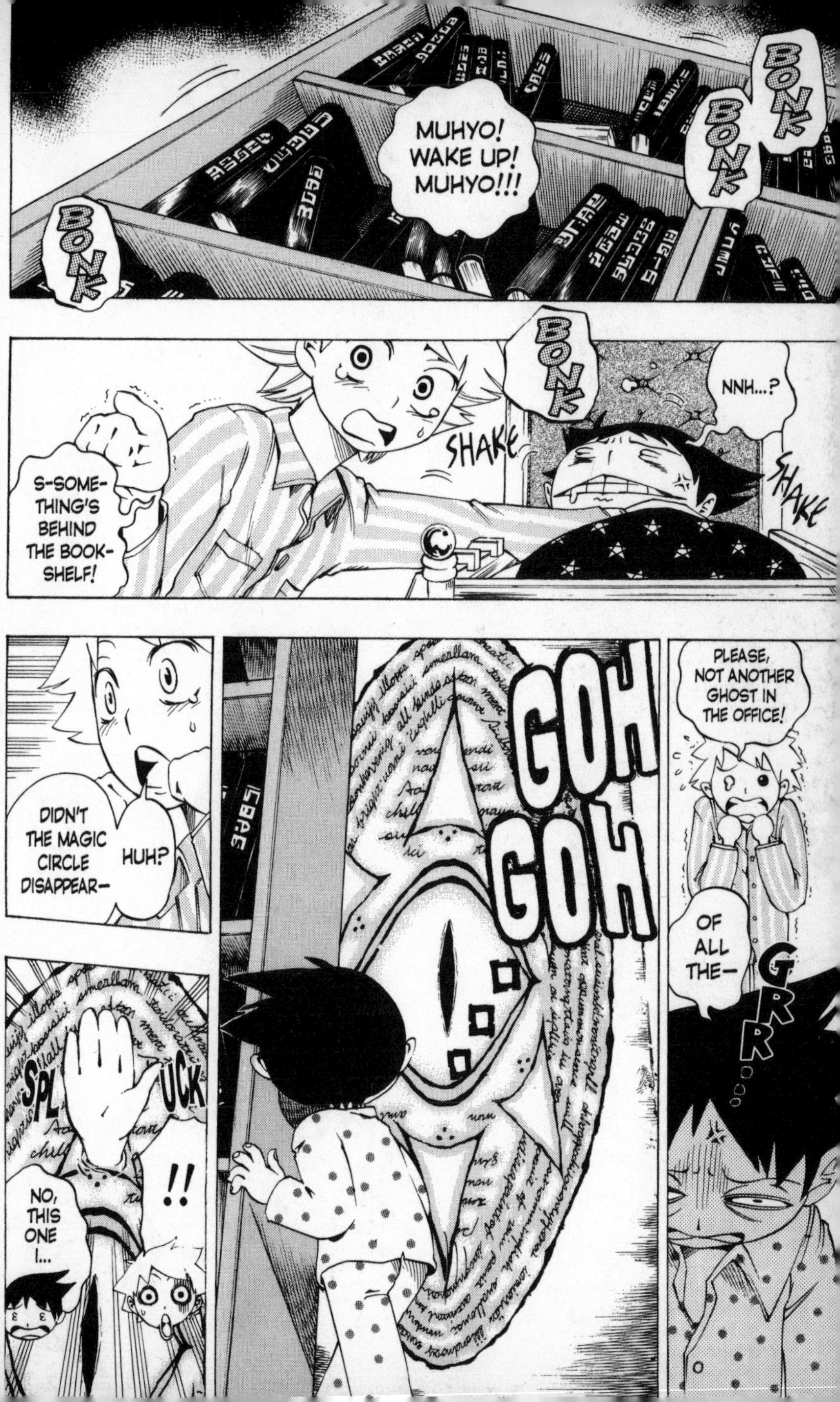
BONK
BONK
MUHYO! WAKE UP! MUHYO!!!
BONK
NNH...?
BONK
SHAKE
SHAKE
S-SOME-THING'S BEHIND THE BOOK-SHELF!
PLEASE, NOT ANOTHER GHOST IN THE OFFICE!
OF ALL THE—
GRR
GOH GOH
HUH?
DIDN'T THE MAGIC CIRCLE DISAPPEAR—
SPLUCK
!!
NO, THIS ONE I...

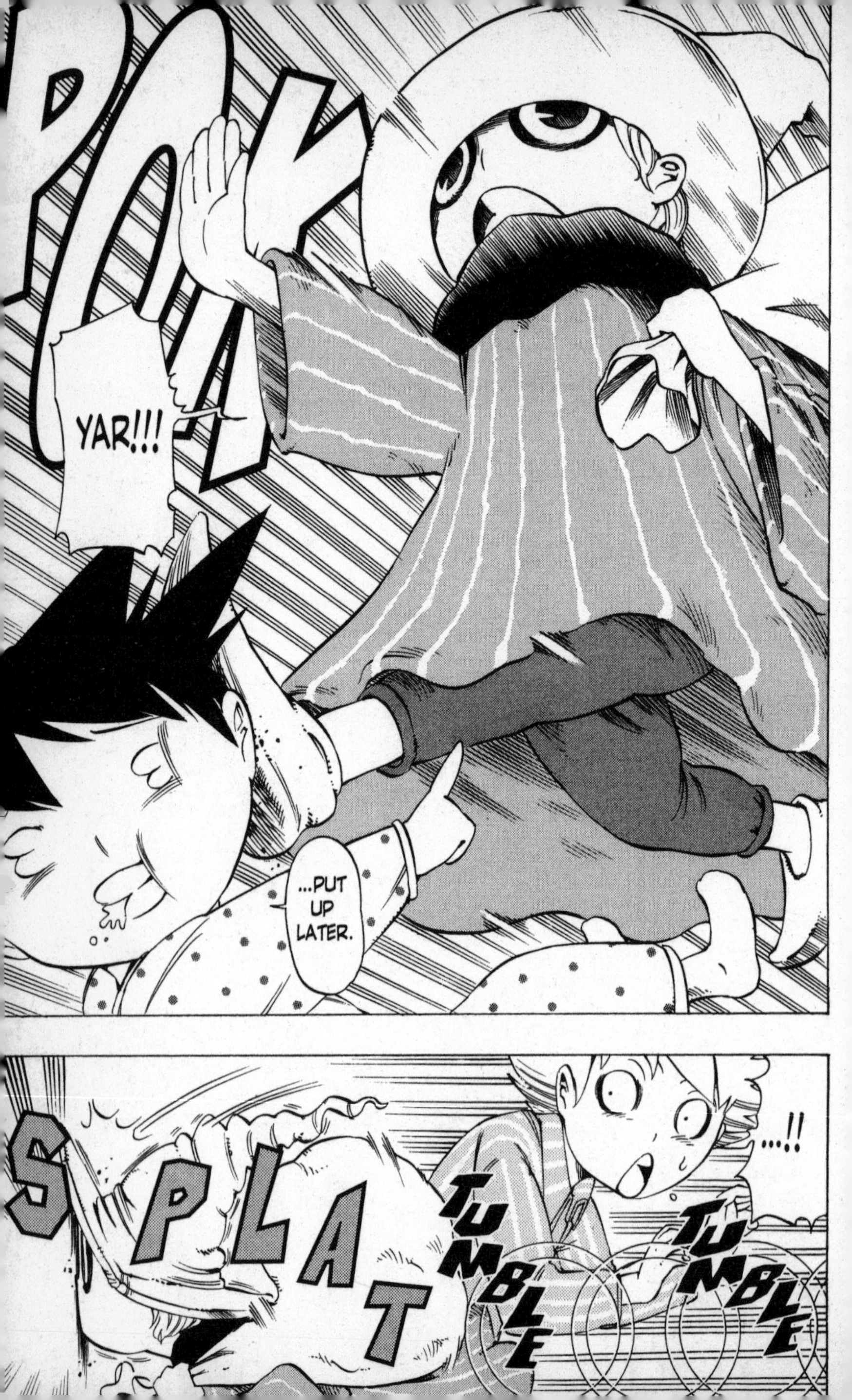
YAR!!!
...PUT UP LATER.
...!!
TUMBLE
TUMBLE
SPLAT

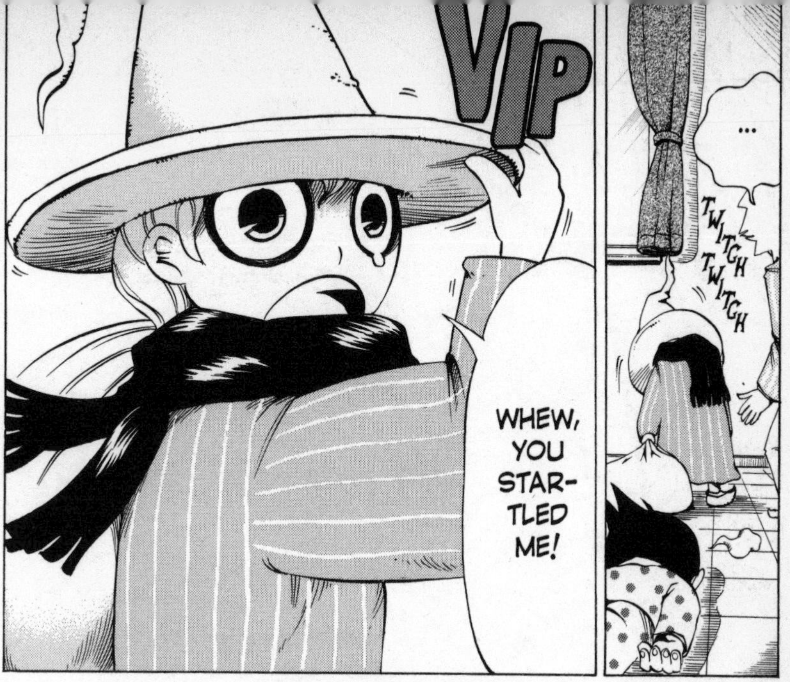
...
TWITCH TWITCH
VIP
WHEW, YOU STAR-TLED ME!

ARTICLE 20
ARTIFICER BIKO

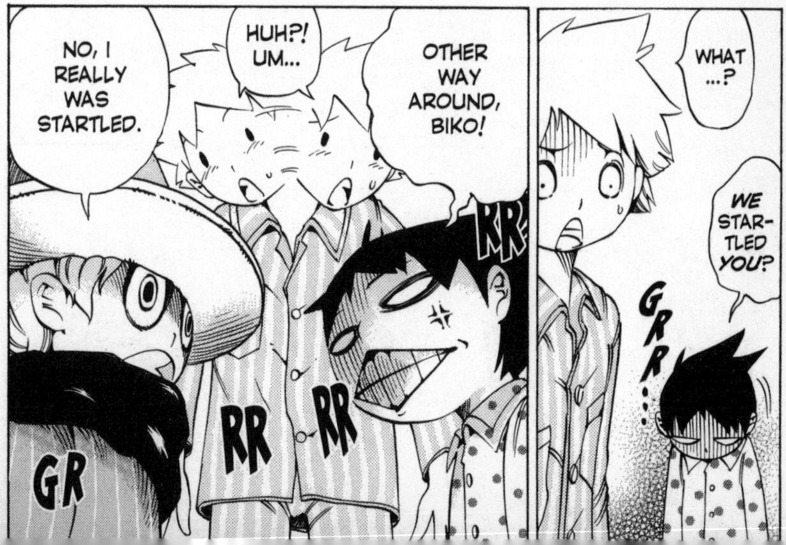
WHAT ...?
WE STAR-TLED YOU?
GRR...
OTHER WAY AROUND, BIKO!
RR-
HUH?! UM...
NO, I REALLY WAS STARTLED.
RR RR
GR

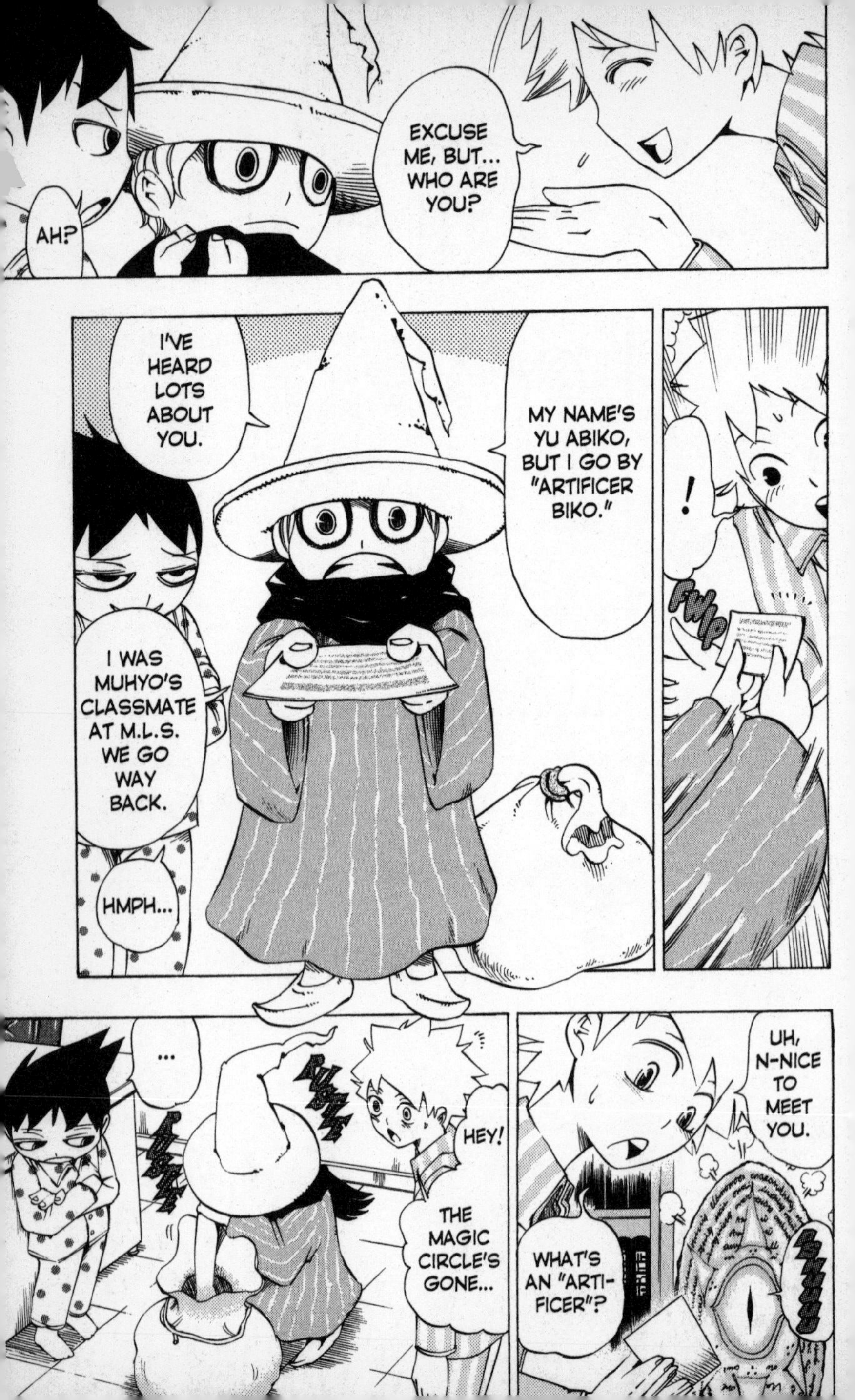
EXCUSE ME, BUT... WHO ARE YOU?
AH?
!
FWIP
MY NAME'S YU ABIKO, BUT I GO BY "ARTIFICER BIKO."
I'VE HEARD LOTS ABOUT YOU.
I WAS MUHYO'S CLASSMATE AT M.L.S. WE GO WAY BACK.
HMPH...
UH, N-NICE TO MEET YOU.
WHAT'S AN "ARTIFICER"?
HEY!
THE MAGIC CIRCLE'S GONE...
...

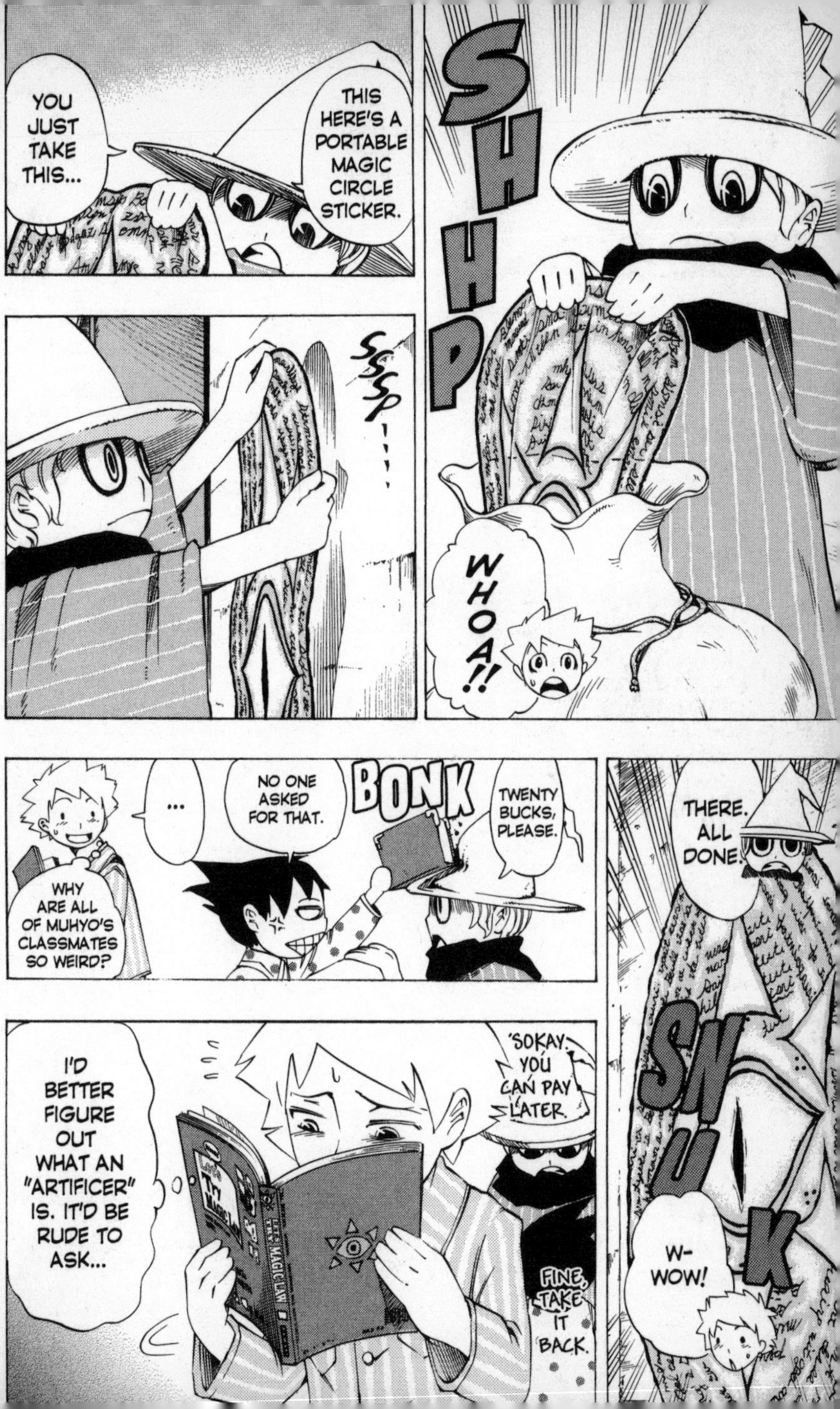
SHHP
WHOA!!
THIS HERE'S A PORTABLE MAGIC CIRCLE STICKER.
YOU JUST TAKE THIS...
SSSP
THERE. ALL DONE.
SNUK
W-WOW!
TWENTY BUCKS, PLEASE.
BONK
NO ONE ASKED FOR THAT.
...
WHY ARE ALL OF MUHYO'S CLASSMATES SO WEIRD?
'SOKAY. YOU CAN PAY LATER.
FINE, TAKE IT BACK.
I'D BETTER FIGURE OUT WHAT AN "ARTIFICER" IS. IT'D BE RUDE TO ASK...

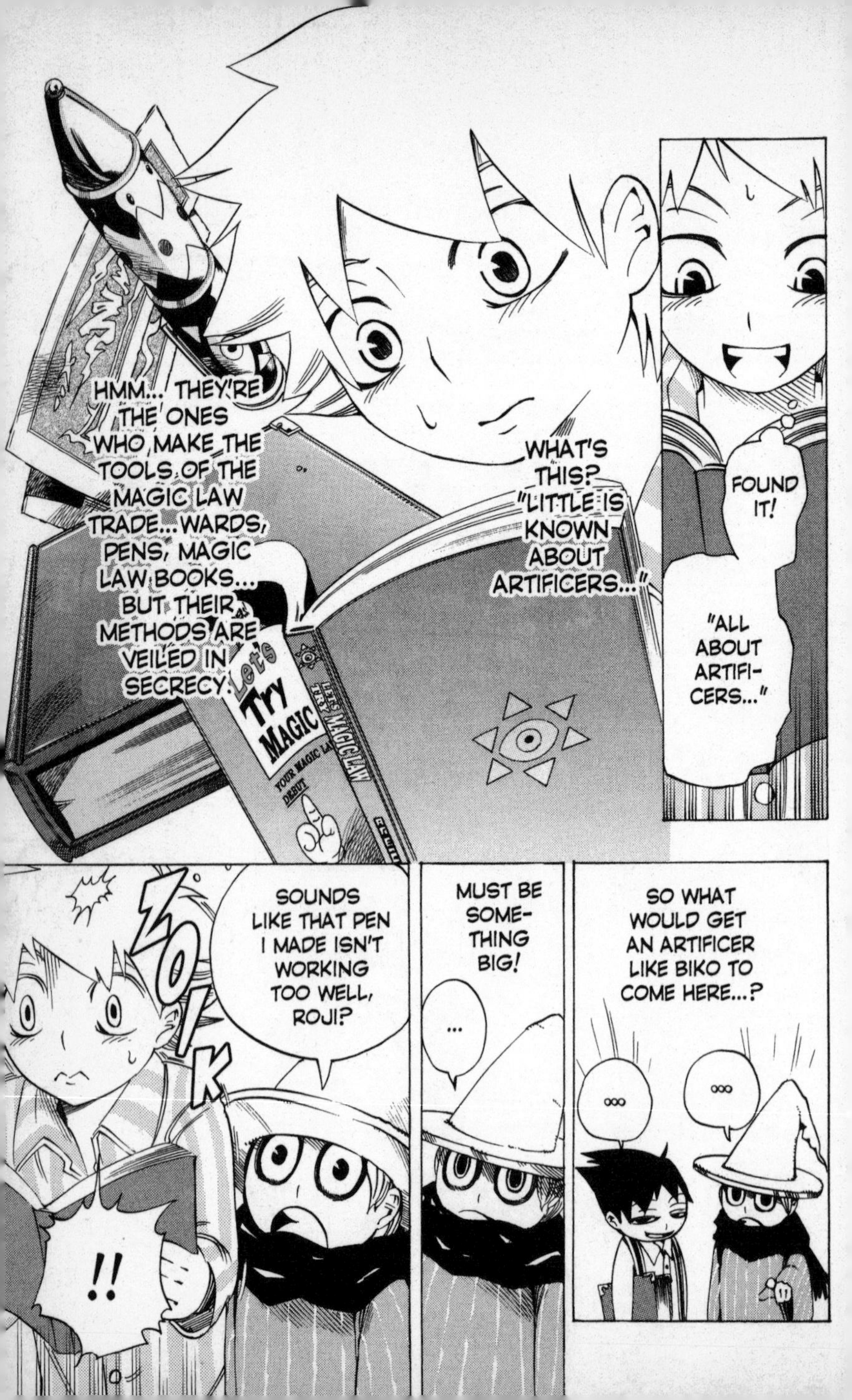
FOUND IT!
"ALL ABOUT ARTIFICERS..."
WHAT'S THIS? "LITTLE IS KNOWN ABOUT ARTIFICERS..."
HMM... THEY'RE THE ONES WHO MAKE THE TOOLS OF THE MAGIC LAW TRADE... WARDS, PENS, MAGIC LAW BOOKS... BUT THEIR METHODS ARE VEILED IN SECRECY.
Let's Try MAGIC
SO WHAT WOULD GET AN ARTIFICER LIKE BIKO TO COME HERE...?
ooo
ooo
MUST BE SOMETHING BIG!
...
SOUNDS LIKE THAT PEN I MADE ISN'T WORKING TOO WELL, ROJI?
ZOIK
!!

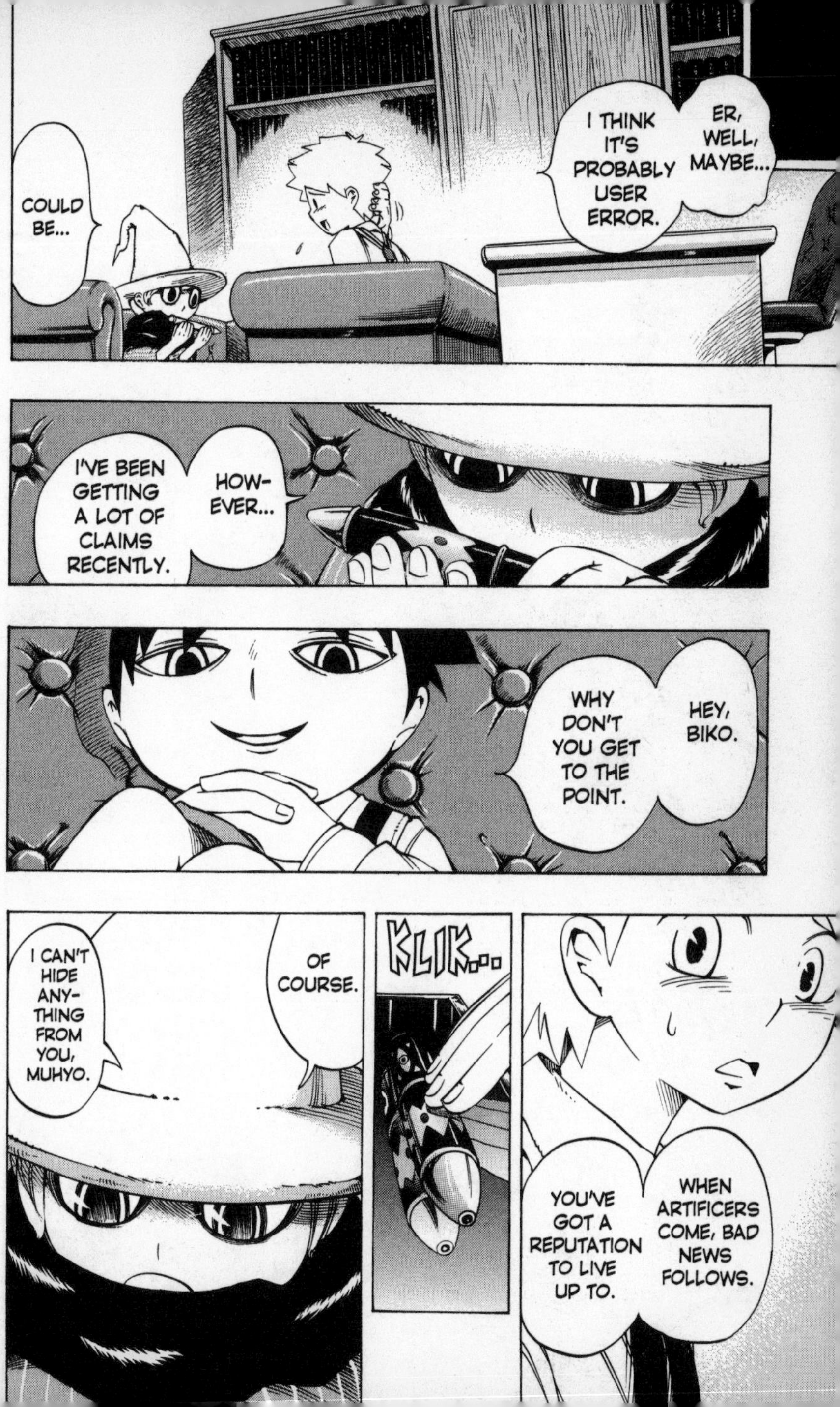

ER, WELL, MAYBE...
I THINK IT'S PROBABLY USER ERROR.
COULD BE...
HOW-EVER...
I'VE BEEN GETTING A LOT OF CLAIMS RECENTLY.
HEY, BIKO.
WHY DON'T YOU GET TO THE POINT.
WHEN ARTIFICERS COME, BAD NEWS FOLLOWS.
YOU'VE GOT A REPUTATION TO LIVE UP TO.
KLIK...
OF COURSE.
I CAN'T HIDE ANY-THING FROM YOU, MUHYO.

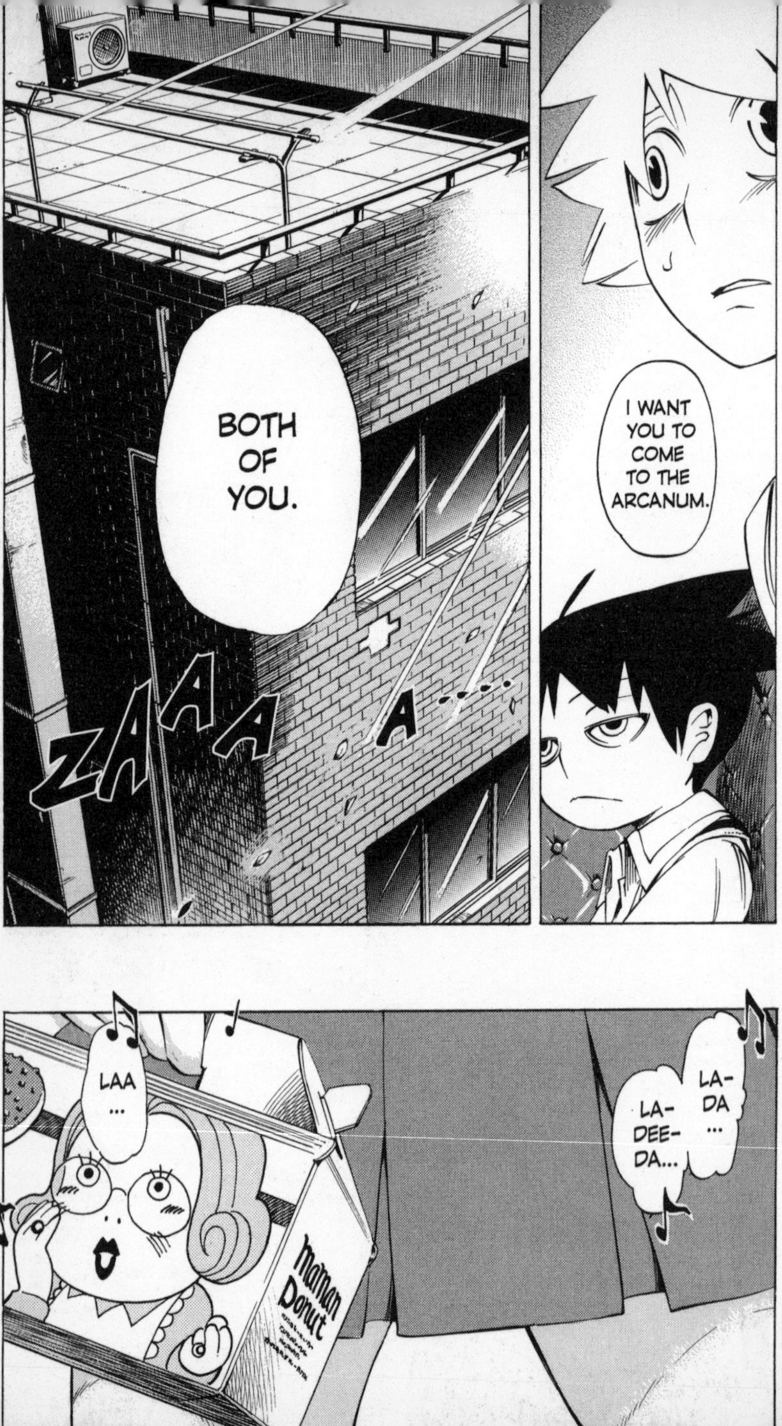
I WANT YOU TO COME TO THE ARCANUM.
BOTH OF YOU.
ZAAAA
A...
LA-DA...
LA-DEE-DA...
LAA...
Maman Donut

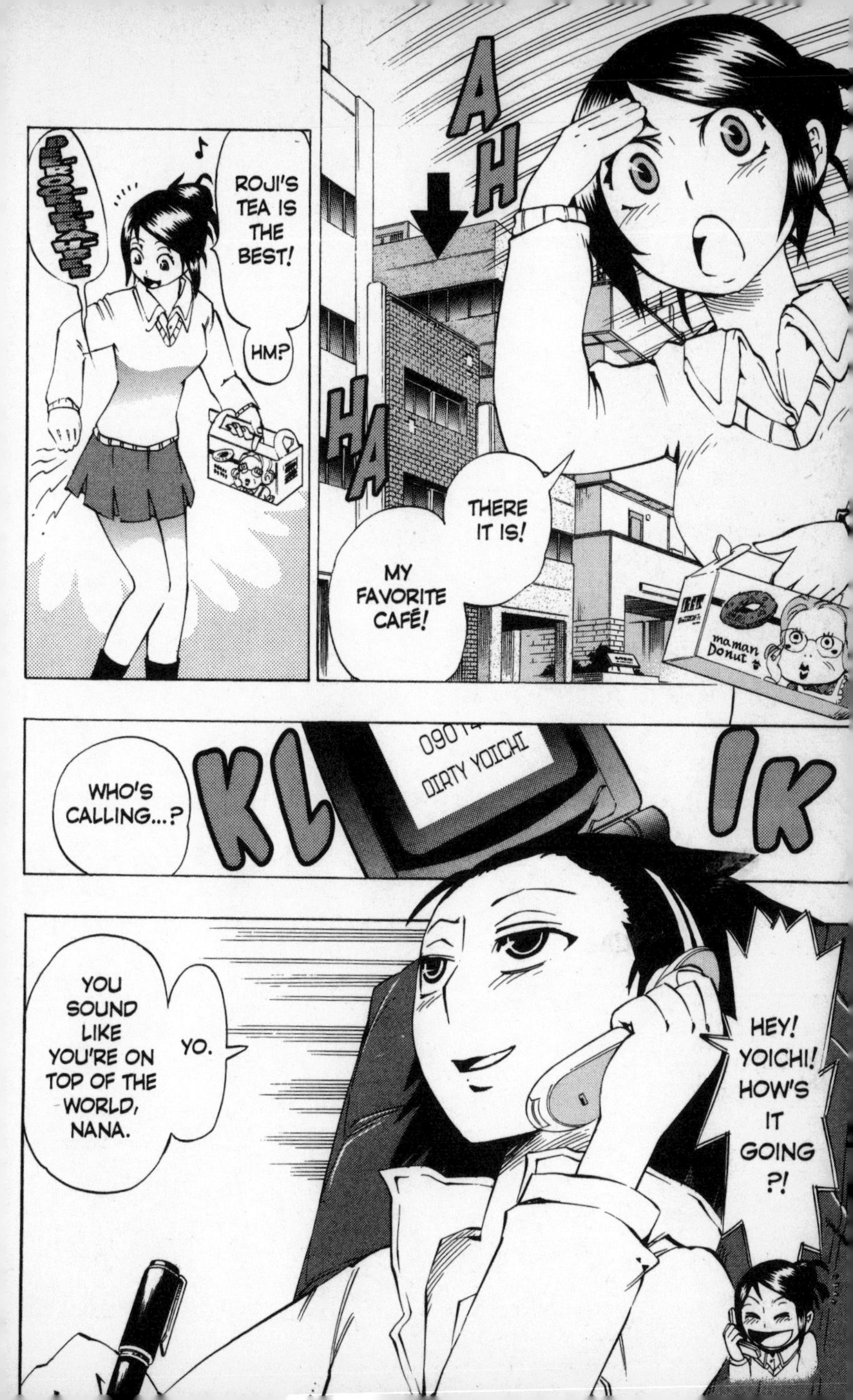

AH
THERE IT IS!
MY FAVORITE CAFÉ!
HA HA
maman Donut
ROJI'S TEA IS THE BEST!
HM?
DIRTY YOICHI
KLIK
WHO'S CALLING...?
HEY! YOICHI! HOW'S IT GOING?!
YO.
YOU SOUND LIKE YOU'RE ON TOP OF THE WORLD, NANA.

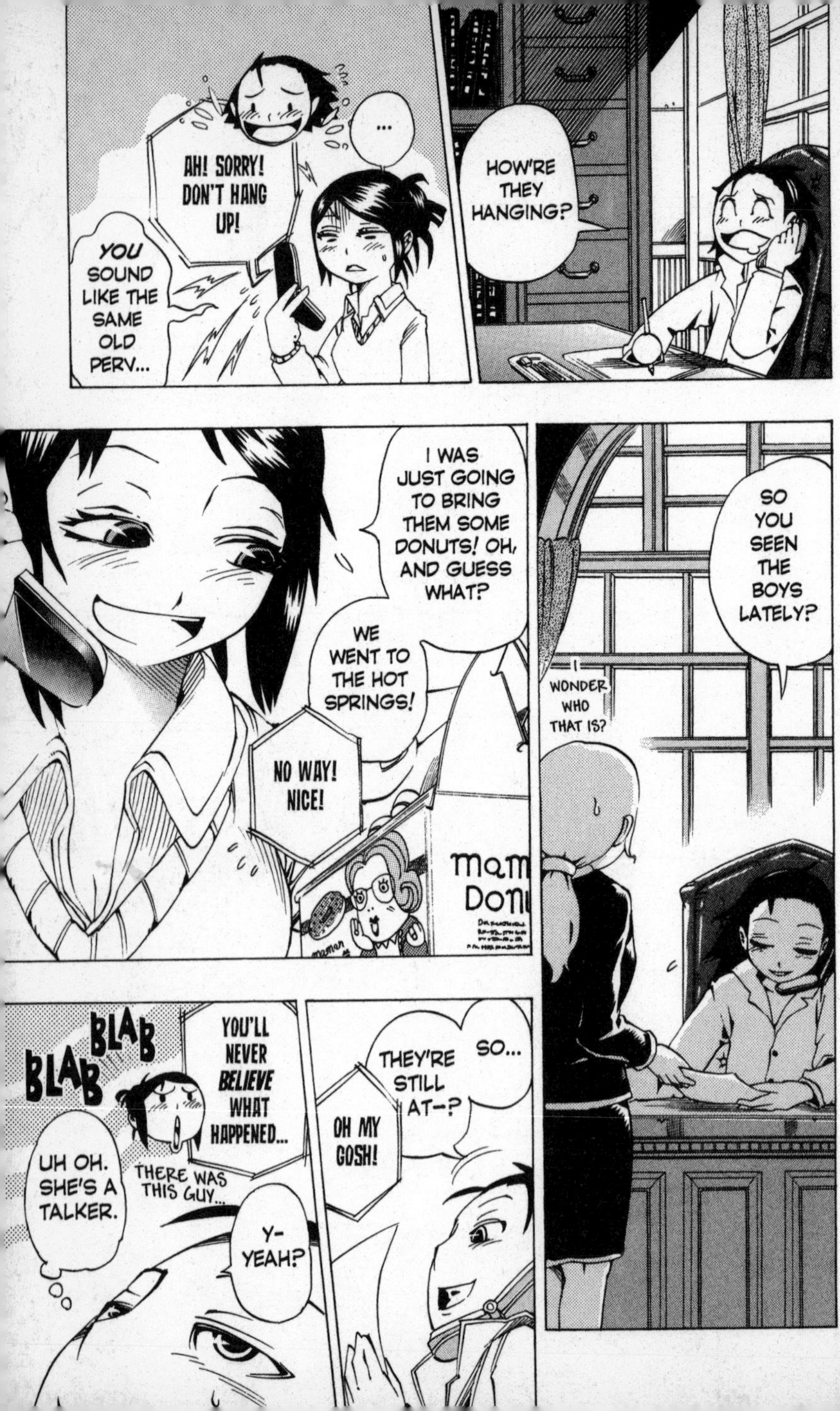
HOW'RE THEY HANGING?
...
AH! SORRY! DON'T HANG UP!
YOU SOUND LIKE THE SAME OLD PERV...
SO YOU SEEN THE BOYS LATELY?
I WONDER WHO THAT IS?
I WAS JUST GOING TO BRING THEM SOME DONUTS! OH, AND GUESS WHAT?
WE WENT TO THE HOT SPRINGS!
NO WAY! NICE!
SO...
THEY'RE STILL AT-?
OH MY GOSH!
YOU'LL NEVER BELIEVE WHAT HAPPENED...
BLAB BLAB
Y-YEAH?
THERE WAS THIS GUY...
UH OH. SHE'S A TALKER.

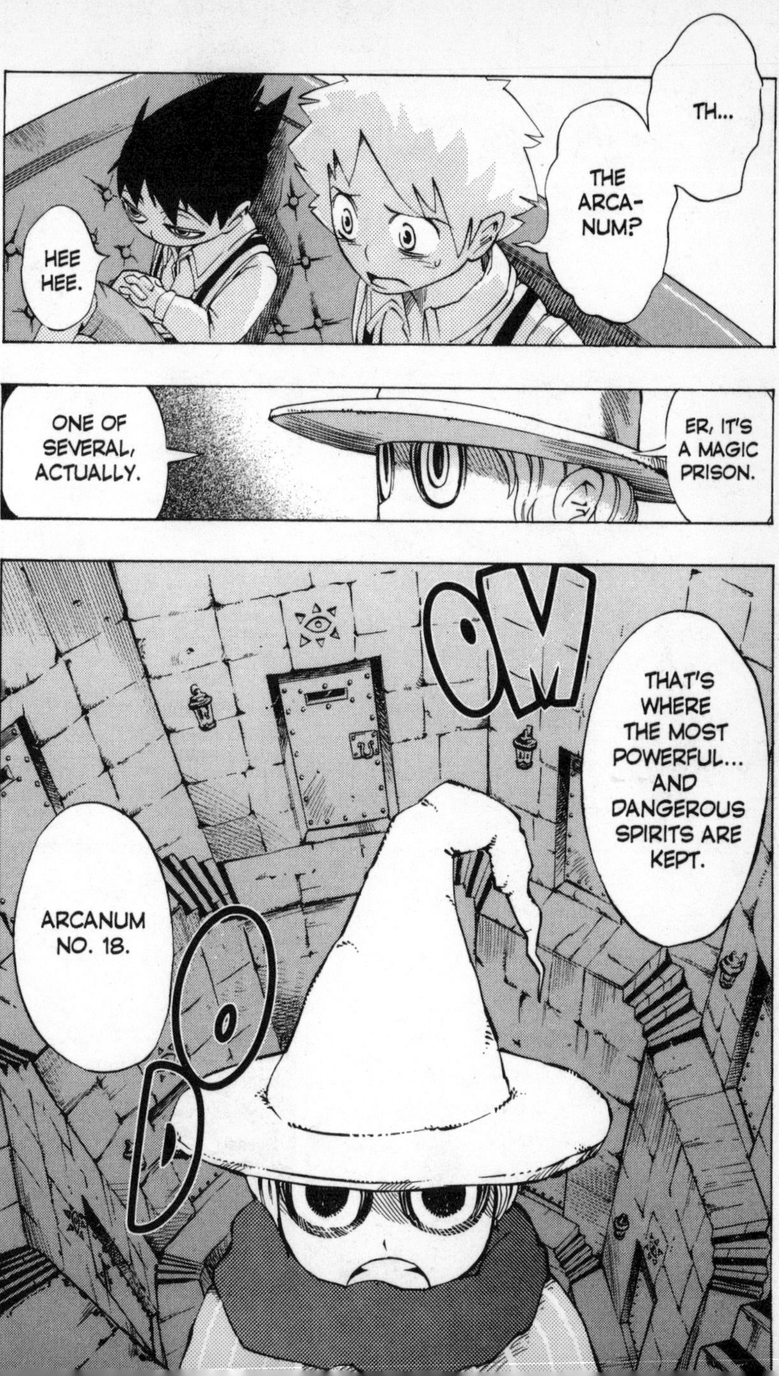
TH...
THE ARCA-NUM?
HEE HEE.
ER, IT'S A MAGIC PRISON.
ONE OF SEVERAL, ACTUALLY.
DOOM
THAT'S WHERE THE MOST POWERFUL... AND DANGEROUS SPIRITS ARE KEPT.
ARCANUM NO. 18.

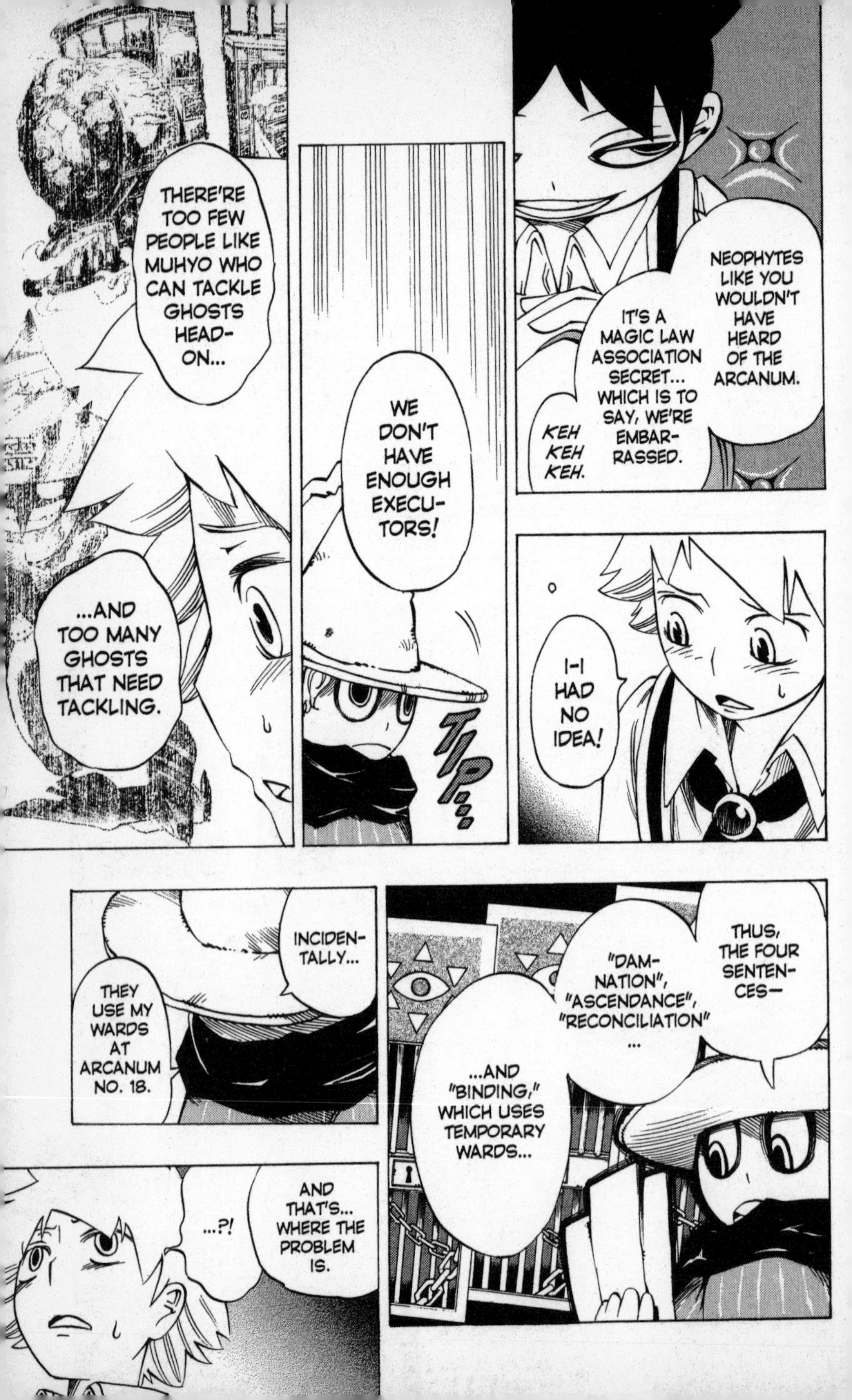
NEOPHYTES LIKE YOU WOULDN'T HAVE HEARD OF THE ARCANUM.
IT'S A MAGIC LAW ASSOCIATION SECRET... WHICH IS TO SAY, WE'RE EMBARRASSED.
KEH KEH KEH.
I-I HAD NO IDEA!
WE DON'T HAVE ENOUGH EXECUTORS!
TIP...
THERE'RE TOO FEW PEOPLE LIKE MUHYO WHO CAN TACKLE GHOSTS HEAD-ON...
...AND TOO MANY GHOSTS THAT NEED TACKLING.
THUS, THE FOUR SENTENCES—
"DAMNATION", "ASCENDANCE", "RECONCILIATION"...
...AND "BINDING," WHICH USES TEMPORARY WARDS...
INCIDENTALLY...
THEY USE MY WARDS AT ARCANUM NO. 18.
AND THAT'S... WHERE THE PROBLEM IS.
...?!

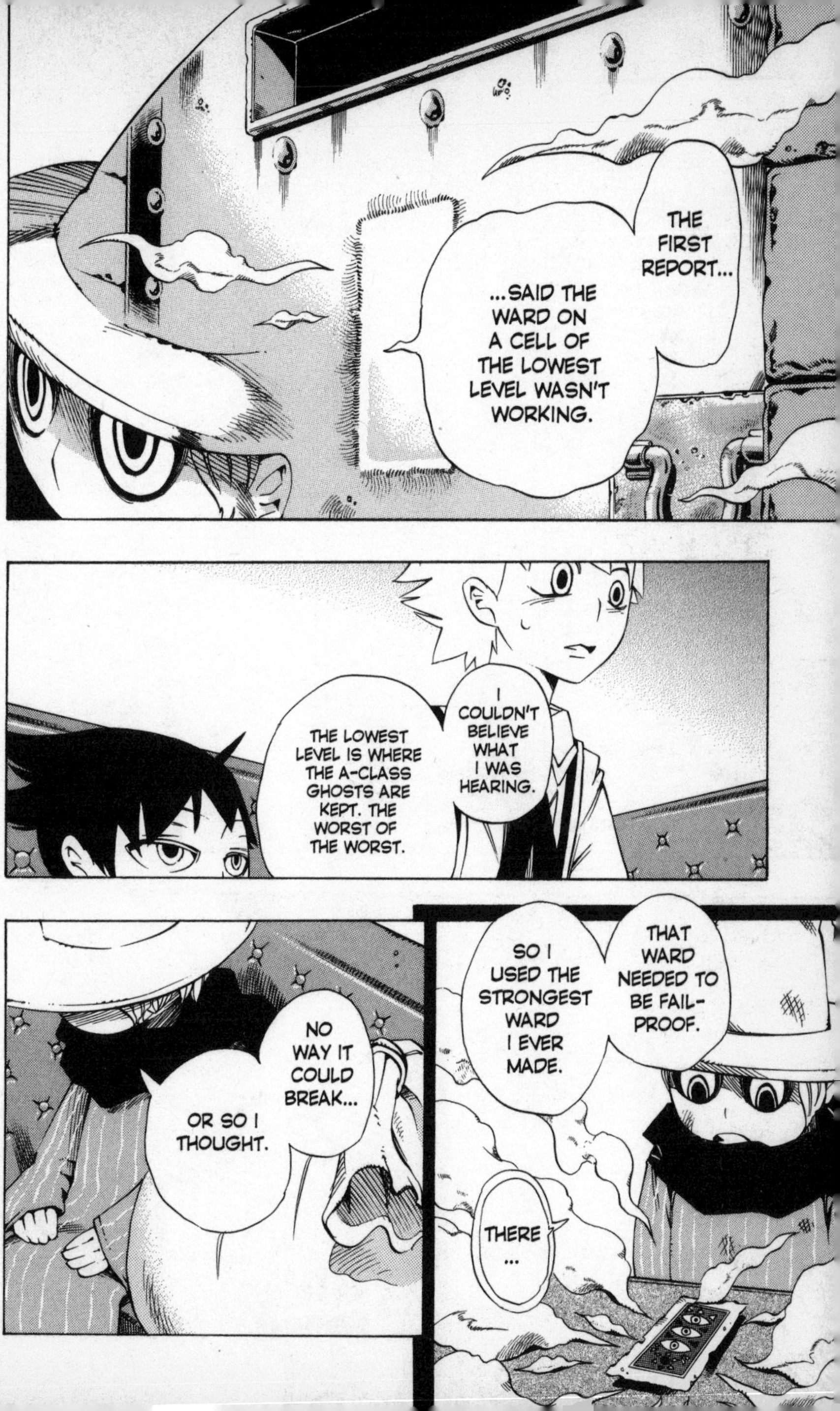
THE FIRST REPORT...
...SAID THE WARD ON A CELL OF THE LOWEST LEVEL WASN'T WORKING.
I COULDN'T BELIEVE WHAT I WAS HEARING.
THE LOWEST LEVEL IS WHERE THE A-CLASS GHOSTS ARE KEPT. THE WORST OF THE WORST.
THAT WARD NEEDED TO BE FAIL-PROOF.
SO I USED THE STRONGEST WARD I EVER MADE.
THERE ...
NO WAY IT COULD BREAK...
OR SO I THOUGHT.

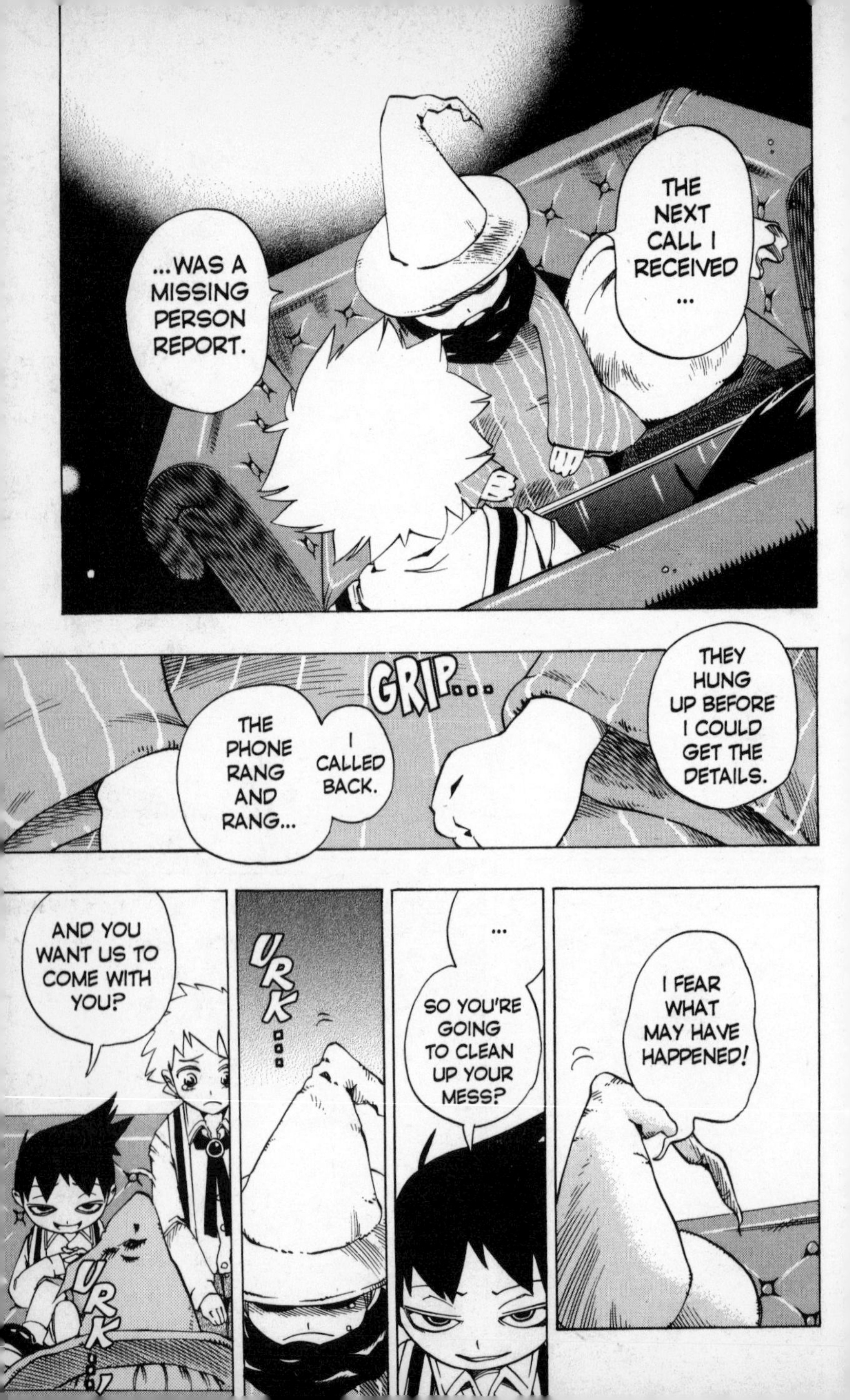
THE NEXT CALL I RECEIVED ...
...WAS A MISSING PERSON REPORT.
THEY HUNG UP BEFORE I COULD GET THE DETAILS.
GRIP...
I CALLED BACK.
THE PHONE RANG AND RANG...
I FEAR WHAT MAY HAVE HAPPENED!
...
SO YOU'RE GOING TO CLEAN UP YOUR MESS?
URK...
AND YOU WANT US TO COME WITH YOU?
URK...!

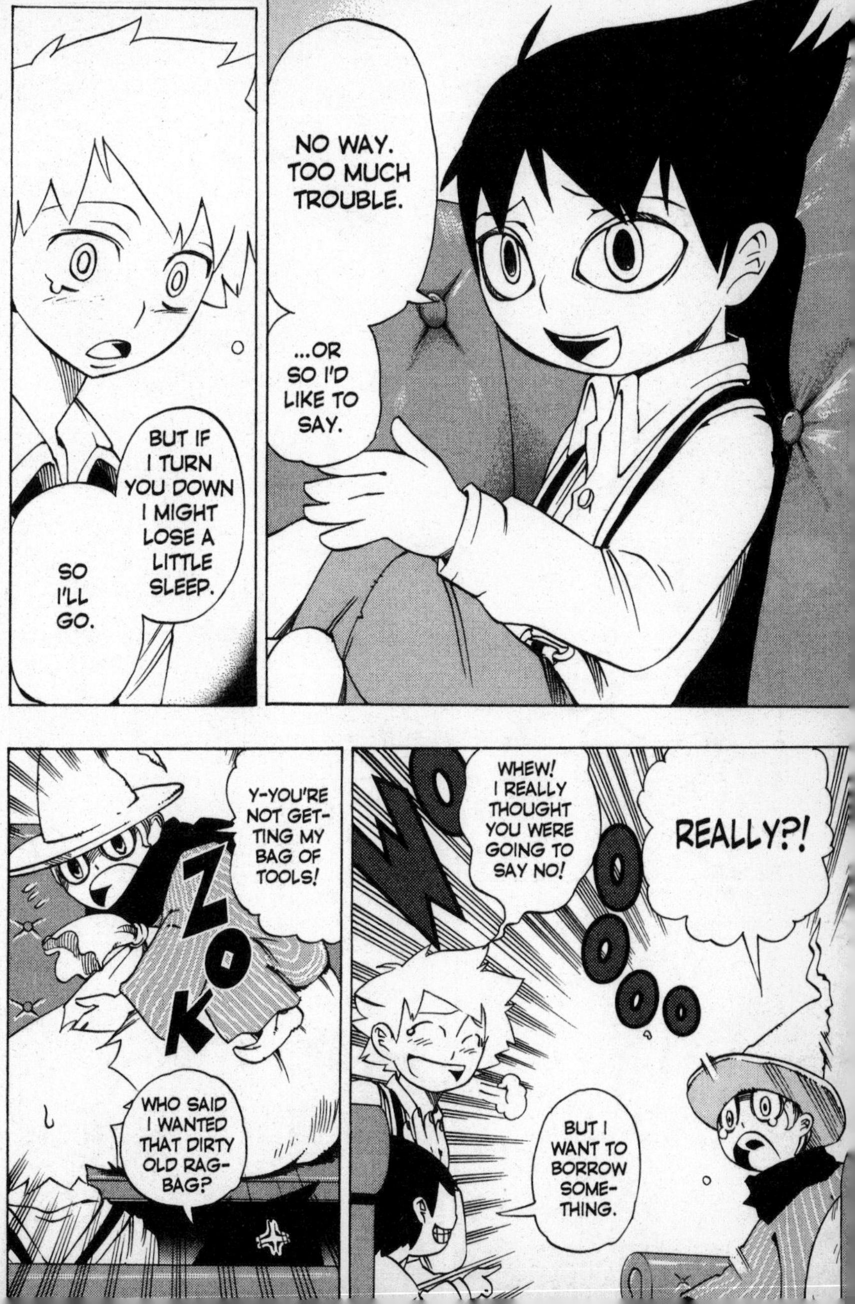
NO WAY. TOO MUCH TROUBLE.
...OR SO I'D LIKE TO SAY.
BUT IF I TURN YOU DOWN I MIGHT LOSE A LITTLE SLEEP.
SO I'LL GO.
REALLY?!
WHEW! I REALLY THOUGHT YOU WERE GOING TO SAY NO!
BUT I WANT TO BORROW SOME-THING.
Y-YOU'RE NOT GET-TING MY BAG OF TOOLS!
ZOK
WHO SAID I WANTED THAT DIRTY OLD RAG-BAG?

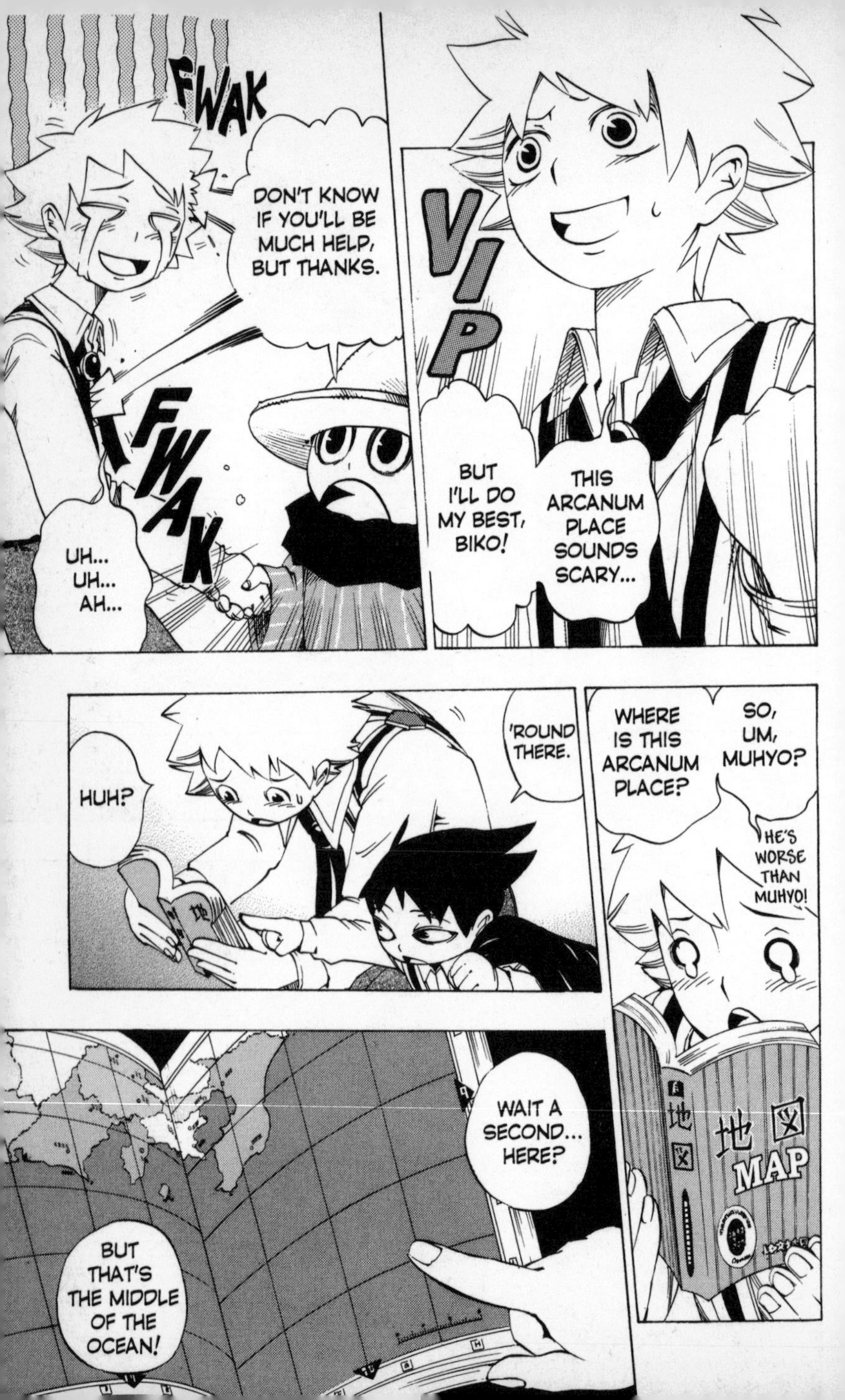
VIP
THIS ARCANUM PLACE SOUNDS SCARY...
BUT I'LL DO MY BEST, BIKO!
FWAK
DON'T KNOW IF YOU'LL BE MUCH HELP, BUT THANKS.
FWAK
UH... UH... AH...
SO, UM, MUHYO?
WHERE IS THIS ARCANUM PLACE?
HE'S WORSE THAN MUHYO!
地図
地図
MAP
'ROUND THERE.
HUH?
WAIT A SECOND... HERE?
BUT THAT'S THE MIDDLE OF THE OCEAN!

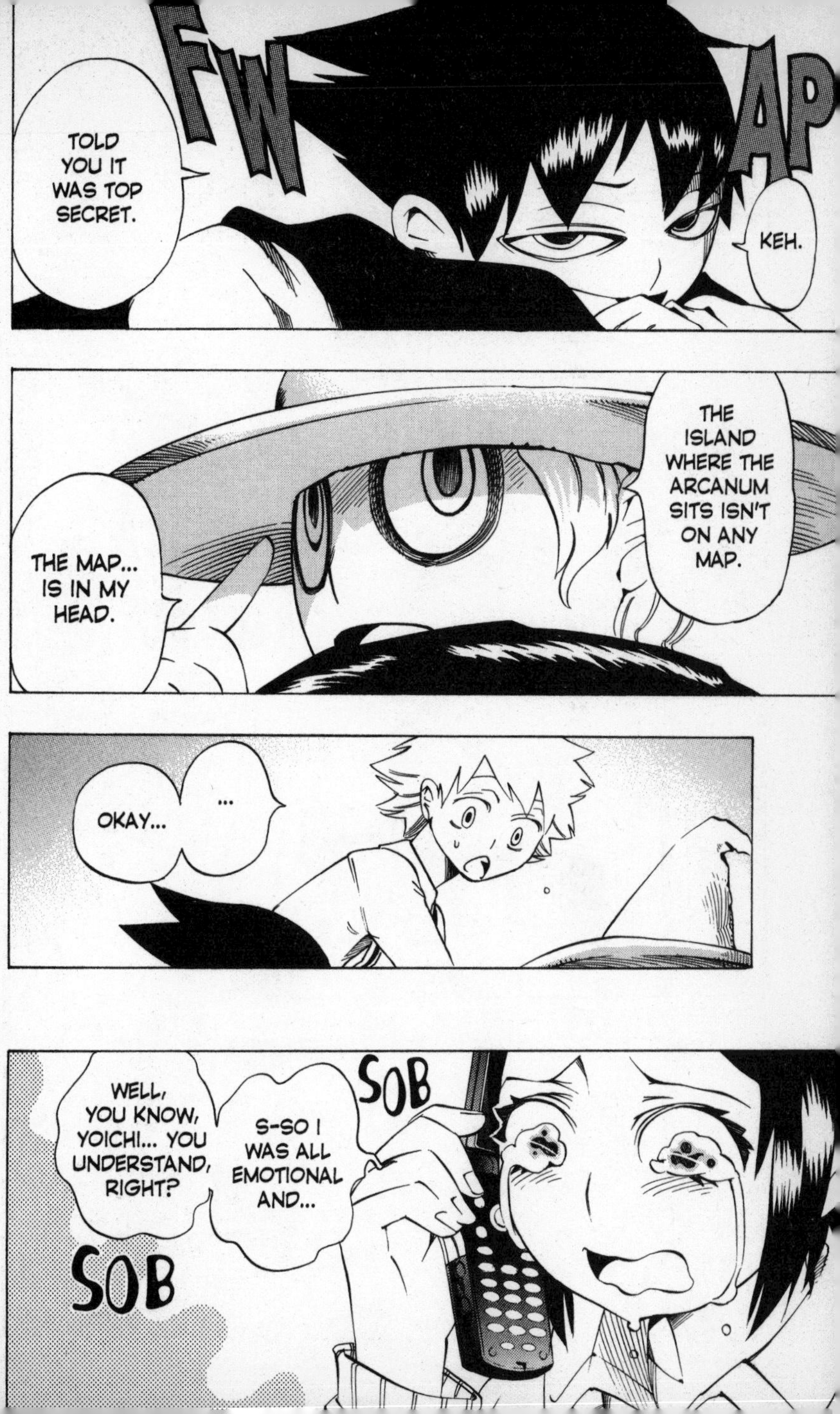
FWAP
KEH.
TOLD YOU IT WAS TOP SECRET.
THE ISLAND WHERE THE ARCANUM SITS ISN'T ON ANY MAP.
THE MAP... IS IN MY HEAD.
...
OKAY...
SOB
S-SO I WAS ALL EMOTIONAL AND...
WELL, YOU KNOW, YOICHI... YOU UNDERSTAND, RIGHT?
SOB

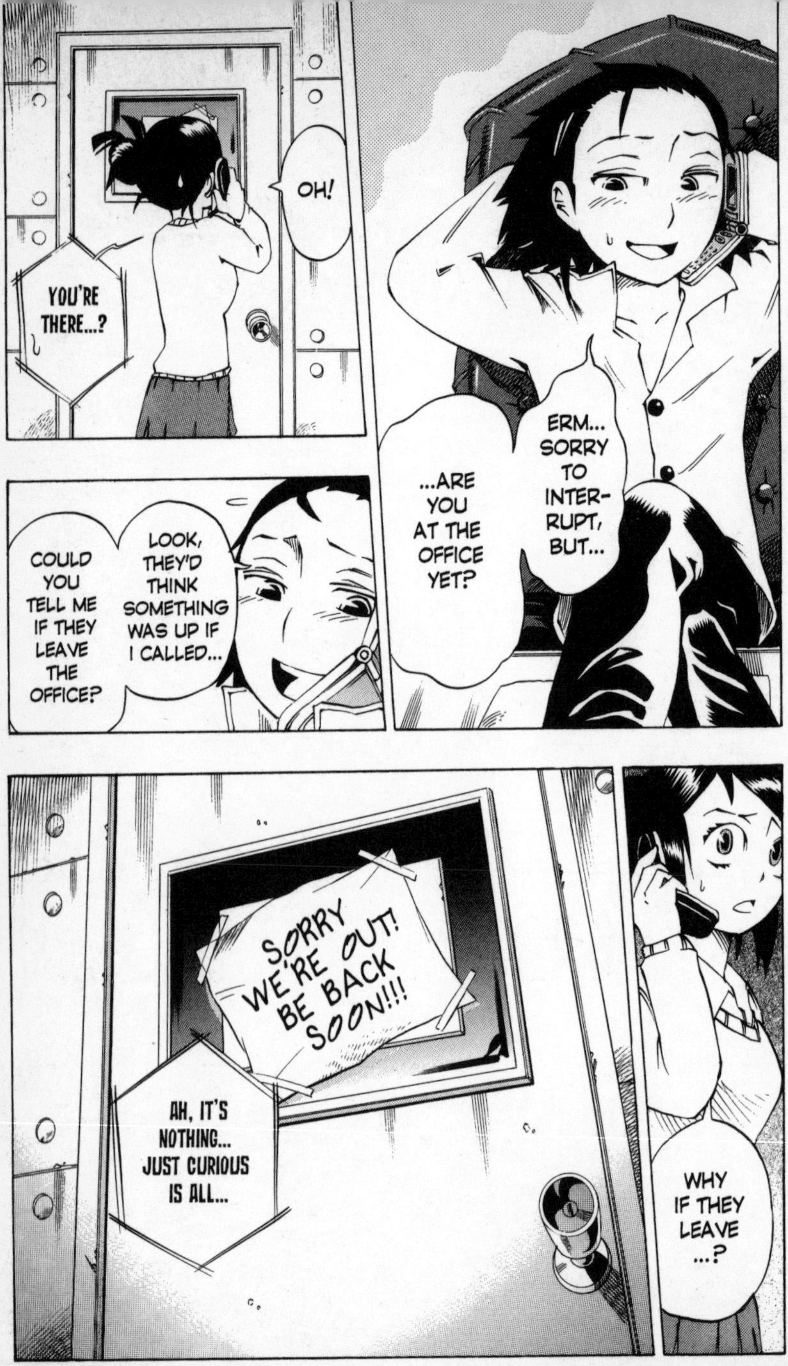
ERM... SORRY TO INTER-RUPT, BUT...
...ARE YOU AT THE OFFICE YET?
OH!
YOU'RE THERE...?
LOOK, THEY'D THINK SOMETHING WAS UP IF I CALLED...
COULD YOU TELL ME IF THEY LEAVE THE OFFICE?
WHY IF THEY LEAVE ...?
SORRY WE'RE OUT! BE BACK SOON!!!
AH, IT'S NOTHING... JUST CURIOUS IS ALL...

Q: HOW OLD ARE MUHYO AND ROJI? PLEASE TELL US!

A: HA HA! THAT'S THE QUESTION I GET THE MOST! ER...28! OH, WAIT, THAT'S HOW OLD I AM. YOU WANT TO KNOW ABOUT MUHYO AND ROJI? HMM... OKAY...
   MUMBLE MUMBLE
   THERE! SATISFIED? NEXT QUESTION!
   (SORRY, IT'S A SECRET FOR NOW. BUT SOMEDAY, ALL WILL BE REVEALED!)

ARTICLE 21
THE LANDING

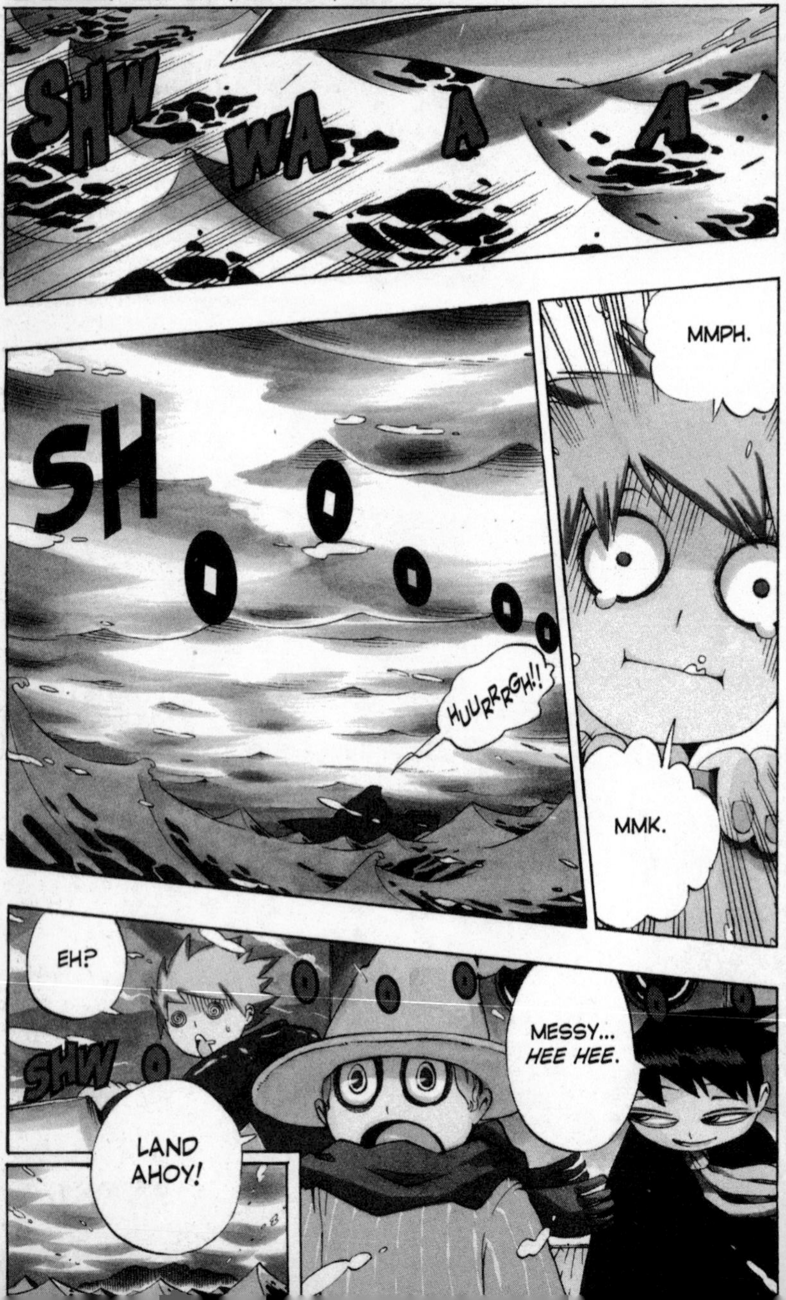
SHWWAAA
MMPH.
MMK.
SHOOOOO
HUURRRGH!!
MESSY... HEE HEE.
EH?
SHW
LAND AHOY!

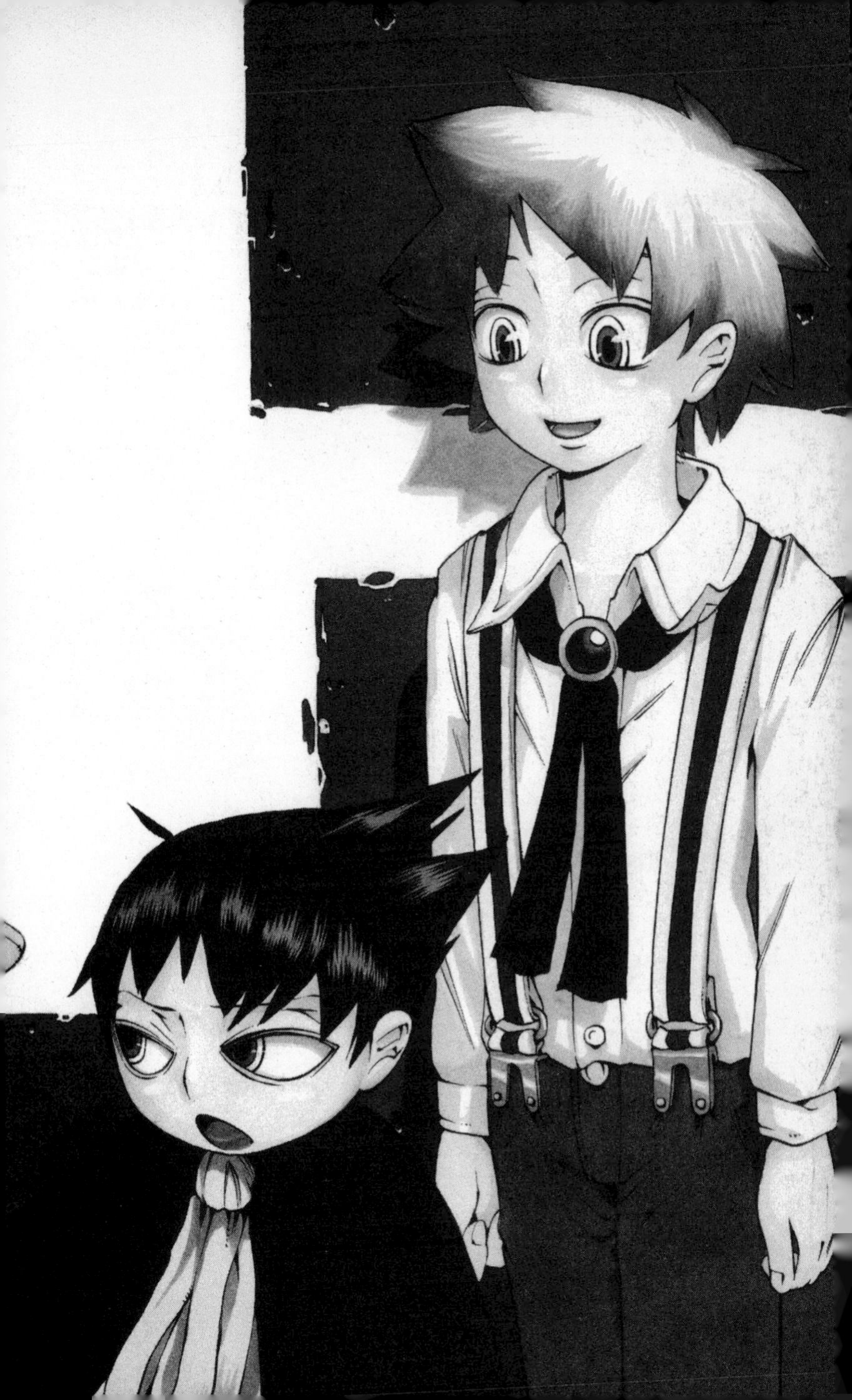

ARTICLE 21
THE LANDING

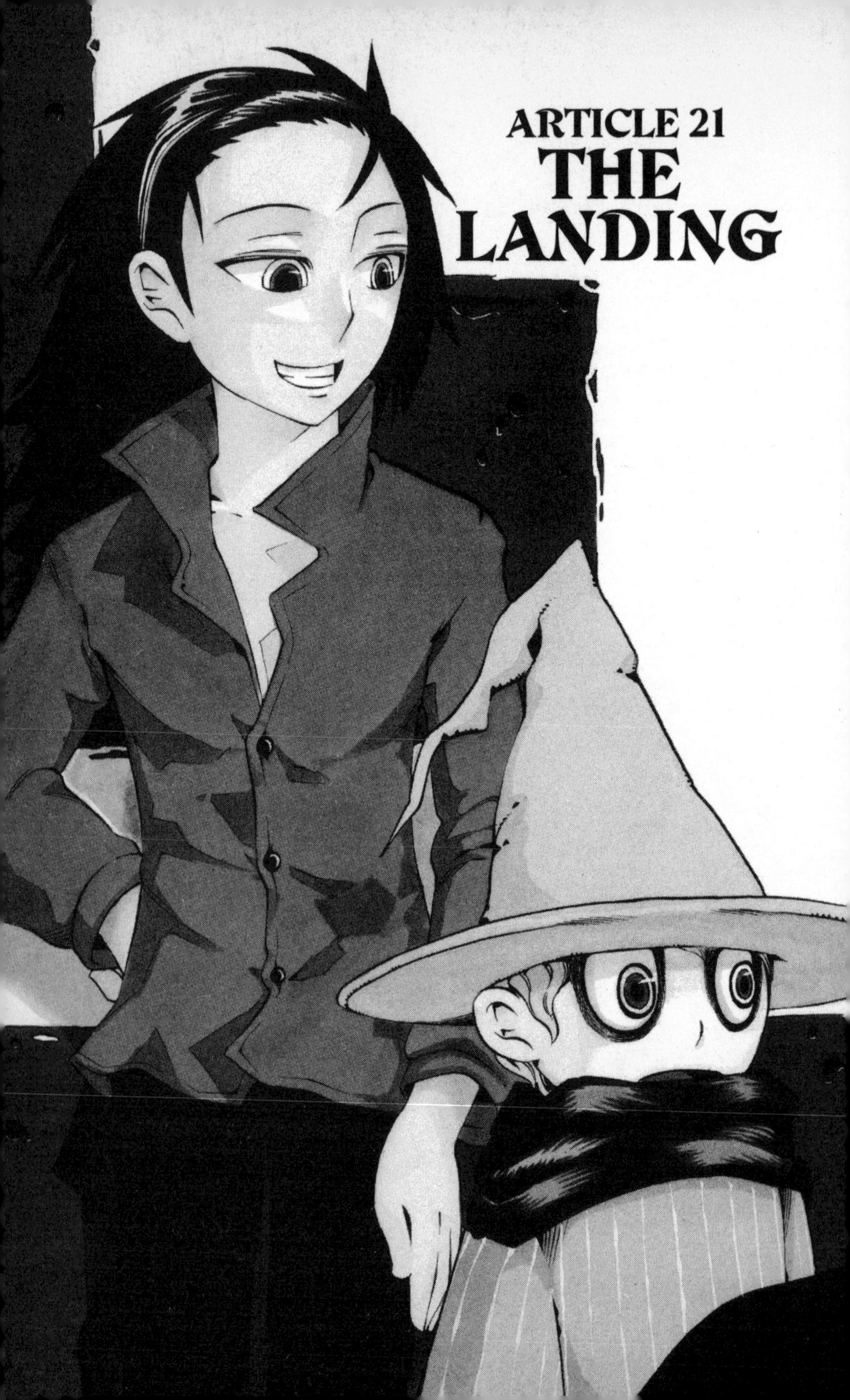

YU ABIKO

BIRTHDAY: FEBRUARY 28
HEIGHT: 126 CM

LIKES: CHEESE GRATIN
(THINKS RIO'S GRATIN IS THE BEST IN THE WORLD)
RAISIN BREAD
ALL FRUITS (ESPECIALLY STRAWBERRIES)

TALENTS: CLEANING
FIXING THINGS (BY TAKING THEM APART)
TAKING GOOD CARE OF STUFF
ZONING OUT (DOESN'T REALIZE IT)

NOT GOOD WITH: RUNNING (BAG'S TOO HEAVY)
CARBONATED DRINKS
LONG DISCUSSIONS

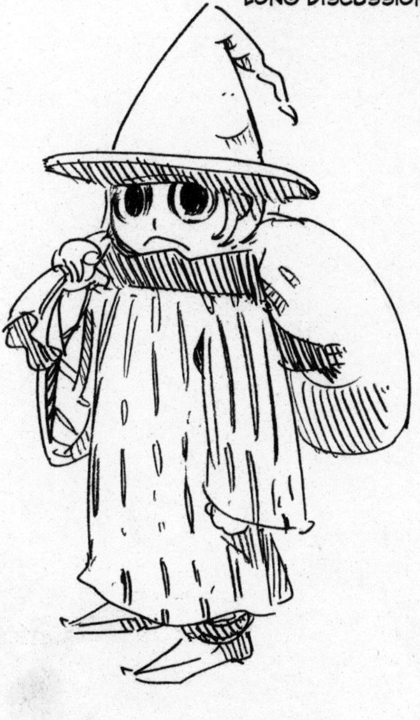

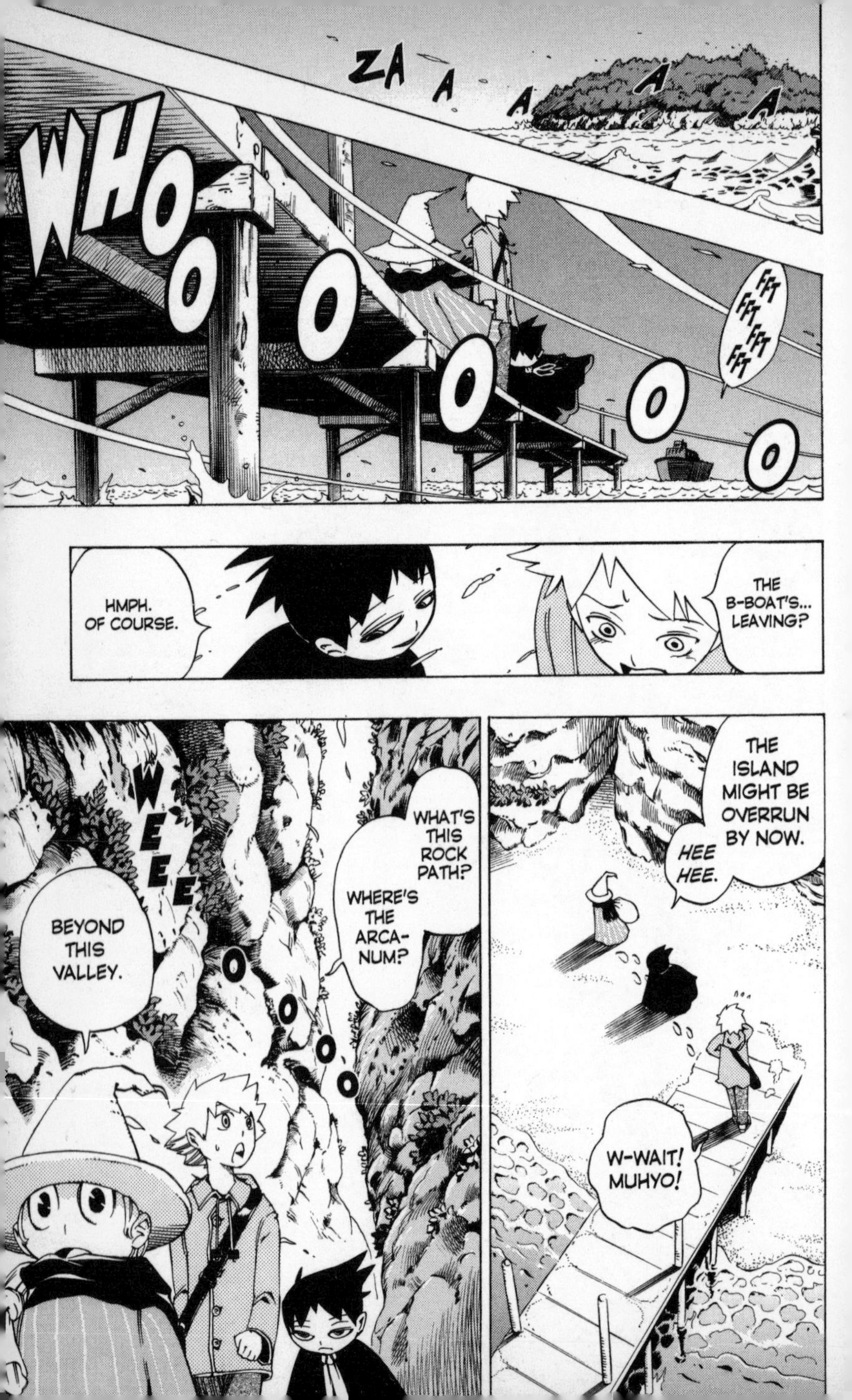
ZA A A A A
FFT FFT FFT FFT
WHOOOOOOOO
THE B-BOAT'S... LEAVING?
HMPH. OF COURSE.
THE ISLAND MIGHT BE OVERRUN BY NOW.
HEE HEE.
W-WAIT! MUHYO!
WHAT'S THIS ROCK PATH?
WHERE'S THE ARCA-NUM?
WEEE
BEYOND THIS VALLEY.
OOOO

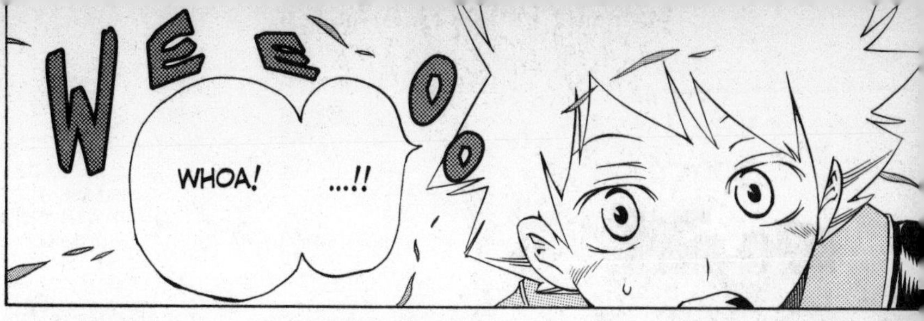
WEEOO
WHOA! ...!!

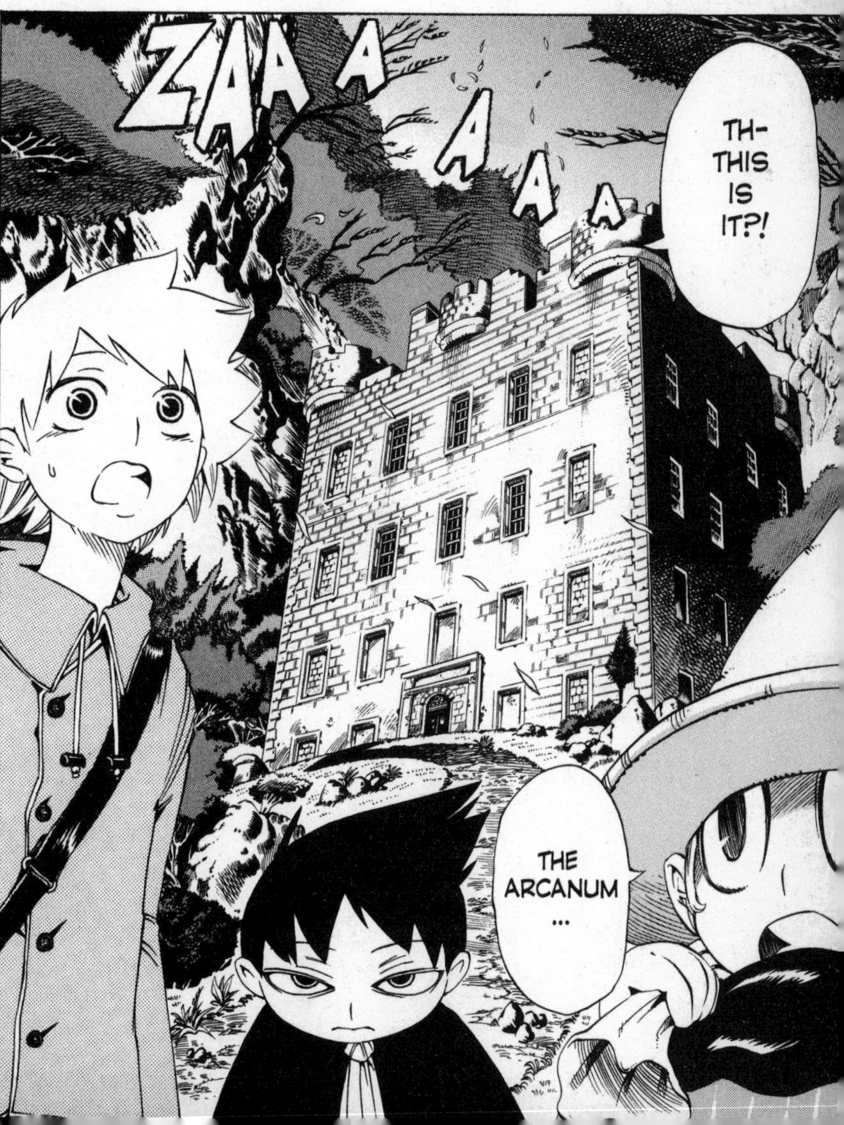
ZAAAAAA
TH- THIS IS IT?!
THE ARCANUM ...

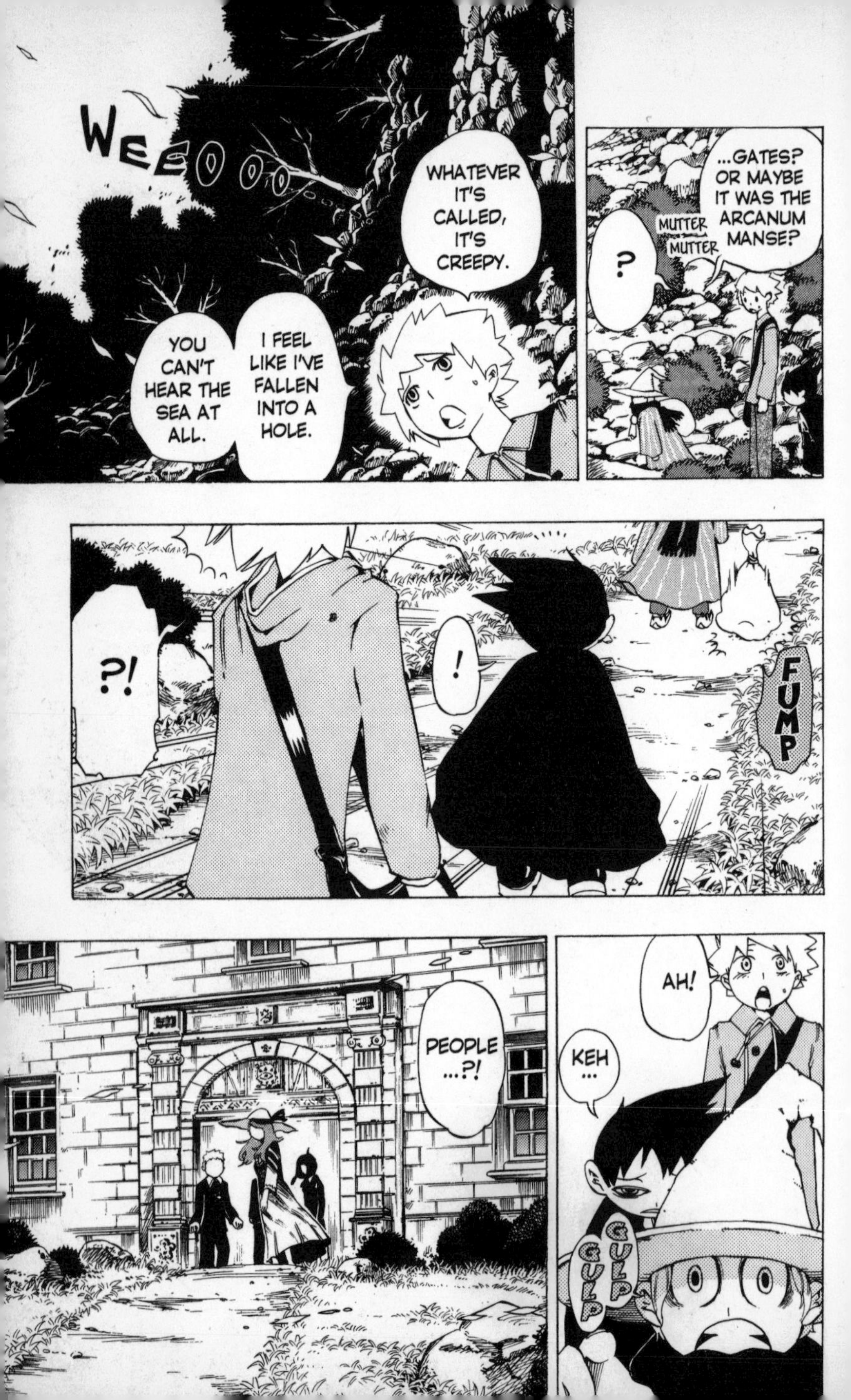
...GATES? OR MAYBE IT WAS THE ARCANUM MANSE?
MUTTER MUTTER
?
WHATEVER IT'S CALLED, IT'S CREEPY.
I FEEL LIKE I'VE FALLEN INTO A HOLE.
YOU CAN'T HEAR THE SEA AT ALL.
WEEOOO
FUMP
!
?!
AH!
KEH...
GULP GULP
PEOPLE...?!

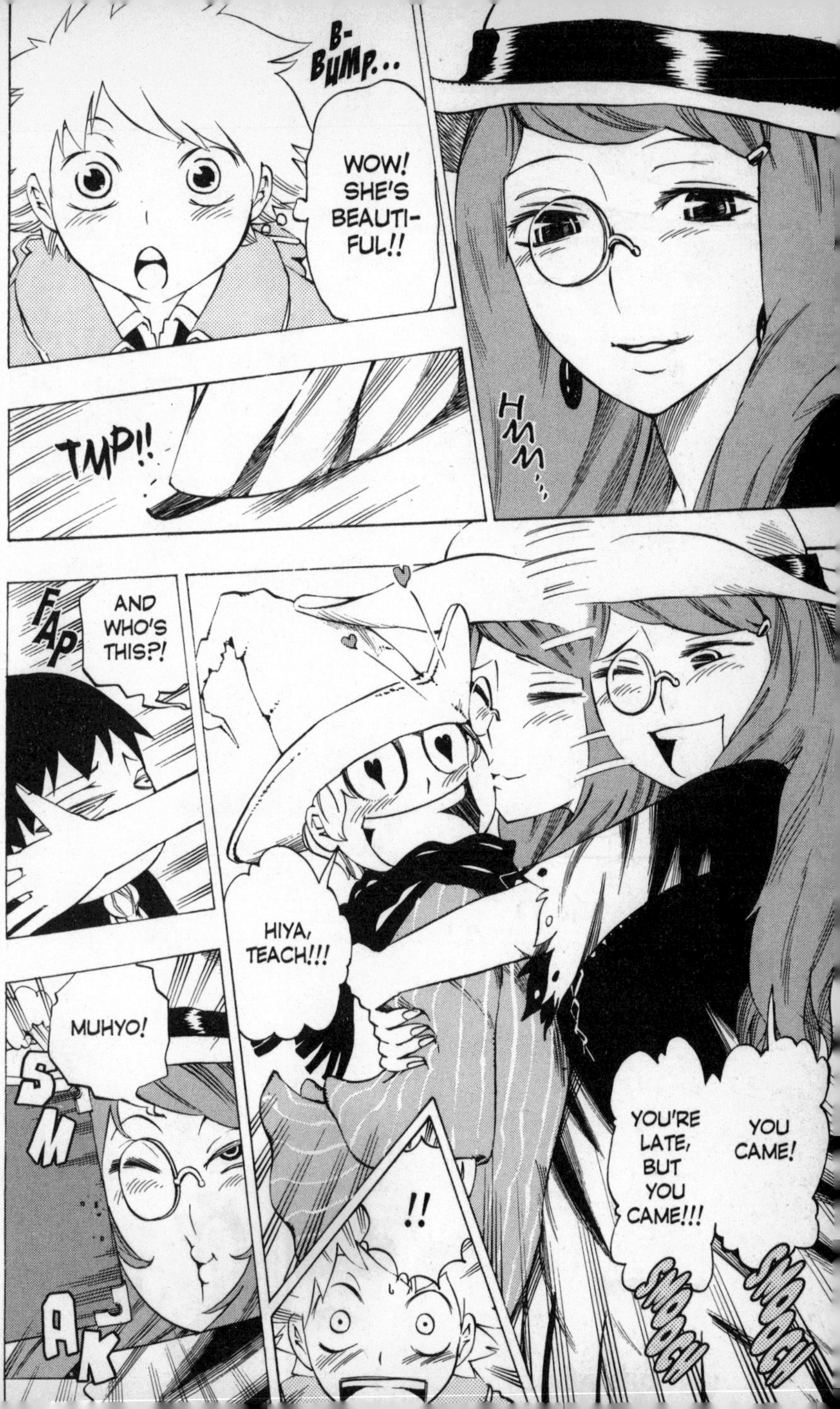
HMMM...
B-BUMP...
WOW! SHE'S BEAUTIFUL!!
TMP!!
YOU CAME!
YOU'RE LATE, BUT YOU CAME!!!
SMOOCH
SMOOCH
HIYA, TEACH!!!
FAP
AND WHO'S THIS?!
MUHYO!
SMJAK
!!

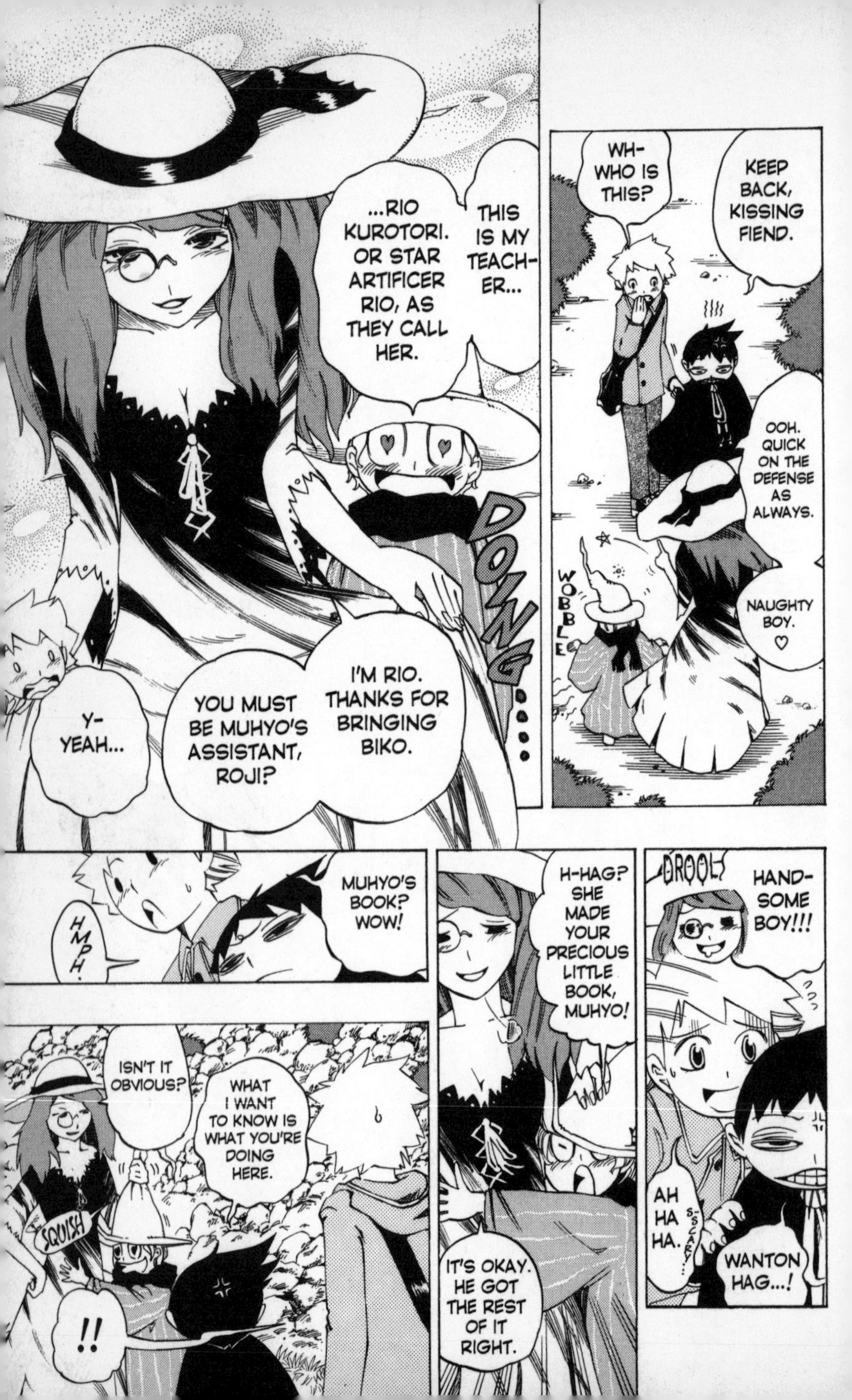
KEEP BACK, KISSING FIEND.
WH- WHO IS THIS?
OOH. QUICK ON THE DEFENSE AS ALWAYS.
WOBBLE
NAUGHTY BOY. ♡
THIS IS MY TEACH-ER...
...RIO KUROTORI. OR STAR ARTIFICER RIO, AS THEY CALL HER.
DOING....
I'M RIO. THANKS FOR BRINGING BIKO.
YOU MUST BE MUHYO'S ASSISTANT, ROJI?
Y-YEAH...
DROOL
HAND-SOME BOY!!!
AH HA HA.
S-SCARY...
WANTON HAG...!
H-HAG? SHE MADE YOUR PRECIOUS LITTLE BOOK, MUHYO!
IT'S OKAY. HE GOT THE REST OF IT RIGHT.
MUHYO'S BOOK? WOW!
HMPH.
WHAT I WANT TO KNOW IS WHAT YOU'RE DOING HERE.
ISN'T IT OBVIOUS?
SQUISH
!!

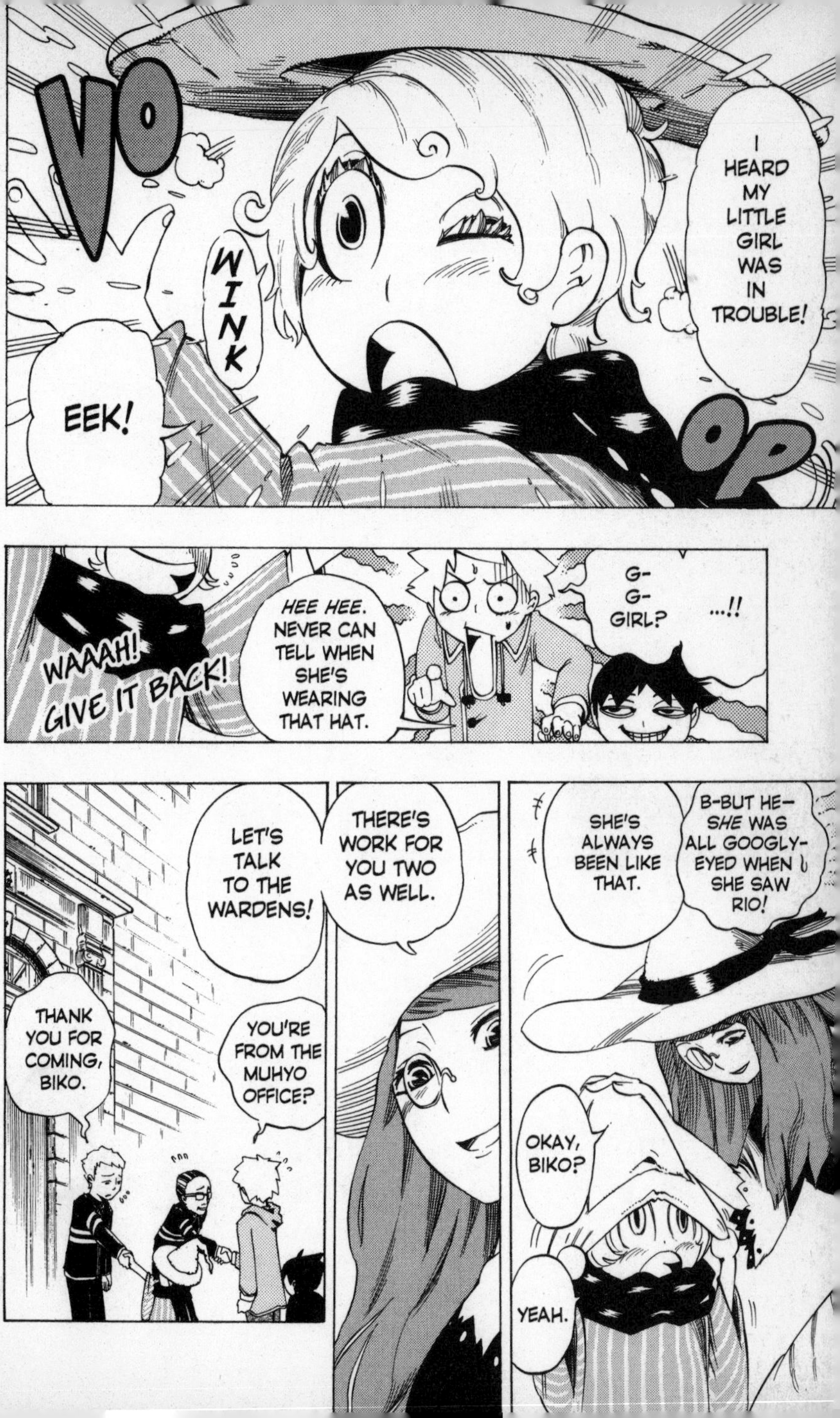
I HEARD MY LITTLE GIRL WAS IN TROUBLE!
VOOP
WINK
EEK!
...!!
G- G- GIRL?
HEE HEE. NEVER CAN TELL WHEN SHE'S WEARING THAT HAT.
WAAAH! GIVE IT BACK!
B-BUT HE— SHE WAS ALL GOOGLY-EYED WHEN SHE SAW RIO!
SHE'S ALWAYS BEEN LIKE THAT.
OKAY, BIKO?
YEAH.
THERE'S WORK FOR YOU TWO AS WELL.
LET'S TALK TO THE WARDENS!
YOU'RE FROM THE MUHYO OFFICE?
THANK YOU FOR COMING, BIKO.

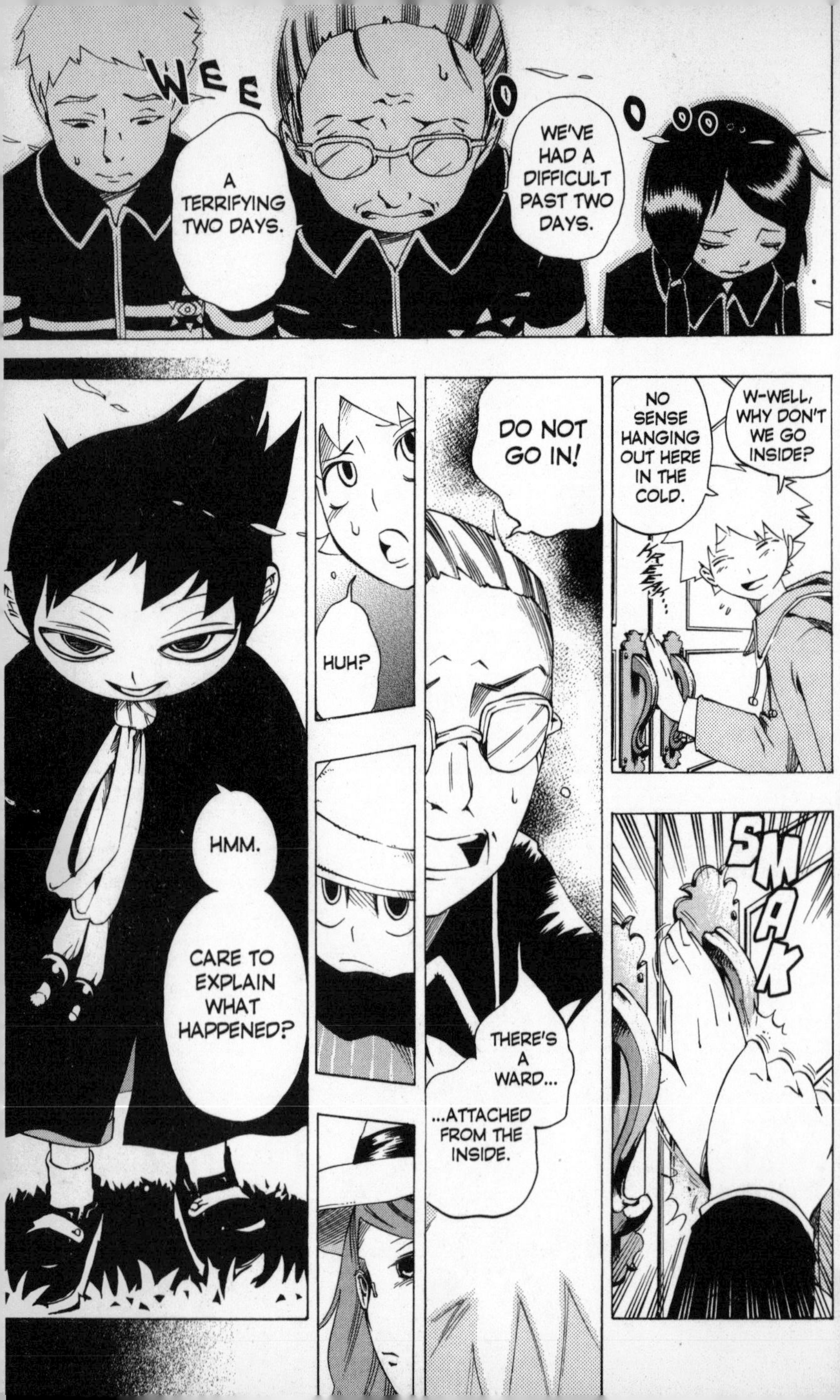
WE'VE HAD A DIFFICULT PAST TWO DAYS.
A TERRIFYING TWO DAYS.
WEE
W-WELL, WHY DON'T WE GO INSIDE?
NO SENSE HANGING OUT HERE IN THE COLD.
KREEAK...
SMAK
DO NOT GO IN!
THERE'S A WARD...
...ATTACHED FROM THE INSIDE.
HUH?
HMM.
CARE TO EXPLAIN WHAT HAPPENED?

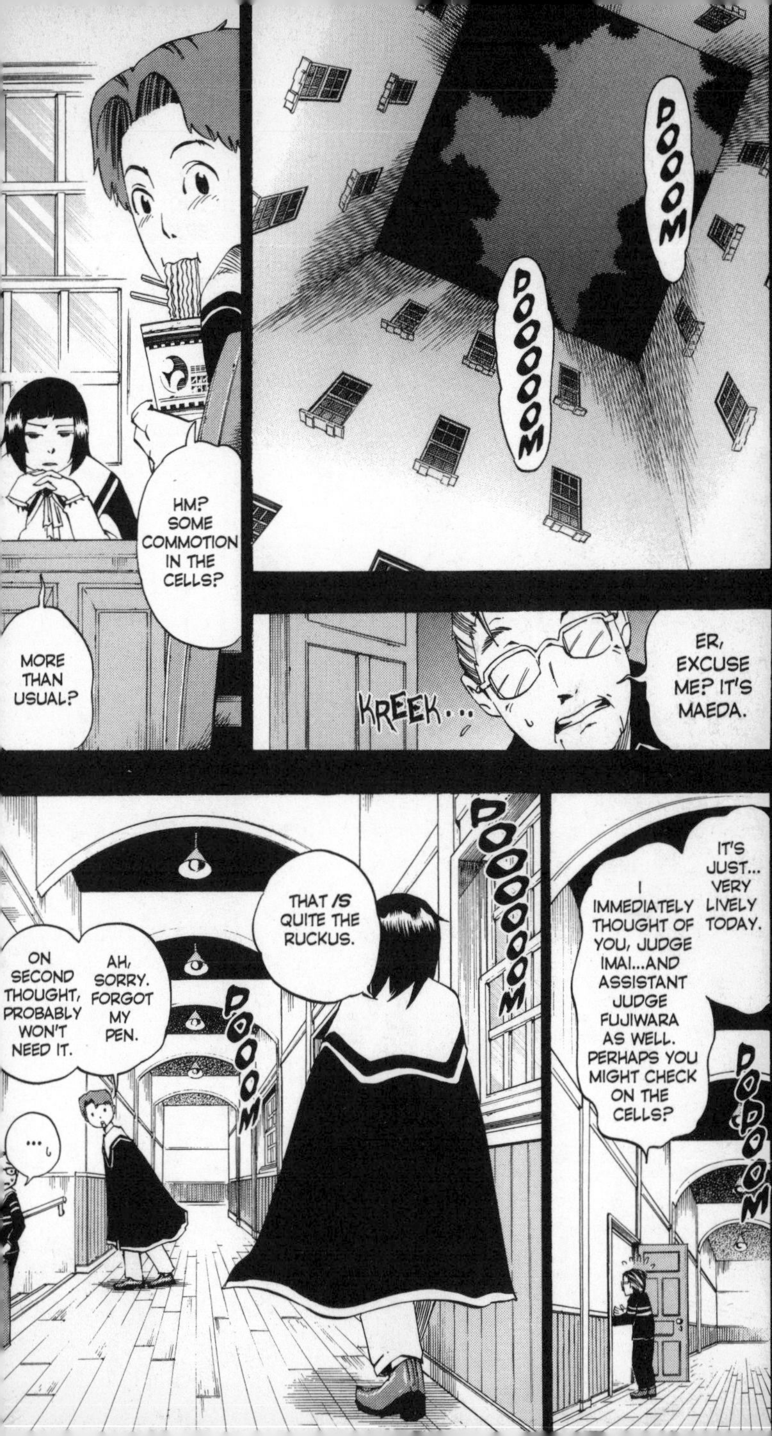
DOOOM
DOOOOOOM
ER, EXCUSE ME? IT'S MAEDA.
KREEK...
HM? SOME COMMOTION IN THE CELLS?
MORE THAN USUAL?
IT'S JUST... VERY LIVELY TODAY.
I IMMEDIATELY THOUGHT OF YOU, JUDGE IMAI...AND ASSISTANT JUDGE FUJIWARA AS WELL. PERHAPS YOU MIGHT CHECK ON THE CELLS?
DODOOM
DOOOOOOOM
THAT IS QUITE THE RUCKUS.
DOOOM
AH, SORRY. FORGOT MY PEN.
ON SECOND THOUGHT, PROBABLY WON'T NEED IT.
...

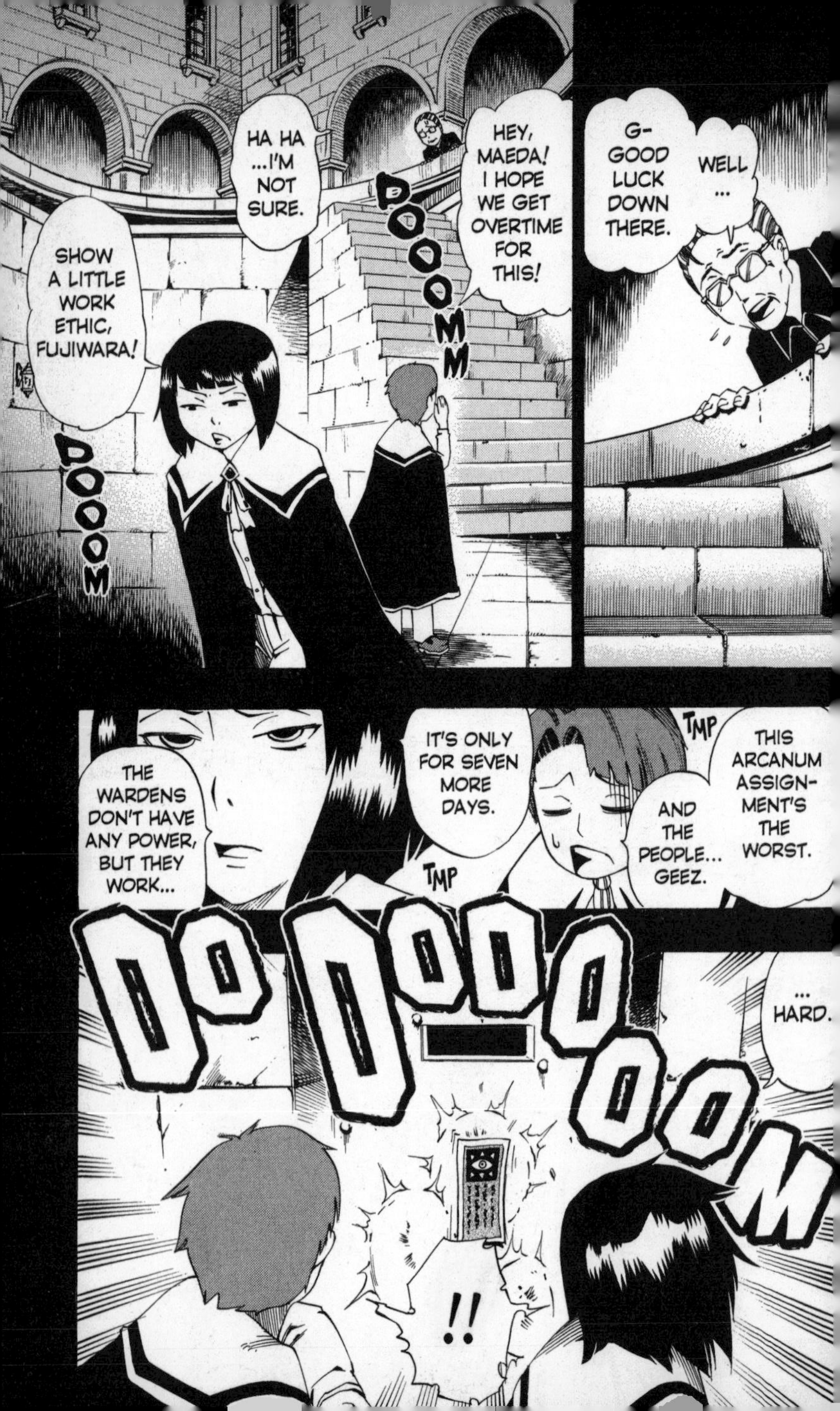
WELL ...
G-GOOD LUCK DOWN THERE.
HEY, MAEDA! I HOPE WE GET OVERTIME FOR THIS!
DOOOMM
HA HA ...I'M NOT SURE.
SHOW A LITTLE WORK ETHIC, FUJIWARA!
DOOOOM
TMP
THIS ARCANUM ASSIGN-MENT'S THE WORST.
AND THE PEOPLE... GEEZ.
IT'S ONLY FOR SEVEN MORE DAYS.
TMP
THE WARDENS DON'T HAVE ANY POWER, BUT THEY WORK...
... HARD.
DO DODOOOOOM
!!

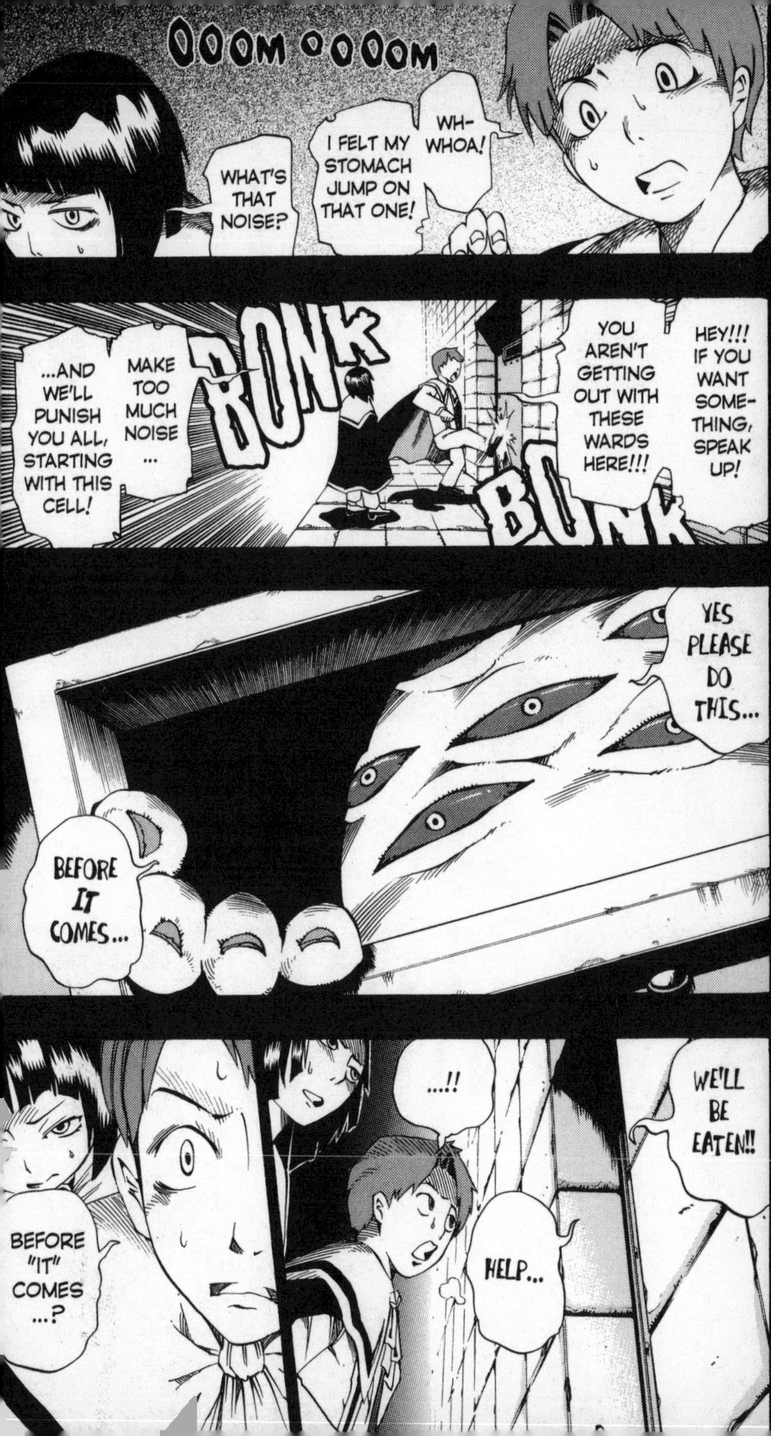
OOOM OOOOM
WH- WHOA!
I FELT MY STOMACH JUMP ON THAT ONE!
WHAT'S THAT NOISE?
HEY!!! IF YOU WANT SOME-THING, SPEAK UP!
YOU AREN'T GETTING OUT WITH THESE WARDS HERE!!!
BONK
BONK
MAKE TOO MUCH NOISE ...
...AND WE'LL PUNISH YOU ALL, STARTING WITH THIS CELL!
YES PLEASE DO THIS...
BEFORE IT COMES...
WE'LL BE EATEN!!
...!!
HELP...
BEFORE "IT" COMES ...?

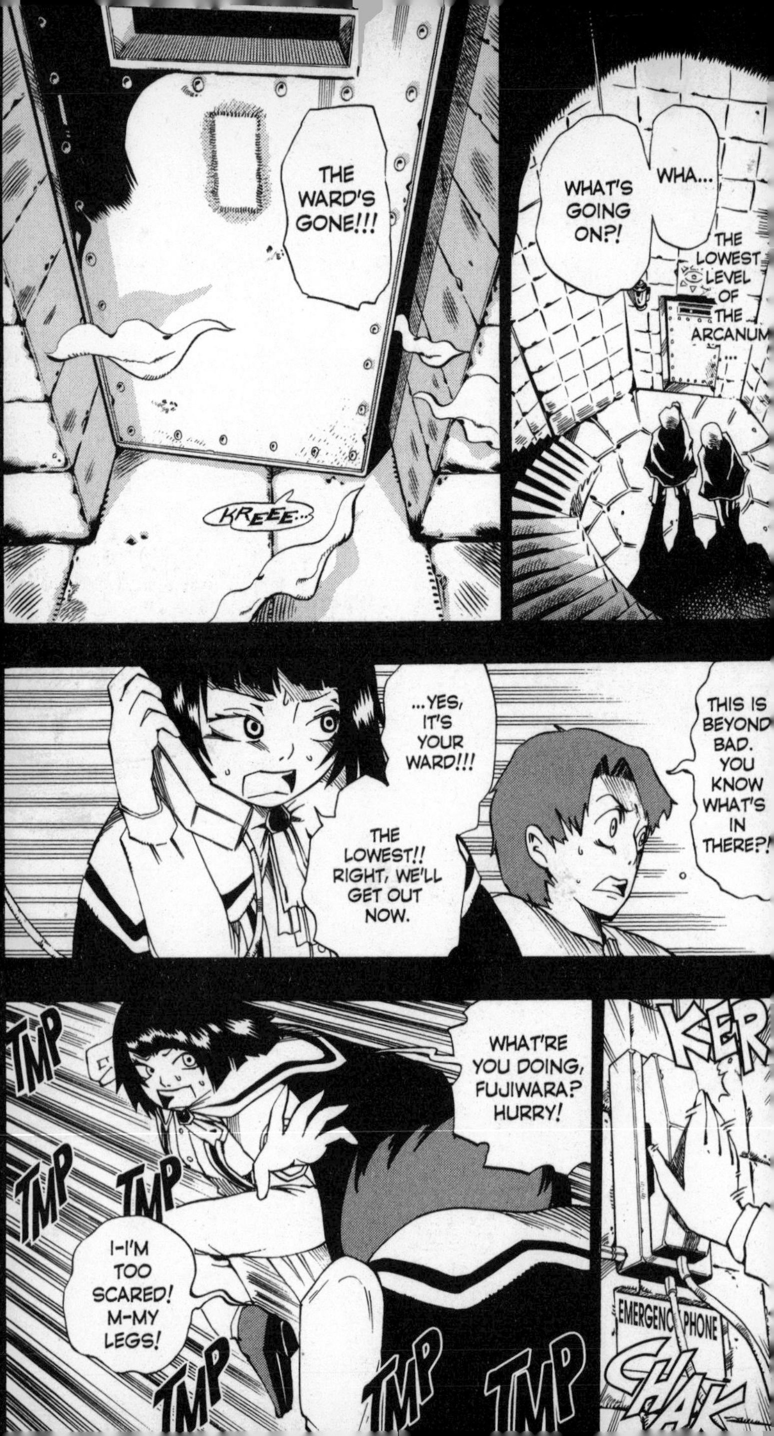
WHA...
WHAT'S GOING ON?!
THE LOWEST LEVEL OF THE ARCANUM...
THE WARD'S GONE!!!
KREEEE...
THIS IS BEYOND BAD. YOU KNOW WHAT'S IN THERE?!
...YES, IT'S YOUR WARD!!!
THE LOWEST!! RIGHT, WE'LL GET OUT NOW.
KER
EMERGENC PHONE
CHAK
WHAT'RE YOU DOING, FUJIWARA? HURRY!
TMP
TMP
TMP
I-I'M TOO SCARED! M-MY LEGS!
TMP
TMP
TMP

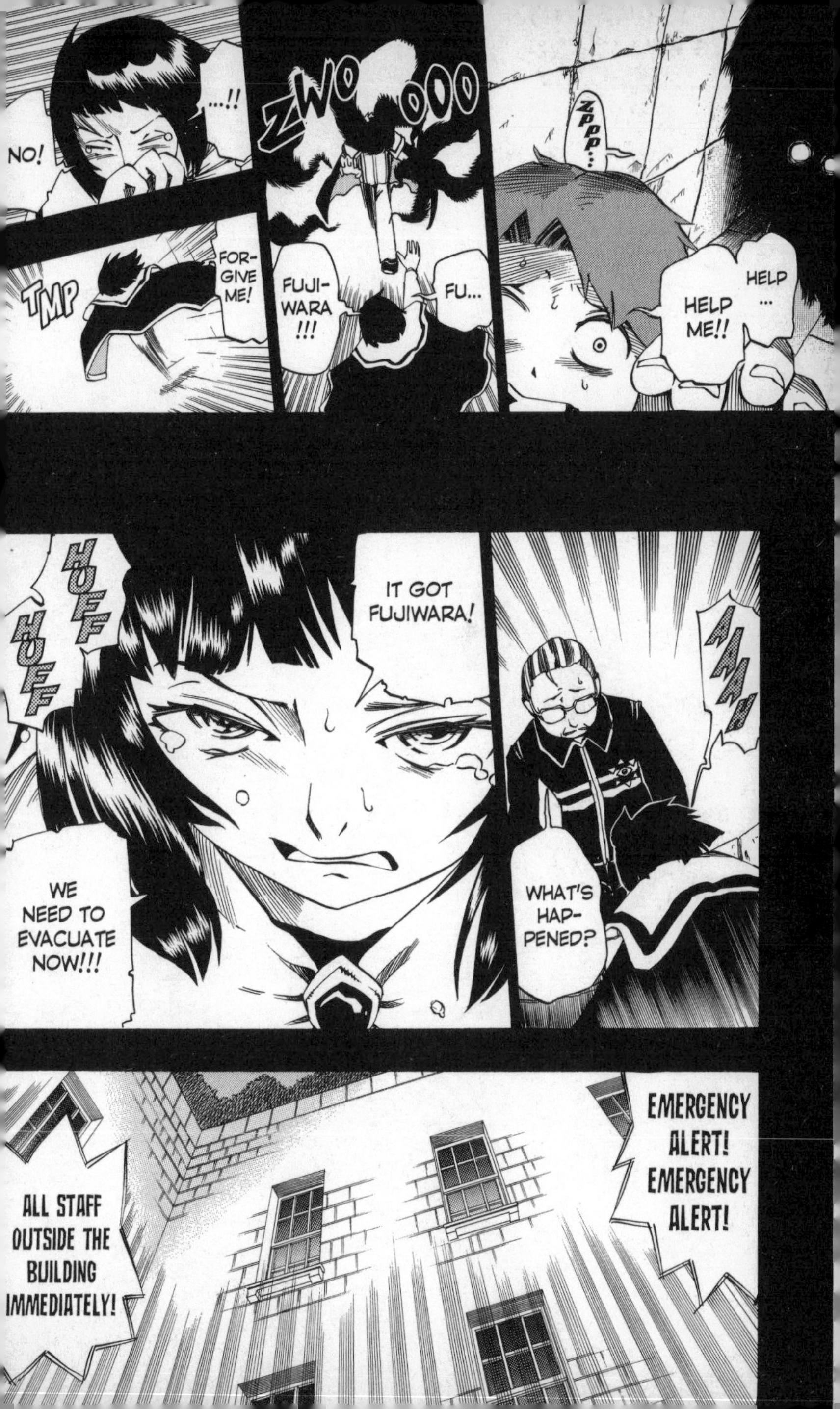
ZPPP...
HELP ...
HELP ME!!
ZWOOOOO
FU...
FUJI-WARA!!!
...!!
NO!
FOR-GIVE ME!
TMP
AAAH!
WHAT'S HAP-PENED?
HUFF HUFF
IT GOT FUJIWARA!
WE NEED TO EVACUATE NOW!!!
EMERGENCY ALERT! EMERGENCY ALERT!
ALL STAFF OUTSIDE THE BUILDING IMMEDIATELY!

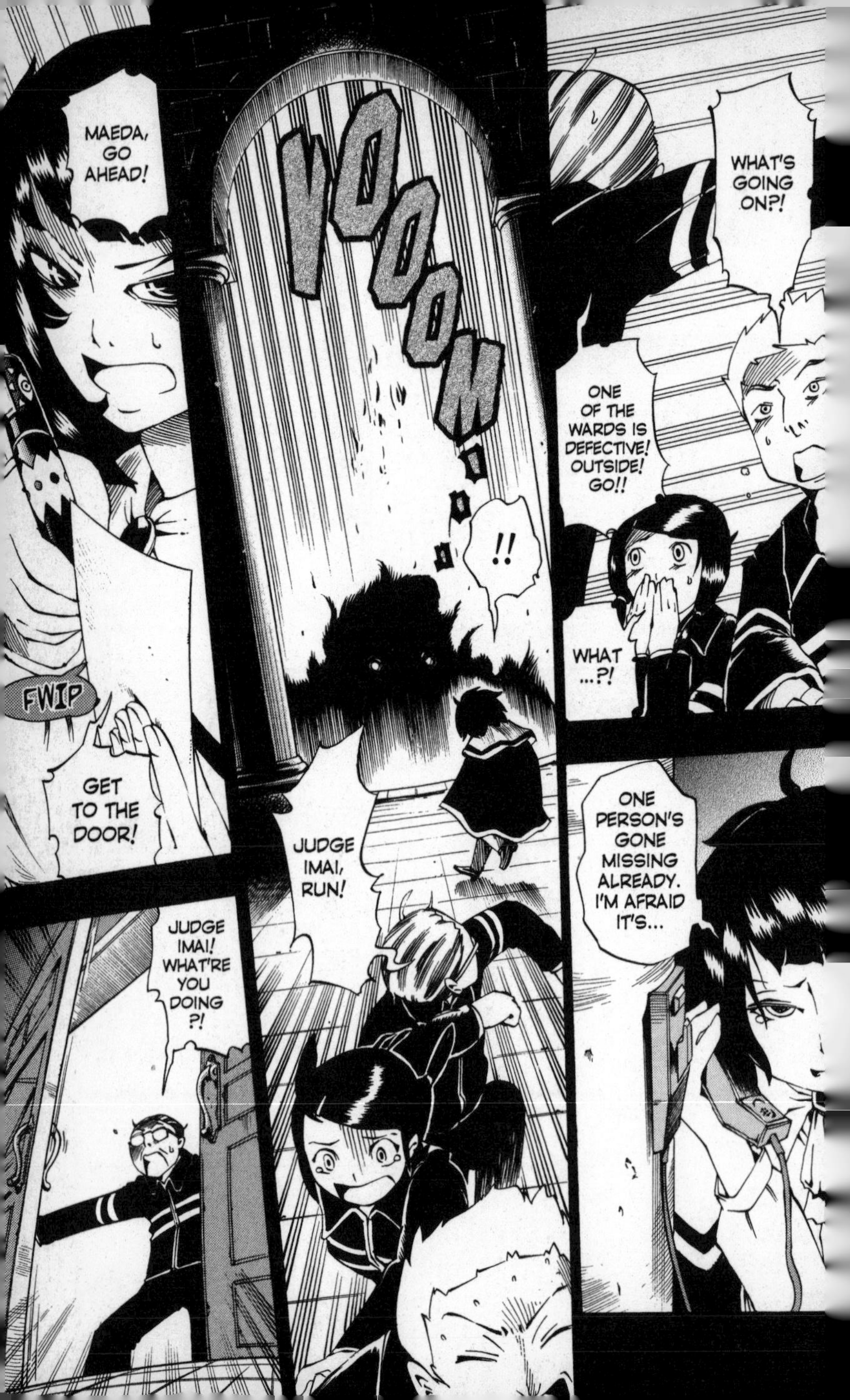
WHAT'S GOING ON?!
ONE OF THE WARDS IS DEFECTIVE! OUTSIDE! GO!!
WHAT ...?!
VOOOOM
!!
JUDGE IMAI, RUN!
MAEDA, GO AHEAD!
FWIP
GET TO THE DOOR!
ONE PERSON'S GONE MISSING ALREADY. I'M AFRAID IT'S...
JUDGE IMAI! WHAT'RE YOU DOING?!

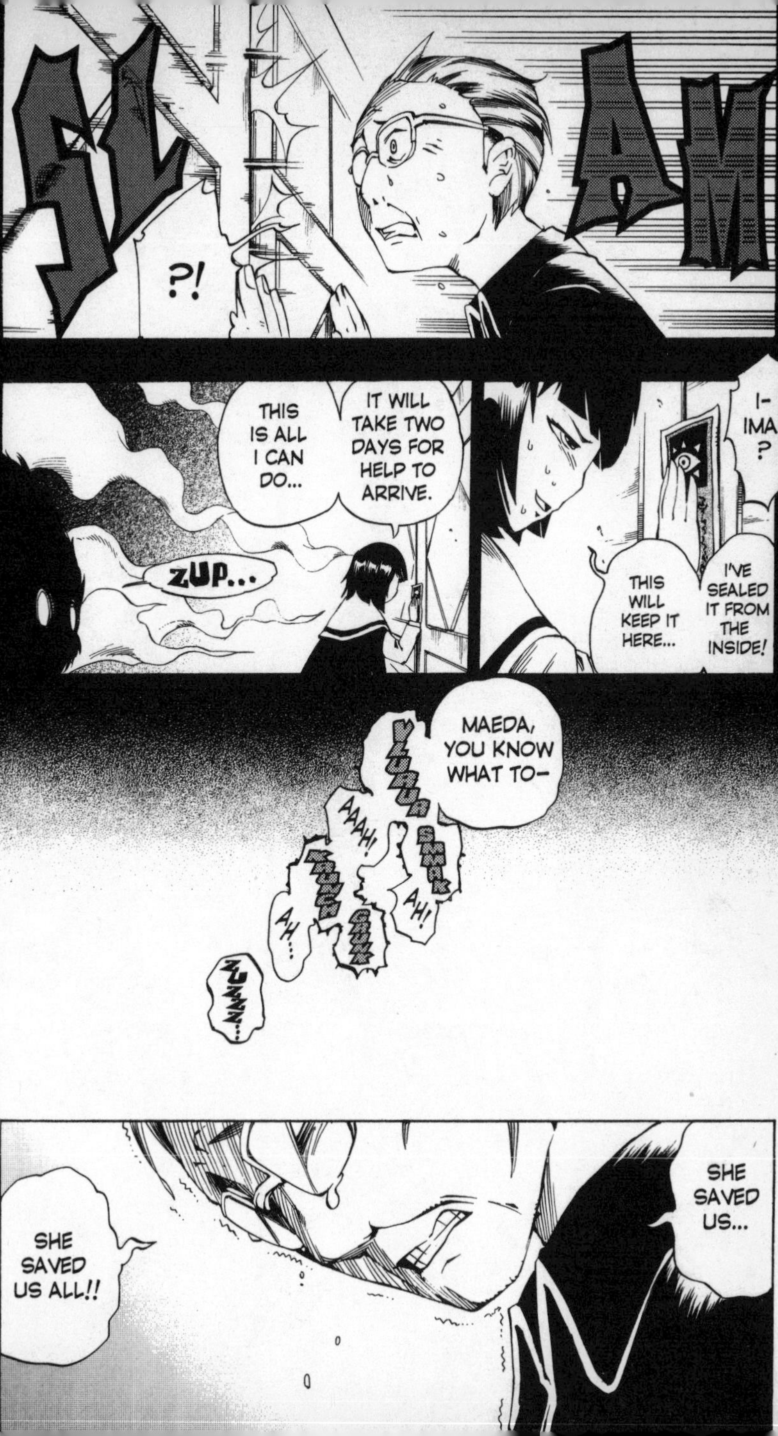
SLAM
?!
I-IMAI?
I'VE SEALED IT FROM THE INSIDE!
THIS WILL KEEP IT HERE...
IT WILL TAKE TWO DAYS FOR HELP TO ARRIVE.
THIS IS ALL I CAN DO...
ZUP...
MAEDA, YOU KNOW WHAT TO—
AAAAH!
AH!
AH...
ZZZZZ...
SHE SAVED US...
SHE SAVED US ALL!!

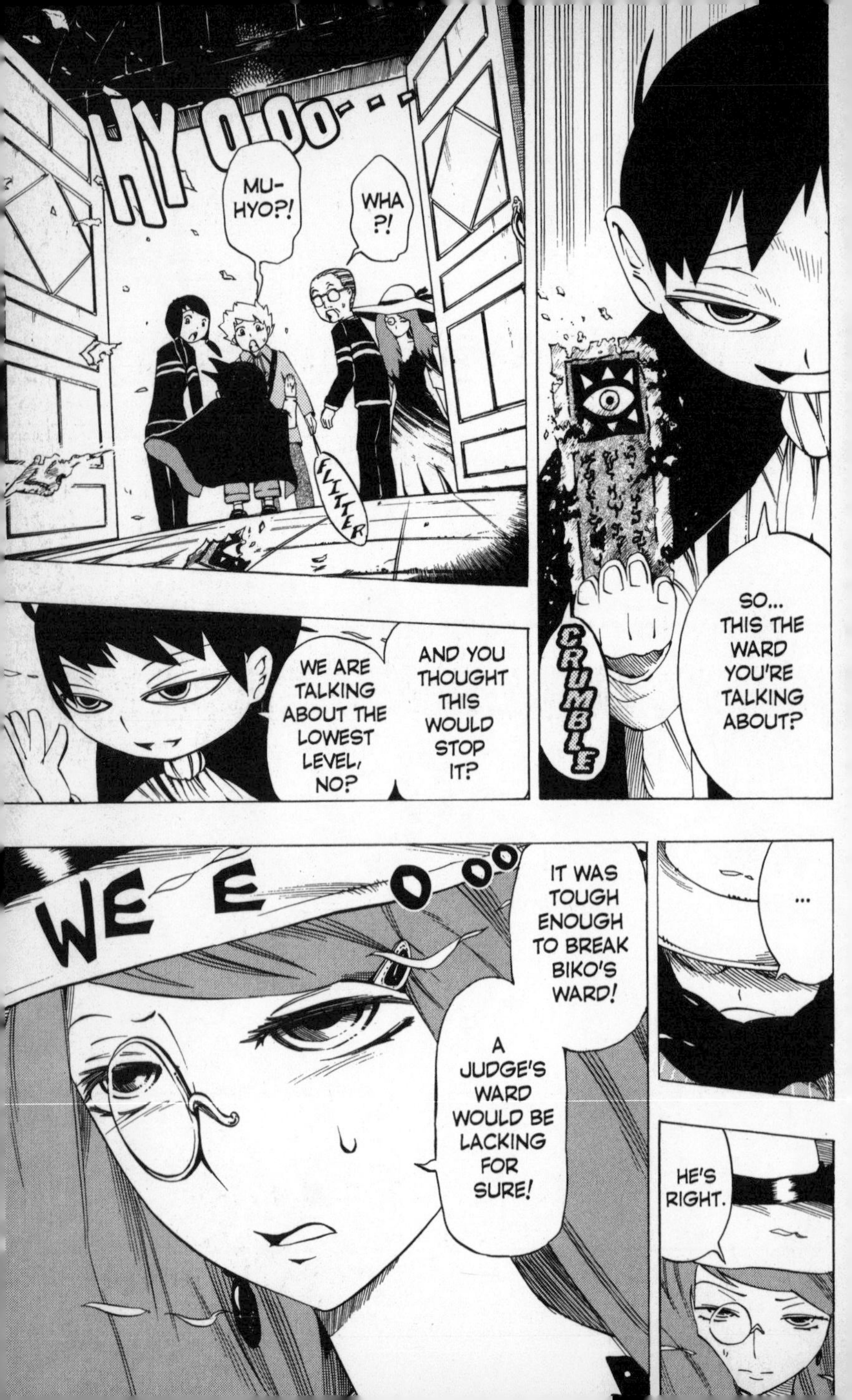
SO... THIS THE WARD YOU'RE TALKING ABOUT?
CRUMBLE
HY O OO
WHA ?!
MU-HYO?!
FLITTER
AND YOU THOUGHT THIS WOULD STOP IT?
WE ARE TALKING ABOUT THE LOWEST LEVEL, NO?
...
HE'S RIGHT.
WE E O OO
IT WAS TOUGH ENOUGH TO BREAK BIKO'S WARD!
A JUDGE'S WARD WOULD BE LACKING FOR SURE!

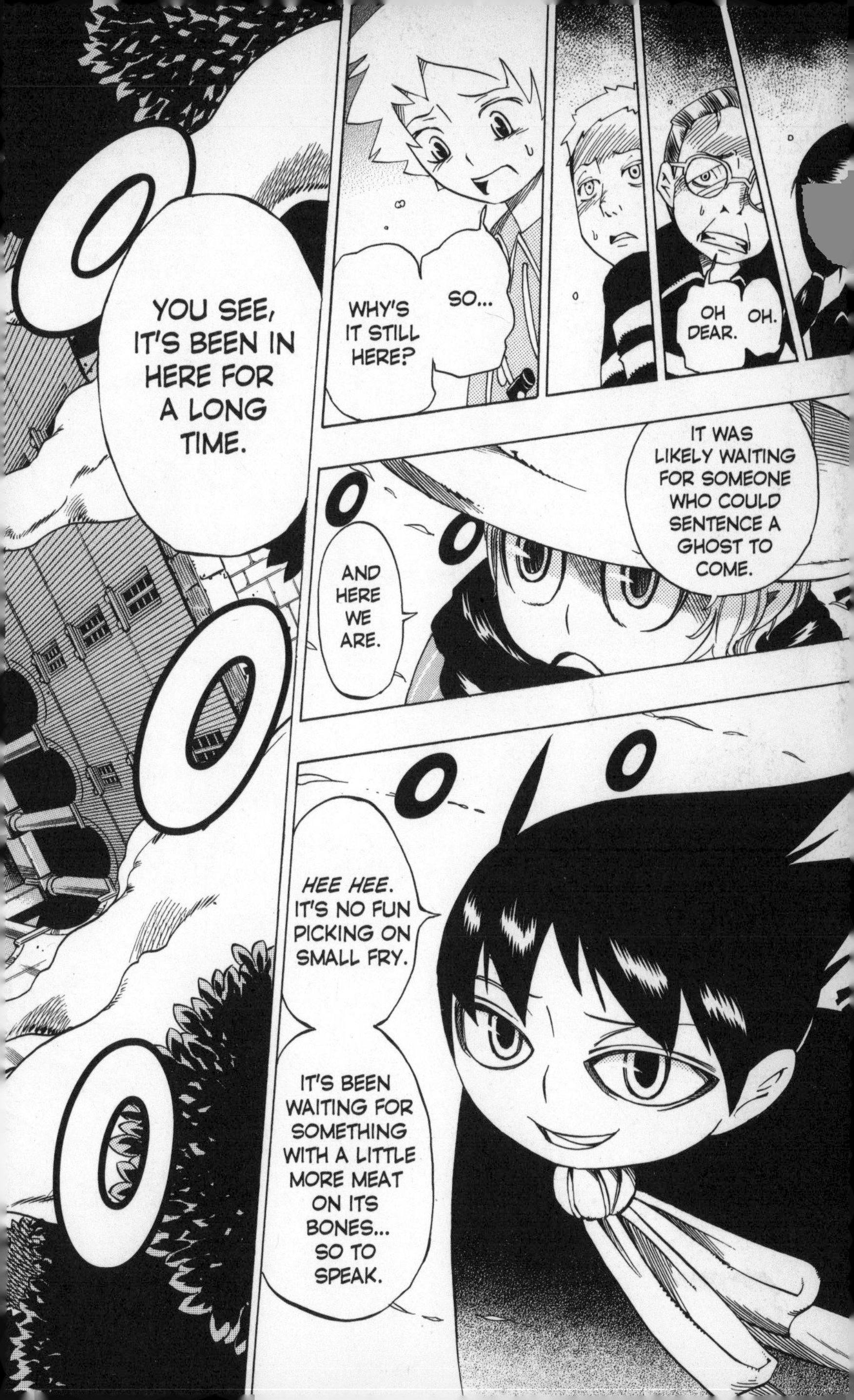
OH.
OH DEAR.
SO...
WHY'S IT STILL HERE?
IT WAS LIKELY WAITING FOR SOMEONE WHO COULD SENTENCE A GHOST TO COME.
AND HERE WE ARE.
HEE HEE. IT'S NO FUN PICKING ON SMALL FRY.
IT'S BEEN WAITING FOR SOMETHING WITH A LITTLE MORE MEAT ON ITS BONES... SO TO SPEAK.
YOU SEE, IT'S BEEN IN HERE FOR A LONG TIME.

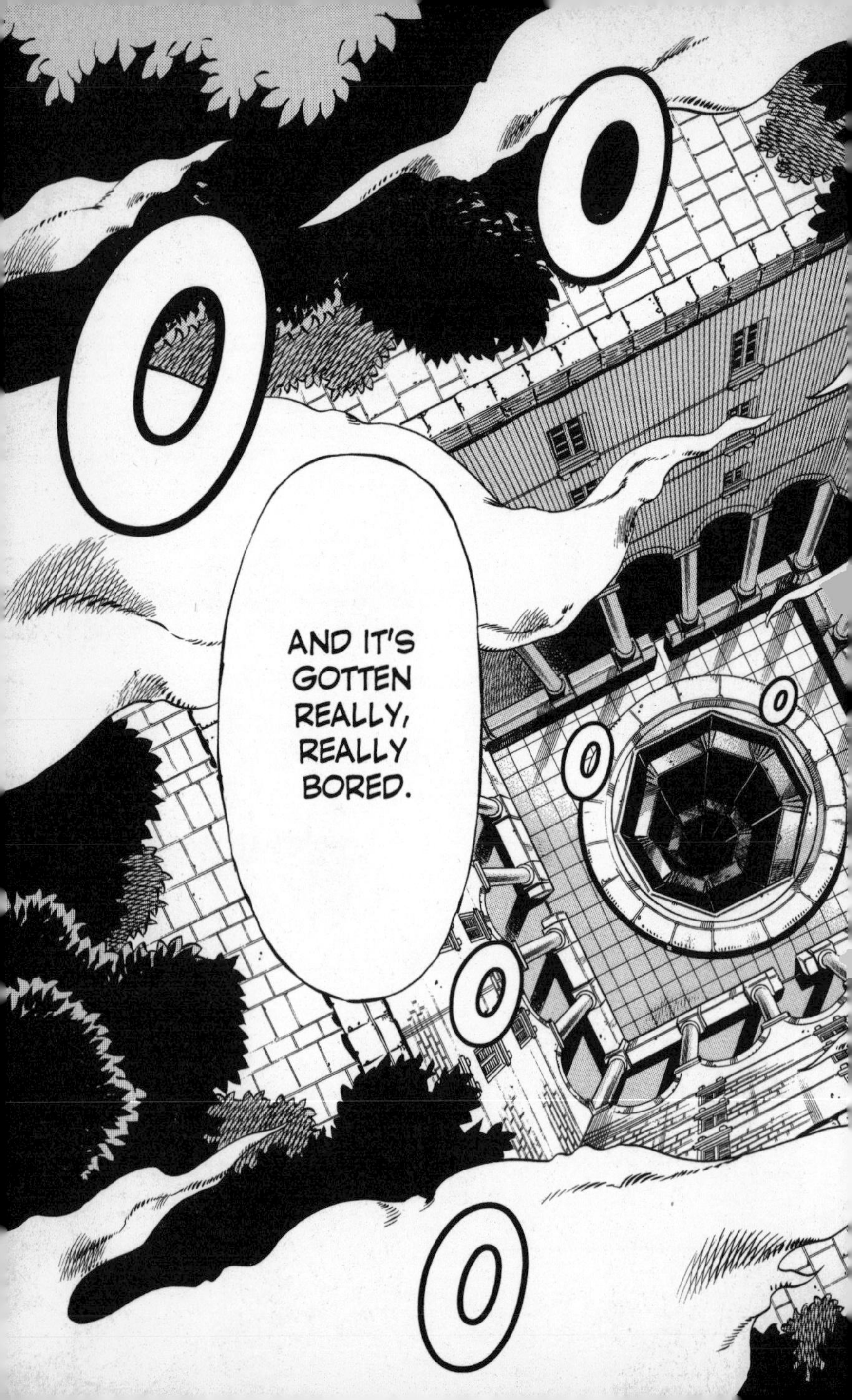
AND IT'S GOTTEN REALLY, REALLY BORED.

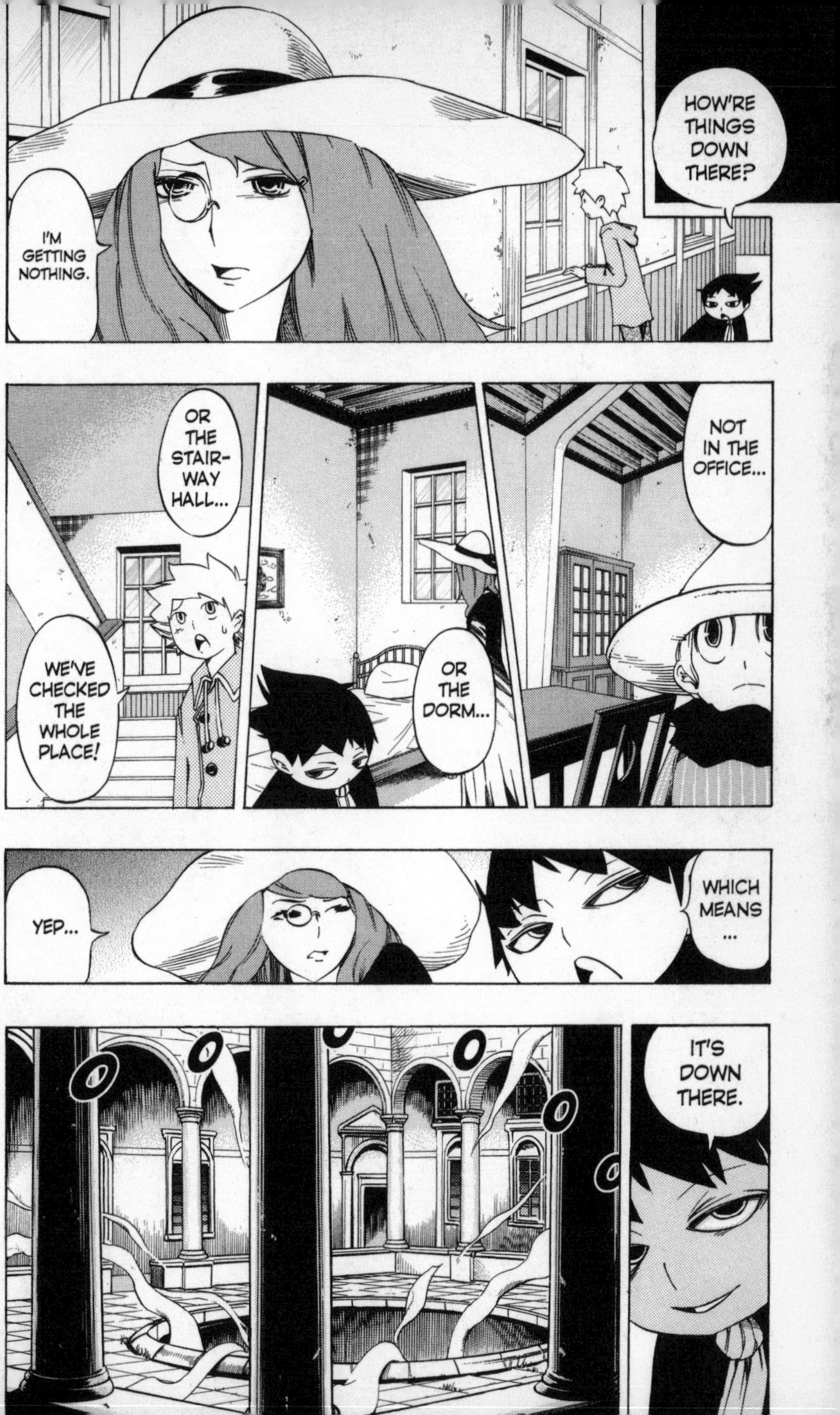
HOW'RE THINGS DOWN THERE?
I'M GETTING NOTHING.
NOT IN THE OFFICE...
OR THE DORM...
OR THE STAIR-WAY HALL...
WE'VE CHECKED THE WHOLE PLACE!
WHICH MEANS ...
YEP...
IT'S DOWN THERE.

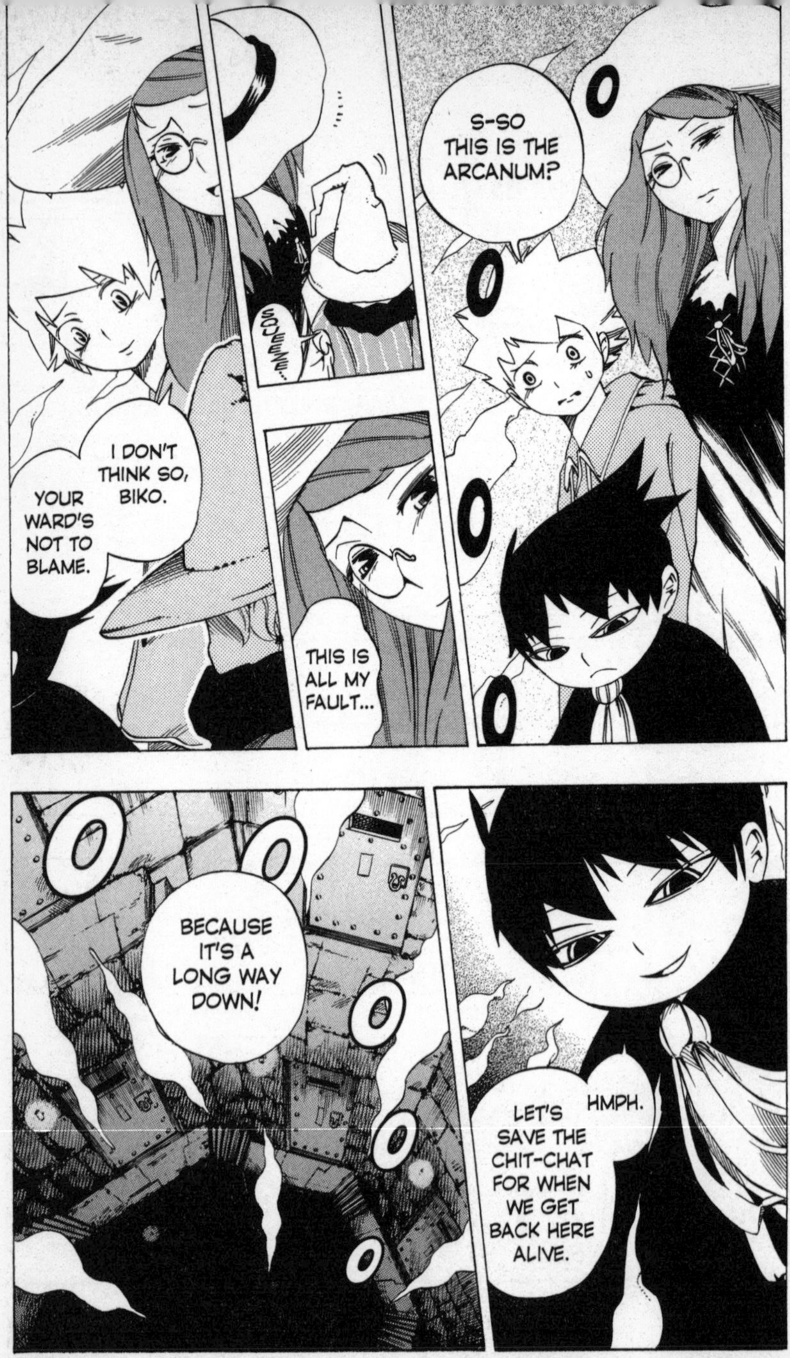
S-SO THIS IS THE ARCANUM?
SQUEEZE...
THIS IS ALL MY FAULT...
I DON'T THINK SO, BIKO.
YOUR WARD'S NOT TO BLAME.
HMPH.
LET'S SAVE THE CHIT-CHAT FOR WHEN WE GET BACK HERE ALIVE.
BECAUSE IT'S A LONG WAY DOWN!

Q: CAN YOU SEE GHOSTS IN REAL LIFE?

A: WELL...
MR. K, MY EDITOR, ONCE WROTE IN A BOOK JACKET THAT I HAD A "STRONG SENSE OF THE SUPER-NATURAL." I'VE SEEN PLENTY OF STRANGE THINGS IN MY DAY, THOUGH IT'S LESS AN ABILITY TO "SEE GHOSTS" AND MORE THAT PLACES TEND TO INFLUENCE ME STRONGLY. ESPECIALLY PLACES WITH A FAMILY CONNECTION, WHERE THE BLOOD RUNS DEEP, SO TO SPEAK. AND I TEND TO GO TO THIS KIND OF PLACE A LOT...AND I SEE THINGS. GHOSTS? MAYBE.

SHIVER

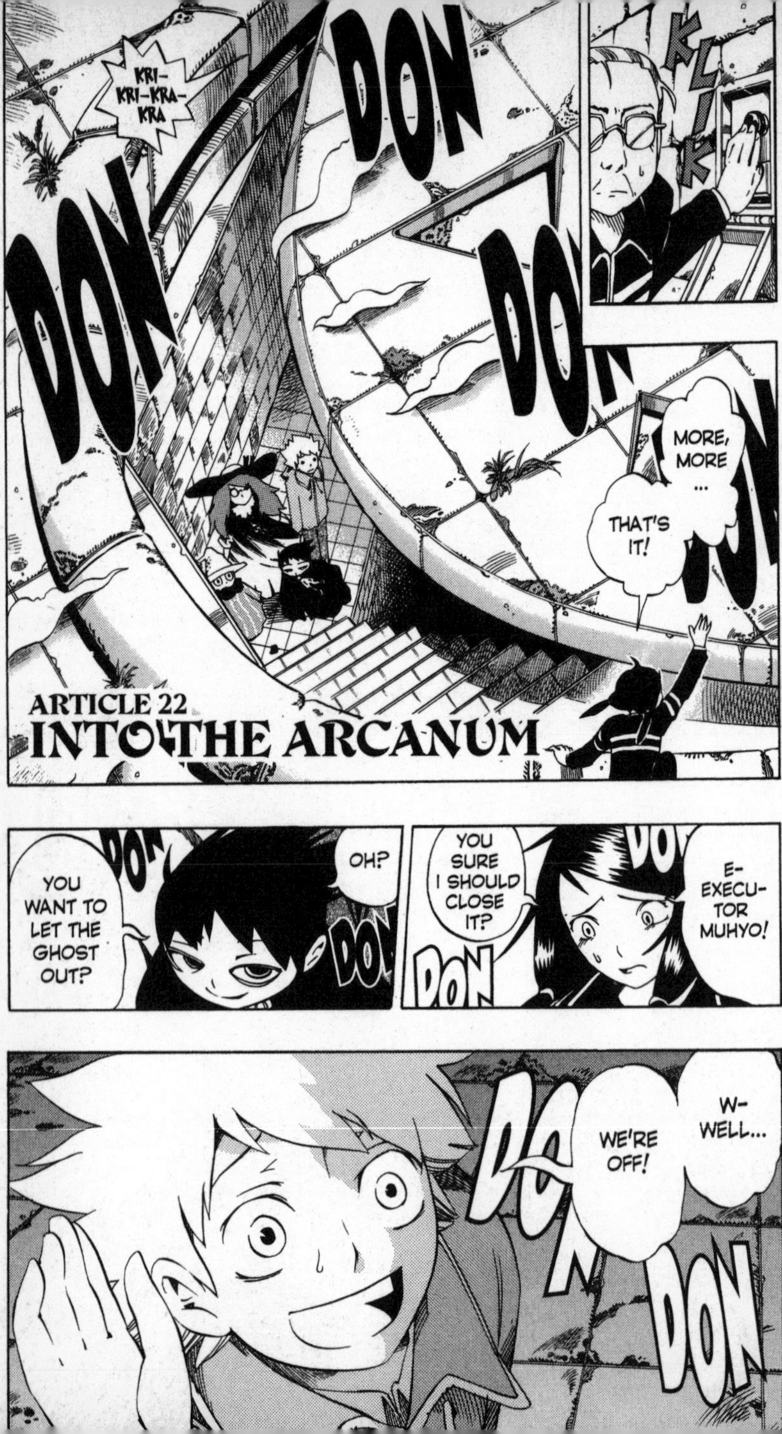
KLICK
KRI-KRI-KRA-KRA
DON
DON
DON
DON
MORE, MORE ...
THAT'S IT!
ARTICLE 22
INTO THE ARCANUM
E-EXECUTOR MUHYO!
YOU SURE I SHOULD CLOSE IT?
DON
DON
OH?
YOU WANT TO LET THE GHOST OUT?
DON
DON
W-WELL...
WE'RE OFF!
DON
DON

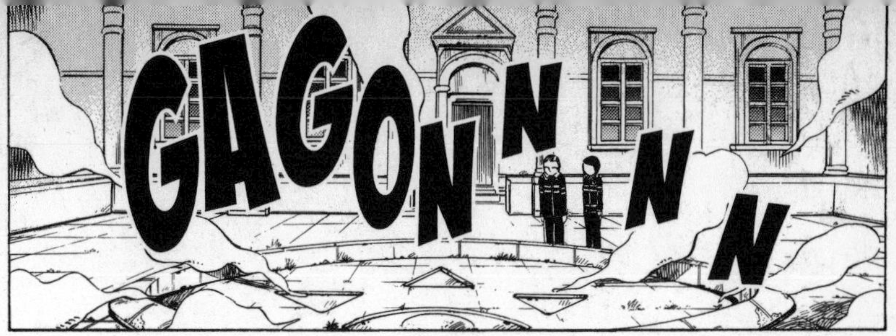
GAGONNNN

ARTICLE 22

INTO THE ARCANUM

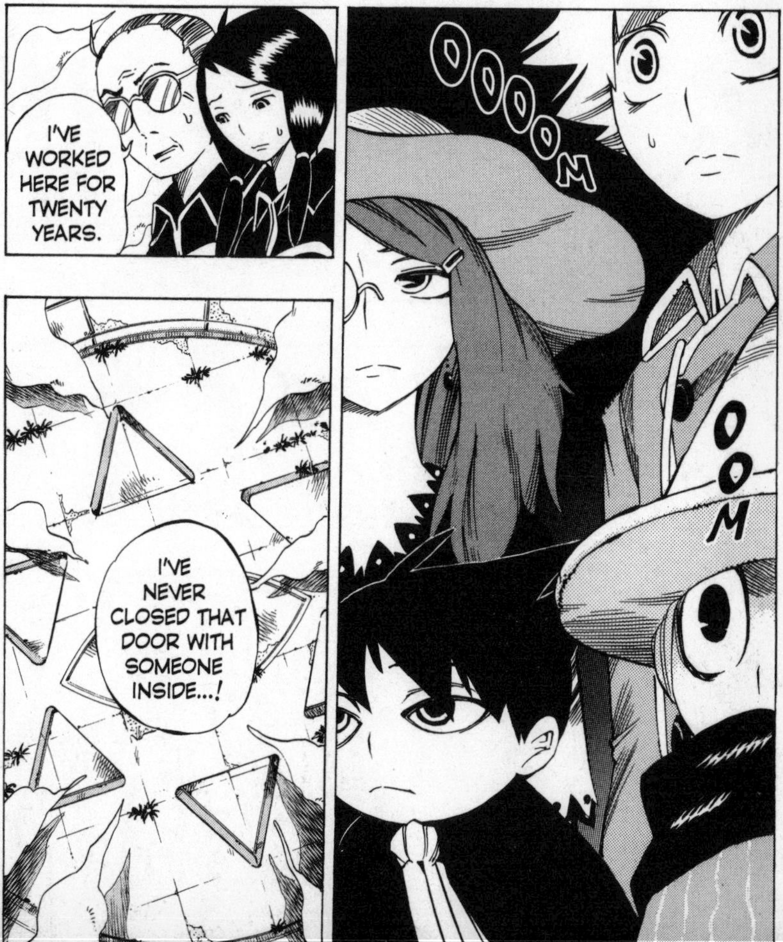
OOOOOM
OOOM
I'VE WORKED HERE FOR TWENTY YEARS.
I'VE NEVER CLOSED THAT DOOR WITH SOMEONE INSIDE...!

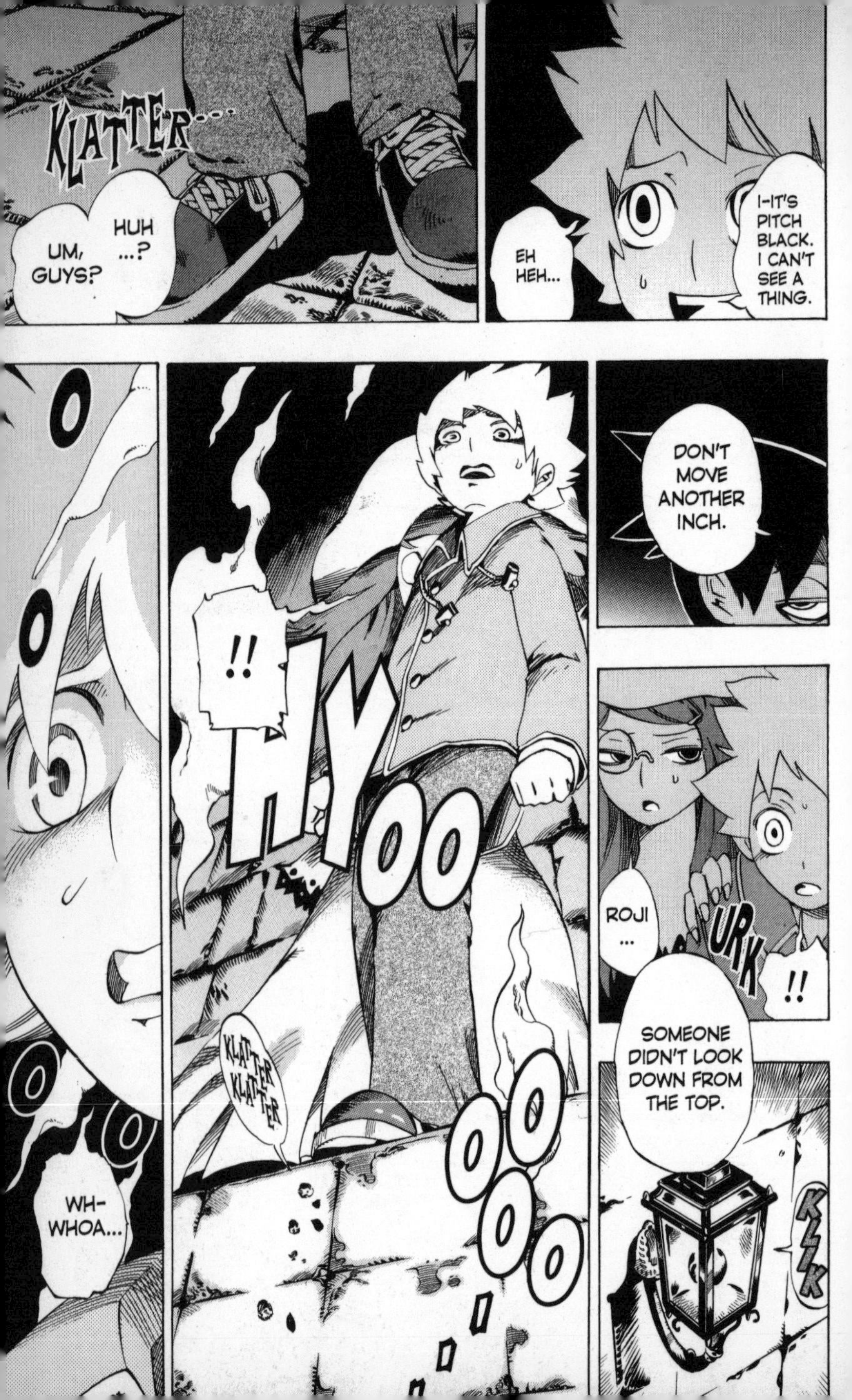
I-IT'S PITCH BLACK. I CAN'T SEE A THING.
EH HEH...
KLATTER...
HUH ...?
UM, GUYS?
DON'T MOVE ANOTHER INCH.
URK
!!
ROJI ...
SOMEONE DIDN'T LOOK DOWN FROM THE TOP.
KLIK
!!
HYOOOOOOO
KLATTER KLATTER
WH-WHOA...

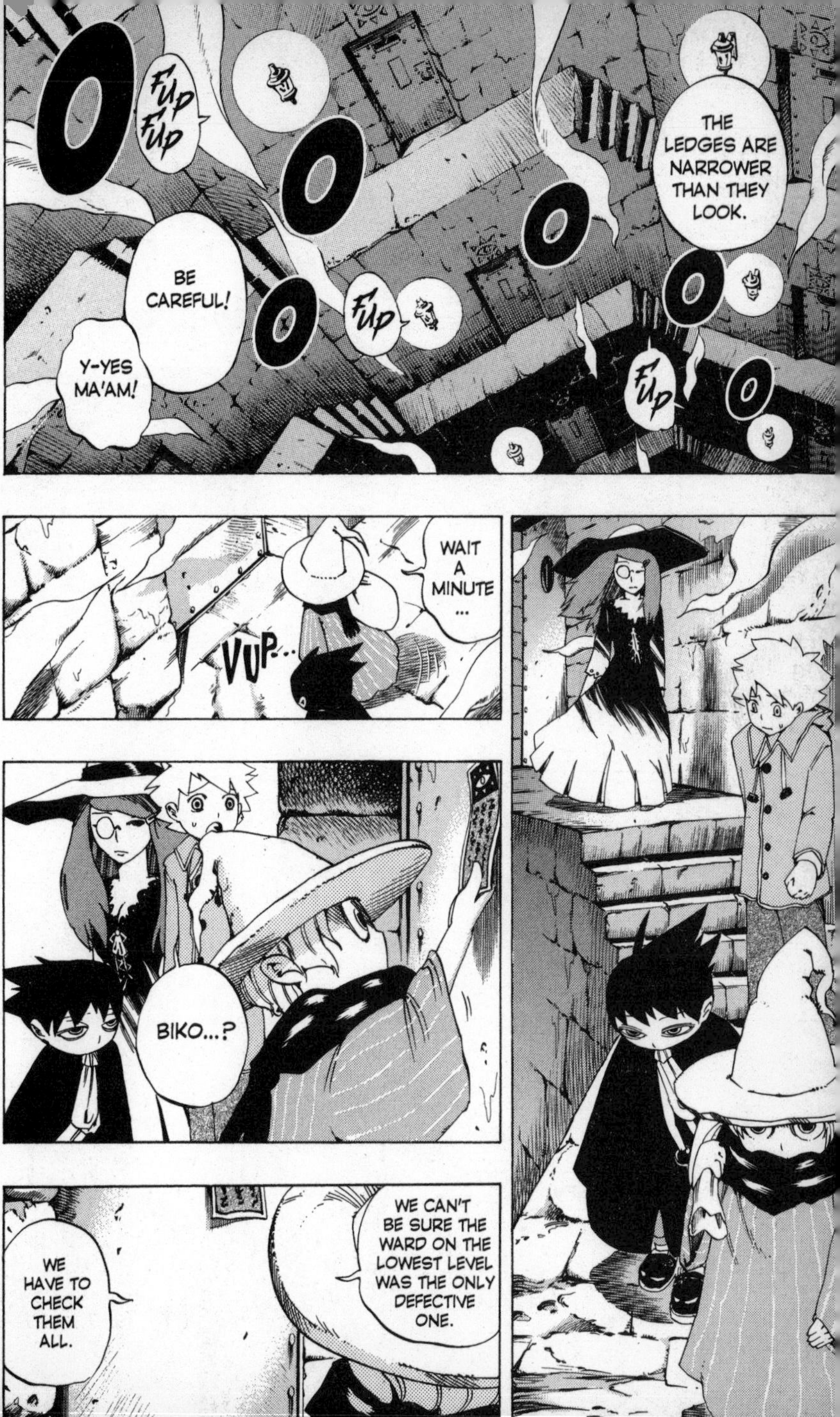
THE LEDGES ARE NARROWER THAN THEY LOOK.
FUP
FUP
FUP FUP
BE CAREFUL!
Y-YES MA'AM!
WAIT A MINUTE ...
VUP...
BIKO...?
WE CAN'T BE SURE THE WARD ON THE LOWEST LEVEL WAS THE ONLY DEFECTIVE ONE.
WE HAVE TO CHECK THEM ALL.

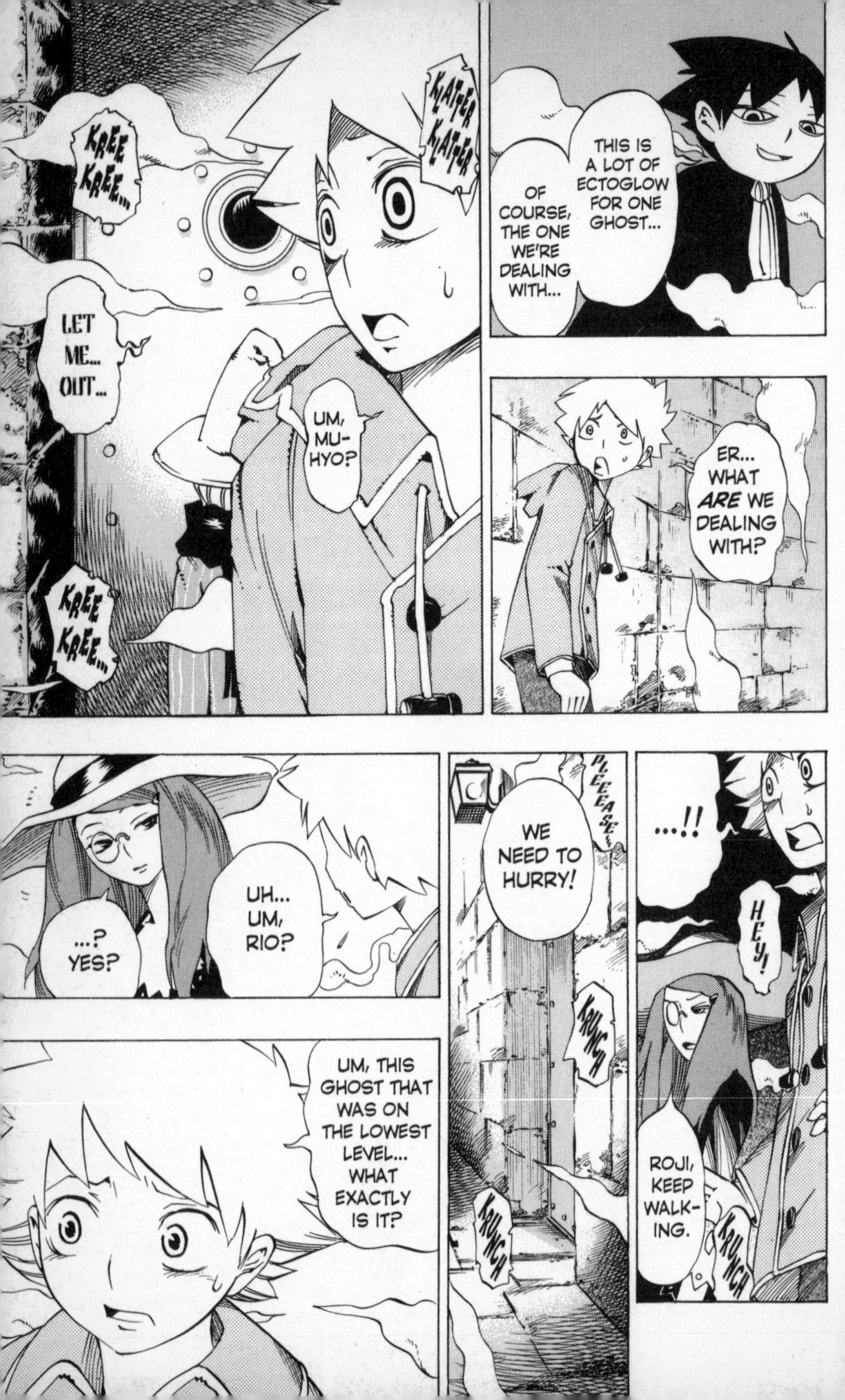
THIS IS A LOT OF ECTOGLOW FOR ONE GHOST...
OF COURSE, THE ONE WE'RE DEALING WITH...
ER... WHAT *ARE* WE DEALING WITH?
KLATTER KLATTER
KREE KREE...
LET ME... OUT...
UM, MU-HYO?
KREE KREE...
...!!
HEY!
ROJI, KEEP WALKING.
KRUNCH
PLEEEASE...
WE NEED TO HURRY!
KRUNCH
KRUNCH
UH... UM, RIO?
...? YES?
UM, THIS GHOST THAT WAS ON THE LOWEST LEVEL... WHAT EXACTLY IS IT?

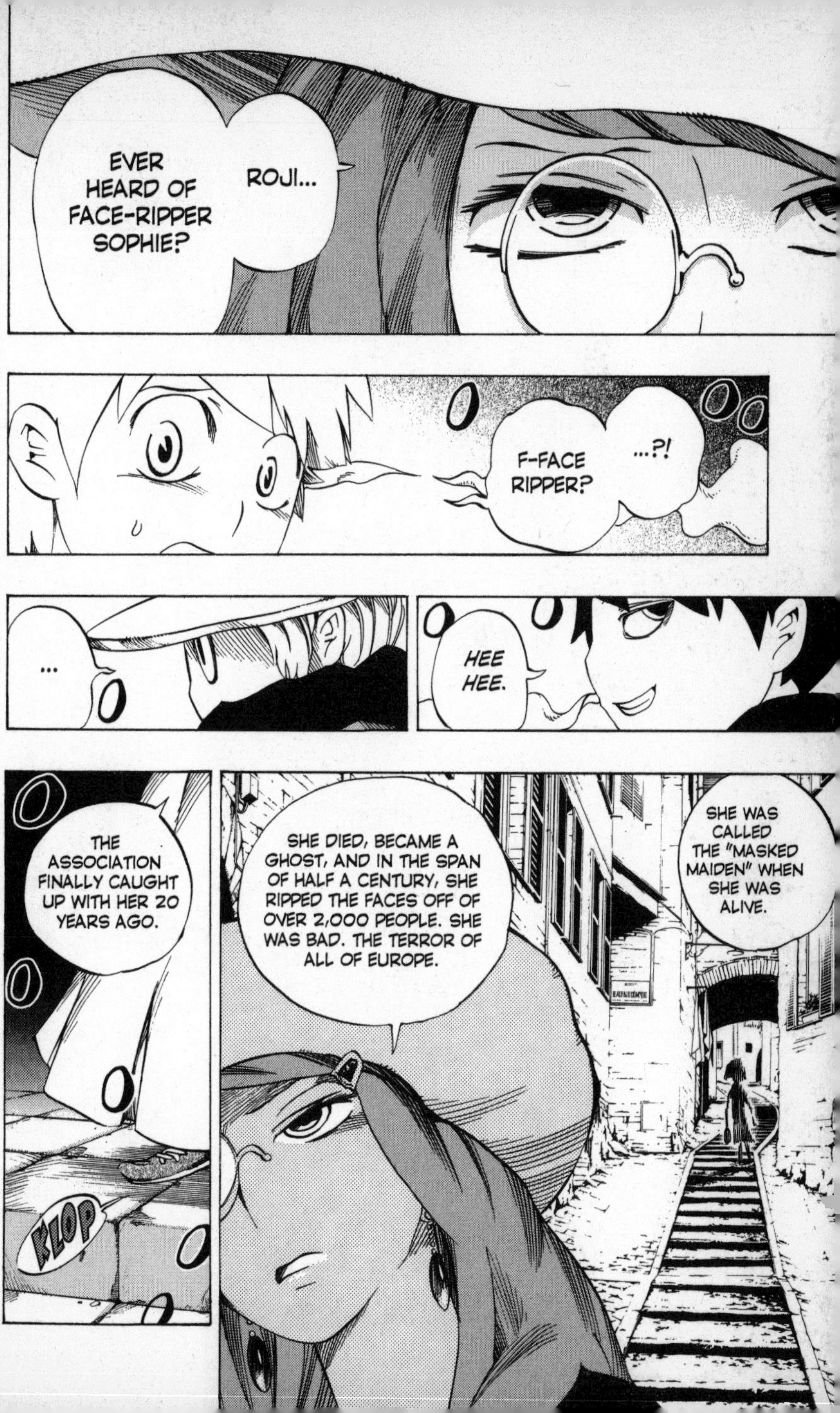
ROJI...
EVER HEARD OF FACE-RIPPER SOPHIE?
...?!
F-FACE RIPPER?
HEE HEE.
...
SHE WAS CALLED THE "MASKED MAIDEN" WHEN SHE WAS ALIVE.
SHE DIED, BECAME A GHOST, AND IN THE SPAN OF HALF A CENTURY, SHE RIPPED THE FACES OFF OF OVER 2,000 PEOPLE. SHE WAS BAD. THE TERROR OF ALL OF EUROPE.
THE ASSOCIATION FINALLY CAUGHT UP WITH HER 20 YEARS AGO.
KLOP

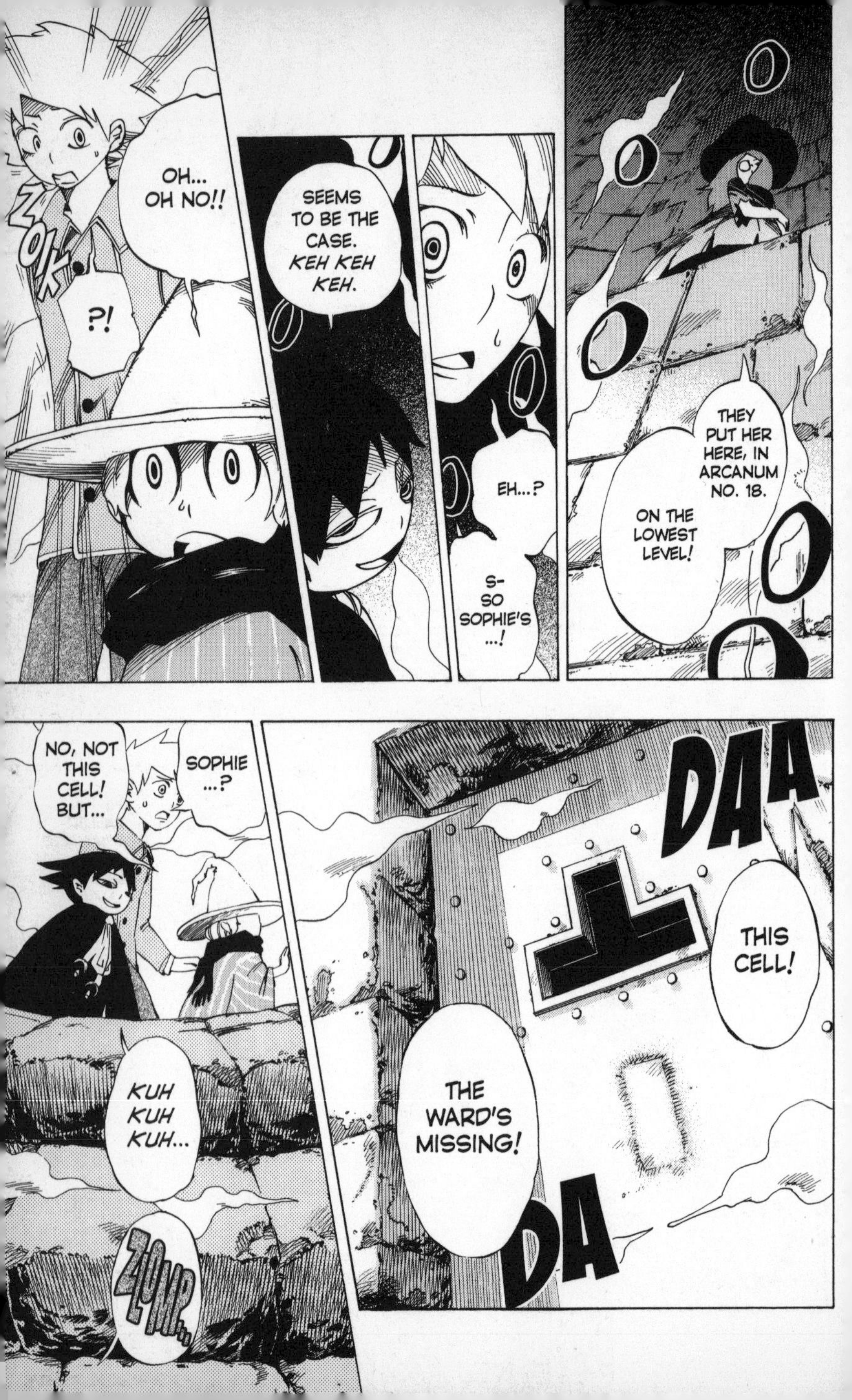
THEY PUT HER HERE, IN ARCANUM NO. 18.
ON THE LOWEST LEVEL!
EH...?
S-SO SOPHIE'S ...!
SEEMS TO BE THE CASE. KEH KEH KEH.
OH... OH NO!!
ZOK
?!
DAA
THIS CELL!
THE WARD'S MISSING!
DA
SOPHIE ...?
NO, NOT THIS CELL! BUT...
KUH KUH KUH...
ZUMP...

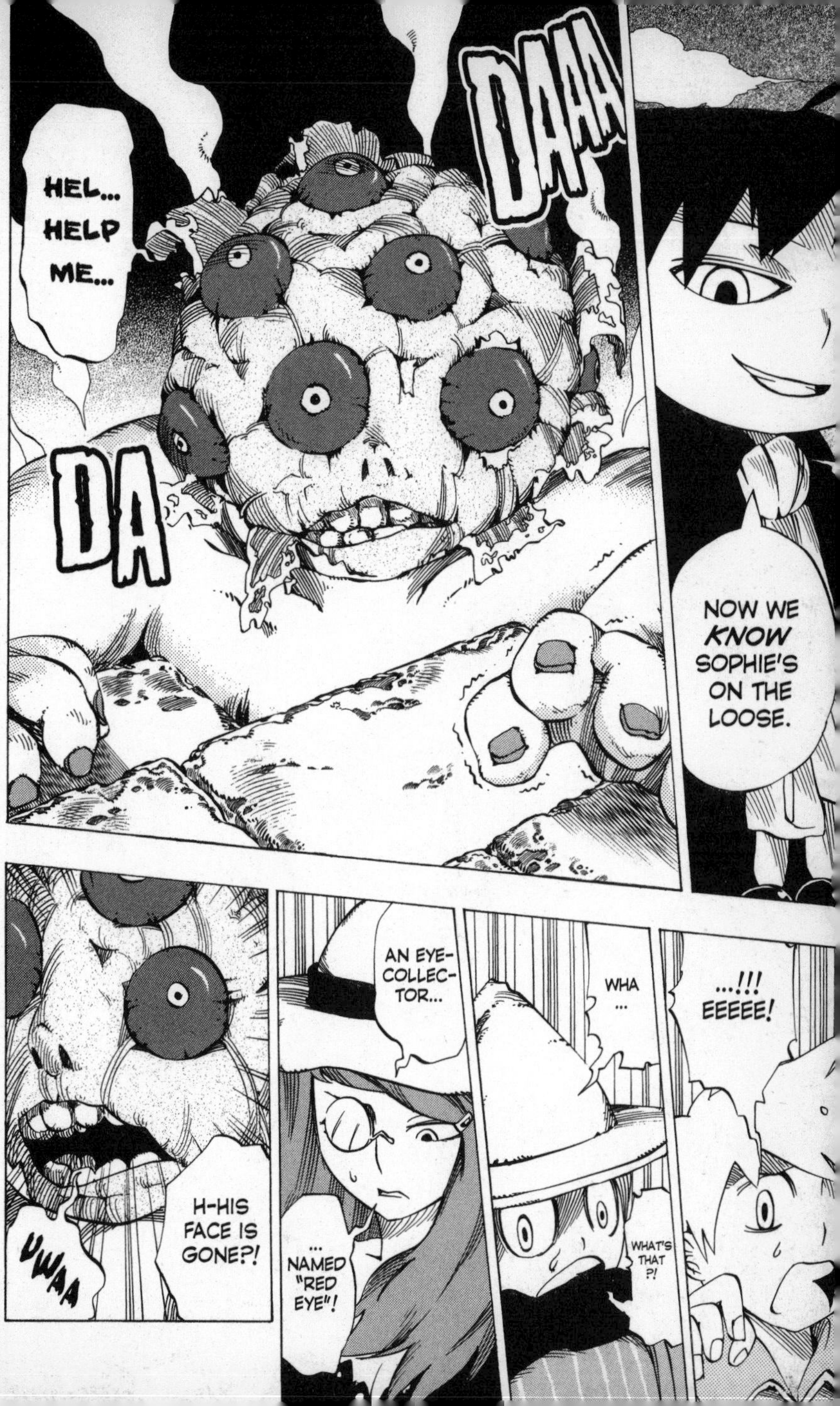

NOW WE KNOW SOPHIE'S ON THE LOOSE.
DAAA
HEL... HELP ME...
DA
...!!! EEEEE!
WHA ...
WHAT'S THAT ?!
AN EYE-COLLECTOR...
... NAMED "RED EYE"!
H-HIS FACE IS GONE?!
UWAA

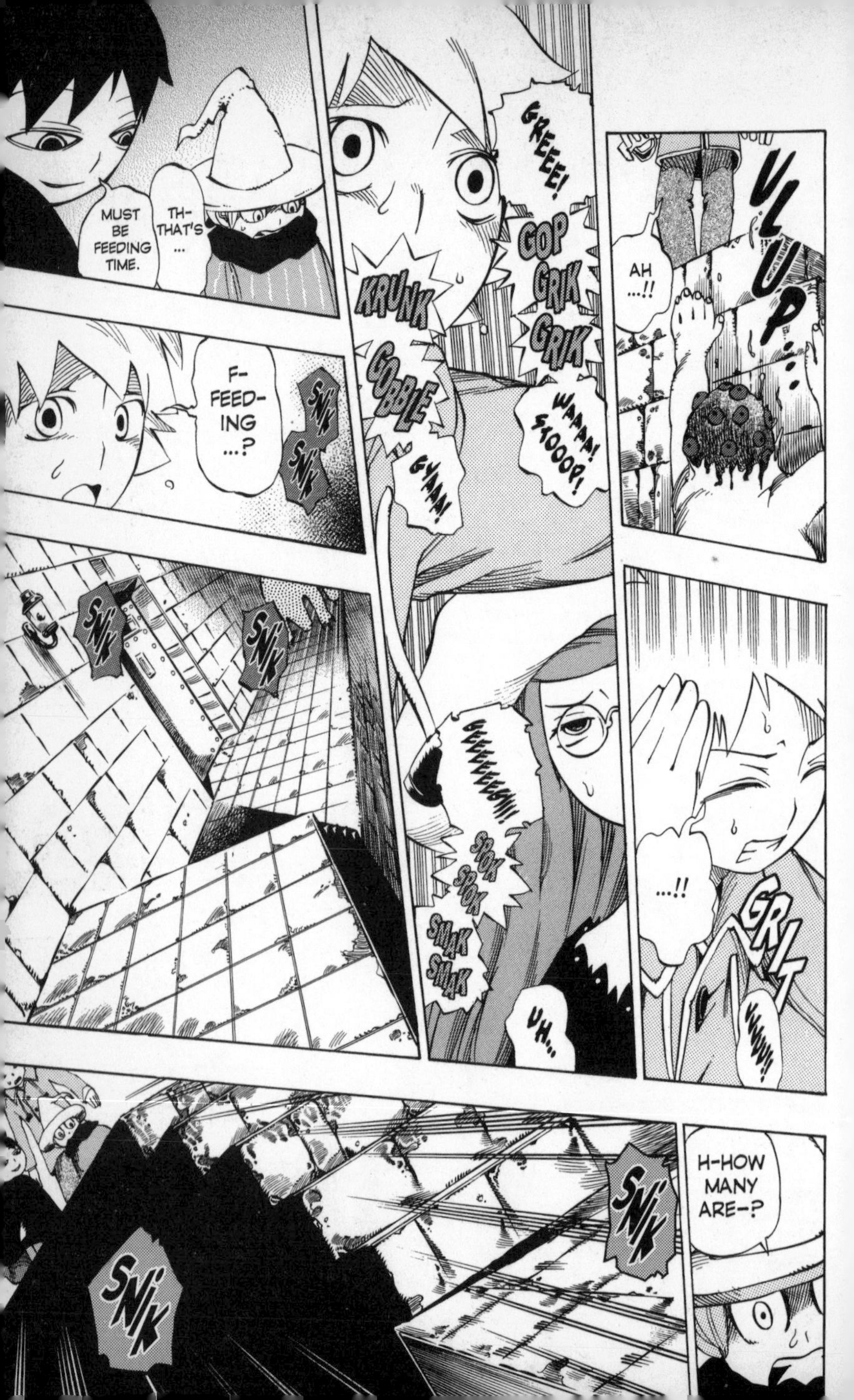
VLUP...
AH ...!!
GREEE!
GOP GRIK GRIK
WAPAA! $1000P!
KRUNK
GOBBLE
TH-THAT'S ...
MUST BE FEEDING TIME.
F-FEEDING ...?
SNIK SNIK
...!!
GRIT
SPOK SPOK
SMAK SMAK
UH...
SNIK
SNIK
H-HOW MANY ARE-?
SNIK
SNIK

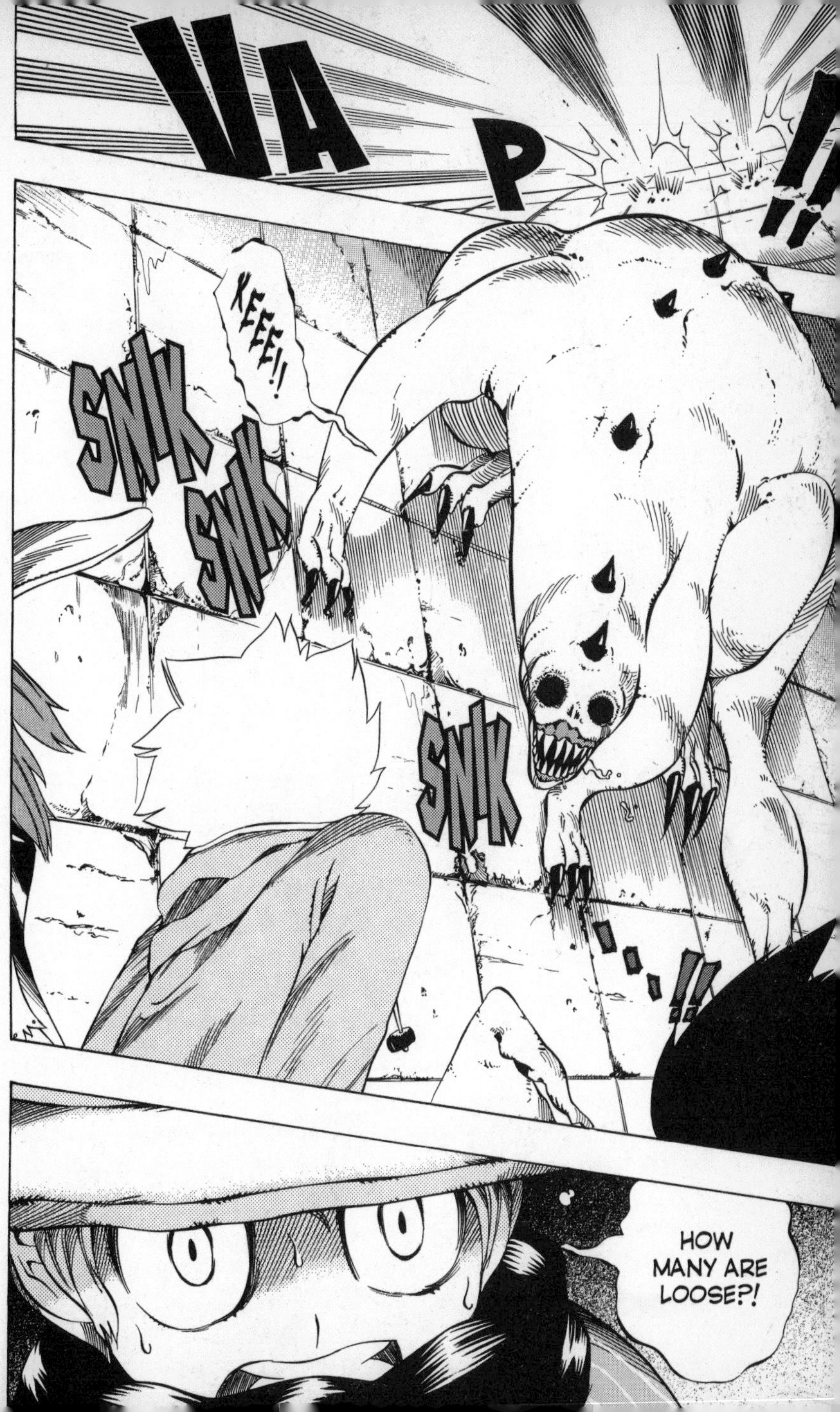
VAP!!
KEEE!!
SNIK
SNIK
SNIK
...!!
HOW MANY ARE LOOSE?!

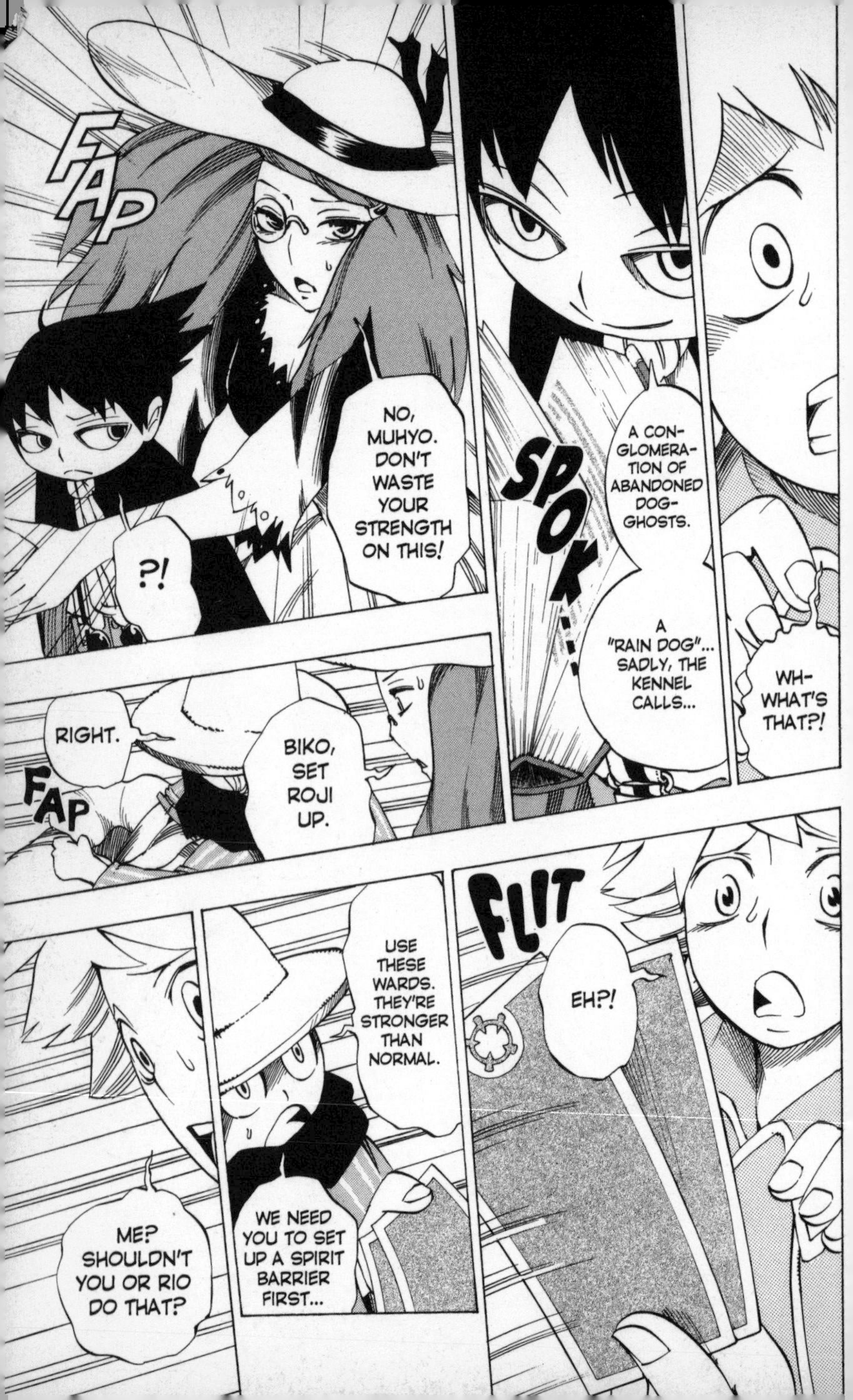
WH-WHAT'S THAT?!
SPOK...
A CONGLOMERATION OF ABANDONED DOG-GHOSTS.
A "RAIN DOG"... SADLY, THE KENNEL CALLS...
FAP
NO, MUHYO. DON'T WASTE YOUR STRENGTH ON THIS!
?!
BIKO, SET ROJI UP.
RIGHT.
FAP
FLIT
EH?!
USE THESE WARDS. THEY'RE STRONGER THAN NORMAL.
WE NEED YOU TO SET UP A SPIRIT BARRIER FIRST...
ME? SHOULDN'T YOU OR RIO DO THAT?

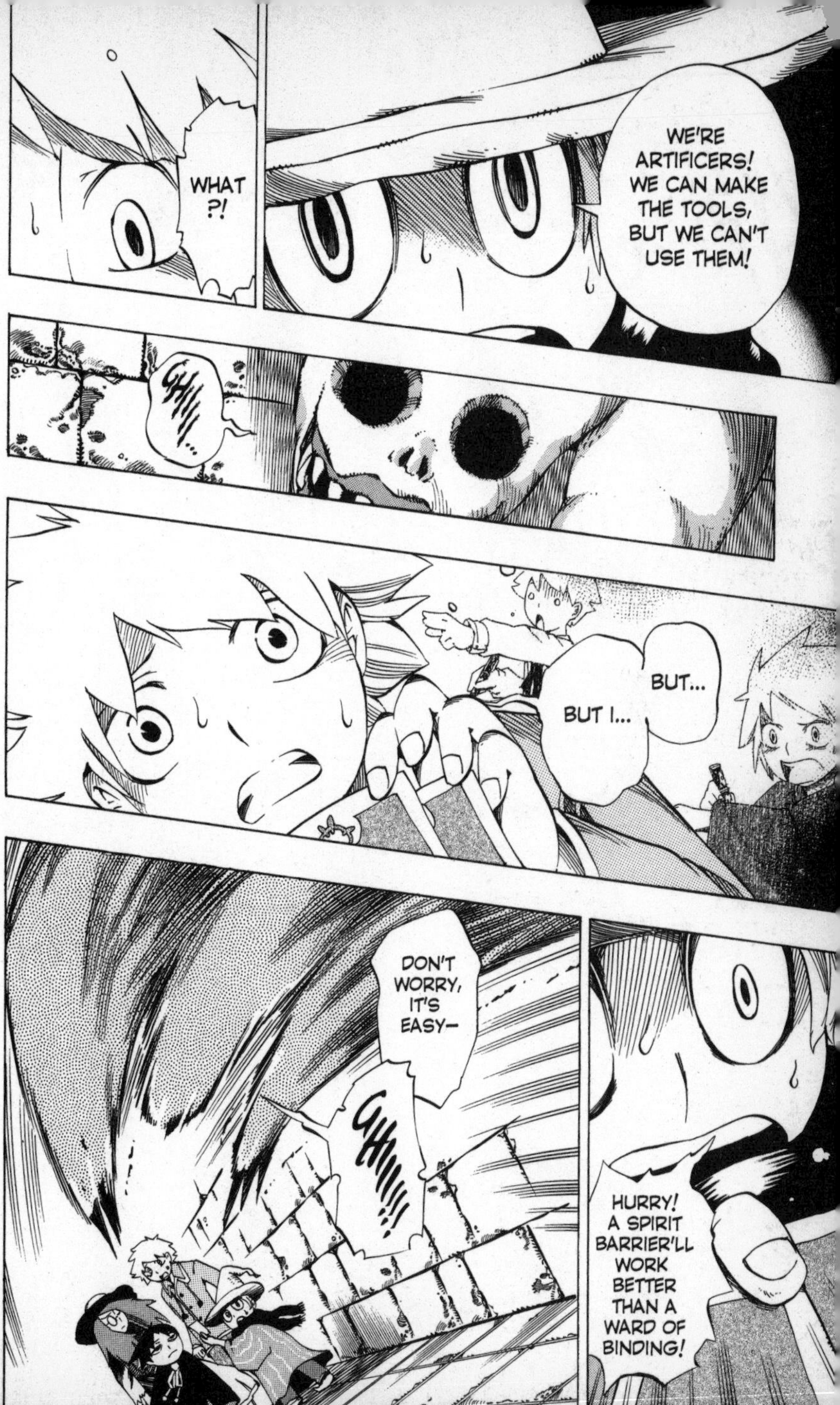
WE'RE ARTIFICERS! WE CAN MAKE THE TOOLS, BUT WE CAN'T USE THEM!
WHAT ?!
BUT...
BUT I...
HURRY! A SPIRIT BARRIER'LL WORK BETTER THAN A WARD OF BINDING!
DON'T WORRY, IT'S EASY—

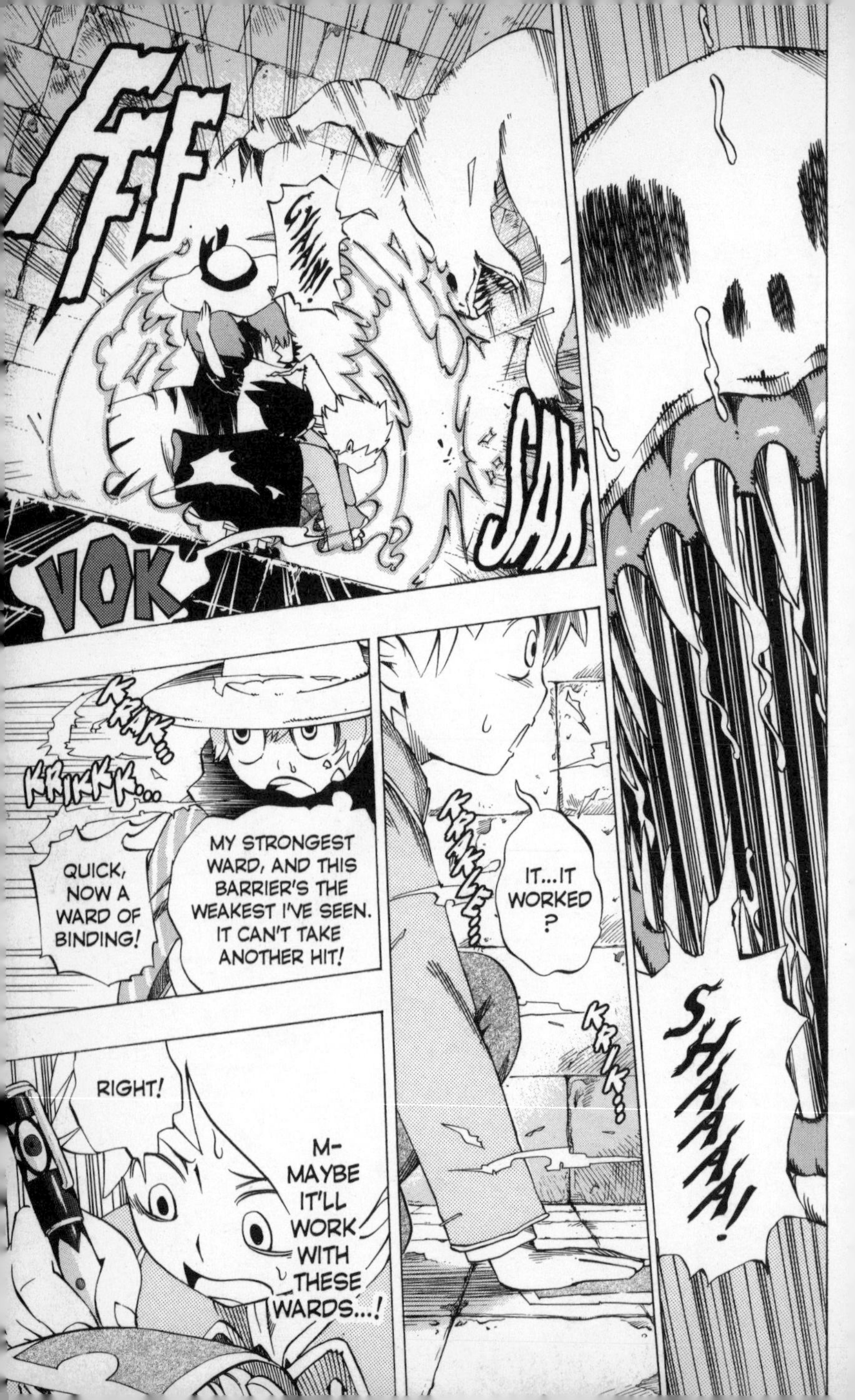
SHAAAAA!
GYAAAN!
SAK
FF
VOK
IT...IT WORKED?
KRAKKLE...
KRIK...
KRAK...
KRIKKK...
MY STRONGEST WARD, AND THIS BARRIER'S THE WEAKEST I'VE SEEN. IT CAN'T TAKE ANOTHER HIT!
QUICK, NOW A WARD OF BINDING!
M-MAYBE IT'LL WORK WITH THESE WARDS...!
RIGHT!

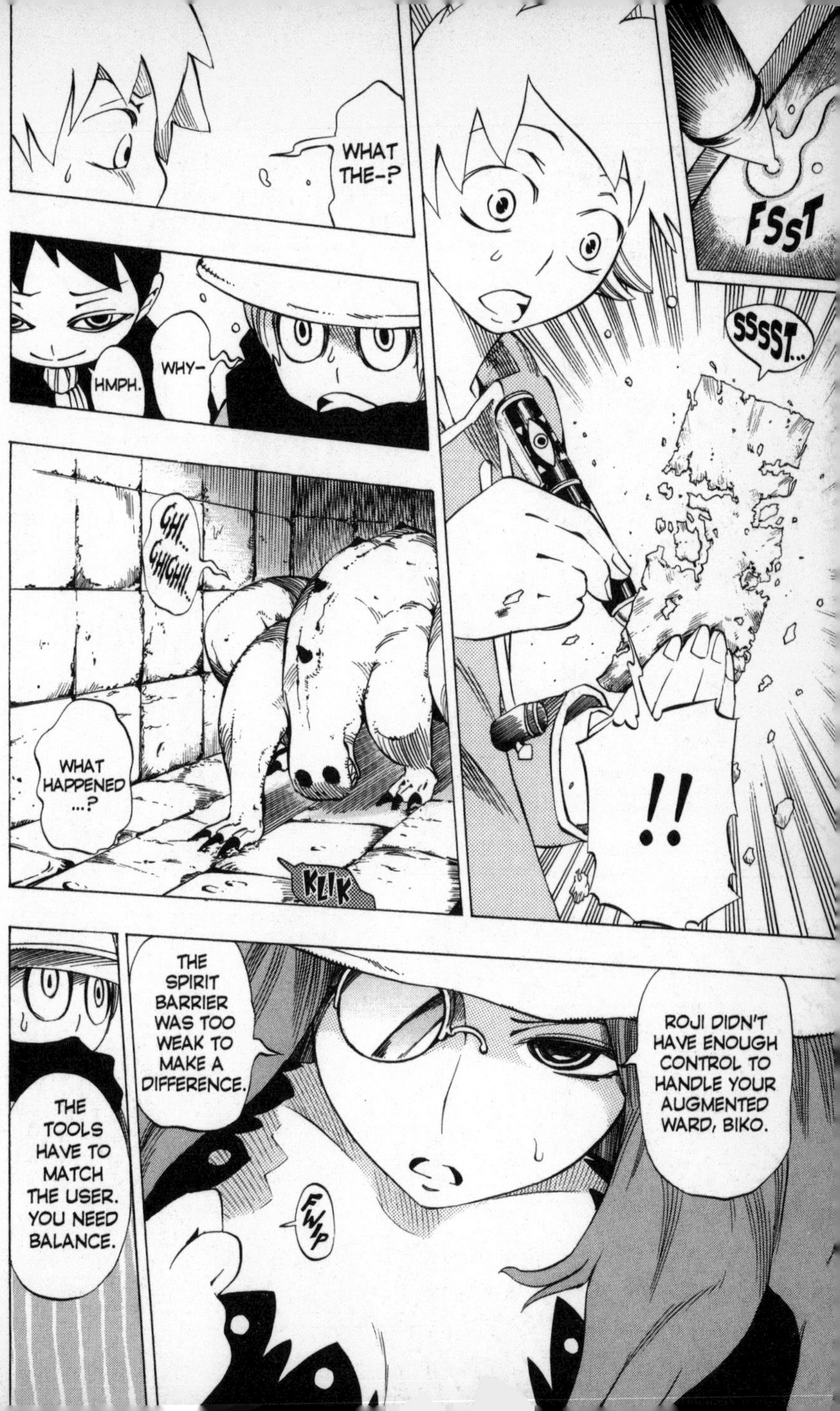
FSST
SSSST...
!!
WHAT THE-?
WHY-
HMPH.
GHI... GHIGH!!
WHAT HAPPENED ...?
KLIK
ROJI DIDN'T HAVE ENOUGH CONTROL TO HANDLE YOUR AUGMENTED WARD, BIKO.
THE SPIRIT BARRIER WAS TOO WEAK TO MAKE A DIFFERENCE.
FWIP
THE TOOLS HAVE TO MATCH THE USER. YOU NEED BALANCE.

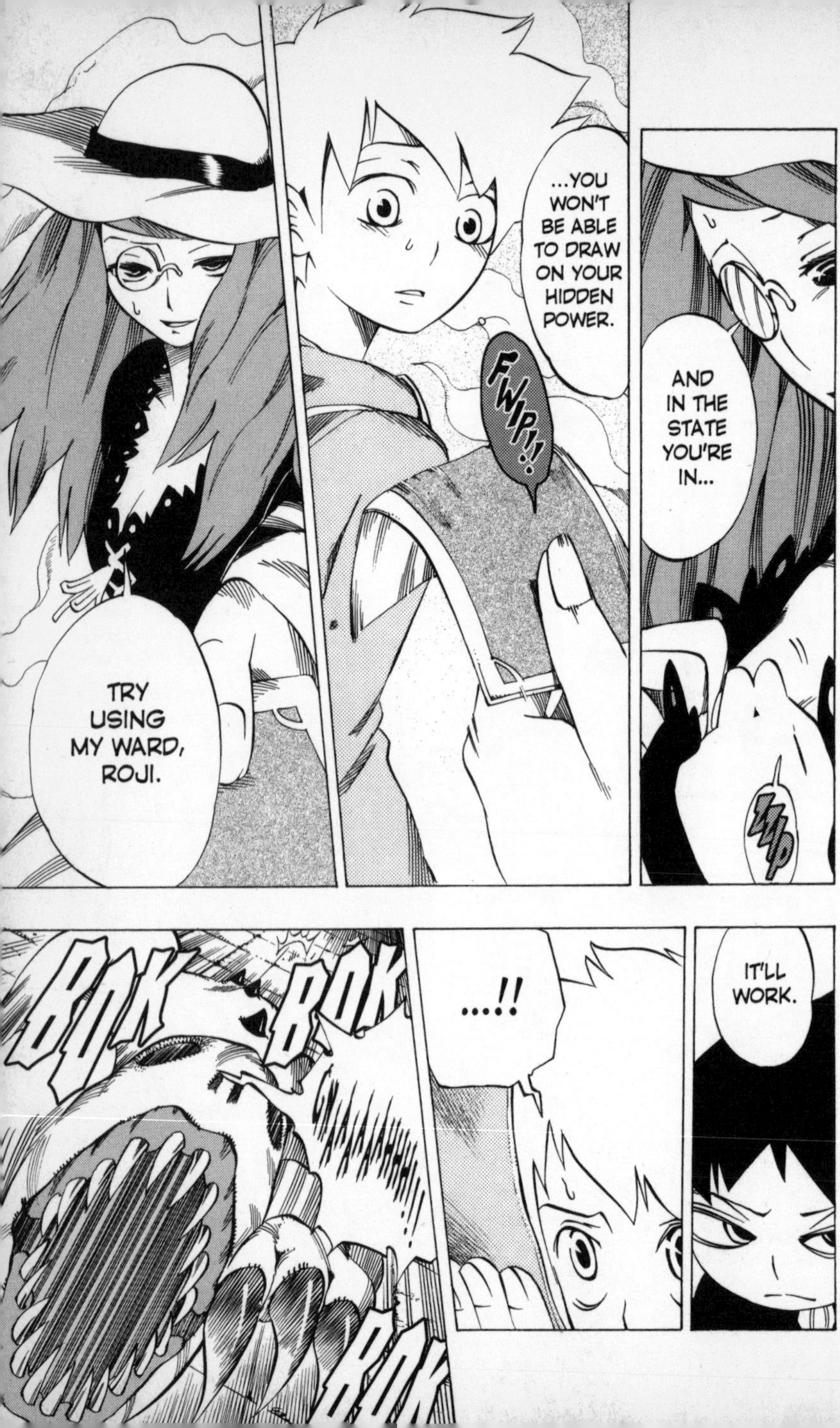
AND IN THE STATE YOU'RE IN...
ZIP
...YOU WON'T BE ABLE TO DRAW ON YOUR HIDDEN POWER.
FWIP!!
TRY USING MY WARD, ROJI.
IT'LL WORK.
...!!
BOK
BOK
BOK

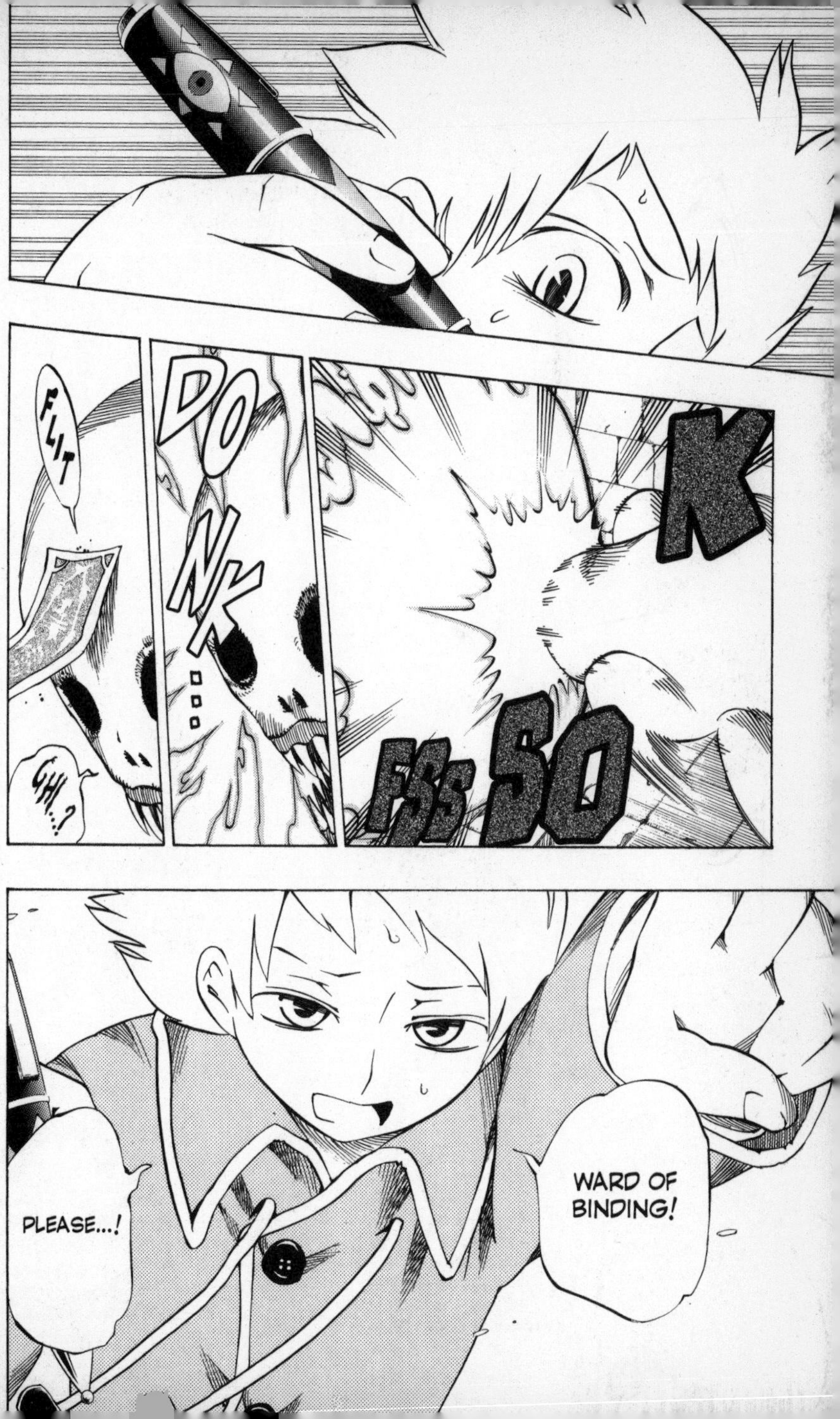
K
FSS SO
DONK...
FLIT
GHI...?
WARD OF BINDING!
PLEASE...!

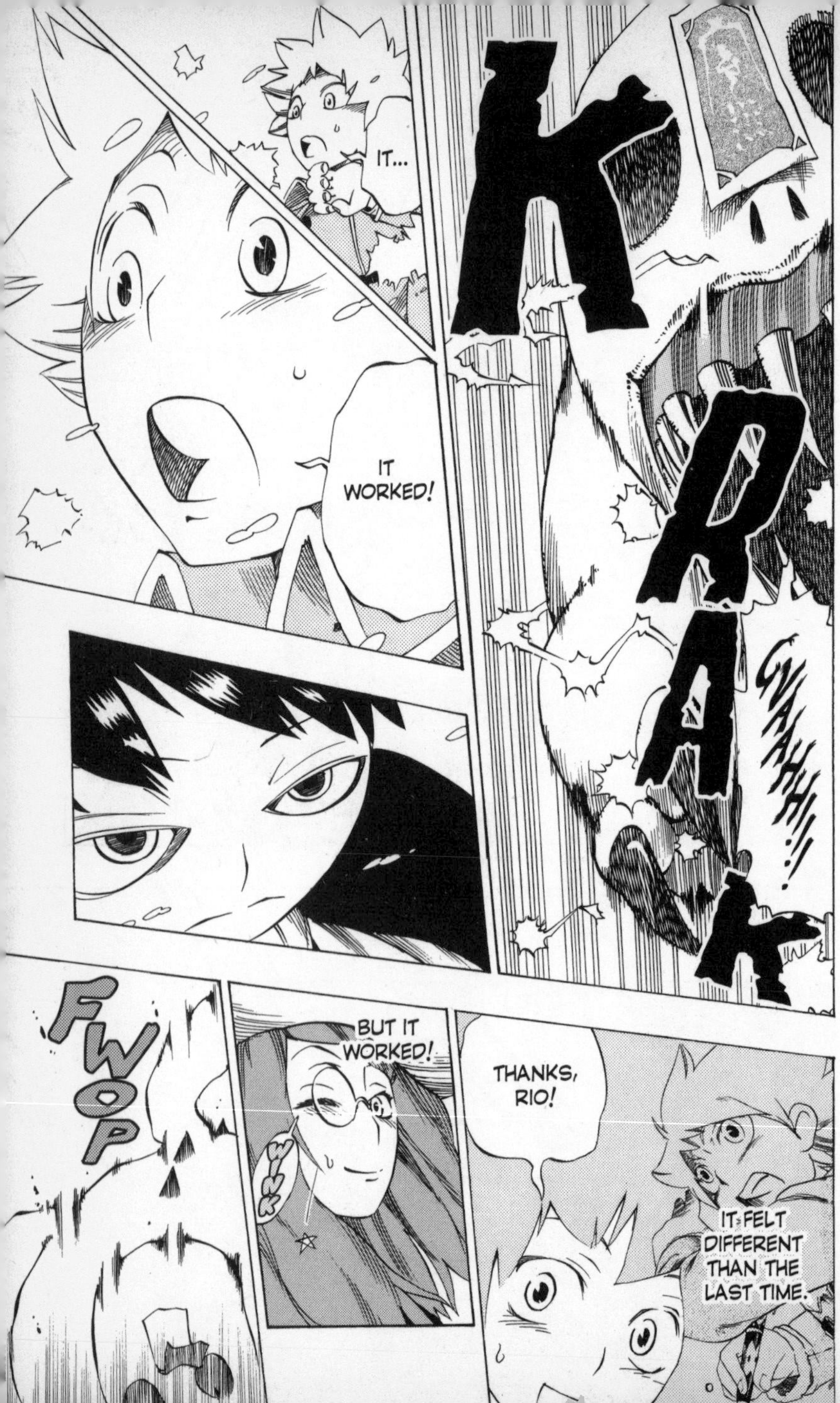
KRAK
GNAAHH!!!
IT...
IT WORKED!
THANKS, RIO!
IT FELT DIFFERENT THAN THE LAST TIME.
BUT IT WORKED!
WINK
FWOP

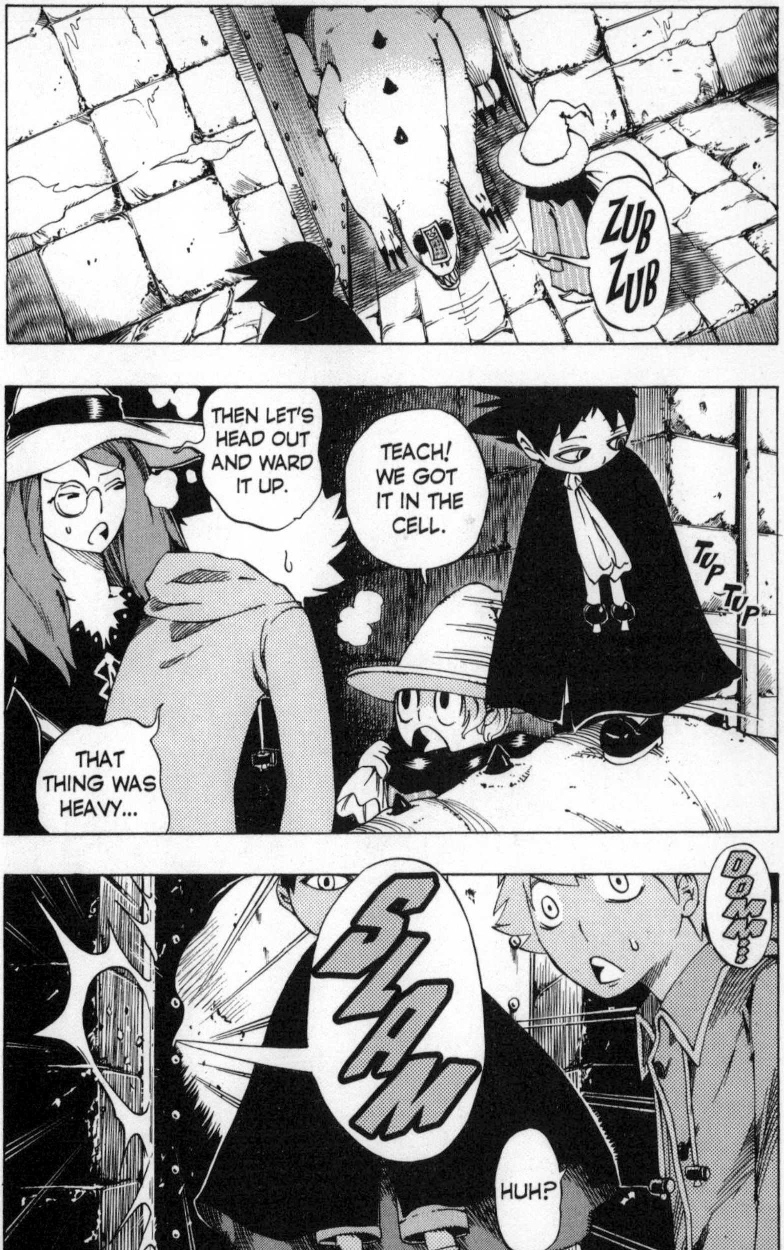
ZUB ZUB
TUP TUP
TEACH! WE GOT IT IN THE CELL.
THEN LET'S HEAD OUT AND WARD IT UP.
THAT THING WAS HEAVY...
DOMM...
SLAM
HUH?

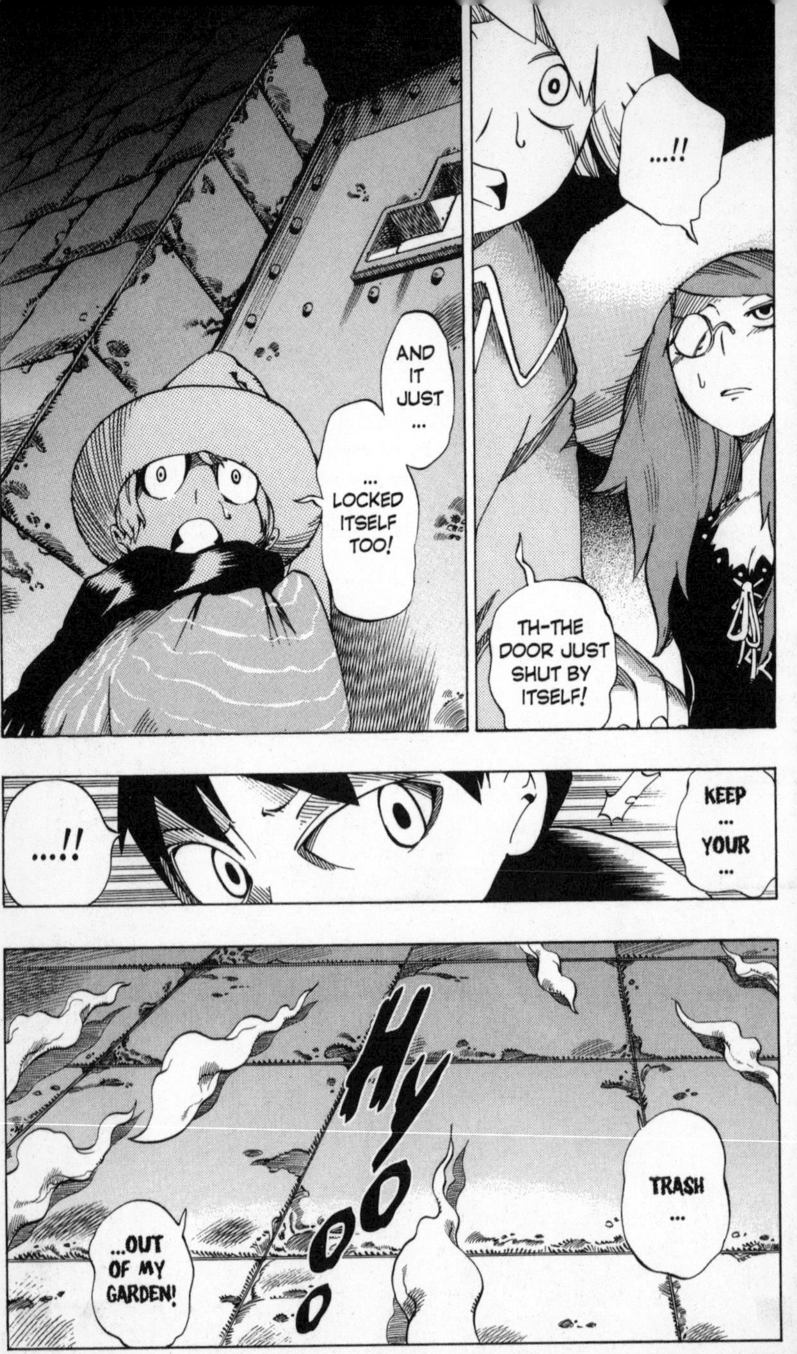
...!!
TH-THE DOOR JUST SHUT BY ITSELF!
AND IT JUST ...
... LOCKED ITSELF TOO!
KEEP ... YOUR ...
...!!
TRASH ...
HYOOOO
...OUT OF MY GARDEN!

Q: DO MUHYO AND ROJI LIVE TOGETHER AT THE OFFICE? WHAT DO THEY DO ON THEIR DAYS OFF?

A: YES, THEY LIVE IN THE OFFICE. ON DAYS OFF? WELL, THEY'RE NOT THAT BUSY NORMALLY ANYWAY... BUT THEY PROBABLY DEVOUR THE LATEST ISSUE OF *JABIN*, THEN ROJI DOES THE LAUNDRY AND SHOPPING, AND MUHYO TAKES A NAP. MAYBE THEY GO FOR A WALK. THEN THEY READ BOOKS AT A USED BOOKSTORE AND SAY "HI" TO THE GHOSTS THEY SEE LURKING AFTER PASSERSBY. HEE HEE! WHO KNOWS WHAT THEY'RE UP TO?! :)

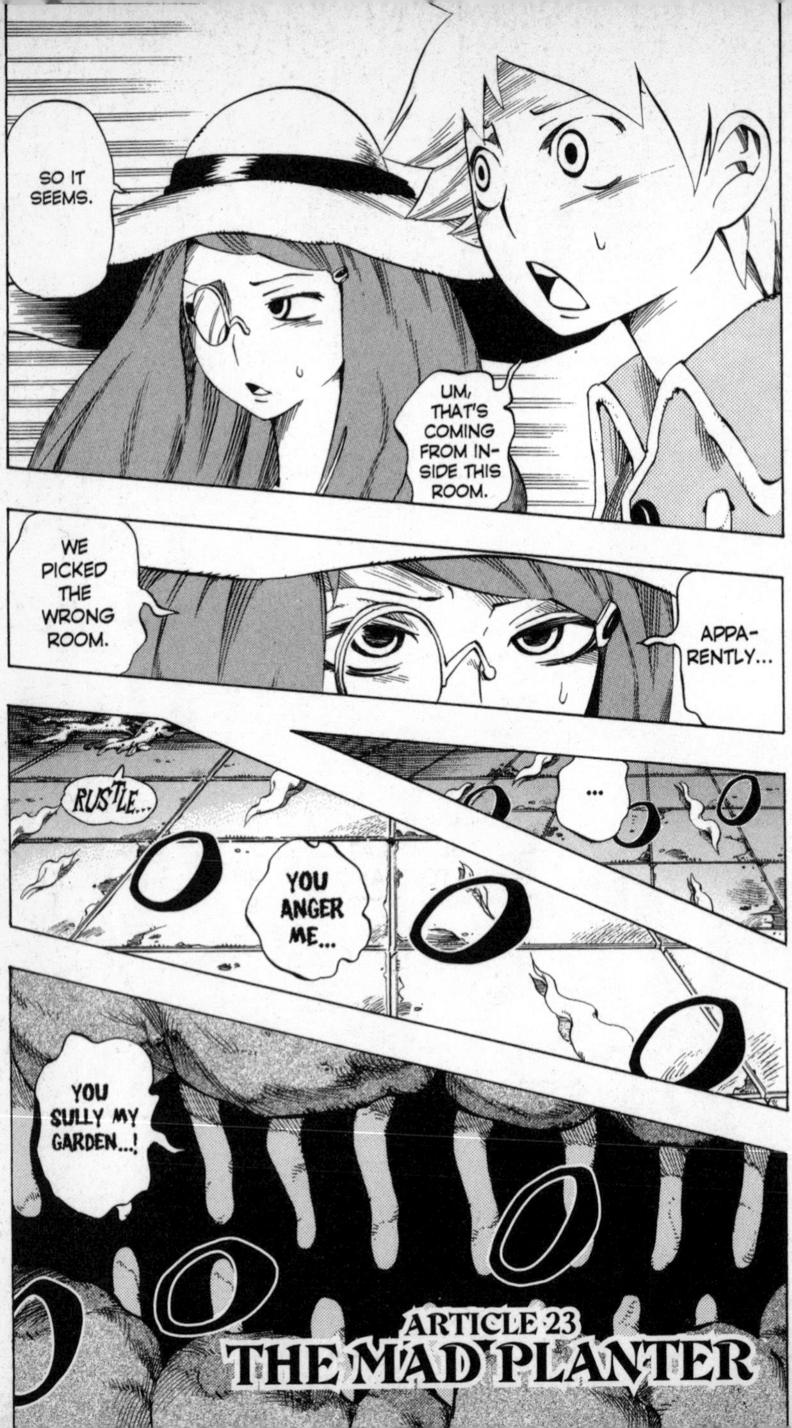
UM, THAT'S COMING FROM INSIDE THIS ROOM.
SO IT SEEMS.
APPARENTLY...
WE PICKED THE WRONG ROOM.
...
YOU ANGER ME...
RUSTLE...
YOU SULLY MY GARDEN...!
ARTICLE 23
THE MAD PLANTER

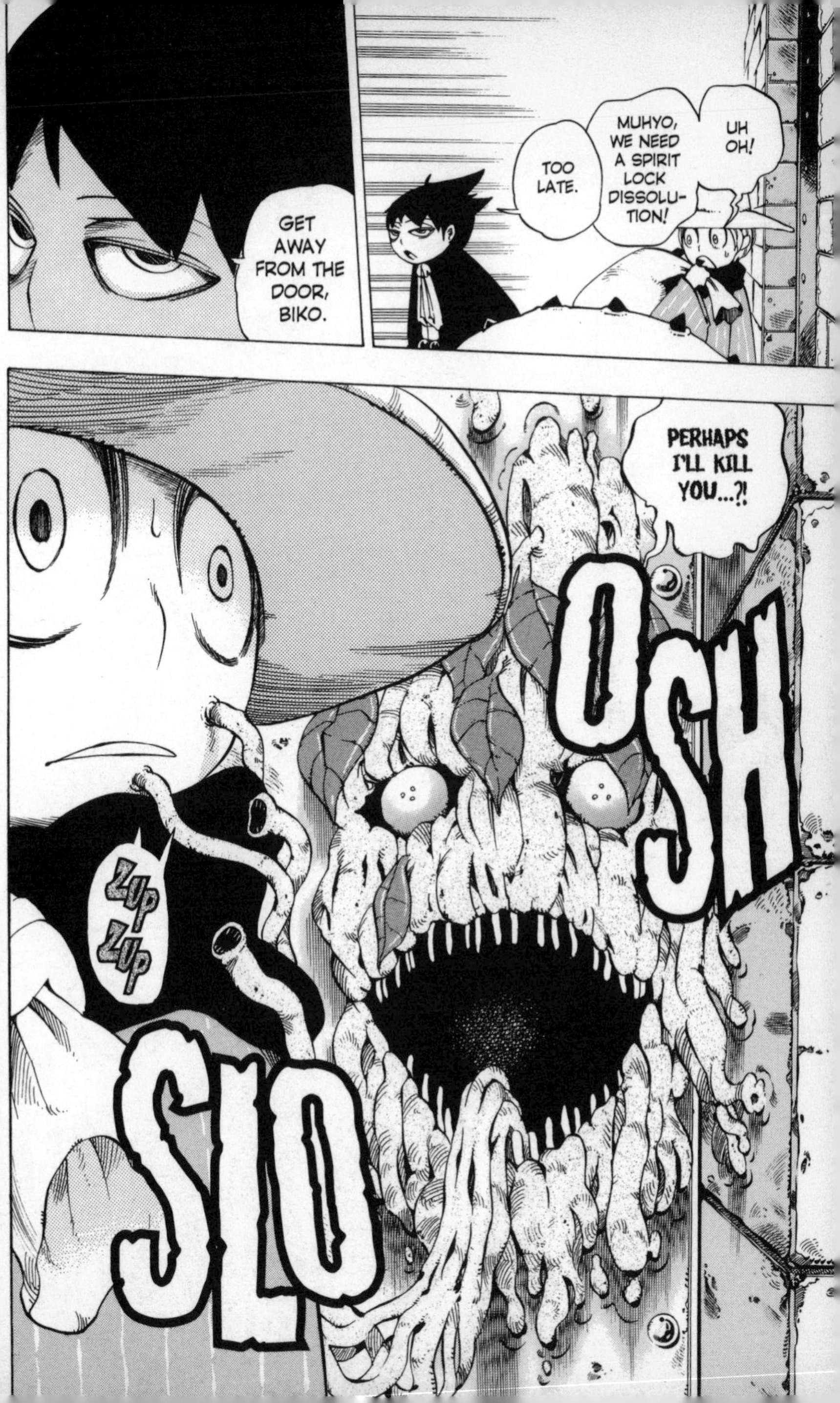
UH OH!
MUHYO, WE NEED A SPIRIT LOCK DISSOLUTION!
TOO LATE.
GET AWAY FROM THE DOOR, BIKO.
PERHAPS I'LL KILL YOU...?!
OSH
ZUP ZUP
SLO

ARTICLE 23
THE MAD PLANTER

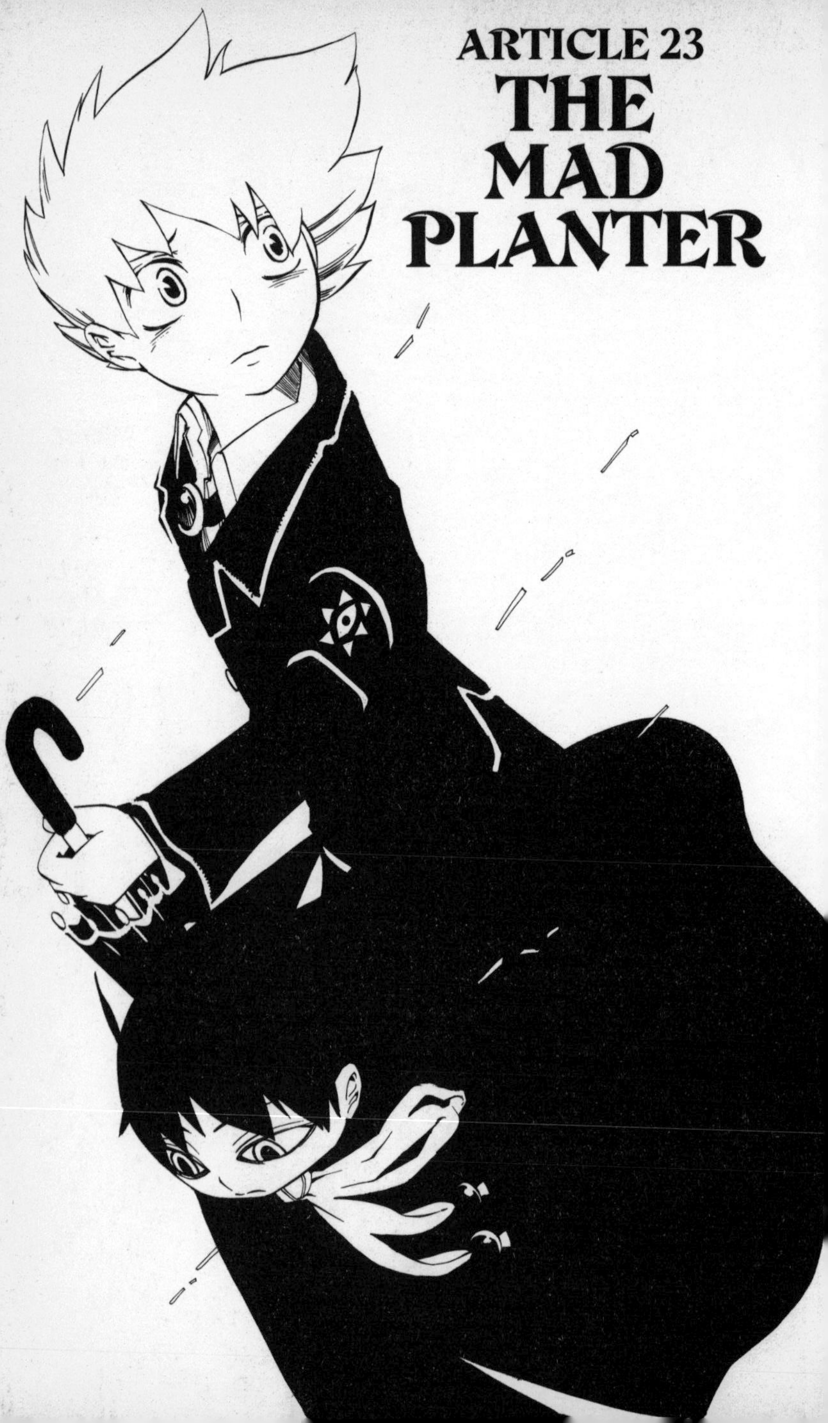

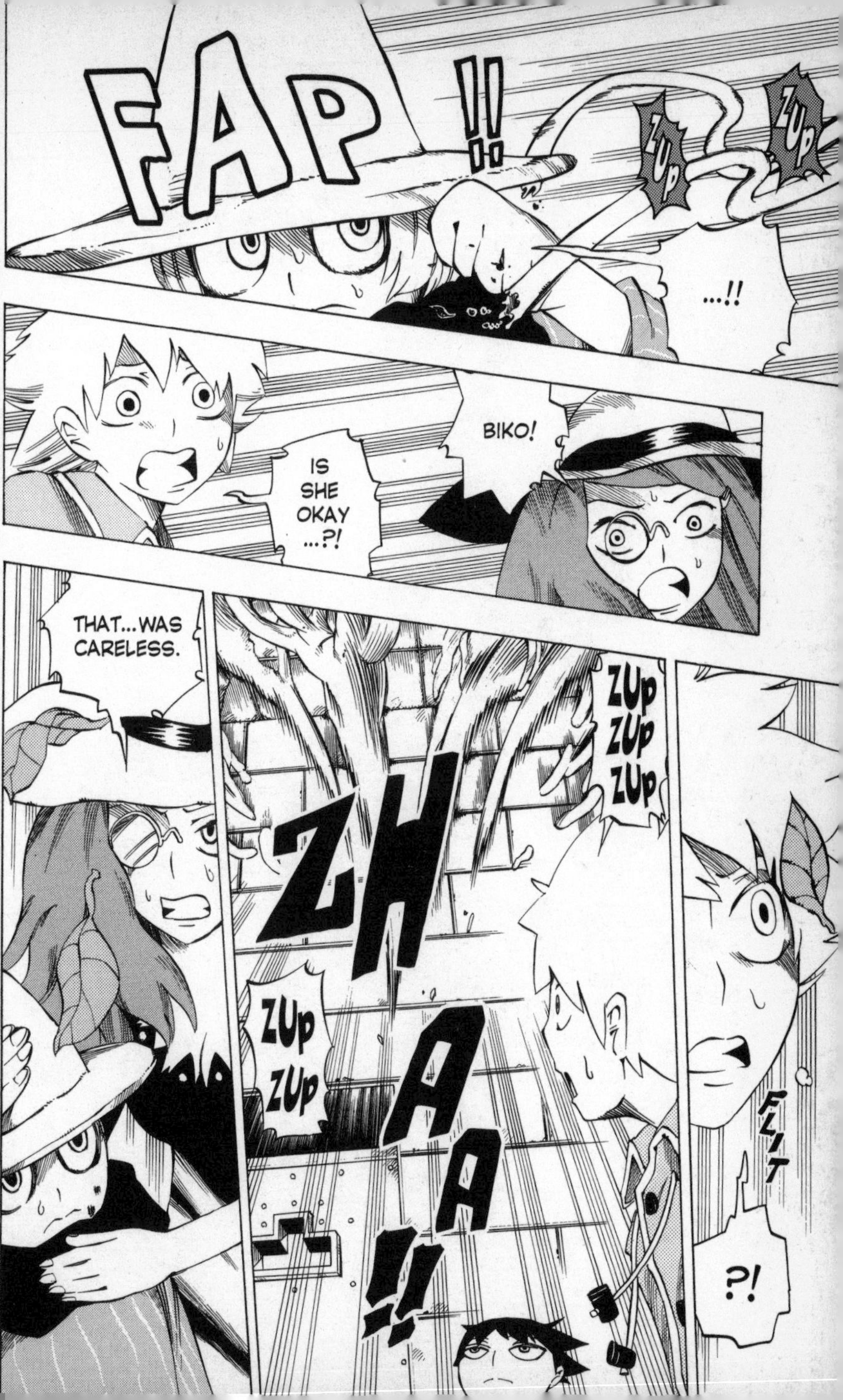
ZUP
ZUP
FAP!!
...!!
BIKO!
IS SHE OKAY ...?!
FLIT
?!
ZUP ZUP ZUP
ZHAA!!
ZUP ZUP
THAT...WAS CARELESS.

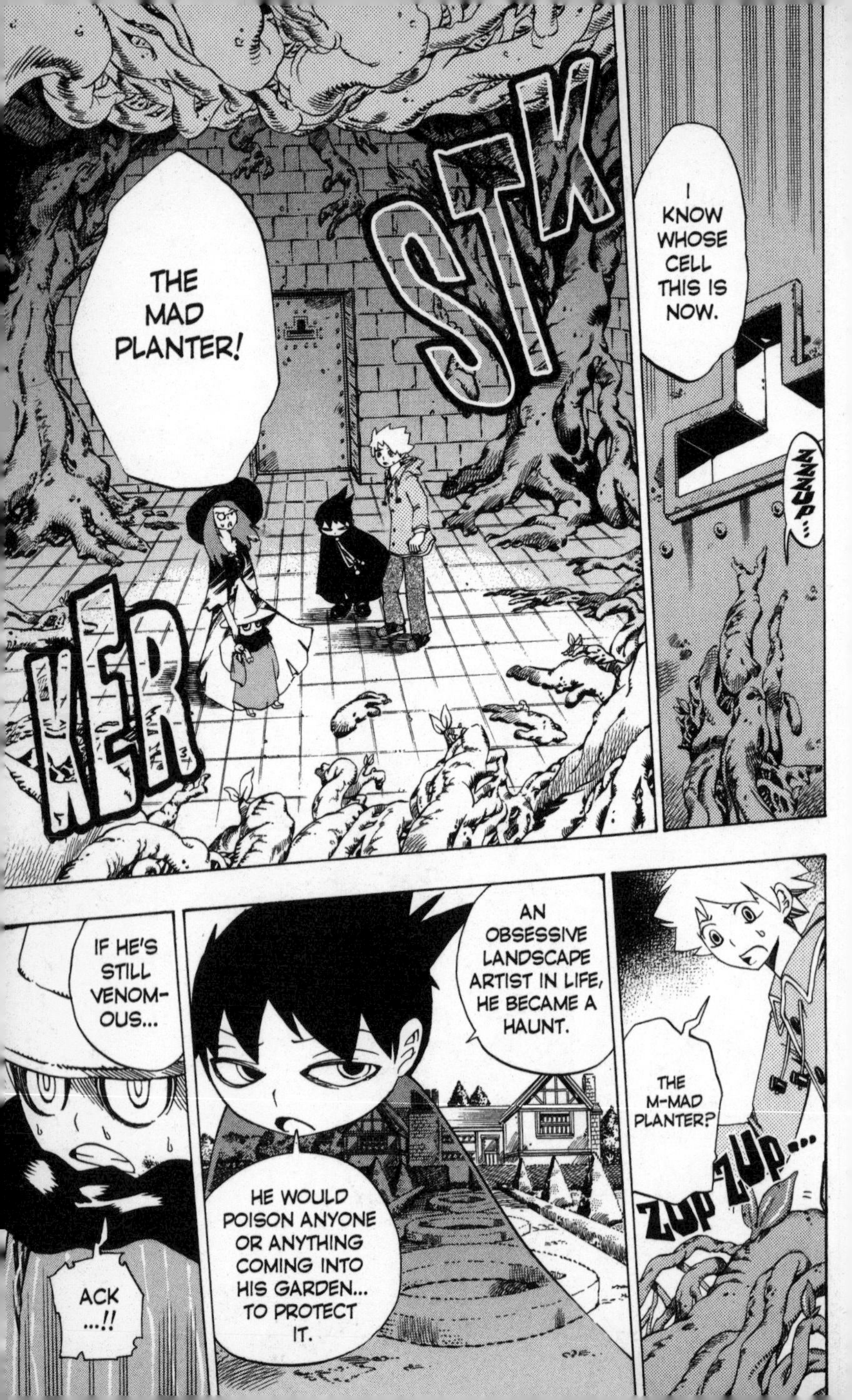
I KNOW WHOSE CELL THIS IS NOW.
ZZZZUP...
STK
THE MAD PLANTER!
KER
THE M-MAD PLANTER?
ZUP ZUP...
AN OBSESSIVE LANDSCAPE ARTIST IN LIFE, HE BECAME A HAUNT.
HE WOULD POISON ANYONE OR ANYTHING COMING INTO HIS GARDEN... TO PROTECT IT.
IF HE'S STILL VENOM-OUS...
ACK ...!!

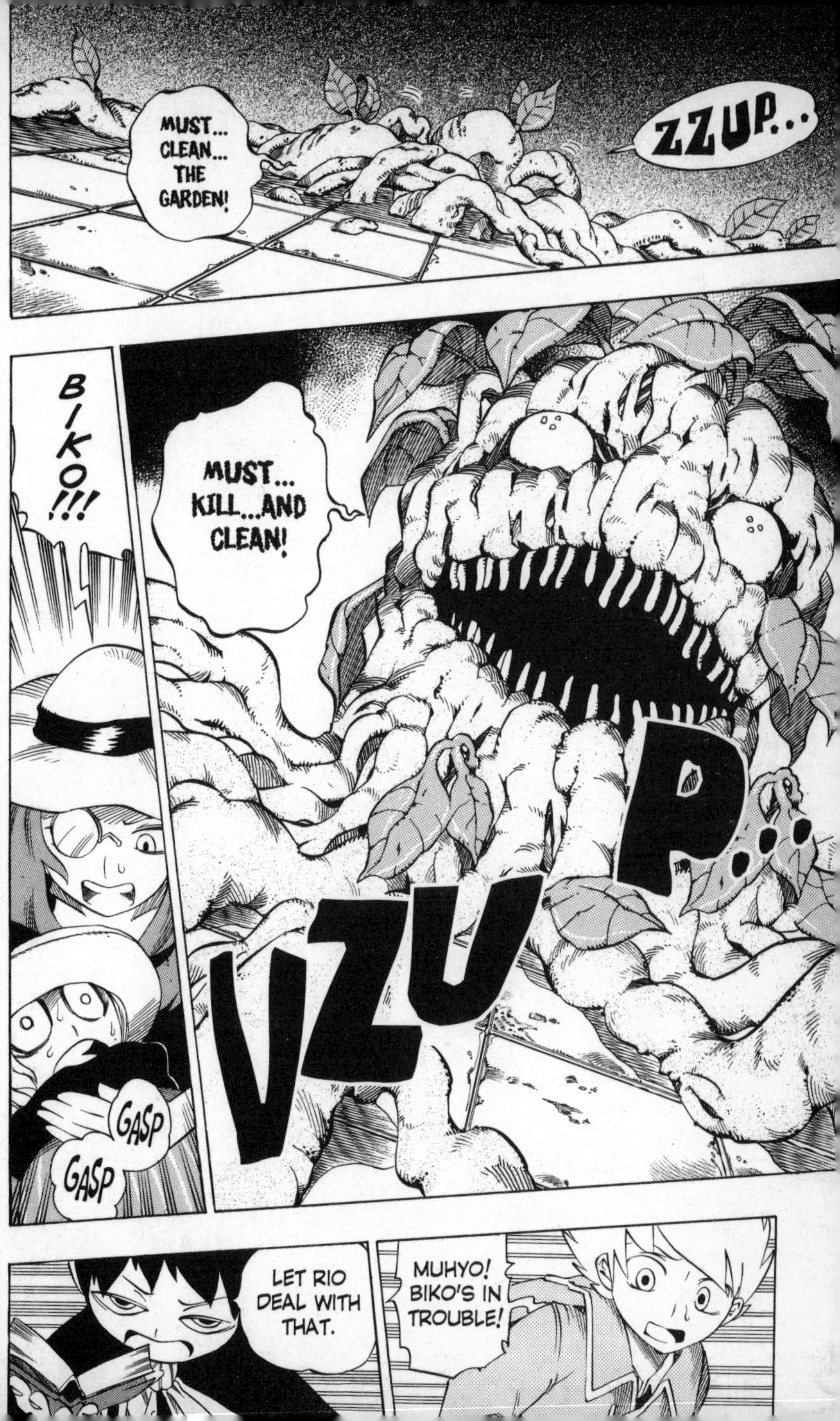
ZZUP...
MUST... CLEAN... THE GARDEN!
MUST... KILL...AND CLEAN!
VZUP...
BIKO!!!
GASP
GASP
MUHYO! BIKO'S IN TROUBLE!
LET RIO DEAL WITH THAT.

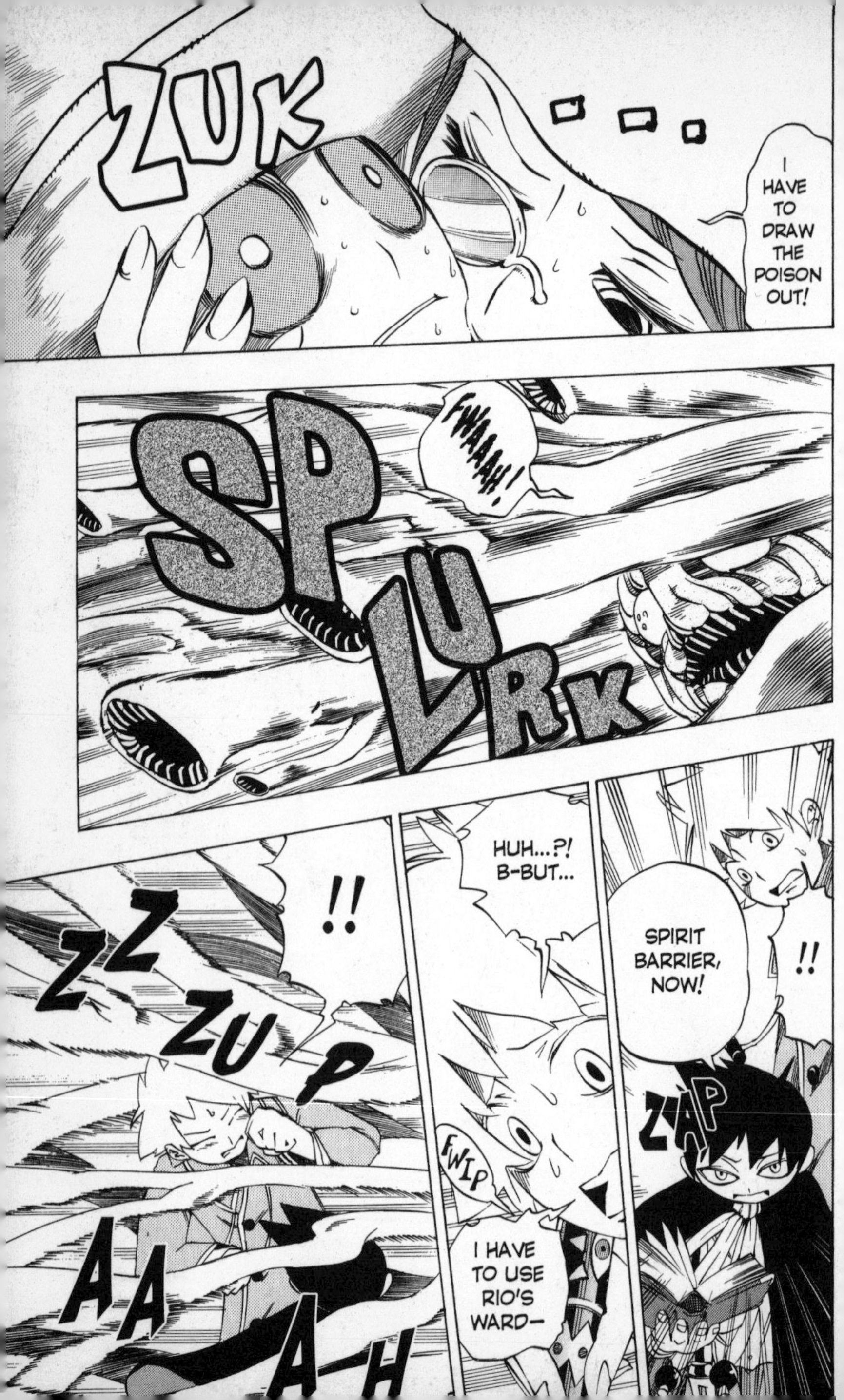
. . .
I HAVE TO DRAW THE POISON OUT!
ZUK
FWAAAH!
SPLURK
!!
SPIRIT BARRIER, NOW!
ZAP
HUH...?! B-BUT...
FWIP
I HAVE TO USE RIO'S WARD—
!!
ZZZUP
AAAAH

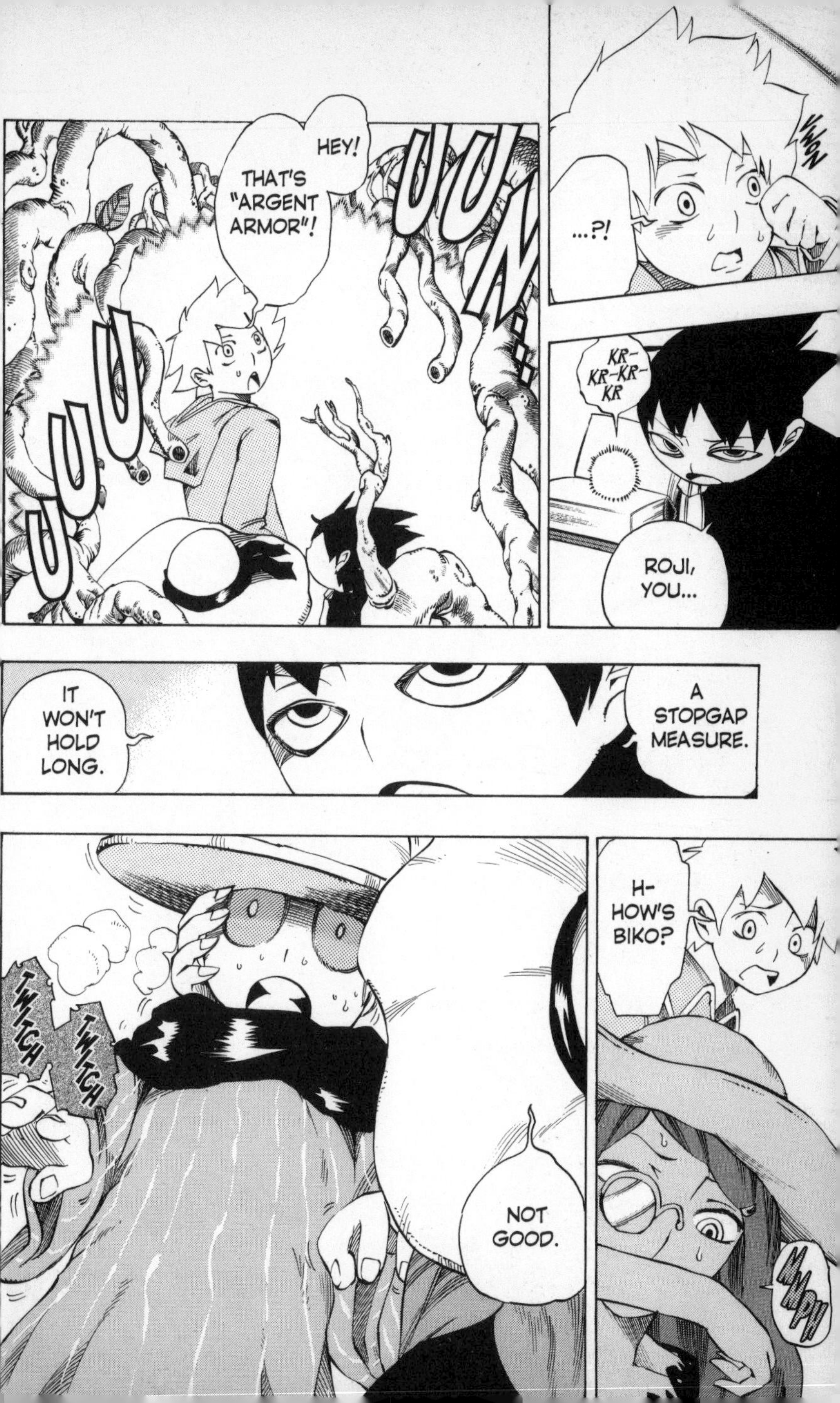

VWON
...?!
KR-KR-KR-KR
ROJI, YOU...
HEY!
THAT'S "ARGENT ARMOR"!
UUN..
UUU
A STOPGAP MEASURE.
IT WON'T HOLD LONG.
H-HOW'S BIKO?
MMPH
TWITCH
TWITCH
NOT GOOD.

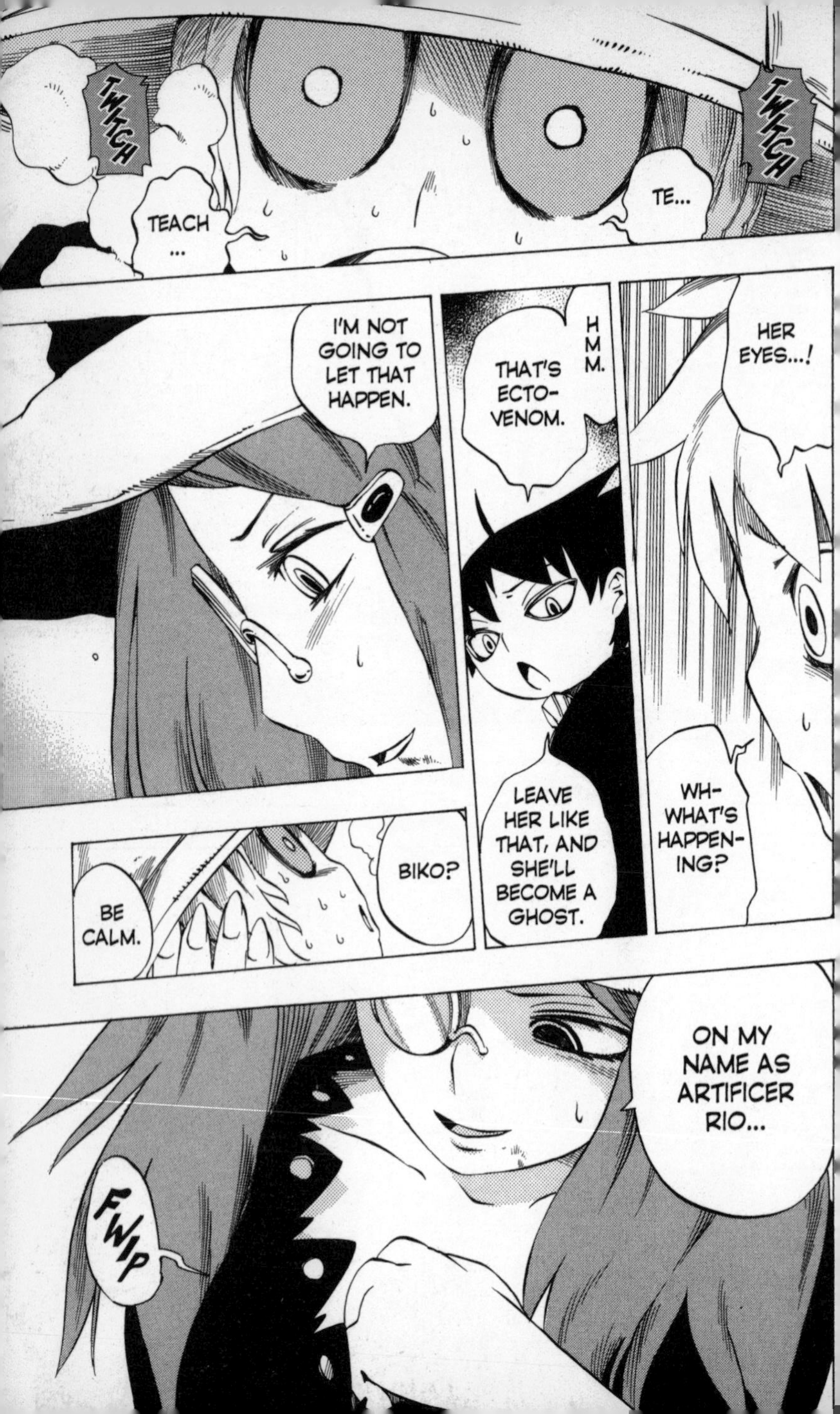
TWITCH
TE...
TEACH ...
TWITCH
HER EYES...!
WH-WHAT'S HAPPEN-ING?
HMM.
THAT'S ECTO-VENOM.
LEAVE HER LIKE THAT, AND SHE'LL BECOME A GHOST.
I'M NOT GOING TO LET THAT HAPPEN.
BIKO?
BE CALM.
ON MY NAME AS ARTIFICER RIO...
FWIP

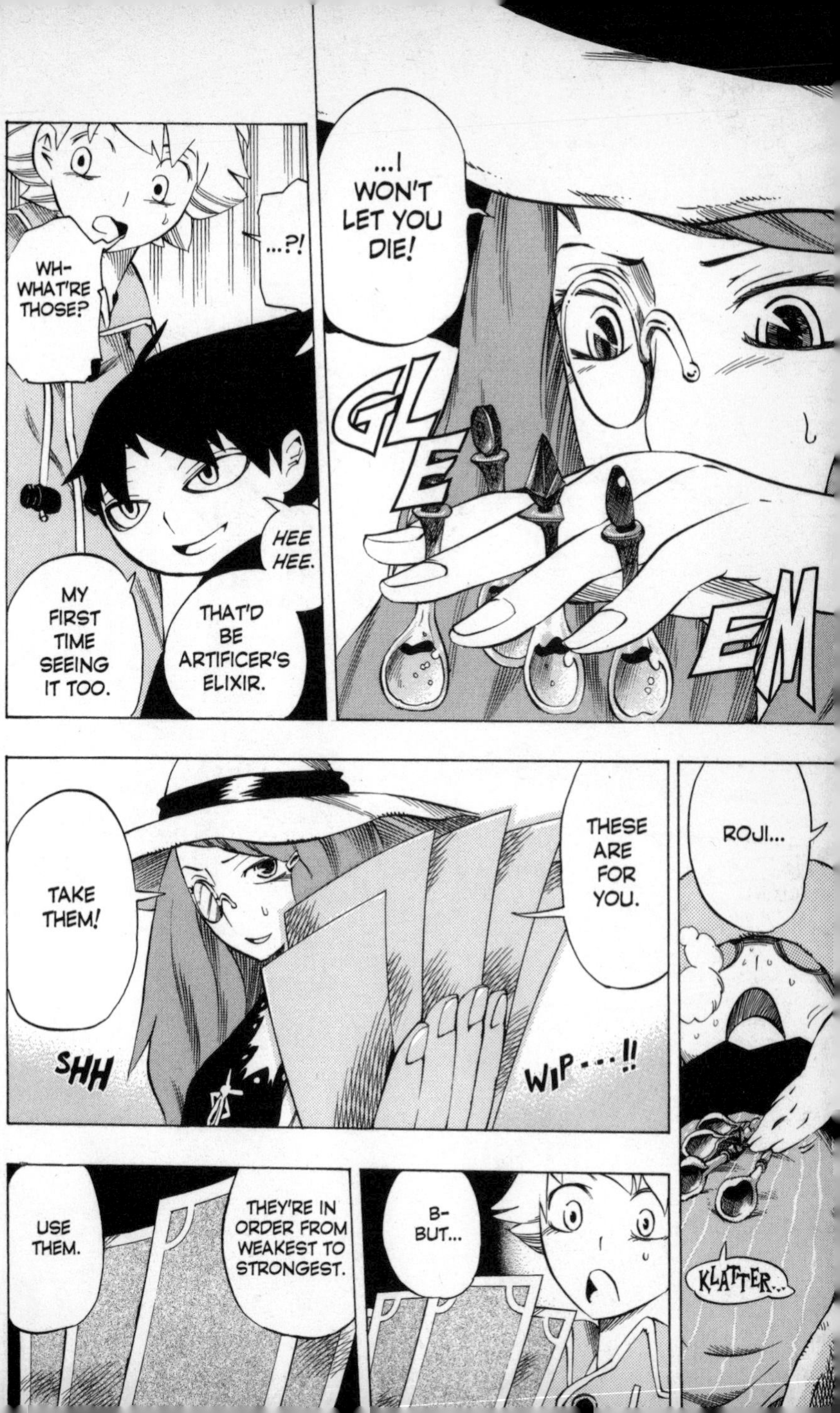
...I WON'T LET YOU DIE!
GLEEM
...?!
WH- WHAT'RE THOSE?
HEE HEE.
THAT'D BE ARTIFICER'S ELIXIR.
MY FIRST TIME SEEING IT TOO.
ROJI...
KLATTER...
THESE ARE FOR YOU.
WIP...!!
TAKE THEM!
SHH
B- BUT...
THEY'RE IN ORDER FROM WEAKEST TO STRONGEST.
USE THEM.

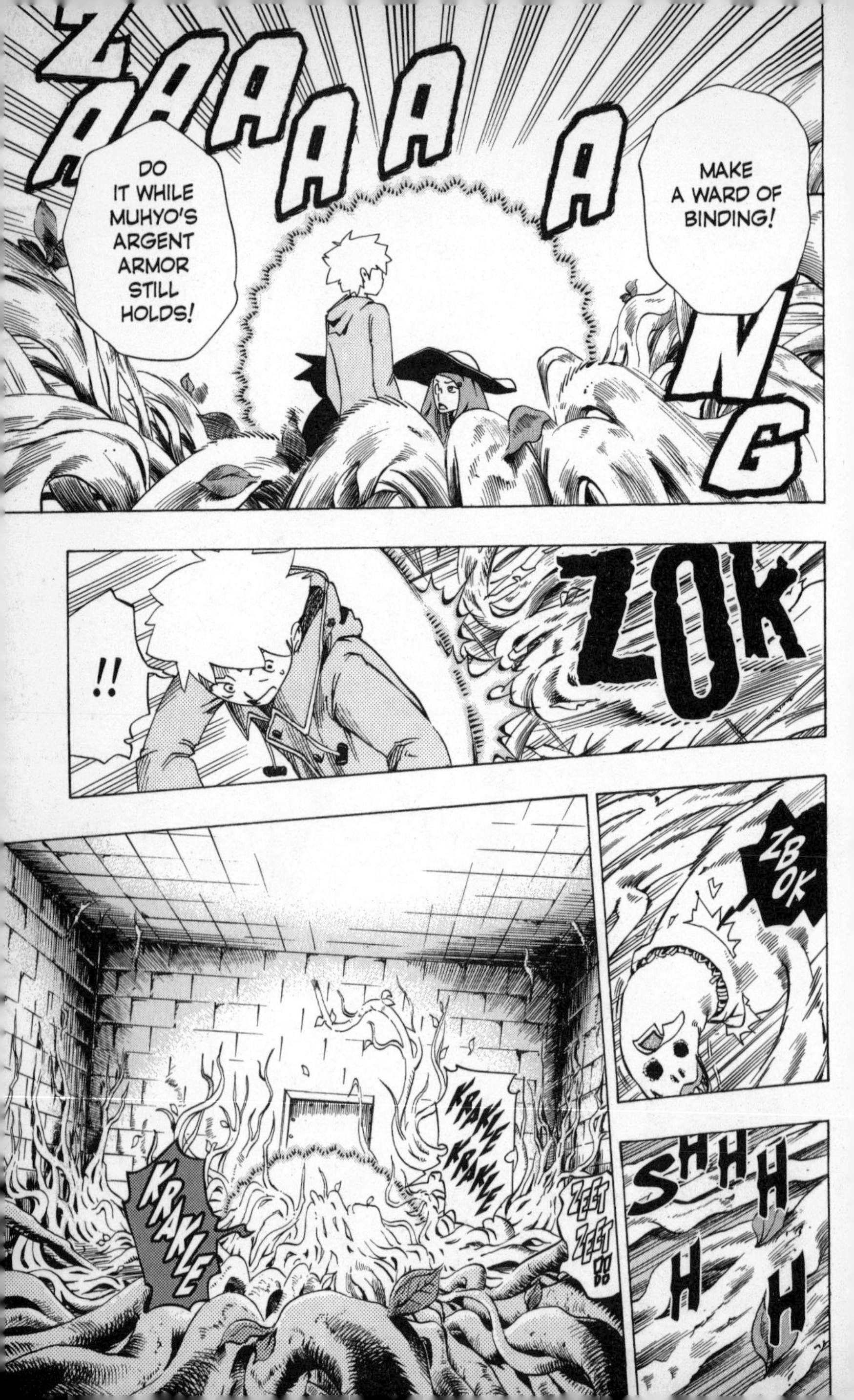
ZAAAAAAANG
MAKE A WARD OF BINDING!
DO IT WHILE MUHYO'S ARGENT ARMOR STILL HOLDS!
ZOK
!!
ZBOK
SHHHHHH
KRAKLE KRAKLE
ZEEST ZEEST
KRAKLE

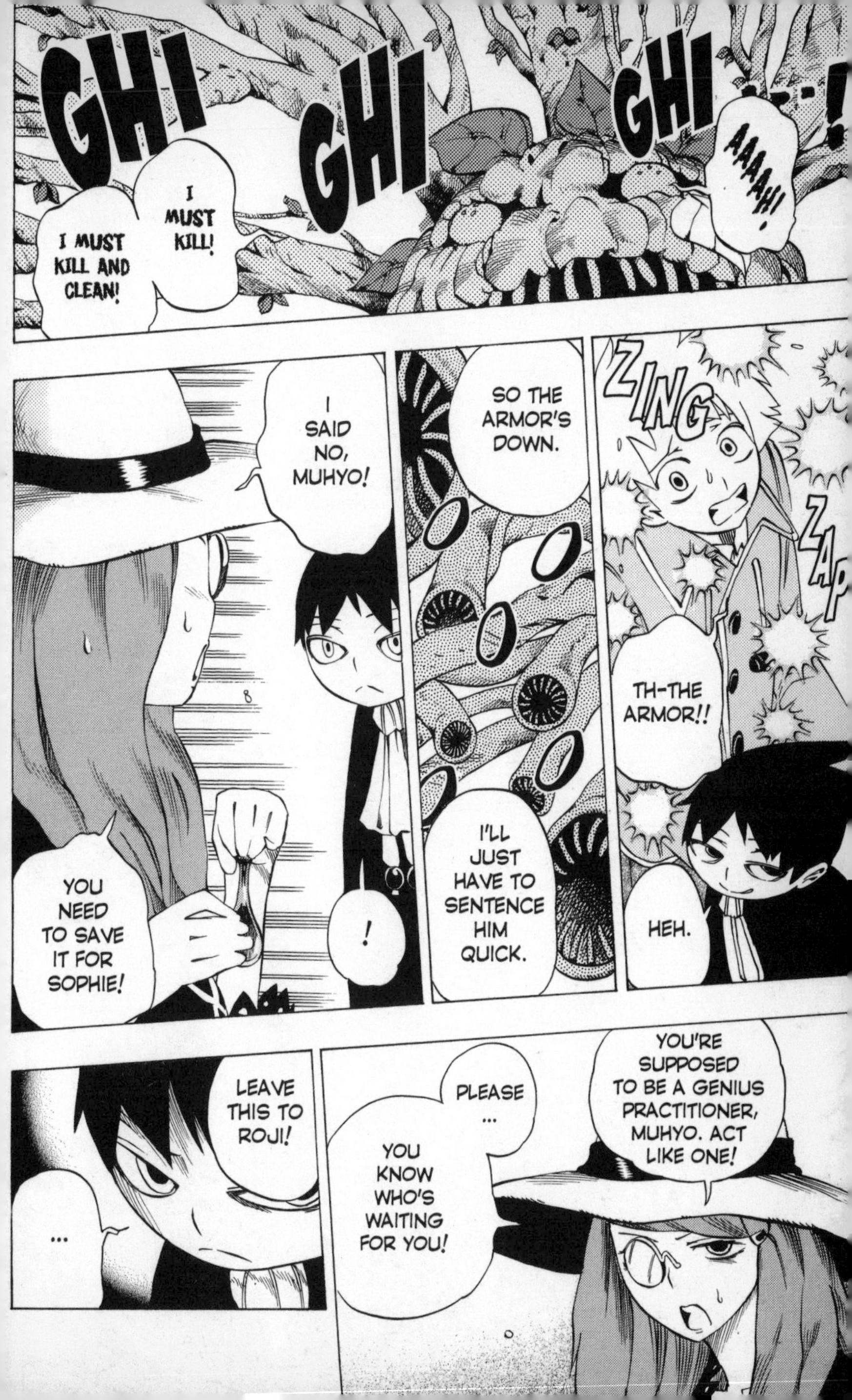
GHI GHI GHI
AAAAAH!
I MUST KILL!
I MUST KILL AND CLEAN!
ZING
ZAP
TH-THE ARMOR!!
HEH.
SO THE ARMOR'S DOWN.
I'LL JUST HAVE TO SENTENCE HIM QUICK.
I SAID NO, MUHYO!
!
YOU NEED TO SAVE IT FOR SOPHIE!
YOU'RE SUPPOSED TO BE A GENIUS PRACTITIONER, MUHYO. ACT LIKE ONE!
PLEASE ...
YOU KNOW WHO'S WAITING FOR YOU!
LEAVE THIS TO ROJI!
...

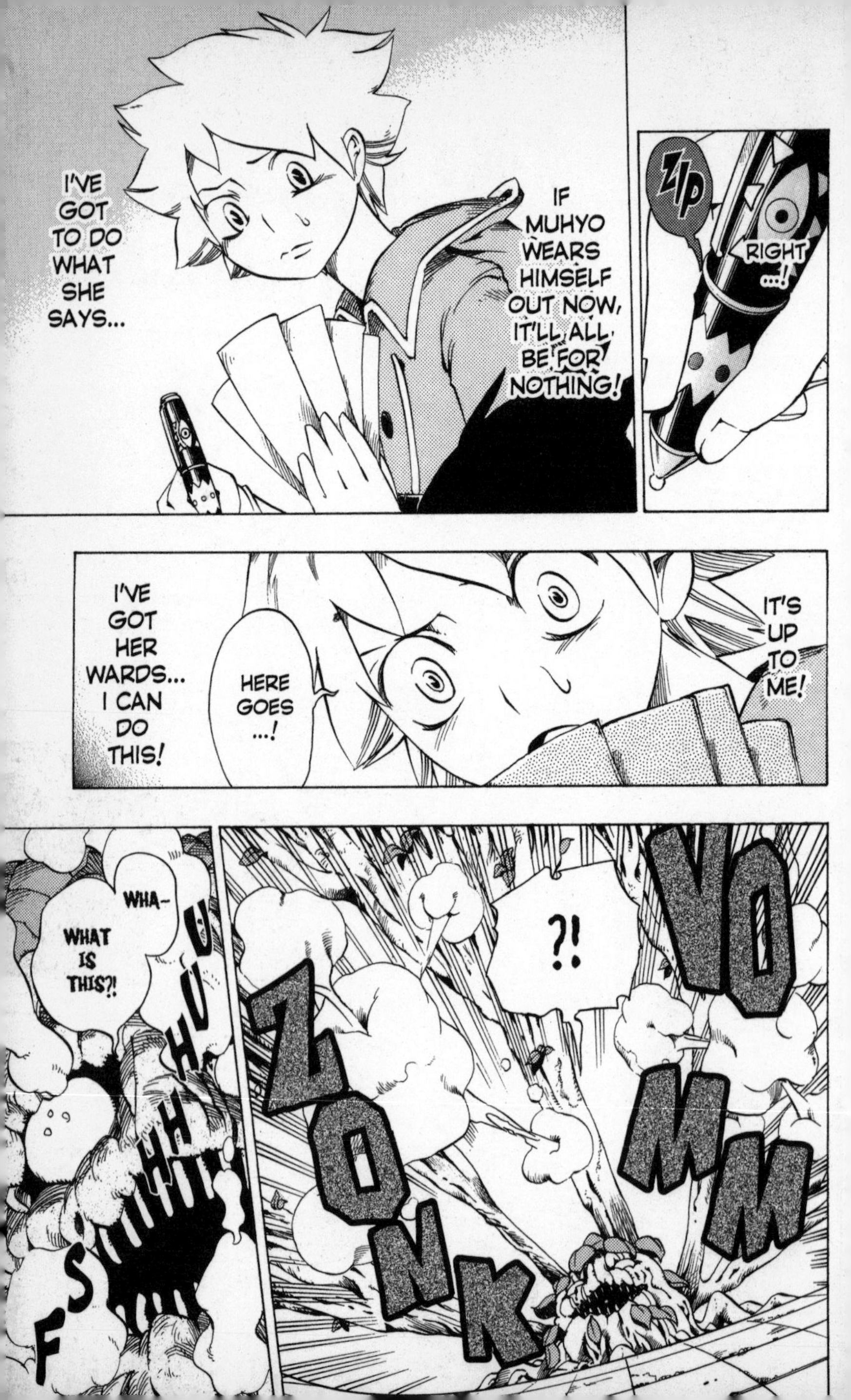
ZIP
RIGHT ...!
IF MUHYO WEARS HIMSELF OUT NOW, IT'LL ALL BE FOR NOTHING!
I'VE GOT TO DO WHAT SHE SAYS...
IT'S UP TO ME!
HERE GOES ...!
I'VE GOT HER WARDS... I CAN DO THIS!
VOMMM
?!
ZONK
WHA-
WHAT IS THIS?!
FSHHUU

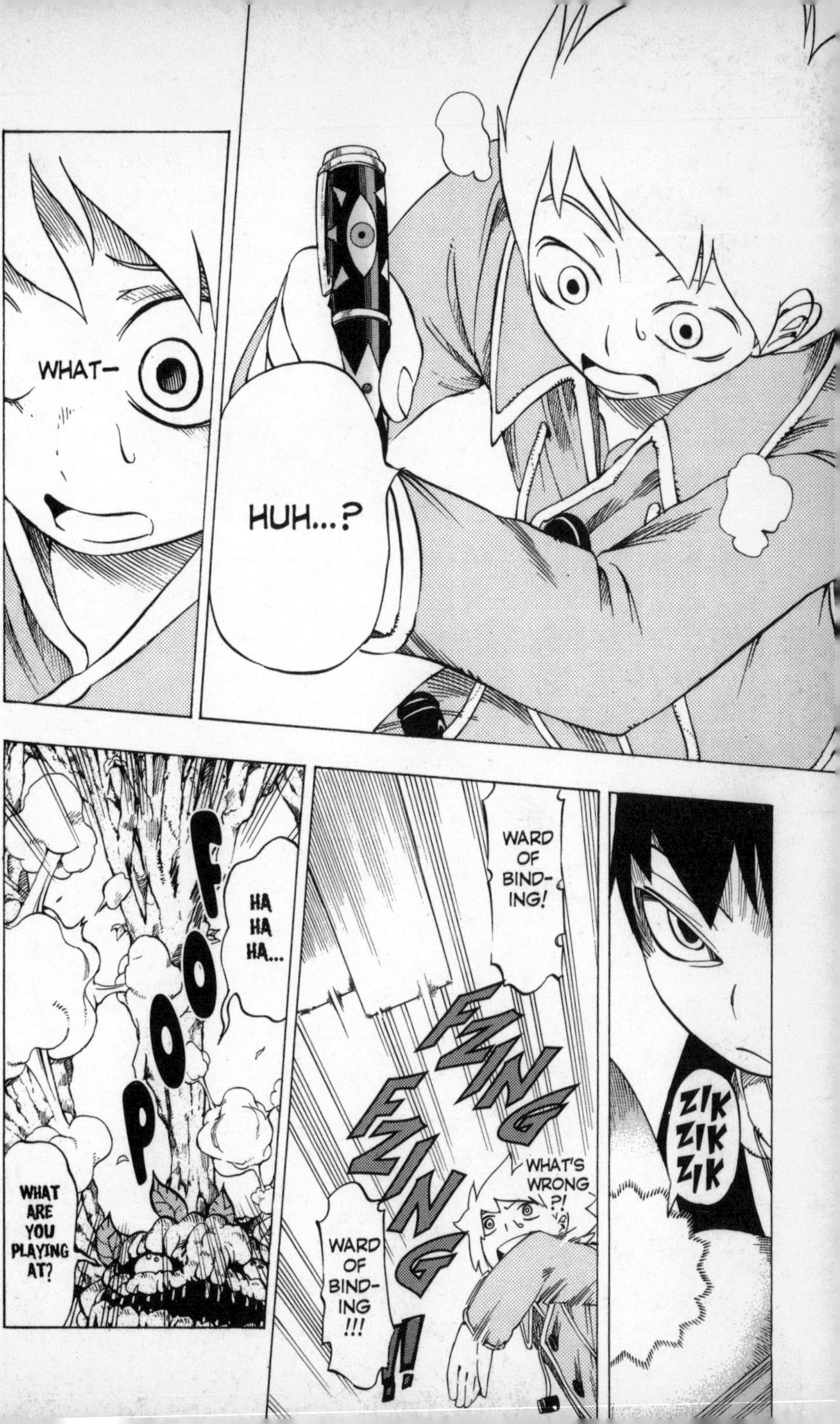
HUH...?
WHAT–
ZIK ZIK ZIK
WARD OF BINDING!
FWING FWING
WHAT'S WRONG?!
WARD OF BINDING!!!
HA HA HA...
POOF
WHAT ARE YOU PLAYING AT?

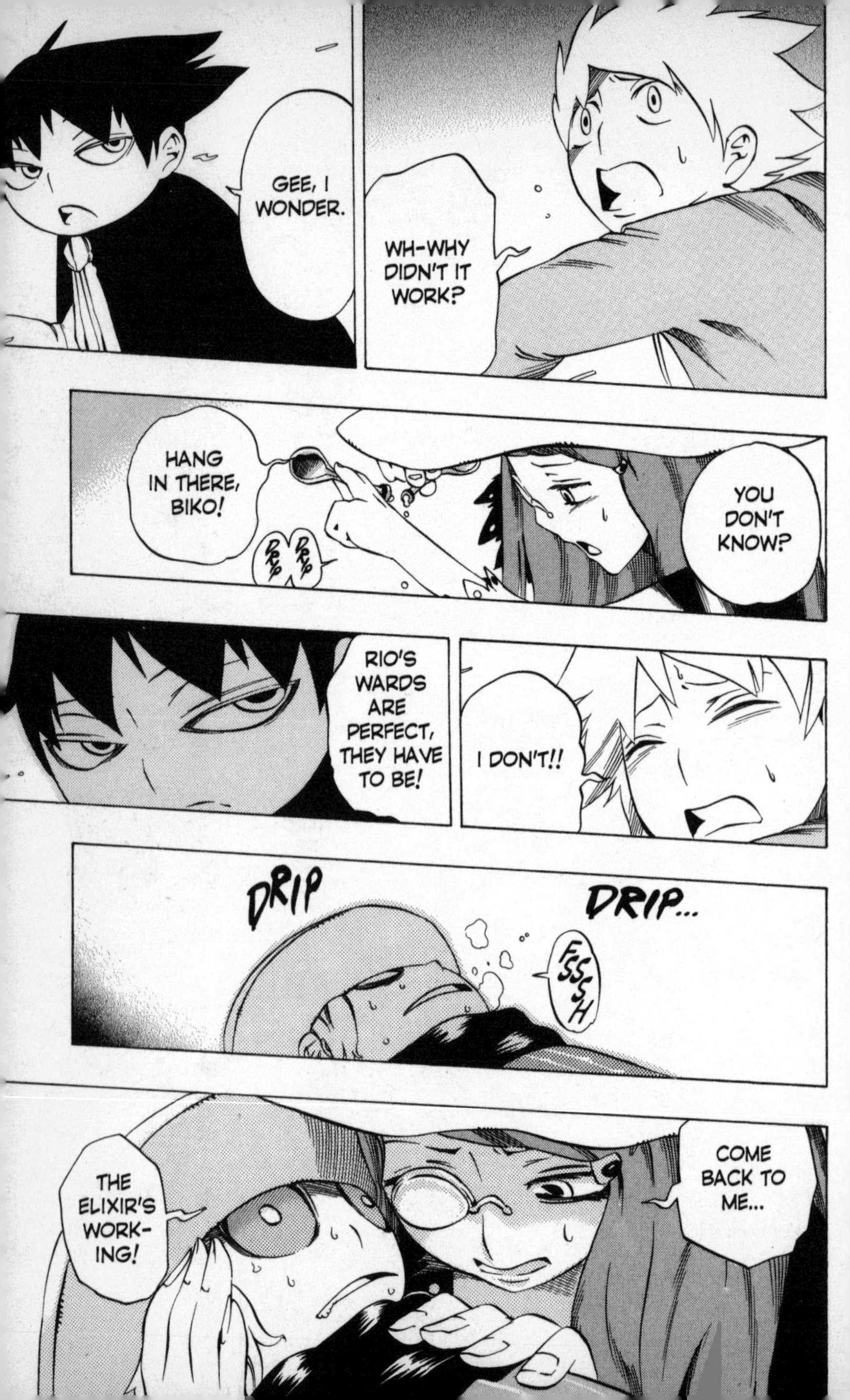
WH-WHY DIDN'T IT WORK?
GEE, I WONDER.
YOU DON'T KNOW?
HANG IN THERE, BIKO!
DRIP DRIP
I DON'T!!
RIO'S WARDS ARE PERFECT, THEY HAVE TO BE!
DRIP...
DRIP
FSSSH
COME BACK TO ME...
THE ELIXIR'S WORK-ING!

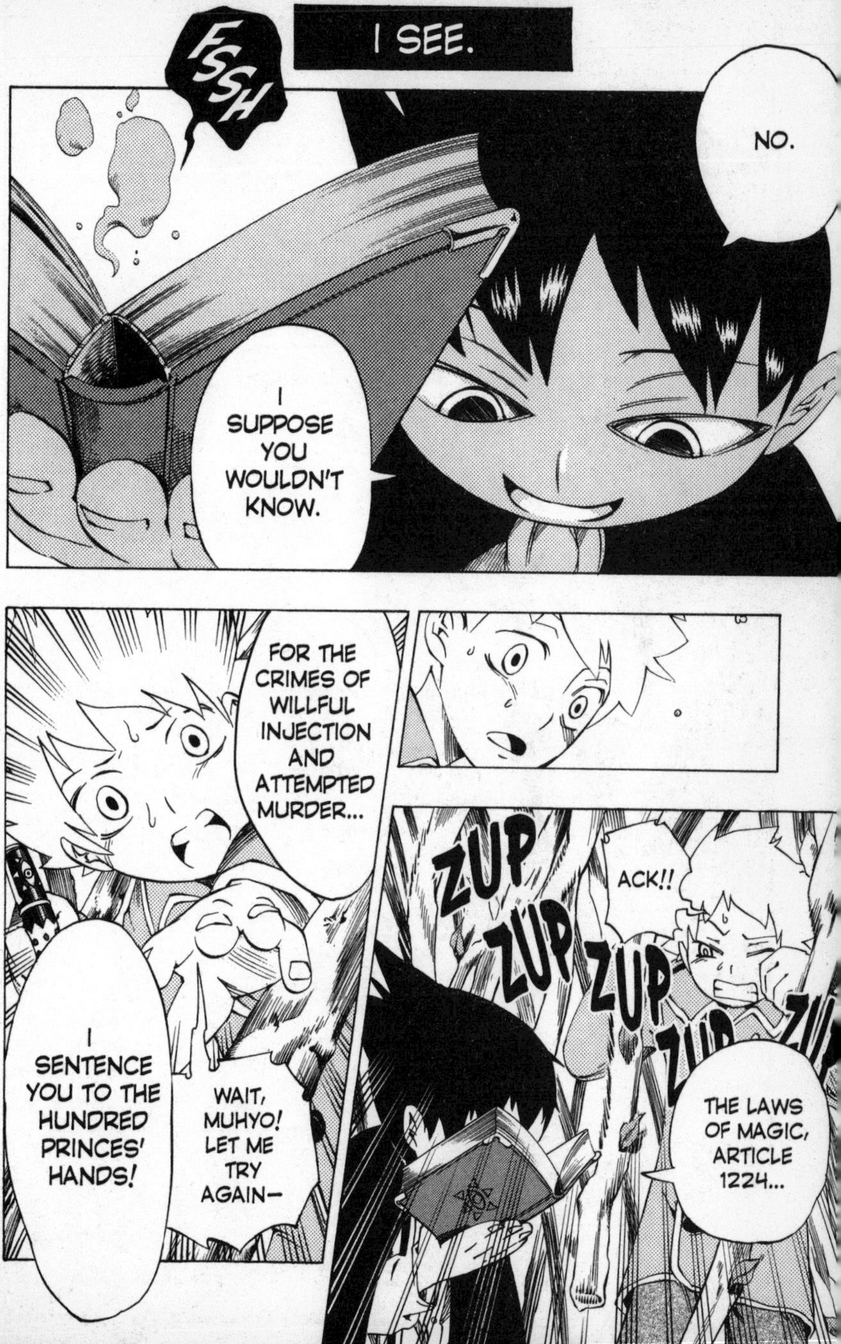
I SEE.
FSSH
NO.
I SUPPOSE YOU WOULDN'T KNOW.
ACK!!
ZUP ZUP ZUP
THE LAWS OF MAGIC, ARTICLE 1224...
FOR THE CRIMES OF WILLFUL INJECTION AND ATTEMPTED MURDER...
I SENTENCE YOU TO THE HUNDRED PRINCES' HANDS!
WAIT, MUHYO! LET ME TRY AGAIN—

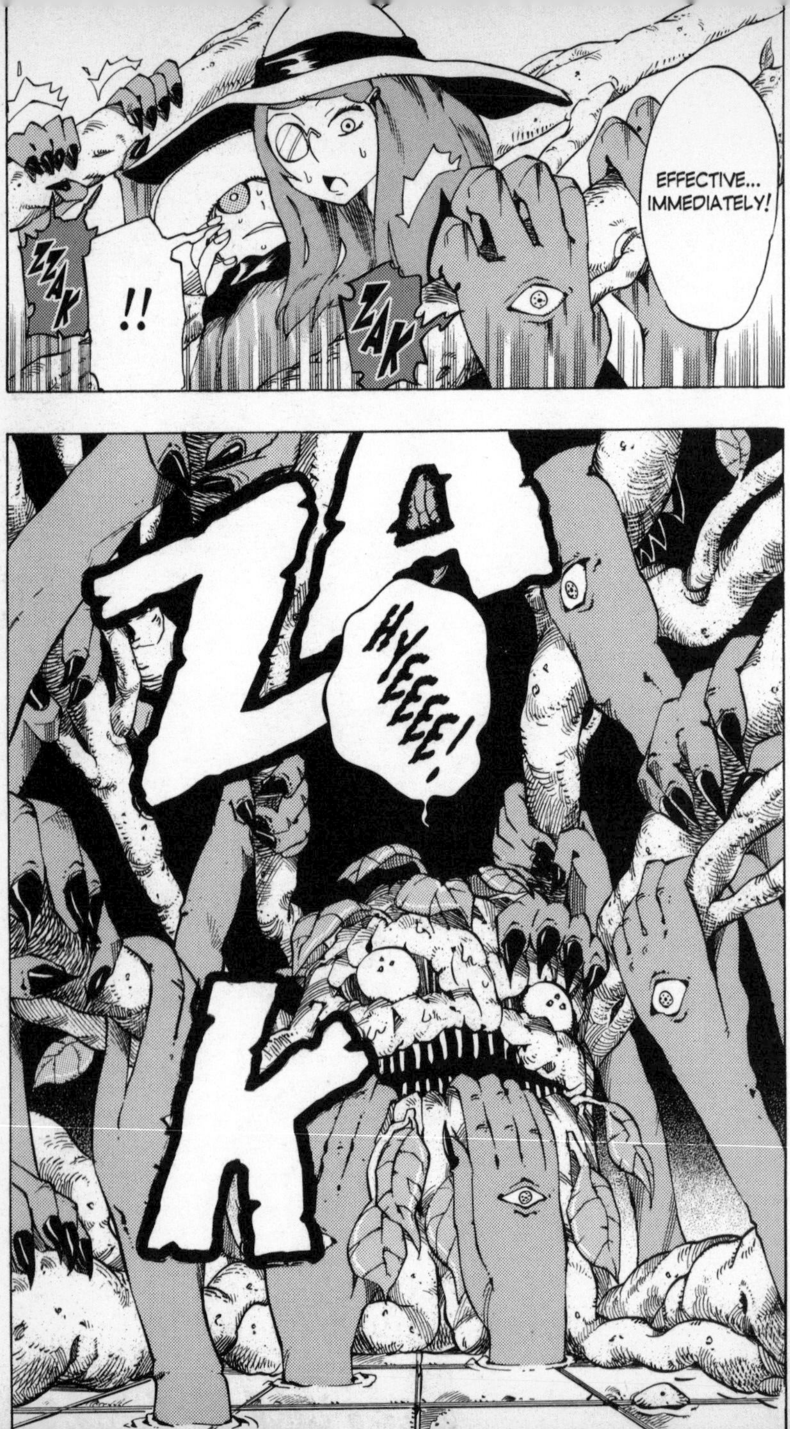
EFFECTIVE... IMMEDIATELY!
ZAK
!!
ZZAK
ZAK
HYEEEE!

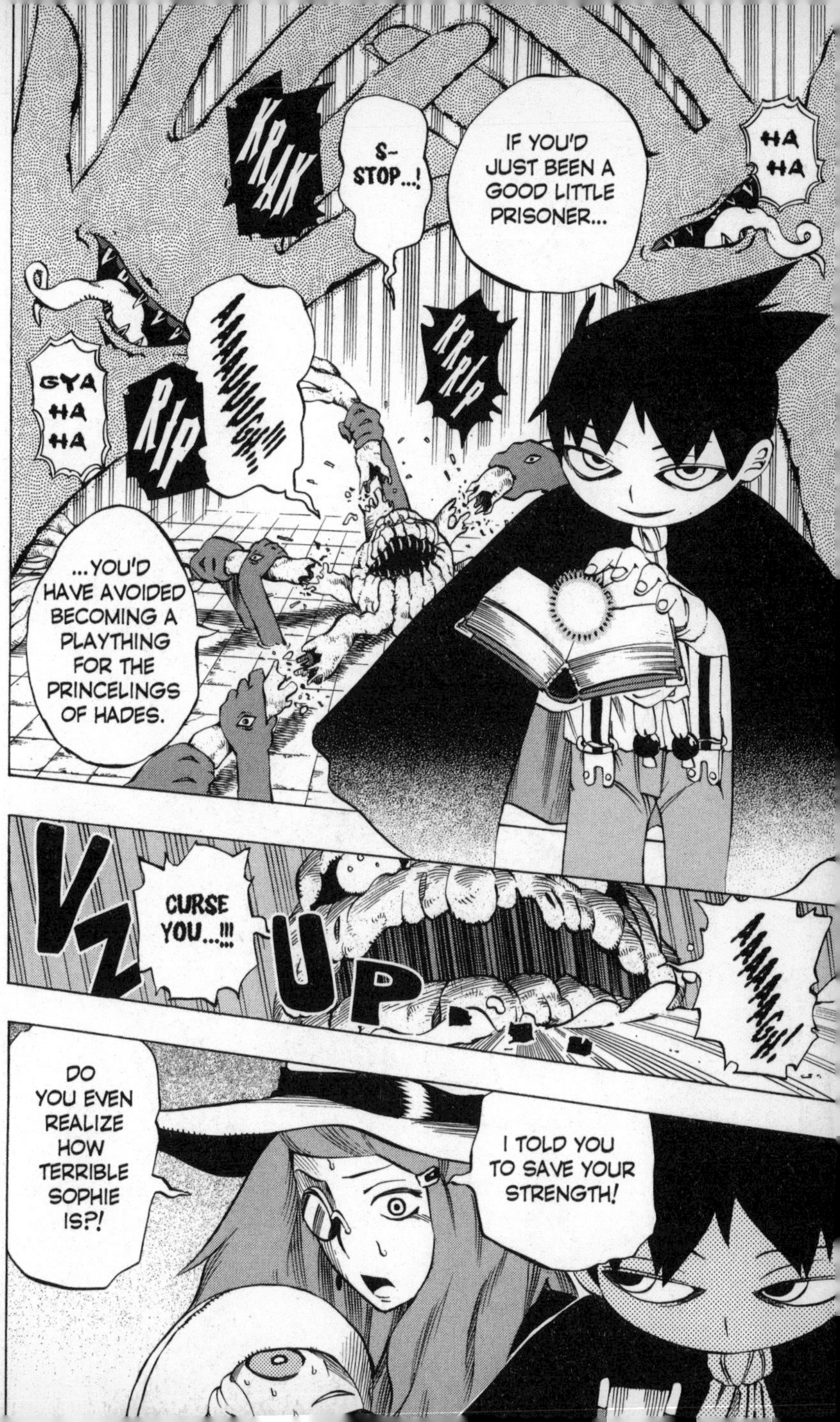
HA HA
IF YOU'D JUST BEEN A GOOD LITTLE PRISONER...
S-STOP...!
KRAK
RRRIP
AAAAUUGH!!!
RIP
GYA HA HA
...YOU'D HAVE AVOIDED BECOMING A PLAYTHING FOR THE PRINCELINGS OF HADES.
AAAAAGH!
UP
CURSE YOU...!!!
I TOLD YOU TO SAVE YOUR STRENGTH!
DO YOU EVEN REALIZE HOW TERRIBLE SOPHIE IS?!

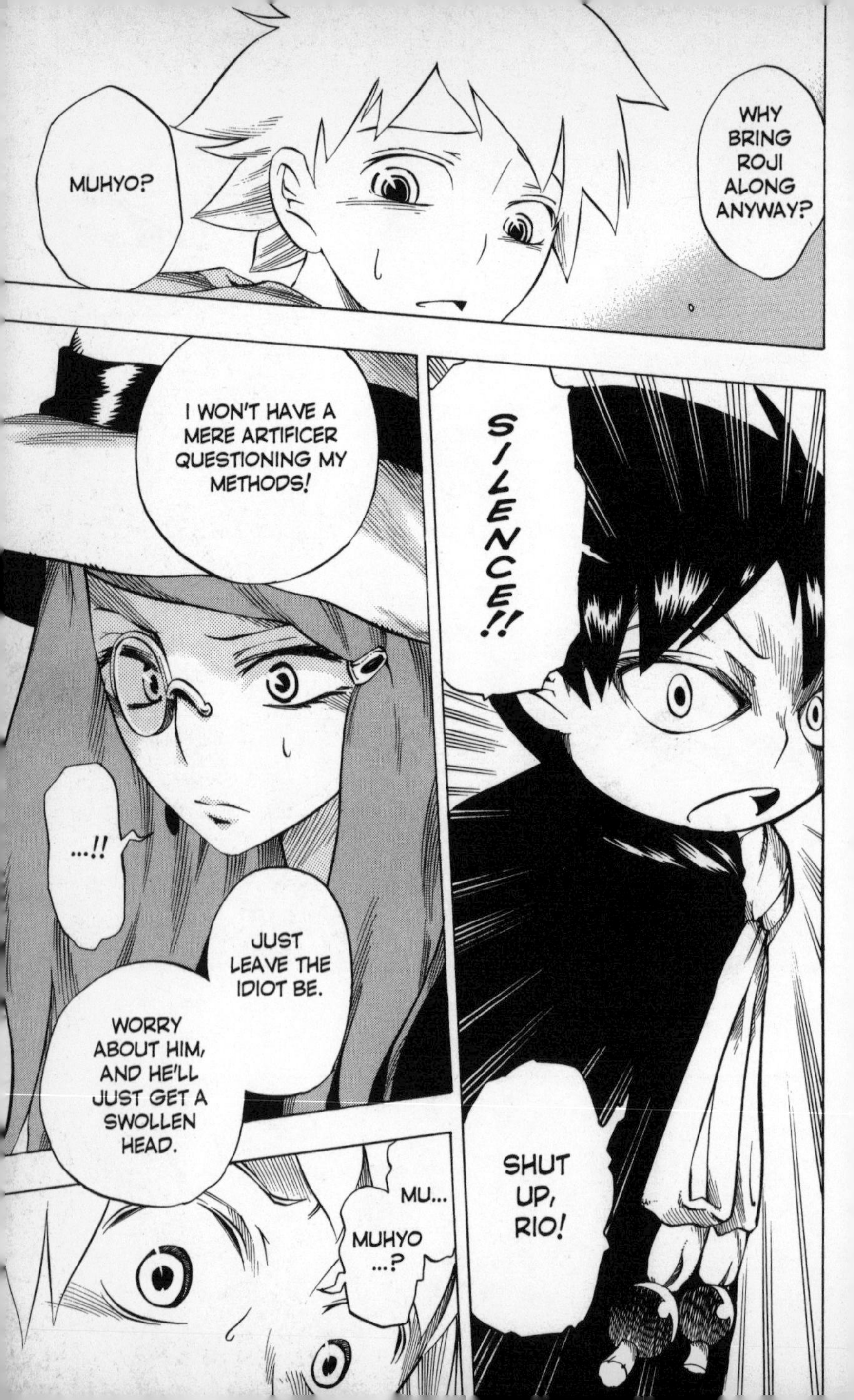
WHY BRING ROJI ALONG ANYWAY?
MUHYO?
SILENCE!!
I WON'T HAVE A MERE ARTIFICER QUESTIONING MY METHODS!
...!!
JUST LEAVE THE IDIOT BE.
WORRY ABOUT HIM, AND HE'LL JUST GET A SWOLLEN HEAD.
SHUT UP, RIO!
MU...
MUHYO ...?

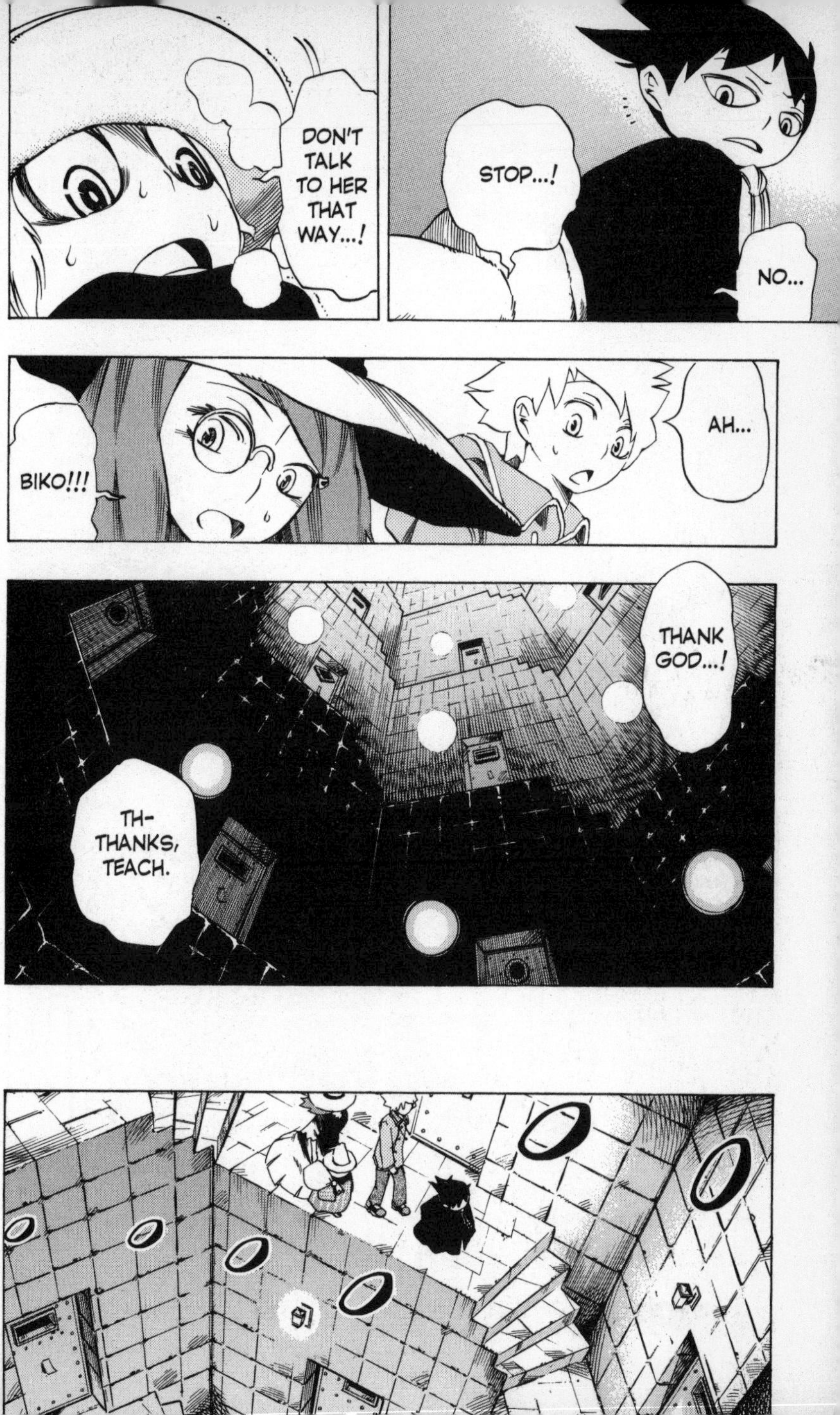
STOP...!
NO...
DON'T TALK TO HER THAT WAY...!
AH...
BIKO!!!
THANK GOD...!
TH-THANKS, TEACH.

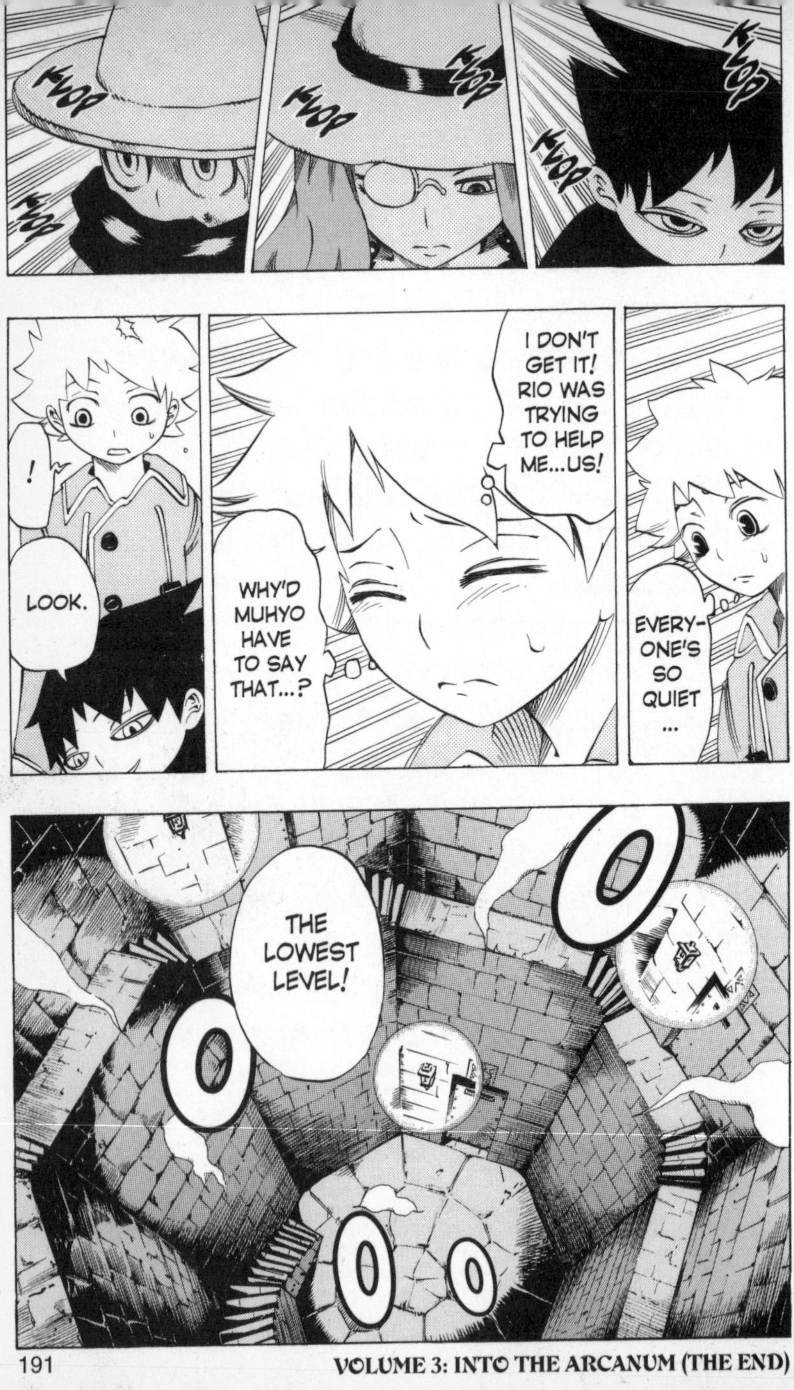
KLOP
KLOP
KLOP
KLOP
KLOP
KLOP
EVERY-ONE'S SO QUIET ...
I DON'T GET IT! RIO WAS TRYING TO HELP ME...US!
WHY'D MUHYO HAVE TO SAY THAT...?
!
LOOK.
THE LOWEST LEVEL!

The following bonus story is something I did for *Akamaru Jump*'s summer special issue.

It was around the end of last March when I said to my editor, Mr. K, "Say, it'd be cool if I could do something with Matsui-sensei. He's at the same office and all..." To which Mr. K. responded, "That'd be cool, but probably impossible..."

Oh well, it was worth a try, I thought. But it turns out that Matsui-sensei was thinking the same thing! And before you know it, it was done. What a lot of fun that was!

Demon Detective Nogami Neuro started around the same time as my manga, so I kind of think of them as being brothers...which means when I hear *Neuro*'s getting popular, it makes me sweat a little. "Ack! I'd better keep up!"

Thanks for the project, Matsui-sensei! Let's do it again sometime!

MUHYO & ROJI'S BUREAU OF SUPERNATURAL INVESTIGATION – BONUS STORY

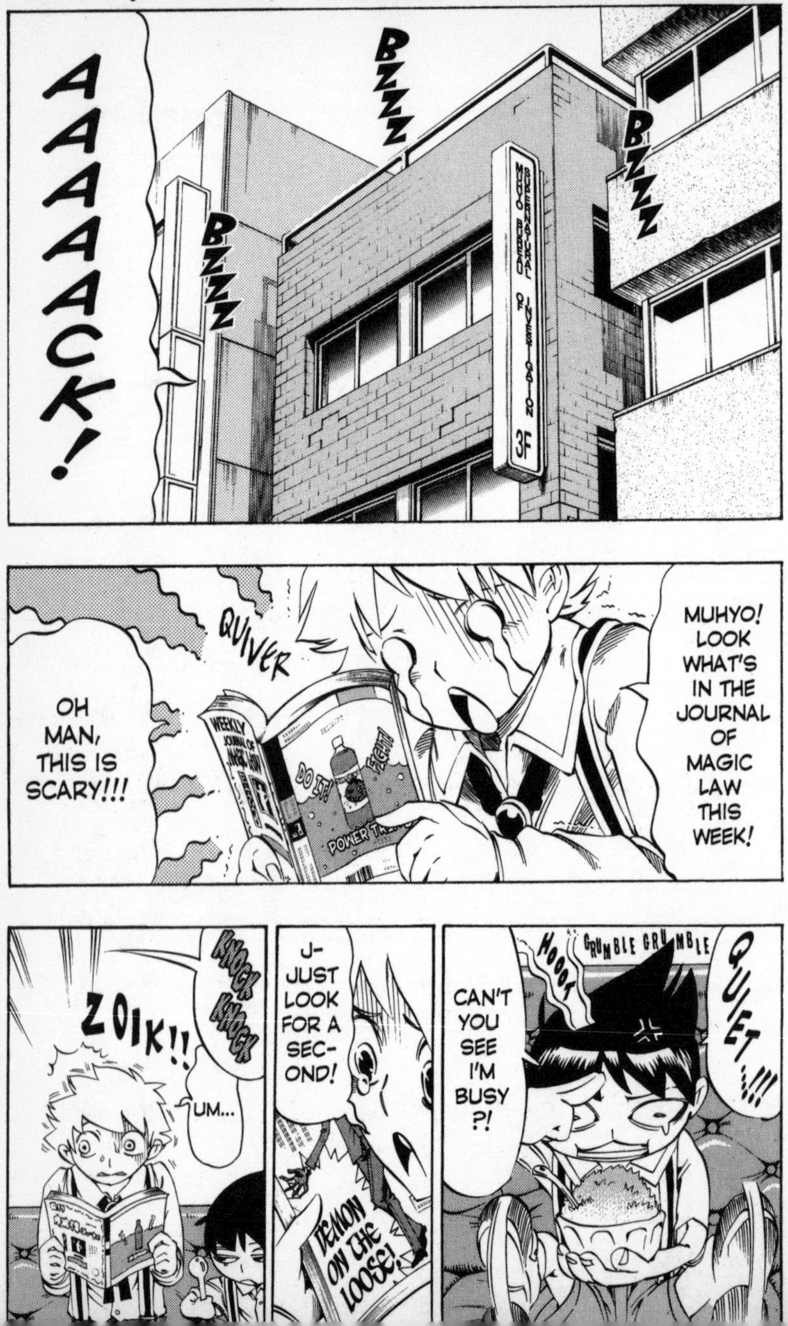
BZZZZ
MUHYO BUREAU OF SUPERNATURAL INVESTIGATION 3F
BZZZZ
BZZZZ
AAAAACK!
MUHYO! LOOK WHAT'S IN THE JOURNAL OF MAGIC LAW THIS WEEK!
QUIVER
DO IT!
FIGHT!
OH MAN, THIS IS SCARY!!!
QUIET...!!!
GRUMBLE GRUMBLE
CAN'T YOU SEE I'M BUSY?!
J-JUST LOOK FOR A SEC-OND!
DEMON ON THE LOOSE!
KNOCK KNOCK
ZOIK!!
UM...

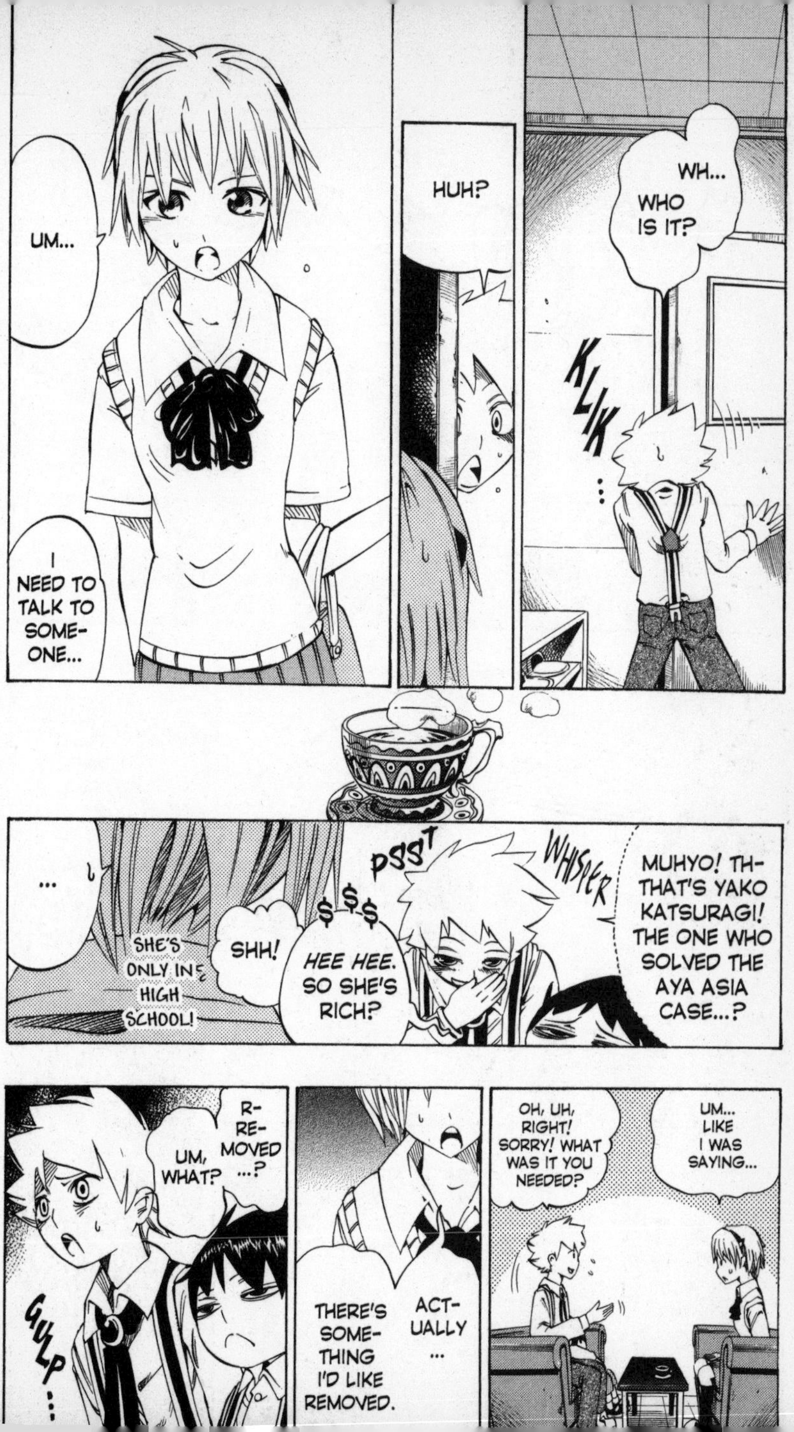
WH... WHO IS IT?
KLIK
...
HUH?
UM...
I NEED TO TALK TO SOMEONE...
MUHYO! TH-THAT'S YAKO KATSURAGI! THE ONE WHO SOLVED THE AYA ASIA CASE...?
WHISPER
PSST
HEE HEE. SO SHE'S RICH?
SHH!
SHE'S ONLY IN HIGH SCHOOL!
...
UM... LIKE I WAS SAYING...
OH, UH, RIGHT! SORRY! WHAT WAS IT YOU NEEDED?
ACTUALLY...
THERE'S SOMETHING I'D LIKE REMOVED.
R-REMOVED...?
UM, WHAT?
GULP...

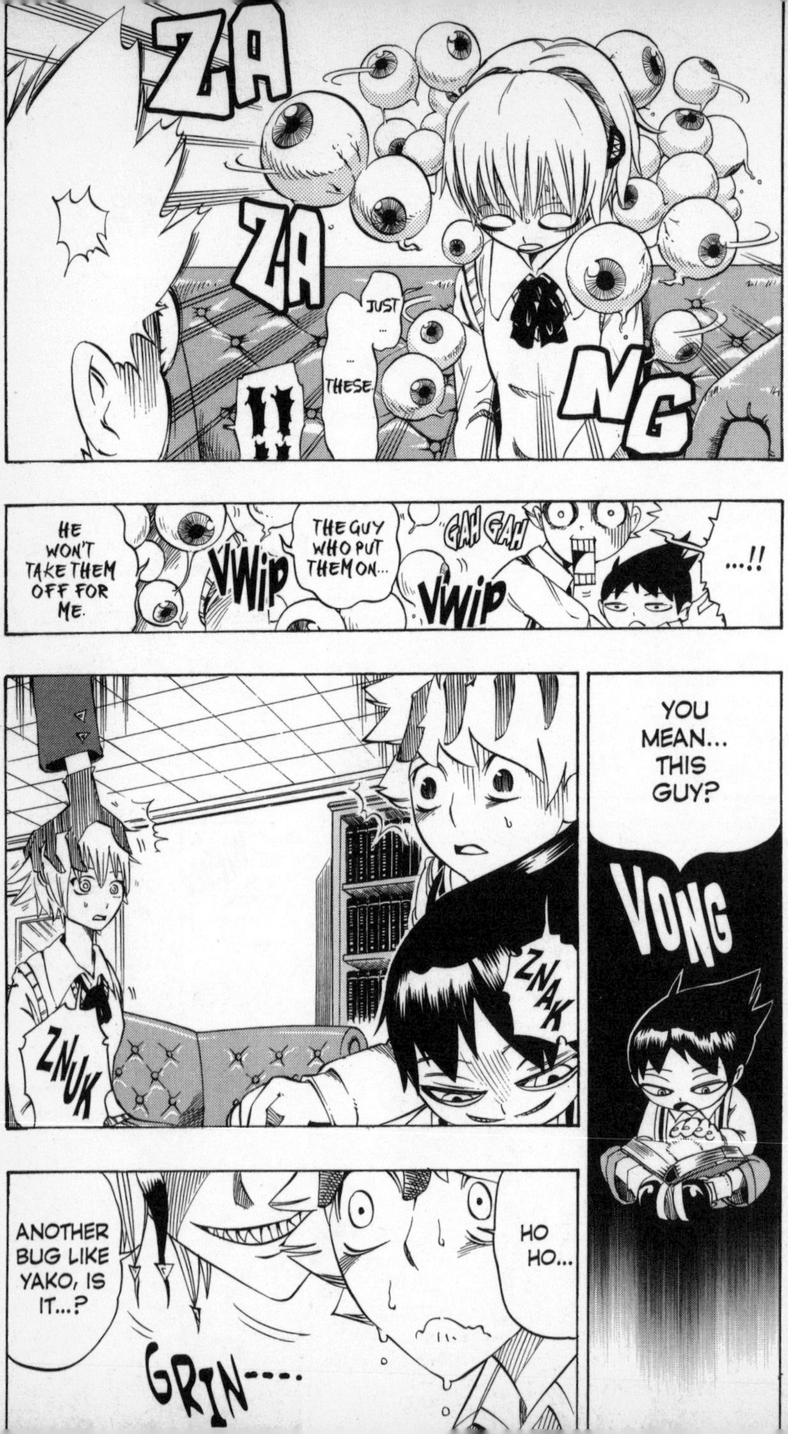
ZA
ZA
NG
JUST... ...THESE.
!!
...!!
GAH GAH
VWIP
THE GUY WHO PUT THEM ON...
VWIP
HE WON'T TAKE THEM OFF FOR ME.
YOU MEAN... THIS GUY?
VONG
ZNAK
ZNUK
HO HO...
ANOTHER BUG LIKE YAKO, IS IT...?
GRIN----.

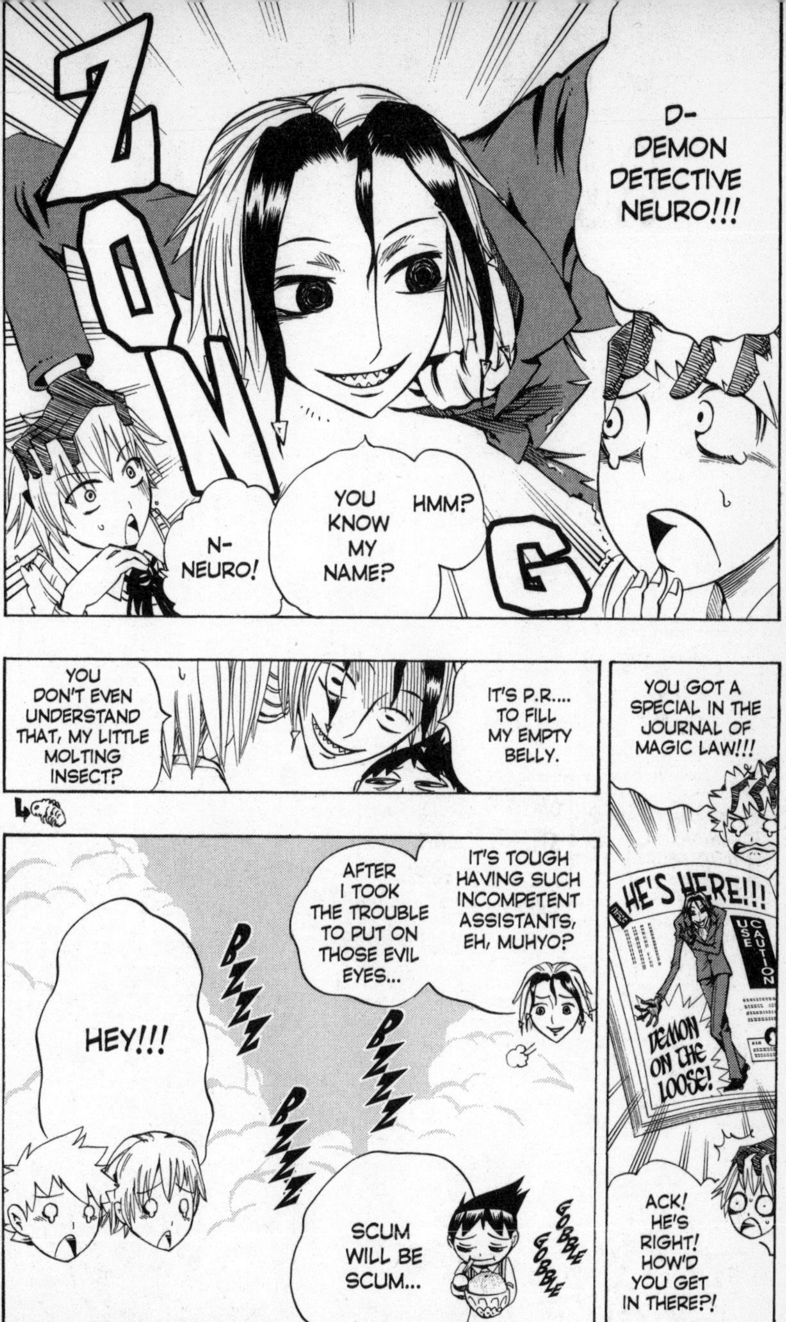
D- DEMON DETECTIVE NEURO!!!
ZONG
HMM?
YOU KNOW MY NAME?
N- NEURO!
YOU GOT A SPECIAL IN THE JOURNAL OF MAGIC LAW!!!
HE'S HERE!!!
USE CAUTION
DEMON ON THE LOOSE!
ACK! HE'S RIGHT! HOW'D YOU GET IN THERE?!
IT'S P.R.... TO FILL MY EMPTY BELLY.
YOU DON'T EVEN UNDERSTAND THAT, MY LITTLE MOLTING INSECT?
IT'S TOUGH HAVING SUCH INCOMPETENT ASSISTANTS, EH, MUHYO?
AFTER I TOOK THE TROUBLE TO PUT ON THOSE EVIL EYES...
GOBBLE GOBBLE
BZZZ
BZZZ
BZZZ
SCUM WILL BE SCUM...
HEY!!!

MUHYO & ROJI'S BUREAU OF SUPERNATURAL INVESTIGATION – BONUS STORY (THE END)

BONUS MANGA

ROJI'S RECIPE

TODAY'S MENU

ONION RICE BOWL

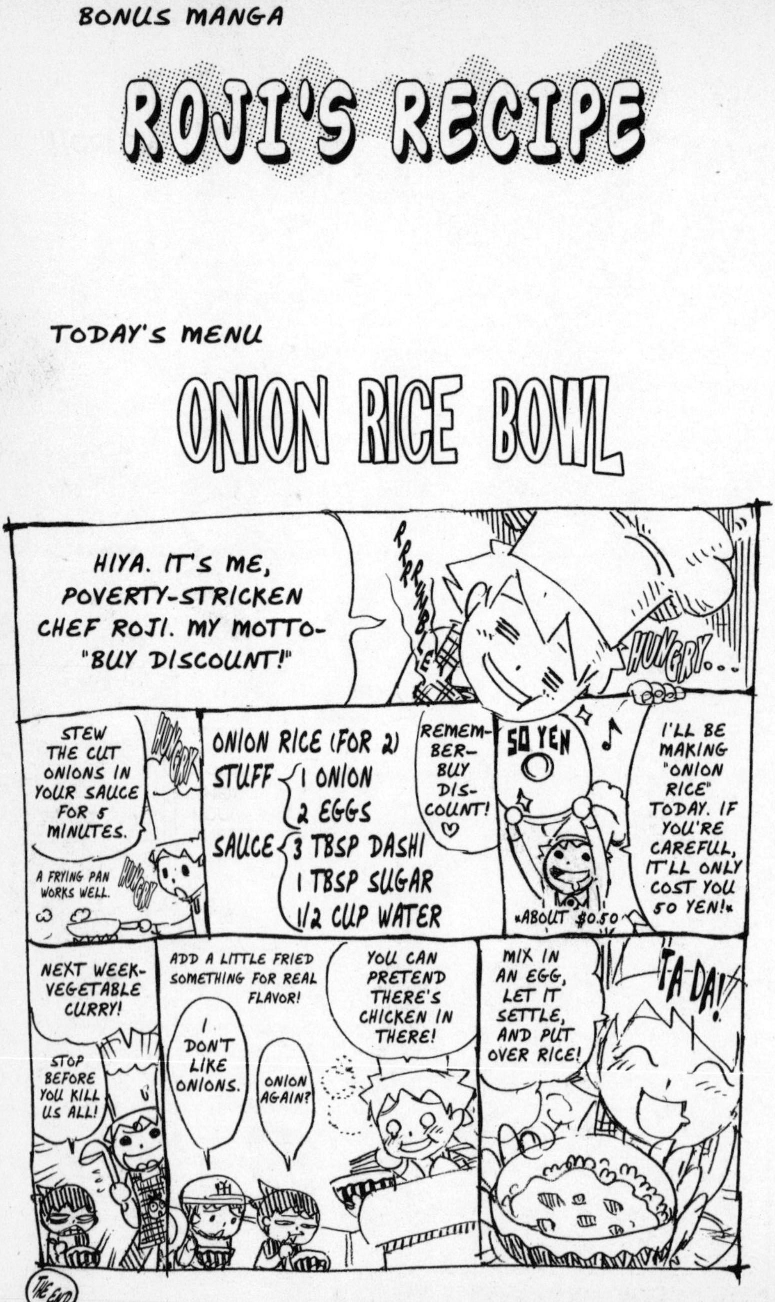

RRRRUMBLE
HUNGRY...
HIYA. IT'S ME, POVERTY-STRICKEN CHEF ROJI. MY MOTTO-"BUY DISCOUNT!"
I'LL BE MAKING "ONION RICE" TODAY. IF YOU'RE CAREFUL, IT'LL ONLY COST YOU 50 YEN!*
50 YEN
*ABOUT $0.50
REMEMBER-BUY DISCOUNT! ♡
ONION RICE (FOR 2)
STUFF { 1 ONION
2 EGGS
SAUCE { 3 TBSP DASHI
1 TBSP SUGAR
1/2 CUP WATER
HUNGRY
STEW THE CUT ONIONS IN YOUR SAUCE FOR 5 MINUTES.
HUNGRY
A FRYING PAN WORKS WELL.
TA-DA!
MIX IN AN EGG, LET IT SETTLE, AND PUT OVER RICE!
YOU CAN PRETEND THERE'S CHICKEN IN THERE!
ADD A LITTLE FRIED SOMETHING FOR REAL FLAVOR!
ONION AGAIN?
I DON'T LIKE ONIONS.
NEXT WEEK-VEGETABLE CURRY!
STOP BEFORE YOU KILL US ALL!
THE END

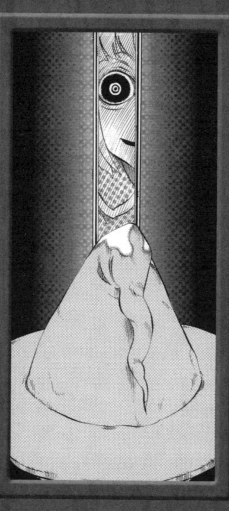

In The Next Volume...

What will Muhyo and his friends find in the bottom
level of Arcanum? And are they prepared to deal
with the horrifying Face-Ripper Sophie?

Available April 2008!